An indispensable public resource in recent years, Matthew McManus has been tracing our everyday political controversies back to the intellectual traditions that help make sense of our times. Now he has turned in the most accessible and useful analysis of conservative thought there is. Incisive, learned, and up-to-date, *The Political Right and Equality* provides desperately needed orientation for anyone who hopes to forge a progressive response.

Samuel Moyn, Yale University

Matt McManus brilliantly surveys two millennia of political philosophy to uncover the oft-misunderstood roots of contemporary conservatism. A must-read for anyone who really wants to grasp the deeper historical and theoretical currents driving today's authoritarian, post-liberal right.

Greg Sargent, The Washington Post

McManus provides a highly readable, intellectual history of the "political right" that underscores the present dangers of reactionary politics and offers a timely reminder about what is at stake for those interested in a better world.

Igor Shoikhedbrod, Department of Political Science,
St. Francis Xavier University

THE POLITICAL RIGHT AND EQUALITY

McManus presents an intellectual history of the conservative and reactionary tradition, stretching from Aristotle and Filmer to Alexander Dugin and Patrick Deneen.

Providing a comprehensive critical genealogy of the intellectual political right, McManus traces its core to a nostalgia for the hierarchical cosmos of antiquarian and scholastic thinking. The yearning for a shared vision of the universe where each part of reality has its place maps onto the conservative admiration for orderly political and social stratification. It stamps even the more moderate forms of liberal conservatism which emerged in the aftermath of the revolutionary 18th century, as the political right struggled to accept and later master first the politics of liberal capitalism and later universal suffrage. In its most radical forms this nostalgia for an orderly and hierarchical existence can harden into a resentment at the perceived shallowness of liberal modernity. McManus argues for those who support the project of modernity to commit themselves to better understanding the depth of the political right's critiques, many of which expose uncomfortable but solvable problems with the quest for equality and freedom.

A critical guide to the history of conservative and reactionary thought for students and scholars of political science and political history.

While there are a lot of competing explanations for the contemporary rise of right-wing forces, Matt McManus' new book suggests that it is hostility to equality that actually unites the right. Zeroing in on key intellectuals and writers, McManus, in a sharply written text, offers a compelling explanation for the disproportionate intensity of right-wing grievance politics.

Matthew McManus is a Lecturer in Political Science at the University of Michigan. He is a contributor to *Jacobin* and *Quillette* online magazines.

THE POLITICAL RIGHT AND EQUALITY

Turning Back the Tide of Egalitarian Modernity

Matthew McManus

LONDON AND NEW YORK

Designed cover image: Designed Cover Image by J. Andrew World

First published 2024
by Routledge
4 Park Square, Milton Park, Abingdon, Oxon OX14 4RN

and by Routledge
605 Third Avenue, New York, NY 10158

Routledge is an imprint of the Taylor & Francis Group, an informa business

British Library Cataloguing-in-Publication Data
A catalogue record for this book is available from the British Library

ISBN: 978-1-032-31084-8 (hbk)
ISBN: 978-1-032-31083-1 (pbk)
ISBN: 978-1-003-30795-2 (ebk)

DOI: 10.4324/9781003307952

To Meaghan and Emily

CONTENTS

ACKNOWLEDGMENTS

In 2010 I won the Carleton Campus Conservative award for "Best Non-Conservative Member of the Carleton Campus Conservatives." This was because—despite my burgeoning leftism—I'd spent an awful lot of time listening to conservatives, attending their events, and, of course, arguing about their views. Naturally the consequence was that I started to learn quite a bit about conservatism in the process, though I'd never have dreamed that one day I would be writing a book like this. The major catalyst was the twin embarrassments of Brexit and the election of Donald Trump in 2016, which above all proved how far you could go as a white scion of privilege who has to pay women to sleep with him. This encouraged me to go back and dust off my old copies of classics like *Reflections on the Revolution in France* and *How to Debate Leftists and Destroy Them* to figure out what happened. The first products of those efforts were my books *The Rise of Post-Modern Conservatism* and *What Is Post-Modern Conservatism: Essays on Our Hugely Tremendous Times*—complemented by a little collection *Myth and Mayhem: A Leftist Critique of Jordan Peterson*. By no means perfect, but a sincere effort to situate these developments in the context of neoliberal post-modernity. One legitimate criticism raised against the argument was that, whatever else their merits as analyses or doorstops, the books tended to approach conservatism generally and post-modern conservatism contextually and pathologically rather than argumentatively. Post-modern conservatisms were diagnosed as the symptomatic forms of reaction distinct to their era, drawing mainly on the examples of Marxist and leftist critics of post-modernity like David Harvey, Wendy Brown, and Fredric Jameson.

I'd hold this was a legitimate route to take, but it does suffer the limitation of not taking the political right seriously on its own terms. One response would be that the political right sometimes simply *is* very hard to take seriously. Having spent a great deal of time reviewing books with titles like *American Marxism*,

Race Marxism, and *The Parasitic Mind*, I can confidently say Albert Hirschman was right in saying a lot of conservative rage is very amusing and very short on substance. One effect of trying to approach these figures seriously is a feeling of migraine-inducing bombast. Followed quickly by a sense of disappointment that not much more is on offer, and then anger at having one's irrecoverable time wasted. This frequent emotional bouncing around left me with a feeling of deflation above all else. Like the preening nobleman who falls into a pile of manure the effect of loud conservative resentments is to make some relentlessly self-serious arguments appear quite funny. Even cute. And no doubt anyone reading this will note there are plenty of passages in this book that echo Hirschman's reaction to the reactionary tradition.

But any progressive who has spent enough time with the political right will tell you that these moments of feeling your eyes roll back to your skull and further are coupled with sensations of genuine unease. Easy as it is to make fun of Joseph de Maistre or Ludwig von Mises in their shriller moments, one can't simply dismiss the substance of their positions wholesale. That goes doubly so for genuinely great intellects like Edmund Burke and Martin Heidegger, who, whatever else they are, deserve top billing in the intellectual canon of the world. They raise legitimate arguments against the egalitarian thrust of modernity whose sweep and power require sustained answers. And progressives need to become better at providing them.

My first tentative effort in this direction was the joint collection *Myth and Mayhem: A Leftist Critique of Jordan Peterson*.[1] As the title indicates this was a pretty focused examination of a major contemporary intellectual on the political right, offering an analysis and a rebuttal of many of his primary arguments. The positive reception to this book encouraged the more ambitious effort that you're perusing right now. Sadly this is (mostly) a solo-authored book, which means there is no one around to share the blame if things go south. However if there are any virtues to this book, very few of them came from me, since I wouldn't be able to write a single thing if it weren't for a lot of special people.

First, I'd like to thank both the University of Calgary and the University of Michigan for employing me. This includes Dr. Robert Franzese and Dr. Fiona Nelson, my TAs Chetna Khandelwal and Evangelina Natynczyk, and the students from whom I learn a lot. Thanks to my colleagues Dylan De Jong, Victor Bruzonne, and Erik Tate on the Plastic Pills Podcast. My friend Ben Burgis is a frequent collaborator and much respected commentator whom I've bounced a lot of these ideas off of. Thanks to Shawn Gude of *Jacobin*, Aaron Anderson of *The Bias*, Iona Italia of *Areo Magazine*, and Paul Crider and Adam Gurri of *Liberal Currents*. Many of the themes discussed here originated in these more popular outlets. I feel a lot of gratitude toward mentors like Nalini Persram, Lesley Jacobs, Trevor Purvis, and Kathleen Kavanaugh. You've always been a source of inspiration and insight. Much gratitude to all my friends, including Taewook Kim, James Williams, Brendan Nickels, Hilary Terrell, Luciana Velloso, Will Norman, Tristan Bradley, Nicholas Young, James W.J. Bowden,

Grant Dingwall, David Hollands, Andrew Thorndyke, Justin Unsworth, Victor Hainagiu, Stacey Freeman, Erik Tate, Leslie Marsh, Dylan DeJong, Manisha Ahmed, Ali Malik, Conrad Hamilton, Aaron Frankruyter, Jeffrey Farncombe, Andrew Fleck, Carrie Duplessis, and more.

And of course thanks as always to my extended family, including all the McLeods and McManuses out there. I think often about the Trejo family, including Melissa, Enrique, Jose-Luis, and Leilani. Thank you to Adam, Kayla, Jean, John, Chris, and Matt for their unyielding patience. Warmth to Thor and Loki. Of course, my love always goes to Marion Trejo—my wife and eternal partner in all our endeavors. Finally this book is dedicated to my sisters Meaghan and Emily, who were among the first to bring true joy into my life.

FOREWORD

The right is back! No, not the center right of British Tories, mainstream US Republicans, and various Christian Democrat parties in Europe. Rather the ferociously anti-egalitarian, anti-liberal, and anti-democratic radical right of Joseph de Maistre, Charles Maurras, Carl Schmitt, and the fascist movements of the 1920s and 1930s that utterly disfigured the politics of the 20th century. Today, their successor ideologies seem to be everywhere: Trumpism and Bannonism in the United States! Bolsonarismo in Brazil! Swedish Democrats in Sweden! Orbán in Hungary and Meloni in Italy! "Identitarianism" in France, Germany, Austria, Belgium, and the Netherlands! Hindu nationalism in India! "Jewish Power" led by Itamar Ben-Gvir in Israel! And worst of all, Dugin-inspired Putinism in Russia! Ultra-nationalism, an apparent yearning for "Führerpolitik," and a shockingly cavalier attitude toward truth in a host of different settings. Matthew McManus has done us an important service with his effort, stunning in its breadth, to trace the intellectual roots of the radical right as a global ideological movement such as we are experiencing it today. The most dangerous threat to liberalism and egalitarianism is the complacent belief that liberal-egalitarian ideals have triumphed, and our best bet for preventing such dangerous complacency is by continually educating and re-educating ourselves about the abiding appeal of profoundly anti-liberal and anti-egalitarian visions of life. This, clearly, is the purpose of McManus's book.

McManus's study is not limited to the far right. For instance, Chapter 1 features a discussion of Edmund Burke, a theorist whose thought shares much in common with the moderate liberalism of Locke and Montesquieu, notwithstanding Burke's ferocious reaction to the French Revolution. Hume is another liberal conservative included in McManus's historical survey of the right. Hume is obviously not Counter-Enlightenment; on the contrary, he's himself very much part of the 18th-century Enlightenment. If the modern right is defined by a campaign to "turn back the tide of egalitarian modernity," a historical survey of the anti-egalitarian right must ultimately focus its main attention not on mere conservatives like Hume and Burke (or Hegel, who also straddles the liberal and conservative traditions) but on a far more radical sub-tradition—namely, thinkers such as De Maistre, Schmitt, Martin Heidegger, Julius Evola, and, in our own day, Alexander Dugin. These thinkers *are* Counter-Enlightenment, and in a very robust sense indeed. Today, the really dire threats to a liberal-egalitarian social order come not from moderate Burkean conservatives but from political thinkers and political actors driven by much more aggressive forms of anti-liberalism, which is why the trajectory of McManus's book moves from right to far right, culminating in Chapter 5. When one gets to this part of the story, the term "conservative" becomes less and less appropriate, because the fundamental business of these thinkers is not to conserve anything but rather to overturn an egalitarian vision of life that they despise. This of course inevitably points us toward Friedrich Nietzsche, who occupies a pivotal role in the radicalization of the modern right.

Over the last 70 years or so, Nietzsche has been misguidedly and perversely embraced by large swathes of the cultural and intellectual left, but re-reading him as the guidepost of the contemporary right that he clearly intended himself to become can be of immense help to us in clarifying exactly where to situate the meaning of the right's vision of life and politics. The central thought animating Nietzsche is that all societies are ultimately judged by the greatness or feebleness of their cultural achievements. Consider what is required to produce something like the pyramids of ancient Egypt. A way of life lived within liberal or democratic or egalitarian horizons could never produce a culture of this scale of grandeur or enduringness. In fact, the Nietzschean view would be that modern "horizons" aren't binding or enduring enough even to merit the name "horizon." What the Egyptians produced is capable of being beheld in awe for millennia. What we produce will be forgotten almost immediately. That's the standard. They ascended to a genuinely *civilizational* culture, whereas we are, to borrow Heidegger's indelible phrase from the Rectoral Address, a "moribund pseudo-civilization." But it took a slave economy ruled by the most rigid hierarchy imaginable in order to produce what the Egyptians produced. Nietzsche would say: so be it. Willing the end entails willing the means.

Indeed, Nietzsche would go further: the fact that modernity is incapable of willing the means required for the attainment of the uniquely humanly-defining end (a civilizational culture) is in itself a definitive condemnation of modernity. (This Nietzschean theme of the civilizational deficit of "bourgeois modernity" is unmistakably echoed by Greg Johnson, a leading standard-bearer of the alt-right, when he asserts that "democracy is a failure and undermines civilization because it shrinks time horizons down, and that means you can't pursue grand strategies and civilizational goals.") So, if one wants to have pyramids that will be marveled at for millennia, one needs slaves to build these pyramids. You can choose to live in a society that doesn't aspire to build the kind of thing that will be marveled at for millennia, but then one will have chosen to live in a society ruled by those who should be in the slave class. That's a mistaken choice, Nietzsche thinks, and modern societies that have opted to go that route will bore themselves to death and eventually collapse in on themselves. This is, at its core, the meaning of the doctrine of the last man; it was later re-stated quite explicitly in exactly these terms by the arch-fascist, Julius Evola.

Nietzsche looks at the culture of 19th-century Europe and sees it as shabby, vulgar, and spiritually hollow. (And if that is how he sees *19th-century* European culture, how on earth would he respond to the endless banalities of current-day television and the internet!) Nietzsche is determined to trace the problem to its origins. According to his analysis, the problem starts with the egalitarianism of Christianity (all individuals, as children of God, are of equal worth). More specifically, the rot sets in with the Protestant Reformation (the judgments of the common man are of a worth and dignity equal to that of putative elites; no one should defer to the supposedly higher judgment and taste of cultural elites). So, one has to destroy Christianity as well as the democratic culture that it spawned. One has to use all possible intellectual weapons for that purpose, including the rhetoric of deconstructing or "genealogizing" authoritative truths (though Nietzsche himself is not lacking in authoritative truths of his own). One can then reinstate pre-French-Revolution hierarchy, iron discipline, and top-down legislation, by superior individuals, of authoritative cultural norms. One will once again be able to restore real cultures that people can live by and that provide a commanding sense of meaning and purpose, relative to which the culture of liberalism and liberal freedom presents itself as mere void and ennui. In *Twilight of the Idols*, Nietzsche suggested that the cause of civilization would be mightily advanced if liberal Europe were more like czarist Russia, and somehow his legions of defenders have never noticed that that's how he sees the world.

For what reason would Nietzsche find Russian autocracy admirable, and perceive the rights and liberties of bourgeois society as fraudulent? To answer this question, one need merely ponder Georg Simmel's faithful encapsulation of Nietzschean anti-liberalism:

> There is no more severe judge of everything anarchic, undisciplined, and soft than Nietzsche, who finds the reason for the engulfing contemporary decadence in the disappearance of strict discipline, piety, and authority in the face of the ignoble tendency toward equalization and universal happiness.

To the extent that one unflinchingly acknowledges the basic truth of Simmel's description (Nietzsche's contempt for what is "soft" and his demand for the harsh wielding of authority), the question of why Nietzsche belongs fundamentally to the right also easily answers itself.

How does one respond to such a challenge to the democratic-egalitarian dispensation? Of course, the preferable option is to respond via a positive normative vision—such as some version of liberalism or a political philosophy to the left of liberalism—articulating a principled commitment to the intrinsic worth or dignity of all human beings qua human beings. The claim is that there is a key moral truth here that Nietzsche and those influenced by him are blind to or which they wrongly dismiss—although it would be naïve ever to expect an end to the philosophical debate about whether this is indeed an essential moral truth or merely (as Nietzsche and his epigones believe) a fiction invented by the liberal tradition due to their bewitchment by the Christian gospels.

However, there is also a negative argument that in no way lacks force. As sketched above, the accusation that runs through all the anti-liberal reactionaries—Nietzsche, Heidegger, Evola, Dugin—is that the liberal-bourgeois dispensation, privileging human equality and respect for shared human dignity, is culturally empty and vapid, spiritually hollow, weak, decadent, effete, banal, spiritless, and so on. (Hence the outrageous fantasy on the part of Schmitt and Heidegger that their support for Hitler was contributing to the "re-spiritualization" of Europe!) In late Nietzsche especially, this rhetoric gets pretty hysterical, which is exactly what inspired the generation of Oswald Spengler, Ernst Jünger, and Heidegger. Fine: bourgeois liberalism is flat, banal, de-spiritualized, etc. It can't offer us the grandeur of ancient Greece or the Roman Empire. So what do we replace it with? The grandeur of Napoleon, paid for with the blood of millions? Rule by a caste of warrior-priests, à la Evola? The theocratized fascism of ISIS? Putin, with his reactivated dreams of a glorious Russian Empire ruled by a "czar"? Even if the cultural critique of a Nietzsche or Heidegger were not completely off the mark (and let's be honest: there's plenty of banality in liberal culture), the alternatives on offer—which in Nietzsche's case are never spelled out with any specificity—are incomparably worse!

As should be obvious to any reader of McManus's book, "the right" is anything but a unitary intellectual and political tradition. The tensions and cleavages within the right are certainly as important as the consistency of its commitment to repudiating equality. We can see this with respect to what distinguishes the radical right from tradition-oriented conservatism by contrasting Nietzsche with a bona fide conservative like T.S. Eliot. Like Eliot, Nietzsche clearly saw modern democracy as the enemy of high culture. But whereas Eliot responded to what he perceived as cultural decline by clutching on to a waning Christianity, Nietzsche was not averse to completing and radicalizing the Enlightenment's liberation from Christianity in order to open up new, more extreme possibilities. And whereas Eliot was in some measure resigned to the triumph of mediocrity, mass culture, and "the vulgarities of modernity," as McManus phrases it, resignation obviously wasn't an option for Nietzsche. He thought that the French Revolution's establishment of an egalitarian dispensation could be comprehensively reversed; hence he conjured up dangerous visions of a Große Politik (grand or epic politics) that would sweep away existing forms of social and political life. Contrary to images of Nietzsche as apolitical or anti-political, he yearned for a more ideologically bellicose age in which "the concept of politics will become entirely merged with a mode of spiritual warfare," as he put it in *Ecce Homo*. "Starting with me, the earth will come to know grand politics." When Nietzsche, in *Thus Spoke Zarathustra*, appealed to "the other shore," he was writing a blank check cashed by the fascists of the next generation.

Even a humane and in many ways liberal-minded thinker like Rousseau could write in *Emile*: "fanaticism, although sanguinary and cruel, is nevertheless a grand and strong passion which elevates the heart of man, makes him despise death, and gives him a prodigious energy that need only be better directed to produce the most sublime virtues." Yet the truth is that this opens an extremely dangerous door. As Rousseau should have known and probably did know, the cruelty and destructiveness are a 100 times more likely than the sublime virtues. As Robert Kagan has written, "one would think it hard to have a 1930s mentality [by which he means: underestimating the capacity of tyrants to upend the entire liberal way of life] knowing what happened in the 1940s." But alas, human nature is too warped—Kant was right to describe it as "crooked timber" from which nothing straight can ever be made—and human memory is too short. We surely don't want to assume that the horrors of the 20th century will be replayed in the coming decades, but neither do we dare assume that they won't.

Engagement with the radical right entails real risks that cannot be circumvented. Extremists love attention, believing that it helps them win more recruits to their cause. They may well be right in thinking that. But what choice do we have? Frank Bruni, in a *New York Times* op-ed devoted to Tucker Carlson, nicely captured the lose-lose nature of the conundrum:

> Like Trump, [Carlson] has decided that virality is its own reward. And he's being amply rewarded…. I'd prefer to ignore him, but I face the same irreconcilable considerations that all the others who aren't ignoring him do. To give him attention is to play into his hands, but to do the opposite is to play ostrich.

It is painful to give intellectuals of the far right the attention that they crave, but it is no less perilous to pretend that these intellectuals don't exist and to fail to do what we can to warn fellow citizens of the dangers that they pose to the imperfect but improvable liberal democracy that we cherish.

The relevant context for this book, and all similar books, is the shift in the Zeitgeist that seemed to occur around 2016. People refer to it as a crisis of liberal democracy, and a crisis of liberal democracy is indeed what it appears to be. To be sure, it would be absurd to believe that we inhabited some kind of liberal utopia prior to 2016. We clearly didn't. But it was possible to be hopeful about the project of civic democracy. That hope is considerably harder to sustain today, after seeing how democratic politics has been blighted by the likes of Brexit; Trump and the January 6th insurrection; Putin and his evil invasion of Ukraine; the "illiberal democracy" of Orbán and his admirers in the United States; Bolsonaro, Erdoğan, and Modi; and now the electoral successes scored by neo-fascists in Sweden, Italy, and Israel. Democracy (whose literal meaning is ruled by the demos) naturally involves populist challenges to dominant elites, but the forms of populist revolt that we have seen since 2016 have consistently targeted the wrong elites for political purposes that are reactionary rather than progressive.

A well-lived life hangs in important ways on maintaining the right balance between hope and despair. The spark of life is extinguished in the absence of hope for a better world, which in the case of the democratic left means a more egalitarian, and hence more just, civic existence. But sustaining hope on the basis of folly and credulity is winning hope at an unacceptable price. The world has to support our hopes, rendering them at least somewhat realistic rather than just a purely ethereal dream. The right, of course, has its own hopes—for what it conceives as a world embodying less equality but more strength, virility, collective self-assertion, supposed cultural creativity, and a more robust set of convictions about who belongs and who doesn't belong. What represents hope for the right represents despair for egalitarian democrats, and vice versa. We have to educate ourselves about threats emanating from the right so that democrats can fend off despair (again, not so easy these days) and try to ensure that the anti-egalitarian ambitions of the right don't prevail over the hopes for a more just social world on the part of the left. We owe thanks to Matthew McManus for contributing to those essential efforts.

Ronald Beiner, 2023

Note

1 See Matthew McManus and Ben Burgis and Conrad Hamilton and Marion Trejo. *Myth and Mayhem: A Leftist Critique of Jordan Peterson.* (Winchester, UK: Zero Books, 2020)

INTRODUCTION

What Does It Mean to Be on the Political Right?

The Right Side of History?

> It is allegiance which defines the condition of society, and which consti-
> tutes society as something greater than the 'aggregate of individuals' that
> the liberal mind perceives. It is proper for conservatives to be skeptical of
> claims made on behalf of the value of the individual, if these claims should
> conflict with the allegiance necessary to society, even though they may
> wish the state (in the sense of the apparatus of government) to stand in a
> fairly loose relation to the activities of individual citizens. Individuality too
> is an artifact, an achievement which depends on the social life of people.[1]
>
> (Roger Scruton, *The Meaning of Conservatism: Third Edition*)

Since at least Trump's election in 2016, the question of what constitutes the political right—and what distinguishes it from liberalism and socialism—has gained
renewed importance.[2] On the political right, "liberal" has often been used as
a pejorative slur second only to "socialist" in its venom. But however, many
prominent intellectuals on the political right—particularly those who identify
with the Intellectual Dark Web and its successors—proudly identify as "classical
liberals" in between launching their 30th tirade about aggravating college students. Sometimes conservatives are portrayed as the most determined defenders
of liberal values like free speech and association, locked in battle against the
censorious left and its growing list of cultural and market allies. There is also
a burgeoning movement of increasingly influential "post-liberal" conservative
thinkers who resent the left's alleged or real efforts at censorship while being
remarkably less attached to longstanding liberal ideals like market economics and
the neutrality of law.

DOI: 10.4324/9781003307952-1

Thinking through this problem requires us to consider how the political right is fundamentally a response to the moral project of modernity: that society consists of moral equals who should be free to pursue their interests within participatory political institutions. This egalitarian project was of course always conceived in highly unequal ways by the two great modernist doctrines of liberalism and socialism, both of which were responsible for often vicious forms of tyranny, imperialism, and carceral discipline. But what distinguished the modernist doctrines of liberalism and socialism was the constant pressure to reform by activist and even revolutionary movements who insisted that such compromises with inequality and unfreedom were intolerant and even evil. It would be going much too far to conclude from this, in a kind of cheesy left-Hegelian manner, that there is an inexorable telos or arc of history which bends toward the modernist project. And indeed in no small part because of the often successful efforts of the political right, the project of modernity has always been both contested and subject to back-and-forth movements. But Will Kymlicka is broadly right that even if it advanced haltingly, it has advanced, and liberals and socialists both have reason to applaud this development.[3]

The political right does not. This is because political right is simply more comfortable with the idea that people are unequal, and so should be treated unequally. There are more and less extreme forms to this idea, with the most moderate forms of ordered liberty conservatism overlapping closely with right-wing variants of liberalism. However, as I've already discussed elsewhere, the more liberals become convinced that moral equality must entail high levels of material parity, the more likely they are to affiliate with socialist ideals.[4] Because I think ultimately the idea of moral equality necessitates securing for all individuals a comparable—though not equal—set of capabilities needed to live a good life, liberals should gradually come to gravitate more toward these progressive positions.

Modernity and the Idea of Moral Equality

The historical relationship between moral equality, liberalism, and socialism is complex, but can be boiled down relatively simply. In his classic polemic *The Meaning of Conservatism*, Roger Scruton discusses liberal's individualism and its consequent wariness of the notion of "allegiance."[5] Elsewhere he stipulates that this is cashed out as an "attitude of respect towards individual existence—an attempt to leave as much moral and political space around very person as is compatible with the demands of social life. As such it has often been thought to imply a kind of egalitarianism. For by its very nature, the respect which liberalism shows to the individual, it shows to each individual equally." Scruton is exactly right on this point, and as we shall see it is the right's insistence that political respect and power isn't owed to all individuals equally that is at the root of its dispute with both liberalism and socialism.

Clearly, the idea of moral equality has deeper, and less secular, roots than liberalism. The Buddhist Emperor Ashoka reflected the ideal in his injunction to tolerate and learn from sources of wisdom regardless of where they come from. The Roman stoics, who had a profound influence on liberals like Adam Smith, often went out of their way to insist that slave and Emperor live, age, and die alike. And, the best elements of the Christian scholastic tradition taught that all of God's children were equal in his eyes. But these doctrines confronted a broader consensus of learned opinion that people were, either by nature or by divine fiat, fundamentally unequal. Consequently, it is both inevitable and desirable that society reflects these inequalities in how wealth and power are allocated. In his *Republic*, Plato famously distinguished between people with souls of bronze, silver, and gold and insisted only the latter were fit to rule. If the wrong souls were somehow to rule, the city would be doomed. Aristotle similarly ranked people according to their virtues and natural capacities, infamously declaring many to be "natural slaves" fit largely for the manual labor which would enable their betters to pursue higher and more virtuous ends.[6] In the medieval and early modern era, religious defenses of both feudalism and later absolutism stressed both the naturalness and divine necessity of social stratification. Sir Robert Filmer's *Patriarcha*, scathingly criticized by none other than John Locke, defended the divine right of kings through a mix of both: arguing that God granted initial authority to a series of Biblical patriarchs, who passed it along through their biological descendants.

Proto- and early liberals attacked these positions from a variety of different angles, in effect attempting to undermine the claim that society should maintain calcified distinctions of wealth and power. At the basis of their argument was the claim that, at least in the proverbial beginning, all human beings were in principle morally equal. This did not mean society required everyone be equal in fact, but it did problematize the idea that the proper kind of social stratification was set once and for all by natural or divine ordinance. Hobbes—not a liberal himself but one who had a deep influence on the tradition—mocked the aristocratic ethos of Plato and especially Aristotle as so much nonsense, and insisted that in the state of nature all of us were conspicuously equal in both bodily and especially mental faculties. Contra the ancients, Hobbes insisted that "as for the faculties of the mind: I find that men are even more equal in these than they are in bodily strength."[7] In the *Second Treatise of Government,* Locke reiterates his critique of Filmer and insists that the state of nature "is also a state of equality in which no-one has more power and authority than anyone else; because it is simply obvious that creatures of the same species and status, all born to all the same advantages of nature and to the use of the same abilities, should also be equal..."[8] Later on in her *Vindication of the Rights of Women*, Mary Wollstonecraft very eloquently chided her liberal counterparts for not applying such principles with the barest consistency, claiming that if "liberty is the mother of virtues, and if women be, by their very constitution, slaves, and not allowed to breathe the sharp invigorating air of freedom, they must ever languish like exotics, and be reckoned beautiful flaws in nature."[9]

This latter point brings us to the most noxious feature of liberalisms' history, which is precisely the self-serving tendency of its exponents to preach moral equality before carving out gigantic exceptions wherever it was expedient. The American founders were a spectacular example, with many of them being slave-owners, and pious democrat Thomas Jefferson seeing nothing wrong with sexual abuse to boot. The post-colonial theorist Uday Mehta has drawn attention to the fact that J.S. Mill, a highly admirable liberal socialist in most other respects, nevertheless adopted condescending views toward the colonized peoples of the British Empire.[10] These compare unfavorably to the conservative Edmund Burke, who was more sensitive to the cultural differences of the Indian subcontinent. And most notably the commitment to moral equality did not mean that liberals were initially committed to material or even political equality for all. Echoing C.B. Macpherson, one could say most early liberals were "possessive individualists."[11] They felt that the old, naturalized hierarchies should gave way to a more dynamic society where social stratification would be determined through competition in the market, rather than something more arbitrary like aristocratic privilege. This persists down to the present day, with neoliberalism constituting the most radical form of possessive individualism we've yet seen. Liberal possessive individualists may have accepted the need to end legal discrimination against groups which keep them from participating as formal equals in the market. But they are generally wary of taking too many steps to compensate members of discriminated groups on the basis of abstract "social justice," and absolutely did not accept that there was any entitlement to the political provision of high levels of material well-being for all where that would contravene the efficient mechanisms of the market.

Between the 19th and 20th centuries, socialism emerged as the other great modernist doctrine, offering pressing critiques of liberalism and capitalism whose relevance persists today. Early socialists like Robert Owen and St. Simon were primarily figures in the vein of the early Enlightenment, drawing up charming but often fanciful blueprints on how property could be distributed in a more egalitarian manner while still preserving economic efficiency and development. They were motivated first and foremost, as Terry Eagleton would put it, by the sentiment that it was wrong "that most people who have lived and died have spent lives of wretched, fruitless, unremitting toil."[12] By the time of Mill and Dickens, such objections began to have some force. But of course the most substantial objection came from Karl Marx, whose epochal critique of political economy remains in some respects the climax of the modernist project. It tightly links human freedom to emancipation from necessity for all, arguing that a scientific analysis of capitalism's dynamics shows how its stunning productivity neverthe-less carries within itself the seeds of its own destruction. Marxism became the chief theoretical outlook for most of the major socialist movements and parties by the end of the 19th century, with many achieving important reforms. But its reputation was seriously tarnished by the totalitarian movements in the Soviet

Union, China, Cambodia, and elsewhere which appealed to Marx's legacy to advance tyranny while taking serious liberties with his thought. With the collapse of the Soviet Empire in 1989, many thought socialisms' days were numbered, though it has since enjoyed a resurgence in popularity as the inequalities and vulgarities of neoliberalism became increasingly scrutinized.

On some of these points liberals and socialists can surprisingly find common ground with conservatives which go beyond mere alliances of expediency. For many socialists and conservatives, the liberal emphasis on manic individualism is atomistic and a bastardization of our true nature. As an ideology spread through institutions and politics, it has generated a profound sense of alienation and detachment. The political right has even found some intriguing points of inspiration in the work of the devil Marx. In the 1920s Carl Schmitt found Marxism's emphasis on class conflict and a utopian world yet to come more inspiring than the endless chatter of liberal parliamentarianism. Post-liberal conservatives like Patrick Deneen and Peter Lawler have also come to begrudgingly acknowledge the Marxist claim that capitalism is a "revolutionary mode of production" which invariably upends the cultural traditions and former hierarchies on which it was initially parasitic. On the other end right-wing liberals like F.A. Hayek and Michael Oakeshott returned the love by emphasizing the importance of law, order, and tradition in stabilizing capitalist societies and providing a sense of humanistic attachment above and beyond market relations. They also sometimes worried, like Alexis de Tocqueville in *Democracy in America*, that liberalism would give into a leveling impulse that would gradually erode the striving for excellence and status upon which social progress and high culture depended. This would need to be countered by the maintenance of quasi-aristocratic and competitive mechanisms which prompted striving.

But these affinities do not mean that liberals or socialists are conservatives. The reason being that for both modernist doctrines, some commitment to the principles of equality and freedom was always crucial. Or as Hayek puts it in "Why I am Not a Conservative," even right-wing liberals must reject the conservative position "...that in any society there are recognizably superior persons whose inherited standards and values and position ought to be protected and who should have a greater influence on public affairs than others."[13] Or to put it in a positive sense, James Fitzjames Stevens once claimed that

> "...the attitude of mind engendered by continual glorification of the present time, and of successful resistance to an authority assumed to be usurped and foolish, is almost of necessity fatal to the recognition of the fact that to obey a real superior, to submit to a real necessity and make the best of it in good part, is one of the most important of all virtues—a virtue absolutely essential to the attainment of anything great and lasting."

It is this rejection that there are "recognizably superior persons" that makes one committed to the modernist project and not to the political right.

The Political Right and Inequality

Oddly enough the political right was the second, not the first, major modernist doctrine to emerge. This is unexpected since conservatives often hold themselves to be defending more ancient and enduring values than their liberal and certainly socialist counterparts. And indeed, the political right generally finds more use in the authors of antiquity than liberals or socialists, whether one talks about Aristotle, Confucius, or a million strands of quasi-Thomism. But as a distinct body of thought, the modern political right emerged in response to the liberal and democratic movements of the 18th century, which they initially saw as a concerted threat to well-established political hierarchies. With the later rise of socialism and its calls for economic democracy and redistribution of property, these disputes took on a renewed vigor that could often become deeply venomous.

This responsiveness to agonism, the "reactionary disposition" as it is sometimes called, means that the political right is far more eclectic than either liberalism or socialism. This is sometimes explained away as arising from theoretical differences. According to Russell Kirk, unlike liberals and socialists who are committed to abstract principles, the conservative is framed more by a disposition or attitude than anything else. In "On Being Conservative" Michael Oakeshott framed it more nostalgically, claiming

> to be a conservative, to be conservative... is to prefer the familiar to the unknown, to prefer the tried to the untried, fact to mystery, the actual to the possible, the limited to the unbounded, the near to the distant, the sufficient to the superabundant, the convenient to the perfect, present laughter to utopian bliss.[14]

This preference for the familiar and "actual" is indeed emblematic of conservative thought, which is why they often rightly claim to be more "realistic" in a very narrow way than their liberal or conservative counterparts.

Since intellectuals on the political right tend to be attracted to defending existent divisions of wealth and power, they can usually claim to be merely upholding the world as it is rather than speculating on an "abstract" (there is that word again) or utopian world to be. But this realism doesn't run very deep, since the world never simply "is" but is in fact always in a process of becoming. When Marx critiqued his opponents for their philosophical "idealism" this is what he had in mind; right-wing intellectuals idealize a state of affairs they take to be reflective of some deeper, more natural, or holier reality and resist any tendency on the part of the material world to transition away from this idealization. Consequently, the alleged "realism" of the political right often turns out to be a kind of sublimated idealism, which not coincidentally is why conservatives since Edmund Burke have always been attracted to aesthetic and religious imagery and ideas which seem to sacralize their preferred social order.[15] This view is something that must be felt and venerated rather than questioned, or as Joseph de Maistre puts it,

> government is a true religion: it has its dogmas, its mysteries, and its min-
> isters. To annihilate it or submit it to the discussion of each individual is
> the same thing; it lives only through national reason, that is to say through
> political faith, which is a creed. Man's first need is that his nascent reason
> be curbed under this double yoke, that it be abased and lose itself in the
> national reason, so that it changes its individual existence into another
> common existence, just as a river that flows into the ocean always contin-
> ues to exist in the mass of water, but without a name and without a distinct
> reality.[16]

Consequently, the political right has always been uncomfortable with the idea of universal critical thinking and permissive free debate, so beloved by the liberal tradition. Power is preferably sublimated into authority, and consequently either to be unquestioned or at best justified through apologias. Any effort to intellectualize power risks desublimating its authority and turning it into a matter of debate, or worse, voluntarism. This is one of the reasons J.S. Mill cheekily claimed "stupid people are generally conservative." And indeed conservatives can dismiss intellectuals as everything from "sophisters, economists, and calculators" in more elitist moments, and to the "anointed" in more populist ones. Oftentimes this wariness of intellectuals is more of a visceral reaction than the product of a thought process; it is a kind of instinctive response to those who would question the perceived inherited and embedded wisdom found in conservative traditions and institutions. Sometimes it is theorized on in a rather partisan and one-sided manner, as with Thomas Sowell's *Intellectuals and Society*.[17] But few are as honest as Roger Scruton in stating the primary reason: too much intellectualism results in people becoming unwilling to accept the problems of life and to seek remedy through potentially radical political action. Consequently, many conservatives prefer and occasionally idolize an "unthinking" population.

> There is a natural instinct in unthinking people—who, tolerant of the
> burdens that life lays on them, and unwilling to lodge blame where they
> seek no remedy, seek fulfillment in the world as it is—to accept and
> endorse through their actions the institutions and practices into which
> they are born. This instinct, which I have attempted to translate into
> the self-conscious language of political doctrine, is rooted in human
> nature...[18]

A little more eloquent than Trump's claim to "love" the uneducated, but the affection is the same.

In moments of political quietism or populism, conservative intellectuals will sometimes heap praise on these "unthinking" masses who know their place and keep the trains running on time, often by contrasting them with ungrateful and resentful "elites"—which typically means liberal and leftist intellectuals and activists. The problem emerges when those same liberal and leftist intellectuals and activists convince the masses through abstract sophistry and other witchcraft that they should seek remedy for their problems in political and economic change. At this point the people quickly become the "swinish multitude" or Nietzsche's "herd," driven by resentment, envy, and a yearning to upset the sublimated idealizations of hierarchy dear to the conservative heart. In such moments the real emphasis of the right on maintaining hierarchies of power and wealth becomes most exposed, and it is at greatest risk of appearing as an unpalatably elitist and inegalitarian doctrine that either naturalizes or mythologies social differences which can ultimately be overcome through determined reform or revolution.

These differences can take many forms: differences in wealth and political status were the first to be critiqued by liberals and later socialists. But since then other social injustices, such as gender-based inequities, the unequal status of LGBTQ individuals, the usurpation of ethnic and religious minority rights, racially based hierarchies, the reduction or elimination of migrant rights, and countless other egalitarian causes, have been recognized in the list of human rights that the political right has at one point or another sought to oppose. Where actions to protect these rights become sufficiently to the fore, the political right tends to become self-conscious and recognize the need to reflect intellectually on their preferred hierarchy to defend it. This is in some respects an uncomfortable position, since it means desacralizing the hierarchies and rendering them open to analysis and consequently criticism. But failing to do this cedes the intellectual high ground to liberals and socialists, who will inevitably use it to inspire critical reflection leading to demands for reform 20 years down the line. When too much change has occurred, many on the right will also adopt more radical postures which seem at odds with their usual claim to be persons of moderation and slow reform. This will be accompanied by some of the more creative efforts of conservative intellectuals to condemn the failure of other elites to sufficiently exercise power and maintain the proper hierarchy. At its peak this can lead to calls for conservative revolution or counter-revolution.

One of the reasons illiberal post-modern conservatives like Donald Trump and Victor Orban became popular was the feeling that too many privileges and too much status had been granted to the unworthy; their success owed a lot to their ability to convince citizens that too many unworthy people—immigrants, feminists, minorities—had cut in line and obtained benefits and government-mandated advantages that they did not deserve. The same was true of Reagan and his tirades against "welfare queens" in the 1980s. In circumstances where too many gains have been achieved by liberals and leftists, the political right will engage in anything from radical reforms to outright counter-revolutionary efforts to create the right kind of social hierarchy appropriate to society.

An Intellectual History of the Political Right

Throughout the history of right-wing thought, different figures have tried to ground it in many interesting, contradicting, and sometimes maddening ways. Around the same time as Leo Strauss and Harry Jaffa were resuscitating the concept of natural right and condemning historicism, Michael Oakeshott and Lord Patrick Devlin were arguing that the roots of British conservatism lay in respect for, and veneration of, a longstanding history of traditions. This is precisely what made them comprehensible to the "man on the Clapham omnibus" who had little interest in Plato or Nietzsche, but plenty in restricting homosexuality.[19] Joseph de Maistre compared the French Revolutionaries' destruction of the aristocracy to a Luciferian rebellion against God, while just a few decades later Friedrich Nietzsche declared that God was dead and a new aristocratic caste of supermen was inbound. Conservatives like William F. Buckley and Jordan Peterson condemned utopian progressives for failing to understand the near scientific laws of the capitalist market, while Martin Heidegger condemned capitalism as "metaphysically the same" as socialism and mourned the arrival of a new technical age.[20]

None of these views was held insincerely, and none can uniformly claim to better embody the thrust of right-wing thinking than any other. Much depends on the historical and social context within which a conservative thinker is embedded, what arguments his egalitarian opponents put forward, and his own creative inclinations. Fusionism and Straussianism resonated in an American context where appeal to universal rights and eternal Christian standards were a matter of course. Neither enjoyed as much traction in the United Kingdom and many of its colonies, where religious evangelism could be as much of a threat as a prop to monarchial authority. Nietzsche and Heidegger wanted to speak to a new generation of the radical right who were convinced that conservative elites were not up to the job of defeating egalitarian modernity, while to Christian conservatives like George Grant or Patrick Deneen their veneration of the will and power is precisely what makes the two Germans emblematic of the modern world at its absolute worst. What identifies each of these philosophers as figures of the political right is their intellectual defense of inequality and authoritative hierarchy, and a wariness that can turn into contempt for those who challenge these ideals or lack the stomach to defend them effectively.

More significant than the philosophical grounding of the right is the potency of this inegalitarianism. The most moderate forms of conservatism insist that the inequality they prioritize is contingent, not metaphysical. For instance proponents of ordered liberty capitalism maintain that they accept equality under the law, and even admire the dynamism of the market which allows individuals to rise and fall on their merits and efforts. While there will always be stratification between rich and poor, the powerful and the weak, these will not be constant for individuals and class mobility will be the order of the day. This is what Margaret Thatcher meant when she claimed to support a "classless society." Other moderate forms of Burkean conservatism contend that we are entitled to morally prioritize the needs of members of our own national, religious, or cultural group. This is not because our own culture is necessary superior; some Burkean conservatives even claim to admire to diversity of groups in the world. It is purely because of the contingent fact that one is born into, or is at least a longstanding member of, the particular group, which necessitates the members of the group being granted moral priority. Much like our parents might have been anyone, we owe special fidelity to those who are actually our parents. In fact, it is acceptable to morally prioritize those who are more proximate to our identity and share our values. And of course, many moralistic conservatives believe that hierarchies of virtue or grace are necessarily fluid, since much is determined by personal character and choice.

What distinguishes the more far-right forms of politics from moderate conservatism is a hardening of their inegalitarianism, which is typically associated with casting inequality in more essentialized or enduring terms, some of them quaint, others dark and disturbing. The De Maistres and Carlyles of the world regarded inequities as resulting from immaterial forces, whether divine order or the heroic character of the truly great. By contrast the most noxious figures on the early far right, like John Calhoun, Arthur de Gobineau, and a host of social Darwinists, were adamant in appealing to history and even pseudo-scientific racism to dignify their prejudice with the veneer of factual immutability. This of course reached its peak with fascism and Nazism, which held that modernist inegalitarianism violated the "aristocratic principle of nature" and never shied away from insisting on its contempt for the weak and idolization of the racially superior. For the far right, the preferred hierarchy is conceived as both just and usually ascribed with immutable characteristics.[21] The kind of dynamic, upwardly mobile hierarchy favored by moderate conservatives is then conceived as conceding too much to modernist egalitarianism. Of course this mania for essentialized immutability will invariably be disappointed when it becomes clear that human society and hierarchy are far more plastic and open to contestation than the far right is prepared to tolerate. But rather than reframing their fundamental outlook, deviations from the proper hierarchy are invariably seen as the result of either external or, more likely, internal antagonists who bring about decay and decadence to the proper ruling caste. This inevitably generates an agonistic disposition toward politics which can climax in militarism and even the demand for extermination. It is believed that these conflicts would not only help overcome one's enemies but also curb the tendency toward decline and slack humanism on the part of the proper elite.

The intellectual history of the political right therefore pivots around this transition from moderate and contingent to harder and more uncompromising forms, depending on a huge variety of personal and contextual factors. One very common factor in determining the transition from the moderate to the far right is, as Corey Robin observed in *The Reactionary Mind*, the presence of—or at least the perception that there exists—a powerful and intellectually vibrant political left.[22] One rarely sees a De Maistre rise to prominence without the French Revolution, or a Carl Schmitt and Heidegger without Karl Marx inspiring the SPD and Bolshevik parties in Germany. A significant factor in the emergence of post-liberalism and the alt-right in the early 21st century was the perception that, even if socialist egalitarianism was defeated, the spread of liberal multiculturalism and permissiveness had continued unabated or even accelerated with the fall of Communism.

Conclusion

> The doctrine of equality!... But there is no more venomous poison in existence: for it appears to be preached by justice itself, when it is actually the end of justice... 'Equality to the equal; inequality to the unequal'—that would be true justice speaking: and its corollary, 'never make the unequal equal'.[23]
>
> (Friedrich Nietzsche, *Twilight of the Idols*)

My project in *The Political Right and Inequality* will be to develop an (inevitably partial) analysis of the intellectual right that both accounts for these theoretical shifts and situates them within their proper context. But it is not simply an exegesis on the right, but a critique of its primary convictions and arguments from the standpoint of one who is faithful to the modernist project. That human beings are morally equal is a vital precondition for holding that we should also be free, since it is on the basis of equality that we can deny the right of political power to impose itself on us without serious justification. This is not to say that liberalism or socialism have been anything but deeply imperfect in their commitments to equality and freedom, either in theory or practice. But Will Kymlicka is right in saying that the force of these principles is such that it imposes pressure upon us both to expand our horizons of moral consideration and to undermine those forms of power and domination which deny respect to all.[24] The political has been the most compelling intellectual opponent of this drive, endlessly reinventing and re-establishing itself to defend and counter-attack against egalitarians in the drive to level the world.

There are some who may find this approach dissatisfying, since it provides a highly intellectualized and theoretical take on the political right. The book does situate the various authors in their historical and socio-political context, including providing some biographical details (and pot-shorts here and there if I'm being honest). Indeed one of the guiding frameworks of the book is the political right's response to the egalitarian project of modernity.[25] But unlike earlier works[25] by me this background context is primarily there to help guide an interpretation of these authors' major arguments and texts in relation to the moral thrust of liberal and socialist arguments that aspire to more equal conditions for all. Those left critics who feel historicization and contextualization are the only sure paths away from the twin hells of idealism and ideological sublimation (a fancy way of saying platforming and consequently legitimating) will probably be dissatisfied. They will see this way of approaching the political right as flawed and even dangerous, insisting that any approach must ground their arguments in a critique of material and social conditions. This has the effect of not only delegitimating the specific claims; by situating right-wing authors in a broader explanatory framework we diagnose their ideas as symptoms of social contradictions and tensions.[26] Many would claim this has the effect of undermining the whole tradition by, in effect, explaining it away. To paraphrase Wittgenstein, the problem of the right is dissolved along with its intellectual and political potency.[27]

I'm enough of a materialist to think there is plenty to be said for such an approach, and critics from Marx through Jessica Whyte have proven its continued critical efficacy.[28] For a while I was tempted to write just such a text, extending some of my arguments in *The Rise of Post-Modern Conservatism* and making the whole edifice bigger, badder, and bolder. But upon reflection it occurred to me that this effort to dissolve through contextualizing and diagnosing did have the effect of often leaving the substance of right-wing claims untouched. Why right-wing intellectuals make their arguments about hierarchy and inequality, traditionalism and a wariness of democracy, the relationship between revolution and counter-revolution, and why we actually need 10,000 books written about how annoying campus activists are may be explained through well-conducted historical analysis. But this does not actually respond to those arguments by pointing out why they are flawed, wicked, or even just not arguments at all. In other words historical contextualization leaves a lot of argumentative room left to the right. So I decided to write a book that was in many respects much more straightforward. It does explain the project of the political right in terms of a reaction to egalitarian modernity but takes it seriously as a cogent intellectual tradition that has often marshaled many bad—but often impressive and creative—arguments which have contributed to standing athwart its march. The hope is that by undermining those arguments *The Political Right and Equality* helps clear a wider path for the march to carry on.

Notes

1 Roger Scruton. *The Meaning of Conservatism: Third Edition.* (South Bend, IN: St Augustine's Press, 2002) at p. 24
2 See also Matthew McManus. *Liberalism and Socialism: Mortal Enemies or Embittered Kin?* (Cham, Switzerland: Palgrave MacMillan, 2021)
3 Will Kymlicka. "Multiculturalism's Moral Impulse." *Carnegie Council for Ethics in International Affairs,* November 25th, 2014. https://www.youtube.com/watch?v=2W689QD849Y&t=6s
4 Matthew McManus. *Liberalism and Socialism: Mortal Enemies or Embittered Kin?* (Cham, Switzerland: Palgrave MacMillan, 2021)
5 Roger Scruton. *The Meaning of Conservatism: Third Edition.* (South Bend, IN: St Augustine's Press, 2002) at Ch. Two
6 Aristotle. *The Basic Works of Aristotle.* (New York, NY: The Modern Library, 2001) at p. 1132

7 Thomas Hobbes. *Leviathan*. (London, UK: Penguin Books, 2017) at p. 100

8 John Locke. *Second Treatise on Government*. (Indianapolis, IN: Hackett Publishing, 1980) at p. 8

9 Mary Wollstonecraft. *A Vindication of the Rights of Women*. (New York, NY: Norton Library, 1967) at p. 72

10 Uday Singh Mehta. *Liberalism and Empire: A Study in Nineteenth-Century British Liberal Thought*. (Chicago, IL: The University of Chicago Press, 1999)

11 C.B. MacPherson. *The Political Theory of Possessive Individualism: Hobbes to Locke*. (Don Mills, ON: Oxford University Press, 1962)

12 Quoted in Meagan Day. "Socialists Identify With Humanity As a Whole: An Interview With Nathan J. Robinson." *Jacobin Magazine*. December 26th, 2019

13 F.A. Hayek. *The Constitution of Liberty: The Definitive Edition*. (Chicago, IL: University of Chicago Press, 2011) at p. 523

14 Michael Oakeshott. *Rationalism in Politics and Other Essays: New and Expanded Edition*. (Indianapolis, IN: Liberty Press, 1991) at p. 408

15 Peter Augustine Lawler. *Postmodernism Rightly Understood: The Return to Realism in American Thought*. (Lanham, MD: Rowman and Littlefield, 1992)

16 Joseph De Maistre. *The Generative Principle of Political Constitutions: Studies on Sovereignty, Religion, and Enlightenment*, ed. Jack Lively. (London, UK: Routledge, 1965)

17 Thomas Sowell. *Intellectuals and Society*. (New York, NY: Basic Books, 2009)

18 Roger Scruton. *The Meaning of Conservatism: Third Edition*. (South Bend, IN: St Augustine's Press, 2002) at p. 111

19 Patrick Devlin. "The Enforcement of Morals." *The Maccabean Lecture in Jurisprudence*, March 1959

20 Martin Heidegger. *Introduction to Metaphysics*, trans. Greogry Fried and Richard Polt. (New Haven, CT: Yale University Press, 2000) at p. 40

21 Though by no means all, and even some forms of biological racism conceive of the struggle for supremacy dynamically. See Mark Sedgwick. *Key Thinkers of the Radical Right: Behind the New Threat to Liberal Democracy*. (Oxford, UK: Oxford University Press, 2019)

22 Corey Robin. *The Reactionary Mind Second Edition: Conservatism from Edmund Burke to Donald Trump*. (Oxford, UK: Oxford University Press, 2018)

23 Friedrich Nietzsche. *The Twilight of the Idols and the Antichrist: or How to Philosophize with a Hammer*. (London, UK: Penguin Classics, 1990) at p. 113

24 Will Kymlicka. "Multiculturalism's Moral Impulse." *Carnegie Council for Ethics in International Affairs*, November 25th, 2014. https://www.youtube.com/watch?v=2W689QD849Y

25 See Matthew McManus. *The Rise of Post-Modern Conservatism: Neoliberalism, Post-Modern Culture, and Reactionary Politics*. (Gewerbestrasse, Switzerland: Palgrave MacMillan, 2019) and Matthew McManus. *What Is Post-Modern Conservatism: Essays on Our Hugely Tremendous Times*. (Winchester, UK: Zero Books, 2019) and Matthew McManus and Ben Burgis and Conrad Hamilton and Marion Trejo. *Myth and Mayhem: A Leftist Critique of Jordan Peterson*. (Winchester, UK: Zero Books, 2020)

26 A contemporary master of this approach was Domenico Losurdo. See Domenico Losurdo. *Liberalism: A Counter-History*, trans. Gregory Elliot. (London, UK: Verso Press, 2014) Domenico Losurdo. *Nietzsche, The Aristocratic Rebel*, trans. Gregor Benton. (Chicago, IL: Haymarket, 2020)

27 For an engaging explanation of how this Wittgensteinian critique connects to left-analysis more generally see the sections on Wittgenstein in Terry Eagleton. *Materialism*. (New Haven, CT: Yale University Press, 2016)

28 See Jessica Whyte. *The Morals of the Market: Human Rights and the Rise of Neoliberalism*. (London, UK: Verso Books, 2019)

PART I
The World Without Seam

1

THE DANGER OF THE SWINISH MULTITUDE

Introduction

Nothing is more certain than that our manners, our civilization, and all the good things which are connected with manners and with civilization have, in this European world of ours, depended for ages upon two principles and were, indeed, the result of both combined: I mean the spirit of a gentleman and the spirit of religion. The nobility and the clergy, the one by profession, the other by patronage, kept learning in existence, even in the midst of arms and confusions, and whilst governments were rather in their causes than formed. Learning paid back what it received to nobility and to priesthood, and paid it with usury, by enlarging their ideas and by furnishing their minds. Happy if they had all continued to know their indissoluble union and their proper place! Happy if learning, not debauched by ambition, had been satisfied to continue the instructor, and not aspired to be the master! Along with its natural protectors and guardians, learning will be cast into the mire and trodden down under the hoofs of a swinish multitude. If, as I suspect, modern letters owe more than they are always willing to own to ancient manners, so do other interests which we value full as much as they are worth.[1]

The modern political right was born as a protestation of grievance—a feeling not of deprivation but of loss. It hasn't stopped complaining since. This point is often expressed both more eloquently and more ponderously by many right-wing authors. They range from Roger Scruton's artful lamentations about the connection between conservatism and loss—the sense that "conservatism is the politics of delay"[2]—to Jordan Peterson reading the tea leaves and predicting that his having to wait three hours for customer service during the middle of

DOI: 10.4324/9781003307952-3

a pandemic is a sure sign that Western civilization is on the verge of collapse.[3] Why the political right feels so wronged, and what reactionaries feel was taken from them will be the subject of much of this book. But it is worth noting that even though a major thesis of *The Political Right and Equality* is that the political right had nothing taken from them to which they actually had any moral claim, and in fact their efforts to keep or recover or regain what they had or coveted us itself a gross injustice, they did in fact lose something.[4] With the advent of egalitarian modernity they were threatened not only with the loss of political station and power, wealth and social status, but in many respects something much worse. The intellectual thrust of egalitarian modernity not only promised to take those things away from them, but to expose them as undeserved at best and the products of gross injustice at worse. Their ressentiment toward the claim that elevated station is unearned can feel tantamount to seeing the "natural entrails" of society taken out.[5]

Egalitarian modernity posed an existential danger to a world in which differences in station and rank were not just respected and seen as deserved, but derived from a transcendent and even divine order beyond the material world. An order which intended each thing and person to be in their place, and more importantly rejected the notion that rising above one's station was admirable. The nostalgia for this manorial and orderly vision of the world has never left the political right, and a lot of its self-anointed claims to profundity come from an intense yearning to restore it.[6] Much of its originary and sometimes paradoxical anti-intellectualism comes from bitterness toward the long history of modernist intellectuals who had the gall to ask whether this beatific order was actually so beautiful to the serfs digging through the mud. Or, more shocking still, whether there was in fact some transcendent order to which human order and hierarchies mapped? Could it truly be that God didn't much care whether the House of Bourbon remained kept its behind firmly ensconced on the throne of France, engaged as it was in a holy quest to send as many paisans as possible to die for the Dutchy of Wurttemberg?

So to understand the political right and its nostalgia for this time period, we must look back a little bit further.

Antecedents to Conservative Thought I: Aristotle

If Whitehead is right and the simplest paraphrase of the Western philosophical tradition is that it consists of a series of footnotes to Plato then the space taken up by Aristotle would put *Infinite Jest* to shame. The master of those who know, or simply "the Philosopher," occupies a deserved place in the highest pantheon, influencing everyone from contemporary hard-right integralists to the most liberal branches of feminism and even Karl Marx.[7] The immensity of this legacy means that much of contemporary conservative thinking, though by no means all, operates in the shadow of Aristotle and the legacy of Aristotelianism.

My point in saying this is not to claim that Aristotle was fundamentally a conservative or right-wing thinker,[8] as has been commonly put forward by various—mostly American—authors keen to distinguish him from the proto-Communist Plato.[9] Instead I want to foreground those features of Aristotle's thought which have proven seductive to right-wing thinkers over the centuries, and to situate them within a genealogical context. And there is quite a lot in Aristotle for the political right to like. This ranges from Aristotle's essentialism to his taste for organic political metaphors, his emphasis on the cultivation of aristocratic-flavored virtues, and at least a cautious attitude toward political democracy. But, perhaps above all, the right remains attracted to Aristotle because as Strauss reminds us

> ...for Aristotle, political inequality is ultimately justified by the natural inequality among men. The fact that some men are by nature rules and others by nature ruled points in turn to the inequality which pervades nature as a whole: the whole as an ordered whole consists of beings of different rank.[10]

Or as Charles Taylor put it more generally in his excellent *Modern Social Imaginaries*:

> What is peculiar to our modern understanding of order stands out most clearly if we focus on how the idealizations of natural law theory differ from those that were dominant before. Premodern social imaginaries, especially those of the hierarchical type, were structured by various modes of hierarchical complementarity. These needed and complemented each other, but this didn't mean that their relations were truly mutual, because they didn't exist on the same level. Rather, they formed a hierarchy in which some had greater dignity and value than others...
>
> It was clear that each needed the others, but there is no doubt that we have here a descending scale of dignity; some functions were in their essence higher than others.[11]

This point is crucial to an understanding not just of the kind of right-Aristotelianism favored by conservatives and reactionaries, but the argument of this entire book. The ontology of an orderly universe where hierarchy and socio-political inequality are granted pride of place will be a –perhaps even *the*— major fetish object of the political right and especially its intellectuals going forward.

Aristotle's conception of nature—defined in the *Metaphysics* as the "genesis of growing things" —is as an organic whole where each particular thing that exists seeks to fulfill its telos. And in so doing both become more or less of what they are while participating in a whole that either enriches or corrupts.[12] Unsurprisingly for the son of a doctor, Aristotle was fond of medical metaphors and analogies, and frequently referred to the well-functioning of the human body in terms of relations between the whole and its organs as an analog to nature as a whole. When the relations between the whole and its parts are operating well, each thing is able to assume the form and shape appropriate to it through a process of becoming directed toward its intrinsic telos. This becoming is not random but governed by the necessity of each thing to remain in keeping with its essence— an essence that remains constant over time even when a thing goes through profound physical changes.[13] A thing which fulfills its telos through its processes of becoming realizes the potential intrinsic to its essence. In so doing it contributes to both its own flourishing and that of its immediate environment, and, in a cosmic sense, to nature as a whole. A thing which does not become both corrupted and a corrupting influence.

Moreover, while those things which possess more being depend on those which possess less, that does not mean that higher and lower beings are equal. Aristotle regards the ontological order of being as hierarchical in not just a descriptive but an evaluative sense. What has more being is not simply prior to, or inclusive of, what has less. What has more being is superior to what has less, even more real in a metaphysical sense. This becomes especially apparent when we look at biological entities, where stratification between and within species—for instance between the sexes—becomes clear. The basis for this stratification is that what possesses a higher ontological status is "ungenerated, imperishable, and eternal, while others are subject to generation and decay."[14] Similarly those who direct themselves to the higher ambitions of the soul more adequately fulfill their telos by participating in what is most eternal. Consequently they become a higher order of human being.

Here we must briefly pause. Modern thinkers will still, even in a post-Darwinian universe, deploy the language of teleology to describe both human actions and even nature. A paradigmatic example would be Immanuel Kant in his *Critique of Judgement* or Alasdair MacIntyre in *After Virtue*. However, even for the latter (so keen to resurrect Aristotelianism after centuries of critique), teleological ends are not intrinsic to a particular thing or that greater order of being in which it participates.[15] For modern thinkers, teleological ends are not ontological in the sense of being intrinsic. They are ascribed to nature and particular beings by conscious entities, which demote teleological ends from an ontological to aesthetic, moral, or epistemological status (not such a terrible demotion if I'm being honest). For many critics of modernity, this was a horrifying development since it robs us of the belief that there is an intrinsic end to human life and nature as a whole. But we get a lot of bang for our buck, since the anti-teleological thrust of modernity has left extraordinary room for human freedom and creative will to step in where once ends were set for us.

Human beings, by virtue of their reason, are both distinct and occupy a higher ontological place in Aristotle's zoology than other animals. This is because we have a degree of choice in whether to fulfill this teleology by living a good life committed to the development of character through cultivation of the virtues. These virtues are arranged in a hierarchy, ranging from the comparatively minor ones associated with practical wisdom to the intellectual virtues which are of a more purely contemplative and philosophical bent. Aristotle then goes on to argue that by behaving virtuously at many given moments over time, we develop the habit of doing so and consequently transform our character for the better. This is a lifelong project which doesn't end until death. If we succeed in being sufficiently virtuous we can be said to have led a good life and to have developed a praiseworthy character. Ultimately these are beneficial since we are rewarded for these efforts with eudaimonic flourishing, the end to which all other human ends aim. Eudaimonic flourishing brings the soul into accord with perfect virtue. If we fail at this project we condemn ourselves and potentially those around us to corruption. Because our ethical life has social consequences of this sort, it is of concern to more than just ourselves. This establishes a fundamental link between ethics and politics.

> "By human virtue we mean not that of the body but that of the soul; and happiness also we call an activity of the soul. But if this is so, clearly the student of politics must know somehow the facts about soul, as the man who is to heal the eyes or the body as a whole must know about the eyes or the body; and all the more so since politics is more prized and better than medicine, but even among doctors the best educated spend much labour on acquiring knowledge of the body. The student of politics, then must study the soul, and must study it with these objects is view…"[16]

One of the ambiguous features in Aristotle's writing is the extent to which a capacity to cultivate the virtues—and thus ultimately to achieve eudaimonic flourishing—is largely determined by nature or by an individual's choices.[17] The same is true of our personal character, which is in part set by our natural characteristics and abilities and in part set by our choices to be virtuous or not. There also seems to be some discrepancy in his writings. Book IV of the *Ethics* stresses individual choices, since these are the result of rational deliberation and not compulsion. But of course in the *Politics* Aristotle famously suggests that most people, including slaves, children, and women, naturally lack the capacity for rational deliberation. This would seem to preclude their ever being fully[18] virtuous and thus capable of achieving full eudaimonic flourishing.[19] Aristotle is well aware of this ambiguity and others, rightly pointing out in the opening to the *Nichomachean Ethics* that his discussion will bring "as much clearness as the subject matter admits of, for precision is not to be sought for alike in all discussion, and more than in all the products of the crafts."[20] This puzzle is sufficiently tricky that most of us have heard of it (nature vs. nurture anyone?). And it also has clear implications for politics. As Sheldon Wolin observes:

> Although the Aristotelian universe was one wherein purpose (telos) was writ large, it was still a universe full of tensions and striving summed up in the principle of potentiality "dynamics." Nature itself was defined at one

point as a 'principle of motion and rest, in respect of place, or of growth and decrease, or by way of alteration.' Within this framework, political science was conceived as an art that assisted and completed nature. At the same time, however, it was a practical and not a purely theoretic science. Its end was action, but action within a situation fraught with change, accident, and contingency. To expect mathematical precision in political theory was foolish, and to arm the practitioners of political science with absolute power was dangerously arrogant.[21]

But for all the ambiguity of the subject matter, what is clear is that Aristotle thinks that whether by nature of choice some individuals are more and others less virtuous. And consequently there are better and worse individuals in both an ethical and even ontological sense.[22]

Antecedents to Conservative Thought II: Aristotle Continued

This style of analysis maps a hierarchy of virtues onto a hierarchy of individuals whose ethical and ontological status is predicated on their capacity to behave virtuously in the moment and to develop virtuous character over time. The *Politics* extends this approach but raises the stakes considerably by stressing how it is the political community that aims at the very highest good. The book opens with a stirring statement to that extent.

> Every state is a community of some kind, and every community is established with a view to some good; for mankind always act in order to obtain that which they think good. But if all communities aim at some good, the state or community, which is the highest of all, and which embraces all the rest, aims at good in a greater degree than any other, and at the highest good.[23]

Aristotle goes on to typologize the different constitutions of the state and bracket them according to whether they are to be considered good or bad. This is perhaps his most singular contribution to political science and theory, though it is remarkably more obscure than one might expect. While he is critical of the three bad constitutions of tyranny, oligarchy, and extreme democracy, Aristotle also claims that these are perversions of three good constitutions. Those being monarchy, aristocracy, and polity. This obviously leads temptingly to the question of what is the best of the best? The Jack White of constitutions if you will. Aristotle's answer is legendarily ambiguous, as he proceeds to offer a menu of arguments on the pros and cons of each of the good constitutions.

Aristotle's understanding of a constitution is framed once more in hierarchical terms, since he thinks the most important feature of a constitution is that it sets out who is to rule and who is to be ruled. Here Aristotle compares the question of the ruler of the state to the relationship between the master and slave and households, arguing that in these cases the master or patriarch considers the good of his subservient—accidentally in the former case and deliberately in the latter—and claims that what determines the quality of rulers is whether they are committed to the highest goods of the principles of justice and the common interest.[24] Whether the one, the few, or the all should rule is an important question, but ultimately secondary to this higher one. The issue is whether the one, the few, or the many in general and in any particular case give us just government.

Throughout Book III of the *Politics* Aristotle tightly associates these questions with those of class. Indeed he claims that the constitutional "form of government" is determined by who rules, with monarchy "exercising the rule of a master over the political society"; aristocracy or oligarchy being when "men of property have the government in their hands" and finally democracy being "the opposite [of aristocracy/oligarchy], when the indigent, and not the men of property are the rulers."[25] So constitutional forms of government are determined by which class rules, raising the question of which class is best? Or, if you prefer the technical language, which class, if any, can effectively rule the state in line with justice and the common interest? This is a remarkably blunt series of questions that should highlight the absurdity of critics who believe consciousness is solely the purview of the revolutionary left. Indeed, contra those conservatives for whom Satan is second only to Karl Marx as a revolutionary agitator of the lower orders, Aristotle demonstrates a degree of class consciousness that often manages to outdo Marx.

At points Aristotle seems to anticipate democrats in arguing that it is quite possible for the masses to determine what is best, rather than an aristocratic or monarchial elite. This obviously gives democracy a serious sex appeal. Aristotle argues that there is "an element of truth" in the argument that the multitude ought to be supreme. He compares this to how a feast provided by one wealthy benefactor is typically inferior to one where each person brings something. For while

> each individual among the many has a share of virtue and prudence, and when they meet together, they become in a manner one man, who has many feet, and hands and senses; that is a figure of their mind and disposition. Hence the many are better judges than a single man of music and poetry; for some understand one part, and some another, and among them they understand the whole.[26]

A far cry from snide disdain for the swinish multitude.

But, as is typical with Aristotle, there is an "on the other hand." While he thinks that all who possess deliberative reason have a certain claim to political power, none—including the demos as a whole—have an absolute claim and some individuals clearly have a greater one than others. He argues that the landowning class claims to be citizens in a truer sense than the ignoble, and Aristotle agrees. He also thinks that "those who are sprung from better ancestors are likely to be better men." But above all "education and virtue" are what give individuals the most superior claim to rule. To paraphrase his famous observation, those who are unequal in the most important characteristics needn't have an equal share of the power. Aristotle follows Plato in chastising democracy for its ressentiment-driven yearning for equality at the cost of excellence, giving mythological and historical examples of how democracies "since equality is above all things their aim" would ostracize and banish "from the city for a time those who seemed to predominate too much through their wealth, or the number of friends, or through any other political influence."[27] This would obviously be a serious problem given how wealth and nobility are conducive to the production of virtuous persons. In the end Aristotle, eminent ethical and political particularist that he is, concludes by arguing that the best form of government is government by the best: whether that be the one, the few, the many, or some mixed regime.[28]

This ambiguity has enabled many different commentators to find resources in his writings to agitate for their preferred political form.[29] This includes the political right. But there is more to the attraction than that. What we find in Aristotle is a richly nuanced and holistic argument for an orderly ontologically cosmos where lower iterations of being have their teleological ends, and can even be considered "wonderous" in their own right. But they should never be confused with the higher orders of being.[30] Human beings occupy an important place in the Aristotelian system since our deliberative capacities seem to give us the power to both pursue the highest kinds of ends out of all animals and so achieve eudaimonic flourishing, or deliberately choose not to and so fall into decay. So too do human societies.

What determines these choices is vague. At points Aristotle tilts in a more egalitarian direction by suggesting that social circumstances like the possession of material wealth and fortunate circumstances are not decisive, and he even concedes that the mass of individuals may be wiser than even a singularly excellent one. This could imply that political stratification by class and power is unjust since it denies many people capable of leading good lives what they need to pursue higher human enterprises.[31] But Aristotle rarely goes in that direction, always pulling back from the egalitarian inclinations of his analysis and toward a kind of reverence for those who already possess the capabilities to lead good lives and so are entitled to a bigger slice of the political pie. He acknowledges that this is due to their greater wealth, but blunts the critical edge of any objection on that basis precisely by arguing that this superior wealth is what allows individuals to become superior in other ways as well. Getting rid of wealth and power disparities would throw a permanent wrench in the engine which produces the more virtuous and aristocratic classes, and so deny to the city its most natural and useful citizens. This led him to any number of ambiguous claims about the relative status of individuals, which, as Ryan points out, border on contradictions at points:

> Aristotle has the same difficulties with slavery as with the authority of husband over wife. If the relationship is not arbitrary and based on brute

force, the superior party must be more rational than the inferior; but not only is the inferior likely to be as rational as the superior; it is implicit in the theory that the inferior must be intelligent enough to be governed as a rational human being. If slaves and women are intellectually indistinguishable from their owners and husbands, Aristotle's framework is threatened. His mode of justifications creates more problems than he can admit to.[32]

Of course Aristotle always insisted there was no guarantee virtue flowed from wealth and power, and he rejected the idea that non-democratic governments were necessarily better. But as it turned out this would be a thin shield against the aristocratic appropriation of his thinking—often in banalized and popularized form—by those who rightly saw its elitism, however caveated, as an auspicious resource to defend their own elite status.

By acknowledging, then sidelining, the egalitarian implications of his thinking and foregrounding its more elitist strands, Aristotle gifted the immense power and prestige of his thinking to generations of aristocrats and their simps. And since he elevated the concern of politics to such an auspicious height—the ministering of the souls of the polis—Aristotle also raised the stakes for anyone perceived to be challenging this thinking in any fundamental manner. Since the aim of politics was to fulfill the project of nature through making good souled peoples, and these aims transcended human choice and full understanding, fostering alternative viewpoints could be seen as not simply disagreement but dangerous. It risked undermining the natural order of being and bringing with it the prospect of individual decay and social vice. And because Aristotle's thinking leaned in that direction, it was quite easy to characterize any challenge to the existent social order as also being a threat to this natural order, signifying that an attack on wealth and privilege was to ring the bells of the apocalypse for all.

Moreover, since Aristotle's conception of nature was one in which ontological change took place only at the temporal level and was indicatory of a lower order or being, this meant that the unchanging was revered as better than the changing. The superficial contribution of this to conservative thought was the well-known denunciation of "revolutionary" change in favor of reform which maintained the Aristotelianized "essence" of what society was. Meaning of course its basic structures, vulgarities, and hierarchies. More importantly, later conservative thinkers went beyond Aristotle in positing that the social structure itself existed as a kind of transcendent truth—reflective of an enduring human nature, or God's will, or the natural division of humanity—which could no more be argued with than the truth that there can be no square circles.[33] This is of course an ideological gesture par excellence which Aristotle himself would never be guilty of, since his own conception of human politics was always more open to the transformative power of deliberative human reason. In this sense much of the political right can be understood as a fall from Aristotle, since this postulation of an unchanging social order mapping the natural order calcifies the far more dynamic Aristotelian system for the purposes of providing intellectual ammunition for those in positions of power. But it cannot be doubted that the influence of Aristotle's metaphysics and natural philosophy provided a template for this way of thinking going forward, and so profoundly shaping the history of the political right.

Antecedents to Conservative Thought II: Scholasticism

> For Aquinas, natural law had meant transcendental equity and therefore precisely that which conjoined the particular instance of justice to the divine and eternal in the surpassing of all mere regularity of convention. But now, for modernity, natural law transcribes the sealed-off totality of nature, where eternal justice consists in the most invariable rules. These are not derived (as for Aquinas) from the inner tendencies of the Aristotelian practical reason towards the telos of the good, but rather from the purely theoretical reflections on the necessity for every creature to ensure its own self-preservation. Because nature, since the Renaissance, was regarded as an 'open book' which might be exhaustively read, Grotius, Hobbes and Spinoza can be confident that the self-preserving conatus provides the universal hermeneutic key for both nature and society.[34]
>
> (John Milbank, *Theology and Social Theory*)

If the Aristotelian universe of hierarchically organized beings and societies is a primary fetish object of the political right then the conservative's God is very much the dom in the relationship; the ultimate guarantor of the transcendent order which permeates both its ontological and moral legitimacy. This is not to say that things need to be this way. As we will see when we discuss Nietzsche's own idiosyncratic take on Christianity, for some on the political right the notion that all individuals enjoy equal dignity and status in the eyes of God—from beggar to King—is precisely where things began to go wrong. Whether this is a more legitimate interpretation of the history of Christianity's influence, or indeed the intrinsic moral thrust of Christian doctrine, are questions I'll sideline here. Whatever the answer, there is no denying the religious overtones, undertones, and every other kind of tone in much of the political right's rhetoric and beliefs. Much of this results from the complicated legacy of Christian scholasticism, which in various forms remains a very active reference point for various social conservative and post-liberal figures to this day.[35]

One feature of scholasticism often held up as a boon for conservatives is its alleged "realism." This is juxtaposed against the nominalism of modernity by post-modern conservatives like Peter Lawler.[36] What they mean by "realism" is that Christian scholasticism deepens Aristotelian essentialism by giving it a firmer basis in the revelation of religious faith. What makes this a form of realism is the conviction that God deliberately chose to make each independent thing what it is as an act of infinite agapeic love. Each being's particular identity, and the universe as a whole, is consequently vested with a level of moral and indeed affective significance which goes well beyond the rather naturalized—even coldly removed—prime mover of Aristotle's *Metaphysics*. This was often given metaphorical expression in the symbolism of God the father, who created the world and each essential thing in it and cherished them individually as what they are. Of course the recurring mirror image of this, well mocked by authors like Nietzsche, is God as the tyrannical and authoritative father who punishes his children for violations of divine law with damnation, hellfire, and a very long eternity listening to Kanye West interviews.

Both sides of God will be influential to the political right, serving as the sublimated guarantor of essentialism and a source of moral reprobation when the nature and ends he accords a being turn out not to be to its taste. In those circumstances many variants of scholasticism conceived a being as not just vulnerable to the decadence of Aristotelian corruption. Because of the extraordinary emphasis on free human will within the Christian tradition, and because the ultimate end of all the ends of human life are God, deviations from nature were conceived as a kind of willed rebellion against God.[37] An attempt to impose one's will upon the form God gave his creation constituted twisted ends and a defiance of his command. This of course creates significant theological difficulties that have haunted the Christian tradition ever since, notably the theodeisic problem that if God is omnipotent and good, and all he creates is good, then how can any person be evil? Aquinas attempts to solve this problem in the *Summa Contra Gentiles* by distinguishing between the incorruptible good each person has in their general being and the corruptible potential attached to their more specific qualities and choices:

> Therefore, although each one is good inasmuch as it exists it cannot be called good absolutely if it lack other things that are required for its goodness. Thus a man who, being despoiled of virtue; is addicted to vice, is said indeed to be good in a restricted sense, namely as a being and as a man; but he is not said to be good absolutely but rather evil. Accordingly in every creature to be and to be good are not the same absolutely, although each one is good inasmuch as it exists, whereas to God to be and to be good are one and the same. [38]

This raises a further question as to how something's being can be intrinsically good and yet still capable of evil. Aquinas' answer is to follow Augustine in arguing that everything that exists is good, and to one up him by arguing that even what could potentially be is good. Evil is consequently a kind of negativity or privation, something which takes away from the form and quality of what is by refusing to pursue the ends which God has set for it.[39] Probably the most advanced form this can take was vividly described by Saint Augustine in his *City of* God where he discusses the *libido domanandi*.[40] This is the yearning for domination and power over the earth, to recreate God's creation in one's own image as it were. What makes this distinct from a mere desire for power in order to enact a given end—including praiseworthy ends—is that as it deepens, the *libido domanandi* becomes the end in itself. One of Augustine's great psychological insights is how, when the yearning for power becomes a mere end for its own sake, this distorts the individual since they are no longer concerned with the rational question of what ends to pursue with their power, but only that they have ever more. Power becomes an empty end in itself. But since the scale of power ranges from virtually nothing to the infinite power of God, in the long run this will lead to a desire to emulate God with none of his goodness or love.

This point is rather abstract and technical, but was given vivid expression in many poetic works produced by Christian tradition. For example in Dante's *Inferno* the many punishments doled out to sinners through the nine circles of hell often mutilate the bodies of the damned through mocking performances of the sins they engaged in life. Here, because of the ontological mutability of hell compared to the earth, sin can literally distort to give a more accurate physical representation of the hollowing out of the soul brought on by evil. Or one can think of Milton's *Paradise Lost* where Satan opens the poem still possessing much of the splendor and power of his tenure as Lucifer the Lightbringer. As his plan progresses to bring about the fall of humankind, he is gradually reduced to a lower form of angel and finally down to a "meer Serpent in appearance, forth was come and on his Quest, where likeliest he might finde the onely two of mankinde, but in them the whole included Race, his purposd prey."

Now there are profound insights here, particularly with regard to Christian psychology and Augustine's account of the lust for power. Even as stalwart an anti-Christian as Nietzsche occasionally expressed grudging respect for the ways in which the discovery (or invention) of Christian psychology contributed to the deepening of the human soul.[41] It is also clear that Christianity as a whole, and even Christian scholasticism, needn't be turned to conservative purposes.[42] As we will see for some on the far right, Christianity's emphasis on the humble, poor, and meek is one of the catalysts for modern egalitarian movements. Nevertheless many on the religious right remain deeply enamored with both the ontology and moralism of the scholastic world. At an ontological level it combines the virtues of Aristotelian holism and hierarchical organization with submission to a divine authority which supersedes the limitations of Aristotle's naturalism. This connects intrinsically to Christianity's moralism, where deviations from the teleological ends set to you by God are conceived as not just corrupt and aberrational, but sinful and wrong. This can very easily map onto demands that one accept the moral judgments of far more human authorities. In its moralistic forms it shrills the pitch from Aristotle's cold discussions about deficient character and a compromised awareness of how natural and social settings can be determinative. At its most judgmental Christian moralism locates the source of sinfulness in the willed choice of an individual to not just give into their worst impulses but to in fact consciously choose to do wickedness; to say, "evil, be thou my good."

What occurs with the conservative appropriation of scholasticism is the extension of the hierarchical ontology ordained by God to the stratified institutions and power dynamics of the feudal era and beyond. This was coupled with an expansion of the moral imperative to obey God's commands into an injunction to obey the commands of God's representatives on earth. Disobedience or resistance to his expectation was not just seen as potentially corrupting but as sinful and expressive of deliberately willed malice on the part of sinners. Consequently when disobedience reached a sufficiently threatening level, it was very easy for political elites to associate challenges to their power with challenges to the ontological order of being wholesale and to compare it bombastically with Satanic insurrection. This might seem fundamentally contrary to Christian notions of the universal equality and brotherhood of all human beings, and indeed there have always been radical arguments to that effect.[43] But in practice these arguments were often easily evaded ideologically by those who could reconfigure notions of equality to mean equal submission to one's allotted station. Or through arguments that all must be treated as equal before God alone, and this says nothing about their appropriate material and political positions. As Barry Goldwater put it, "we are all equal in the eyes of God but we are equal in no other respect. Artificial devices for enforcing equality among unequal men must be rejected..."[44]

Contemporaneously these forms of Christian conservatism are often invoked when disobedience challenges norms related to biological practices, like gender roles and sexuality. These are typically so insulated by often invisible systems of power that even exposing them as related to power is taken as threatening the whole religious outlook.[45] But "in the beginning" the rhetoric of challenging God's will through egalitarian agitation become especially notable in responses to the liberal revolutions. As though rejecting the throne of France was remotely comparable to challenging the throne of God.[46] In fact for one of the founding figures of the political right challenging the thrones of Europe was tantamount to challenging God.

Robert Filmer's *De Patriarcha*

> In all kingdoms of commonwealths in the world, whether the prince be the supreme father of the people or but the true heir of such a father, or whether he come to the crown by usurpation, or by election of the nobles or of the people, or by any other way whatsoever, or whether some few or a multitude govern the commonwealth, yet still the authority that is in any one, or in many, or in all of these, is the only right and natural authority of a supreme father. There is and always shall be continued to the end of the world a natural right of a supreme father over every multitude...

Robert Filmer is little read and little known today—mostly just a footnote in some graduate student's paper on John Locke. From a purely intellectual standpoint this obscurity is well deserved. As an argument *De Patriarcha* belongs firmly in the dreaded "of historical interest" part of the canon. Even by the time we get to Burke and De Maistre one would be hard pressed to find such singularly monological defenses of patriarchal monarchism. Filmer is undoubtedly not a thinker of the right on par with many of the others we will look at. Nevertheless he is an important figure for his role as the founder of a distinct style of reactionary rhetoric: the analogical depiction of society as a family governed from the top down by a benevolent but stern father figure who sometimes needs to bring his unruly children in line. Coupled with this is the disdainful characterization of their fierce desire for independence as flowing from a perverting misunderstanding of the systems which keep them and civil society itself afloat.[47] More importantly Filmer's status as the major adversary of the early liberals gives him some claim to being the grandfather of modern conservatism—a status any man so fixated on lineage might have enjoyed.

More than just a thinker, Filmer was himself a noble (the bloviated "Sir" usually attached to his name is a give-away) who was heavily involved in the major political disputes of the day. While never fighting directly for Charles I, perhaps owing to late middle age, Filmer was nevertheless suspected of Royalist sympathies and had his manor home looted by parliamentary forces during the Civil War. This background contributes to the notably polemical quality of De Patriarcha; one it shares with similarly engaged screeds by later conservative thinkers wary of a forthcoming revolution, or already bemoaning the dark fruits of mass political participation. It is a tedious work, characterized by an exaggerated scholastic style that piles endless references to authoritative texts atop of one another in a manic effort to bury the opposition through sheer refinement. Nevertheless there are two main lines of argumentation worth unpacking, if nothing else due to their emulation.

The first line of argumentation in Patriarcha is that political authority was passed down generationally from Adam to the kings and princes of Europe. Filmer highlights how God granted Adam dominion over the creatures of the earth, and argues that the "command [Adam] had over the whole world, and by right descending from him the patriarchs did enjoy, was as large and ample as the absolutist dominion of any monarch which hath been since the creation."[48] This was transferred from Adam to Noah, then his three sons, and then to the rulers of the divided kingdoms of the world after God split humanity into many nations due to the fiasco of the tower of Babel. This authority then passes to Abraham, and after a brief gap, to Moses and Joshua out of God's "special care" for the Israelites,[49] and so on. In each of these cases there was an original family headed by a patriarch, who passed his authority along to an heir who retained command of the growing political community descended from the initial stud's loins.

On its own terms this becomes problematic as an argument for even 17th-century monarchial authority, as it is quite clear that the European kings of the time were not the literal "fathers" of the people. This risked the claim becoming nothing more than a rather sentimental metaphor inappropriately applied. Filmer was aware of this, but counters that the kings were nevertheless descended from the original fathers, and implies that the very title "King" or "prince" came into being to "express the power of him who succeeds only to the right of that fatherhood which his ancestors did naturally enjoy. By this means it comes to pass that many a child, by succeeding a king, hath the right of a father over many a greyheaded multitude."[50] In circumstances where an original patriarchal line broke down, Filmer denies that power returns to the people since there is always an heir one might find to take up the title of patriarch. Even in circumstances of usurpation, where the crown passes from one family to another—quite important in a British context where 1066 has always been well remembered—Filmer holds that the authority claimed by the new king is sufficiently proximate. This is because for "natural authority of a supreme father" to count, there "is and always will be continued to the end of the world a natural right of a supreme father over every multitude, although, by the secret will of God, many at first do most unjustly obtain the exercise of it."[51] How Filmer knows this is the will of God if it is a "secret" is unexplained. Perhaps God fails at duplicity.

To defend this crucial argument about natural rights, upon which the legitimacy of patriarchal authority is predicated, Filmer appeals to a variety of sources from the *Decalogue* to the Bible. In Chapter Three of *De Patriarcha* Filmer argues that the natural right to power can in no way be compromised, since the "father of the family governs by no other law than by his own will, not by the laws and wills of his sons or servants."[52] Acknowledging that this might seem like a recipe for tyranny, Filmer hastens to add that nevertheless the king will always be

> tied by the same law of nature to keep this general ground, that the safety of the kingdom be his chief law, he must remember that the profit of every man in particular, and all in general, is not always one and the same; and that the public is to be preferred before the private.[53]

He then gives a number of historical and biblical examples which testify to the benevolence of kings.

Filmer's patriarchal line of argumentation is backed by two further claims. The first is the claim that contemporary kings and princes inherit authority over history. The second is that the right to this authority is absolute and natural. Neither is remotely convincing. As Filmer himself acknowledges, even on its own terms the claim about historical lineage routinely breaks down when one looks at the various usurpations, conquests, coups, adulteries, and machinations through which often rather sleazy individuals came to power. This includes the British isles where William of Normandy seized the island by right of conquest, the House of Normandy ruled until the Plantagenet insurgency a century later, and they in turn kept their rears on the throne until Richard III was backstabbed by the Earl of Northumberland at Bosworth Field and made Henry Tudor the last English monarch to win his crown by killing his own subjects. Filmer's response to this is that it was the will of God that made these events happen—though one suspects the tens of thousands of peasants, doubtless grateful for the chance to die for their liege lord's prestige, also played a role. But apparently it could never be God's "secret will if parliamentary forces happened to win the day. The reason is an assertion of the natural right of kings, which apparently supersedes the concurrent claims to the natural rights of the people by the sheer volume of textual references Filmer could marshal compared to his opponents. Too bad the *First Treatise* of Government wound up being even longer and more reference-happy than *Patriarcha*, since that must settle the matter in Locke's favor by sheer girth.

But while Filmer's first line of argumentation may not be interesting on its own merits, his rhetorical efforts to sublimate monarchial authority are. At points Filmer moves dramatically away from the grandiosity of Aristotelian and scholastic thought toward the far more homely analogy of the monarch with the father and the state with the family. But these rustic analogies sit with some aesthetic discomfort next to his far more bombastic appeals to historical grandeur and Biblical stature. It will not be the last time conservatives attempt to combine these two aesthetics together, though it's not until Burke that conservatives will accomplish it. But even in Filmer's work the prospect of an authority presented as both absolute and regal while also being paternalistic and warm, enjoying divine sanction and legitimated through being the one person capable of genuinely looking after the good of his children without private favoritism, has an electrifying ideological appeal. That the ideological contrasts between these distinct aesthetics would be too much for any actually living person to embody explains why so many appeals are made to back up the cosmological order to God, who manages to reconcile them both in his own being as lord and father and legitimate the contradictions through sheer ontological fiat.

Filmer's second line of argumentation is less developed than the one on divinely ordained patrimony, but undoubtedly more convincing to anyone born after 1688. This is because Filmer develops one of the first modern conservative arguments against democracy, and indeed anticipates most of the lines of attack that will be launched by other right-wing authors over the next few decades. In this respect he is something of a pioneer, and not just in the sense of being an antiquity.

Filmer clears his throat early in the book by denying that power ever devolves to the multitude who get to "choose what rulers they please."[54] But the main assault comes in Chapter Two, where Filmer claims it is "unnatural" for the people to govern or choose their governors. The book begins by arguing against those appealing to Aristotle as a proto-democratic thinker, referencing many of the points I highlighted in the section on Aristotle above. Filmer also points out that Plato had similar reservations. This is followed by a long and mostly forgettable debate with the Jesuit Francisco Suarez, who contended with the patriarchal defense of authority. The argument only really gets going about midway through the chapter, where Filmer argues against the idea that it is right that the majority should have their wishes implemented, and that authoritarianism is wrong since it allows the few to "oversway the liberty of their opposites." Filmer begins responding to this by appealing to the laws of nature:

> But in assemblies that take their authority from the law of nature, it cannot be so; for what freedom or liberty is due to any man by the law of nature

no inferior power can alter, limit, or diminish, no man nor a multitude can give away the natural right of another. The law of nature is unchangeable, and howsoever one man may hinder another in the use or exercise or his natural right, yet thereby no man loseth the right itself; for the right and the use of the right may be distinguished as right and possession are often distinct.[55]

Filmer then goes on to point out that majoritarianism only shifts the problem it was originally intended to solve, since a majority is now granting itself the authority to "oversway the Liberty of their Opposites" simply by virtue of numbers.[56] He then expresses a proto-Schmittian skepticism that in any community there isn't a circumstance where one group imposes its views on another, which blurs the distinctions which might exist between monarchy and democracy. Filmer holds that monarchy is the natural form of government, and indeed that God endued "all creatures with a natural propensity to monarchy" because this is the form of government which he desired for his creation.[57] Since one might object that this can hardly be the case if other forms of government have existed, there is a lengthy historical section where Filmer examines the operation of the most well-known democracies. He fixates on the Roman Republic as an exemplar. Filmer asks whether the reader could conclude from the examples given that democracies were better governed than monarchies, and contends the answer is an emphatic no. Finally Filmer asks whether it would be possible for a kind of mixed regime to emerge—ironically very much of the sort that has existed in Britain for three centuries—and concludes that it would be impossible. Because it is in the nature of kingship and sovereignty generally to be defined by absolute authority. If the King "admits the people to be his companions, he leaves to be a King, and the State should be a Democracy."[58] Sovereign authority must be absolute or it ceases to be sovereign authority; Filmer perceives this to approximate a logical contradiction and so be nonsensical as a moral claim.

Independently none of these arguments is made that impressively. One of the clearest examples is Filmer's confused ascription of logical necessity to a political concept whose semantic and moral meaning is socially determined. In part the reasoning for this should be obvious. Arguing that a reconceptualization of sovereign authority as divided isn't to his taste is a weaker claim than arguing it simply cannot be conceived in this way. But not only does a long history of divided government invalidate his claim,[59] it was obviously untrue on the face of it. The concept of sovereign authority approximates what Marx would call a "real abstraction"—it emerges from the social relations of a given period and has genuine effect so long as participants continue to believe in it. But it certainly has nothing like the force of a law of nature or logic, let alone anything as lofty as a divine command.

More impressive is Filmer's arguments about the dangers of strict majoritarianism, and how this wouldn't avoid the dilemma of one group imposing its will on the liberty of another. He is right to make this argument, but it doesn't follow from this that we should efface the distinctions between a more democratic form of government in which at least most have a say and a monarchy in which a singular person governs all. The notion that democratic societies could blunt their worst impulses through the institution of anti-majoritarian constitutional checks and individual rights doesn't come up in Filmer; though of course Locke would make a big deal of it very shortly in his *Second Treatise of Government*.

Nevertheless taken together Filmer's arguments express an exaggerated—but not irrational—wariness of democracy which will become central to the conservative position going forward. Interestingly he never directly addresses the key source of the problem, though Filmer diagnoses it early in *Patriarcha*. He points out that when other defenders of monarchy like Sir John Heywood, Adam Blackwood, and John Barclay "bravely vindicated the right of kings in most points" they nevertheless felt compelled to concede to radical claims about the "natural liberty" and "equality of mankind." Filmer rightly notes that the "Rebellious Consequence which follows this prime Article of the *Natural Freedom of Mankind*" is sufficiently dangerous to warrant interrogation.[60] And he is absolutely right that these twinned principles of belief in freedom and equality are the acid which will gradually erode the ideological pillars propping up the monarchy. But Filmer's response to this is very weak: to simply remind his readers that all children are subject to their parents, that the subjection of children is the fount of regal authority, and so liberty needs to be checked by obedience.[61] Whether this makes the King or the father a superior kind of being Filmer doesn't say; perhaps out of wary deference to Christian humanism and its insistence that highest and lowest are equally children of God. But this is a thin shield against demands for further liberty, since unless it is the case that the king is in fact better, the crude appeals to lineage and patriarchal authority can't carry the conservative cause very far once its ideological luster fades. And it would start to fade very quickly under pressure from the more muscular and sophisticated liberal tradition.

The Ideology of Liberal Modernity

Filmer deserves to be called the father of the modern political right because he was among the first to feel the present's continuity with the past slipping irrevocably away.[62] Whatever his intellectual defects, one can already see in *Patriarcha* many of the standard tropes conservatism would adopt in its conflict with egalitarian modernity. This is a book on the political right, so it would be impractical and tedious to spend a lot of time discussing these movements here.[63] But a few comments will be helpful in framing what is to come.

Liberalism can be understood in a variety of different ways, ranging from the philosophy of freedom to the ideology of market capitalism. The overwhelming viewpoint of conservatives has been to see it as an obnoxious and upstart movement, at times so powerful that one must make peace with its more reconcilable elements, at other times an ally against even more Satanic forces, and at still other times the ultimate source of those same forces.[64] On their end liberals

haven't been shy in launching many attacks on conservatism, often by sentiments ranging from bemusement to righteous indignation. Underpinning most
of these has been J.S. Mill's sentiment that conservatives are overwhelmingly
the "stupid" party, or at least the political ideology that manifests an almost
magnetic attraction to the cognitively challenged. Indeed this style of responding to conservative arguments was already well established by John Locke in his
argument with Robert Filmer, where he pulled no punches in ridiculing the
opposition while refuting his position line by line. As he put it in the opening of
the *First Treatise*:

> Slavery is so vile and miserable an estate of man, and so directly opposite
> to the generous temper and courage of our nation; that it is hardly to be
> conceived, that an Englishman, much less a gentleman, should plead for it.
> And truly I should have taken Sir Robert Filmer's *Patriarcha*, as any other
> treatise, which would persuade all men, that they are slaves, and ought to
> be so, for such another exercise of wit, as was his who writ the encomium
> of Nero; rather than for a serious discourse meant in earnest, had not the
> gravity of the title and epistle, the picture in the front of the book, and
> the applause that followed it, required me to believe, that the author and
> publisher were both in earnest. I therefore took it into my hands with all
> the expectation, and read it through with all the attention due to a treatise
> that made such a noise at its coming abroad, and cannot but confess my
> self mightily surprised, that in a book, which was to provide chains for all
> mankind, I should find nothing but a rope of sand, useful perhaps to such,
> whose skill and business it is to raise a dust, and would blind the people,
> the better to mislead them; but in truth not of any force to draw those into
> bondage, who have their eyes open, and so much sense about them, as to
> consider, that chains are but an ill wearing, how much care soever hath
> been taken to file and polish them.[65]

Meanwhile, conservatives have fired back at the impudence of the liberal tradition. It is an unwritten truth of the right[66] that it often betrays a barely concealed
sense of intellectual inferiority to its modernist opponents—often poorly masked
by a sincere talent for snide putdowns and tantric appeals to being the party of
down-to-earth realism even when talking about magical transcendent realms
and "more than metaphysical" truths.[67] For the rest of this section, I'll discuss
the early liberal tradition which the political right opposed. From a conservative
standpoint early liberalism was broadly committed to two twinned goals, neither
of which was acceptable.

The first goal was achieving victory for the political philosophy of possessive
individualism, now often called classical liberalism.[68] At its philosophical basis
was a commitment to the idea of the rational individual as the fundamental unit
of political life. Rational individuals were perceived to be free and equal by
nature, meaning they possessed certain fundamental rights even upon entry into

civil society which could not be abridged by authority.[69] Possessive individualist liberalism's main political tenets were the replacement of aristocratic social order by a competitive market society complemented by representative and participatory government. Though representative of who and how participatory were and are matters of fierce debate even among liberals themselves.[70] While they would later come to terms with it, right-wing intellectuals were initially opposed to this ambition, with prominent figures like Filmer and Hooker arguing that human rights and freedoms were naturally subject to the authority of natural law. This in practice meant the authority of their preferred authorities. They were more cautious than their later peers in denying ontological human equality, but always circumscribed this limitation by insisting that equality before God didn't require anything remotely approximating equality in this life.

The second main goal of early liberalism was more ephemeral, but in the long run no less threatening and perhaps even more transformative. This was to replace the ontological frameworks of antiquity and the Medieval period with the scientific reason of the Enlightenment. Even at the time Enlightenment came in a huge number of flavors, from Cartesian rationalism to English empiricism and Hobbesian materialism. The legacy[71] of the Enlightenment has never ceased to be controversial. It has been hailed as the ideology of penicillin and the atomic bomb in equal measure. But it was and is very much a threat to the political right. Sometimes this has been misunderstood and misrepresented. Kantian philosophers in particular tend to follow "What is Enlightenment?" in holding that the primary danger of liberal Enlightenment is its insistence of the right and capacity of all individuals to understand the world and consequently to have a say in how it is governed.[72] To an extent this is correct, and we will see how figures like Joseph de Maistre venomously respond to this dangerously corrosive egalitarianism shortly. But possessive individualist liberals never had much difficulty blunting the radical edge of this position by denying that most of the world in fact was sufficiently rational to warrant rights, including the right to participate in politics, often limiting their political imaginations to propertied white men. While over time the blatant exceptionalism in such doctrines would prove a pathetic defense against demands for the consistent extension of liberal rights to all, in the early modern period it was more than enough to convince conservatives like Burke that liberalism could be accommodated and tamed.

The more abiding danger of the Enlightenment philosophy espoused by liberals was how comprehensively it threatened the Aristotelian-Scholastic ordered universe, where a transcendent source of authority immanentized itself through nature and legitimated the division of society and humanity into complementary but unequal ranks. As has been expressed throughout this chapter, this orderly universe of hierarchical complementary is one of the longstanding and nostalgized fetishes of many on the political right. Enlightenment philosophy not only denied that there was any "sense" in understanding nature this way, but that it was positively mystical and even a barrier to reason and consequently to that most esteemed liberal value: progress.[73] Human reason was capable of understanding reality without any need of appealing to transcendence and immanence; or worse yet, human reason was too limited for it to even speak of such things without lapsing into nonsense and "transcendental illusion."[74] Beyond marshaling tremendous intellectual powers to back up these ontological and cosmological claims, Enlightenment modernity gained an undeniable ideological credibility as a consequence of the manifest boons of science and technology to human well-being. Early reactionaries[75] immediately recognized that this risked permanently discrediting the most enduring philosophical and ideological basis for their positions; one of the reasons Burke accepts certain tenets of political liberalism but rejects Enlightenment for the sublime is his (rather intuitive) understanding of this peril. Even to this day a yearning to undo the Enlightenment is so powerful that plenty of conservative thinkers are unafraid to demand it, even if they are usually unwilling to take on rationalistic and scientific metaphysics in a head-on struggle, let alone argue it should be comprehensively replaced with something else.[76]

This connection between Enlightenment philosophy and the emancipatory and qualified egalitarianism of liberal possessive individualism was always contingent and historical rather than logically necessary. As we will see soon the more ingenious and often insidious thinkers of the right and far right have found ways of appealing to Enlightenment dogmas to reinscribe inequality into humankind on a more naturalistic basis. And there are liberal thinkers like Richard Rorty and, at moments, the late Rawls, who deny that their political convictions need to be tied in any deep sense to Enlightenment reason. Some may even think liberalism would be better off without it. But these shifts would occur later in our story, and in the 17th and 18th centuries this mix of possessive individualist philosophy with egalitarian Enlightenment reason would become a heavyweight champion in the battle for hearts and minds.

Humean Communitarianism

> It is not with forms of government, as with other artificial contrivances; where an old engine may be rejected, if we can discover another more accurate and commodious, or where trials may safely be made, even though the success be doubtful. An established government has an infinite advantage, by that very circumstance of its being established; the bulk of mankind being governed by authority, not reason, and never attributing authority to any thing that has not the recommendation of antiquity. To tamper, therefore, in this affair, or try experiments merely upon the credit of supposed argument and philosophy, can never be the part of a wise magistrate, who will bear a reverence to what carries the marks of age; and though he may attempt some improvements for the public good, yet will he adjust his innovations, as much as possible, to the ancient fabric, and preserve entire the chief pillars and supports of the constitution.
>
> (David Hume, "Idea of a Perfect Commonwealth")

David Hume occupies an unusual position in the history of political thought, and conservatism more generally. So much so that despite (perhaps because of?) his reputation as a radical philosophical innovator he rarely enjoys pride of place even in the better guides written by conservatives about their own tradition. Roger Scruton barely has time for Hume in the pre-history of conservatism, preferring to begin the modern tradition with Burke.[77] Russell Kirk gives him a handful of references in *The Conservative Mind*, and mostly saw his skepticism as inimical to the Burkean politics he wanted to defend.[78] Edmund Neill draws a few parallels between Hume's occasionally gloomy views on human political life and the cautious anti-democratic sentiments of the American founders, but has little more to say.[79]

In some respects this is unsurprising. On the face of it Hume embodies many of the characteristics most conservatives have been allergic to. His skepticism goes well beyond the selective anti-rationalism and anti-Enlightenment positions of Burke and De Maistre. Doubting God is kid's stuff. Reading Hume undermines faith in everything from the sun rising tomorrow to the very idea that we have a "self" (I'll leave it to you to ponder who then is writing these words).[80] By itself this might be an intellectual curiosity, but then Hume goes on to attack religious dogmas and transcendent ideas with gusto. This would be bad enough for those conservatives who need their views spiced up with generous doses of onto-theology, but Hume goes even further. His famous guillotine closes the door to those on the political right who would try to reinscribe moral and social absolutes into the world through naturalization, since one cannot derive an "ought" from an "is." With mythologization and naturalization off the table, at least on the surface of things, two of the major weapons of the conservative intellectual are hacked into ploughshares.

And yet Hume consistently argued for caution in changing social mores and political institutions, and ridiculed the ambitions of utopian thinkers from antiquity to modernity.

> All plans of government, which suppose great reformation in the manners of mankind, are plainly imaginary. Of this nature, are the *Republic* of Plato, and the *Utopia* of Sir Thomas More.[81]

He also rejects the ideal of a perfect democracy, concurs with the division of society into different "ranks" which in turn should be accorded distinct and unequal political powers, and argues that legislation should be unhurried and respectful of convention and precedent. Perhaps most importantly, Hume is scathingly critical of the contractarian tradition for reasons that are recognizably conservative. Hume believes that any argument which makes political authority turn exclusively or primarily on the consent of the governed is ahistorical and excessively individualistic. They fail to recognize our embeddedness in differentiated and various societies, where authority and mores are dictated by traditional practices more than any kind of rational deliberation or self-interest.

This is of course a curious mixture, appropriately for so gleefully idiosyncratic a man as Hume. How to explain it? Alasdair MacIntyre[82] offers perhaps the most robust take, carefully analyzing the seemingly paradoxical links between Hume's radical philosophy and surprisingly cautious and conservative traditionalism.[83] And MacIntyre perhaps answers the paradox of the Scottish gadfly's radical philosophical views and conservative political convictions by describing Hume as a "philosophical champion of an essentially unphilosophical culture."[84] Hume often expressed the conviction that the radically skeptical consequences of his philosophical inquiries alerted him to the wastefulness of abstract speculation and the limitations of human understanding. These needn't necessarily be conservative dispositions, as a later host of post-modern skeptical critics would show. But it maps more sympathetically onto a kind of moderate conservatism which is wary of the kind of precision required to specify arguments for equality and accepts that a degree of imperfection is a built-in feature of all human society. This was nicely summarized in his essay "Of the First Principles of Government" where Hume accepted the need to give the lower orders some representation in Parliament, but chastised those who wanted a full democratic or republican system of governance. Hume argued, "let us cherish and improve our ancient government as much as possible, without encouraging a passion for such dangerous novelties."[85] Burke himself could not have put it better.

But Hume's issue goes deeper than a mere disposition. One of the major consequences of Hume's skeptical arguments is that the kind of grandly rationalistic projects and faith in humanity on which much of Enlightenment radicalism flourished were in fact founded on shifting sand. And indeed one of the targets of Hume's ire was against the natural rights and contractarian traditions which—however dominated by possessive individualism they might appear in hindsight—did play an ideological role in mobilizing revolutionary energies through the 18th century. He appreciated the argument that political authority was predicated on the consent of the government and was to be to the people's benefit, but characterized contractarian arguments themselves as fictions.

Hume also acknowledged that while the logic of contractarianism might apply to human beings in their state of "natural equality" it doesn't apply now. This is in part because an examination of history shows that most governments were not empirically predicated on consent. As an argument this isn't especially convincing, since it only challenges the historical and not the normative force of the contractarian argument. More significant is Hume's argument that in a developed social context the inequities which arise from education should be considered significant in the allocation of power. This is in no small part because of the predilection of democratic governments to disrespect property. As he puts it were

> all men possessed of so inflexible a regard to justice, that, of themselves, they would totally abstain from the properties of others; they had for ever remained in a state of absolute liberty, without subjection to any magistrate

of political society; but this is a state of perfection, of which human nature is justly deemed incapable. Again, were all men possessed of so perfect an understanding as always to know their own interests, no form of government had ever been submitted to, but what was established on consent, and was fully canvassed by every member of the society: but this state of perfection is likewise much superior to human nature.

He concludes the essay in a rather ambivalent way, citing with approval Plato's discovery of Tory consequences in the Whig premises of his contractarian argument in the *Crito*. Much the same could be said about Hume's own work.[86]

Hume's political philosophy can be understood as consciously unsystematic and multipolar, drawing on a variety of sources to justify his positions. At times he seems to anticipate the arguments of later historical empiricists, in arguing that the consequences of history need to be taken seriously when assessing political authority. This could of course be weaponized against him by a radical critic, since one could rebut that, taken seriously, the litany of horrors Hume chronicles might demand a more combative approach to established authorities. But in these cases Hume would likely shift his emphasis to an argument from human nature, as ascertained from more general forms of experience. He would argue that individuals submit to authority by habit where government is moderate, gentle, and respectful of property. He would argue that revolutionary upheavals disturb the peace and natural moderation to which the best sides of our nature are inclined. Finally when confronted by the moral arguments of Enlightenment philosophers arguing for the natural equality of humankind, he would agree but qualify it by arguing that natural equality doesn't persist in a social setting where education can mold the intellect and temperament of individuals in politically meaningful ways. If this seems morally inadequate, Hume could turn to a right-communitarian argument with some utilitarian flourishes of the type developed in his *Enquiry Concerning the Principles of Morals* and argue that if

we examine the particular laws, by which justice is directed, and property determined; we shall still be presented with the same conclusion. The good of mankind is the only object of all these laws and regulations. Not only is it requisite, for the peace and interest of society, that men's possessions should be separated; but the rules, which we follow, in making the separation, are such as can best be contrived to serve farther the interests of society.

This includes to keep their promises, and to show allegiance to government for the sake of peace and stability.[87]

Taken individually none of these arguments have much force, and Hume himself occasionally seems uncertain about them. He often goes back and forth on the issues of consent and political participation by the masses, concedes natural but not social human equality, and will appeal to both the common sense views of individuals inhabiting given societies and more truistic claims about human nature in the abstract. This is in sharp contrast to Hume's directly philosophical work, which often shows a striking confidence and assurance in at least the direction if not the conclusion of the questions being asked.

But the most important objection raised at both the philosophical and political level was Kant's, who accepts elements of the skeptical Humean project which would be part and parcel of the mature Enlightenment but tempers their sting in an important way. Most notably Kant's project built on Hume's strict empirical skepticism to make an argument about the universal transcendental structure of human reason, arguing that in fact a degree of scientific certainty at the phenomenal level was possible since empirical reality was apprehended by all in the same way. This mapped in a complex way onto his moral claim that each of us is to be considered an autonomous reasoner of equal moral worth. But more importantly, the sting of Hume's skepticism became more lethal. Kant argued that the appeals to both transcendent authority on which earlier conservatives relied and the myriad empiricisms Hume favored were reduced to phenomenalism and consequently could not be reified and fetishized as sources of political legitimation. Drawing on his egalitarian moral theory, Kant argued people should be free to use their own reason to criticize the heteronymous structures of transcendence and common sense used to justify inequality, leading to his famous claim that all should be allowed to participate in republican politics. Seen from this standpoint, the shifting maneuvers in Hume's politics are a predictable consequence of his being unwilling to push the anti-dogmatic implications of his thinking all the way to practical implications.

As we will see this isn't the last time a conservative thinker will find themselves in this situation, and it won't be the last time there is a substantial evasion of implications. Hume is willing to allow radical thinking at the philosophical level, and it is worth noting by elite philosophers. But this needn't be the case, and Hume was well aware that even at the time philosophy was becoming a corrosive weapon undermining the moderate English blended system he so cherished. In that case thinkers need to back away; radical philosophizing needs to be muted politically and socially through the tempering influence of history, education, and property. But the basis for this demand is contingent and flows more from Hume's predilections than any deep theoretical necessity, in contrast to the more stringent reasoning applied by his more aggressively liberal and egalitarian counterparts.

Nevertheless, it is important to understand Hume's contribution. Taken together his politics laid the template for the kind of proudly syncretic and anti-systematic Toryism which would come to define English conservatism as both a disposition and later a philosophy. That it cannot be fully explicated through reason is almost the point, since it is conceived and portrayed as a kind of lived or embedded wisdom irreducible to rationalistic analysis and drawn from modes of experiencing that more concrete world which abstract intellectuals—of the type Hume was happy to be at other points—are so fond of critiquing. Our next figure will take many of his insights and give them a far more pronounced and theoretically grand form.

The "Burke Problem"

> ...You would have had a protected, satisfied, laborious, and obedient people, taught to seek and to recognize the happiness that is to be found by virtue in all conditions; in which consists the true moral equality of mankind, and not in that monstrous fiction, which, by inspiring false ideas and vain expectations into men destined to travel in the obscure walk of laborious life, serves only to aggravate and embitter that real inequality, which it never can remove; and which the order of civil life establishes as much for the benefit of those whom it must leave in a humble state, as those whom it is able to exalt to a condition more splendid, but not more happy.
>
> (Edmund Burke, *Reflections on the Revolution in France*)

Eddie Burke. What can be said about him that hasn't been said before? For Russell Kirk, Burke is a genius who simultaneously embodied the wisdom of the ages while sadly being continuously out of step with the times.[88] Roger Scruton described Burke as coming to his "rescue" in the 1960s, the peak of decadent pot smoking hippies with topless women emerging as heralds of the fall. Burke's vision of social cohesion brought about by stability, hierarchy, and structure of command made a deep impression on the young Scruton. As did Burke's imperious

> defense of authority and obedience. Far from being the evil and obnoxious thing that my contemporaries held it to be, authority was, for Burke, the root of political order. Society, he argued, is not held together by the abstract rights of the citizen, as the French Revolutionaries supposed. It is held together by authority—by which is meant the right to obedience, rather than the mere power to compel it. And obedience, in its turn, is the prime virtue of political beings, the disposition which makes it possible to govern them, and without which societies crumble into 'the dust and powder of individuality'.[89]

Jesse Norman is no less grandiose when opening his charming intellectual biography by calling Burke both the "greatest and the most underrated political thinker of the past 300 years."[90]

On the liberal and left side of things, the opinion of Burke gets quite a bit dimmer. Macpherson damns with faint praise by calling Burke a "devoted and principled politician, an acclaimed House of Commons orator, and a superb pamphleteer."[91] But his evaluation of Burke as a thinker was damning. Macpherson pointed out that Burke made bombastic claims for which there "was no theoretical basis" except a "rough" utilitarianism, highlighted that his "logic" was often as unclear as his sentiments were transparent, and that many of his actual arguments moved in the dreaded "circle."[92] Honderich lampooned efforts by conservatives to make Burke idolatry stick for the broader intellectual community, mocking those who "bravely said that Burke stands on a level with Karl Marx and John Stuart Mill" despite not being "very good at holding one idea before the mind long enough to explain it."[93] Given Burke's famous description of small ideas as clear ideas, he might have even taken that as a compliment. Corey Robin described Burke as a mess of contradictions, simultaneously filled with petit bourgeois resentment of the aristocracy that didn't appreciate efforts on their behalf while still finding the new monied elites vulgar and unimaginative. In Robin's hands Burke is less Scruton's "romantic" hero and more a resentful firebrand who despised the aristocracy for not letting him fully be a part of it. But Burke nevertheless adores its chivalric ideologies since they glitter so much brighter than the trite utilitarianism of the emerging middle class to which he would ever belong. However much Burke strived to elevate himself by flattering his social betters.[94]

Coupled with these divergent interpretations is the deep ambiguity about how exactly to describe Burke, or, as Macpherson puts it with artful grace, the "Burke Problem."[95] Is he, as I once (inaccurately) thought, a prudentialist? Uday Mehta made an argument to that effect, claiming it explained how Burke was less rigid in his thinking than many of the early Utilitarians. This goes some way to explaining why he could endorse one revolution and condemn another, chastise colonial practices in India and argue for kindness toward slaves while still supporting empire and slavery.[96] But prudentialism is inherently difficult to define, and hardly counts as a theoretical outlook anyways. Prudence can dictate radicalism or caution, violence or peace as the context demands and is disconnected from the crucial question of ends. It may be the case that Burke was a prudent man, but what does his worldly wisdom aim at?

Closely related to the prudentialist interpretation is the Kirkean argument that Burkeanism is a disposition or outlook, a kind of personality which gravitates toward a set of political inclinations rather than a substantiated philosophy.[97] On this view Burke would never offer a rationalistic philosophy precisely because it would run against his experiential philosophy to do so; the Burkean doesn't so much rationalize as feel in his gut what to do, which changes are necessary, and which are too radical by half.[98] But if this is the case then conservatism ala Burke amounts to little more than a pathological assertion of one's own good sense and intuitive judgments, backed by whatever ex post facto evidence can be found to legitimate them. Far from being Kirk's genius Burke appears at best to be a man of good sense to his supporters and an unprincipled crank to the rest of us.

Maybe Burke is, as Edmund Neill claims, a "traditionalist" who is committed to a "relatively systematic conservative position, organized around the ideology's core concepts of controlling historical change, and the importance of influences beyond human agency."[99] This is an attractive way to solve the puzzle since it grants Burke the honor of holding a "relatively systematic" philosophy, and doing so in a way that pays practical dividends through accurate political analysis of current and past events. But if that's the case how to explain why Burke thought the Glorious Revolution was justified, the American Revolution at least understandable, and the emergence of new propertied classes an acceptable challenge to the calcified entitlements of aristocratic authority? Yet modest laws for the relief of the poor, raising taxes to pay for affairs of state, and the toleration of low-scale atheism and even deism were unacceptable? By any metric the former were far more profound or at least immediately consequential breaks with "tradition" than the latter. Some have explained this by coupling Burke's traditionalism with, or retreating back to, the prudentialist or dispositional interpretive. But this only brings us back to the earlier interpretive difficulties while raising the theoretical stakes considerably.

Finally there are those who acknowledge that the theoretical ambiguities in Burke's work cannot be settled through a strict approach to the text, but only by reading him as either embodying or anticipating a more systematic conservatism. Perhaps even without knowing it. There are two major candidates in this regard. Some argue, contra Strauss, that despite his scathing denunciation of "natural rights" as the "imaginary rights of men," Burke is ultimately committed to a classical conception of natural law and possibly even natural right. This claim features prominently in James Matthew Wilson's *The Vision of the Soul* where he claims that Burke provided conservatives with a "specifically modern vocabulary" for understanding cultural ways of life as a "slow pursuit of the good" but criticizes him for offering a "rear guard defense of an ancient and venerable understanding of beauty as convertible with, as bound to, truth and goodness."[100] His approach was rear-guard because Burke already conceded too much to the ontological and egalitarian suppositions of modernity, leaving him vulnerable to critiques of irrationalism by figures like Wollstonecraft. For Wilson, what is needed then is reformulating Burke's key insights through a tradition like Christian Platonism.[101]

This take can appear attractive, and certainly situates Burke closer to such illustrative English conservatives as Coleridge and later the migratory T.S. Eliot. The price for this move is great though. It anachronizes Burke, turning him into an impoverished and deracinated spokesman for a tradition so gutted it can't even make use of its own expressive and technical vocabulary anymore without inviting ridicule. Thus requiring loopdiloops of rhetoric and ellipses in logic to rehash the same points about nasty democratic sophisters Plato made them far more successfully two millennia before. It utterly dethrones Burke from his auspicious place as a founder of modern conservatism and makes him instead the ghoulish remnant of a tradition shambling forth for one last suckle at the brains of the modern world.

Another route is to take Burke as not speaking for what came before but anticipating what is to come. Roger Scruton often describes Burke as giving protean expression to the philosophical ideas which would later be picked up and systematized in the grand work of Georg Hegel.[102] This of course means acknowledging that Burke was, as Strauss claimed, a historicist through and through. But this is only a danger if one buys into the idea that Burkean-Hegelian historicism is inherently anti-conservative, something Marx at least might scoff at. For Scruton, Burke recognized the fundamentally Hegelian point that submission to authority and law isn't a limitation on freedom but rather a necessary precondition for it. Moreover, freedom was best achieved within a society whose authority structures were settled over time, since that generated the kinds of ties of spirit and affection—the affective "ethical life" of the nation—which held individuals together and made them mutually interested in one another's well-being.[103] This also meant that consent to authority is not crucial to secure its legitimacy, let alone efficacy. As Yuval Levin[104] puts it:

> As Burke sees it, each man is in society not by choice but by birth. And the facts of his birth-the family, the station, and the nation he is born into-exert inescapable demands on him, while also granting him some privileges and protections that the newborn has, of course, done nothing to earn. Men can change their circumstances and can garner and lose privileges and obligations in the course of their lives, but even when they do so, they take on in their new stations new obligations that are not simply chosen and cannot simply be discarded at will. 'The place of every man determines his duty'.[105]

By contrast the abstract egalitarian individual of liberal thought conceived of freedom as mere liberation from authority and was consequently universalistic in its outlook, invoking the demand that the demands imposed by traditionalist ties be destroyed at ever higher levels.

This interpretation seems to me to be the most accurate, and it might be fruitful to consider Burke giving implicit expression to the kind of ordered liberty conservatism Hegel later systematizes in the *Philosophy of Right*. But this also comes at the price of undermining Burke, who pays for not being a relic by becoming a way station on the way to a far greater thinker.

Edmund Burke and the Sublimation of Power into Authority

One way to uncharitably interpret these ambiguities in Burkeanism is to simply bite the bullet and nod along when Honderich claims Burke's arguments' are inconsistent or simply bad.[106] But I think this is wrong. Burkeanism is a conservative worldview which cannot be understood as resting on any consistent foundation recognizable to a typical analytical philosopher, or, for that matter, the early Enlightenment thinkers Burke castigated. It needs to be grasped holistically. So it is not anti-republicanism, or the cautious management of history, or reverence for private property which is the Rosetta stone for understanding Burke's worldview, any more than the dialectic of the master and slave is the generative thought out of which Hegel's system springs. But to say Burkeanism is anti-foundational and holistic is not to say it lacks unity. If anything, Burke's worldview is doggedly committed to enforcing a kind of unity on the world even where the world resists it. And it achieves this not through reason but through aesthetics. Burke's core conservative project is the aestheticization of rank by describing it in beatific or sublime terms. In so doing, Burke inaugurates an entire school of conservative romanticism—a politically correct word for irrationalism—which persists to this day.

We need to break from the understanding of Burke's aesthetic theory, as presented most fully in his *A Philosophical Enquiry into the Origin of Our Ideas of the Beautiful and the Sublime* (not a very beautiful title, though perhaps sublime in its endlessness), which is secondary and even juvenile relative to the works of his political maturity.[107] This is because the aesthetic categories developed there, the beautiful and the sublime, provide clues to understanding how Burke will later evaluate political phenomena. It is also the first place where he committed to the idea that he indirectly attacks the Enlightenment ideal of the rational subject. Intriguingly he already connects all these threads together in the *Enquiry*, arguing against materialism and rationalism, and contending that the basis of moral concern is an affective attachment of sympathy which has its origins in aesthetics. As he puts it very early in the book:

> It is by the first of these passions that we enter into the concerns of others; that we are moved as they are moved, and are never suffered to be indifferent spectators of almost anything which men can do or suffer. For sympathy must be considered as a sort of substitution, by which we are put into the place of another man, and affected in many respects as he is affected: so that this passion may either partake of the nature of those which regard self-preservation, and turning upon pain may be a source of the sublime; or it may turn upon ideas of pleasure; and then whatever has been said of the social affections, whether they regard society in general, or only some particular modes of it, may be applicable here. It is by this principle chiefly that poetry, painting, and other affecting arts, transfuse their passions from one breast to another, and are often capable of grafting a delight on wretchedness, misery, and death itself. It is a common observation, that objects which in the reality would shock, are in tragical, and such like representations, the source of a very high species of pleasure. This, taken as a fact, has been the cause of much reasoning. The satisfaction has been commonly attributed, first, to the comfort we receive in considering that so melancholy a story is no more than a fiction; and, next, to the contemplation of our own freedom from the evils which we see represented. I am afraid it is a practice much too common in inquiries of this nature, to attribute the cause of feelings which merely arise from the mechanical structure of our bodies, or from the natural frame and constitution of our minds, to certain conclusions of the reasoning faculty on the objects presented to us; for I

should imagine, that the influence of reason in producing our passions is nothing near so extensive as it is commonly believed.[108]

While Burke rarely returned directly to the subject of aesthetics, as we will see, he continued to routinely appeal to its categories throughout his lengthy political career. The most important of these is the category of the sublime, which for Burke refers to the affective sense of awe and horror toward an object of power, infinite expanse, and grandeur. Jesse Norman goes too far when he claims that for Burke

> the social order is…sublime: it far outstrips human understanding, triggering the instinct for self-preservation, and so feelings of awe and humility, in those who seek to grasp it. It is an inheritance, which imposes on each generation the obligation to preserve and if possible, enhance it, before passing it on to the next generation. And there is no opt out.[109]

This is because the category of the beautiful also plays its role, as what achieves a proportion comprehensible to the average human mind and so becomes potentially subject to human control and manipulation. It is the relationship between the two which is crucial for understanding the varied contradictions within Burke's work.

For Burke, beauty is what stirs the sentiment of love in us by its orderliness and proportion. This is intrinsically linked to our reasoning powers, since in beautiful objects affect and reason are united in being able to recognize and approve their end to such an extent that they induce in us pleasurable feelings of love. This also requires first and foremost that what we consider beautiful be "small," because above all "we love what submits to us."[110] It fills us with a feeling of power and ability, which is one of the reasons many of the most praiseworthy aesthetic activities involve degrees of control and refinement in presentation. These testify to their willed and created quality, brought into being consciously by their makers. To demonstrate grace, for example, what is required is "a small inflection of the body; and a composure of the parts in such a manner, as not to encumber each other, not to appear divided by sharp and sudden angles."[111] Music, the primary example of beauty in hearing, is beautiful when it is soft and orderly, sweet and characterized by

> the unbroken continuance, the easy gradation of the beautiful in other things; and all the diversities of the several senses, with all their several affections, will rather help to throw lights from one another to finish one clear, consistent idea of the whole, than to obscure it by their intricacy and variety.[112]

This aesthetic theory maps with remarkable consistency onto Burke's mature politics, where his admiration for smallness is almost always accompanied by beatific and affective descriptions; sometimes, as with his rather hoary ruminations on the age of chivalry being gone, to a point approaching self-parody.[113] He is profoundly critical of the designs of Enlightenment sophisters and philosophers who take a materialist or "mechanical" view of society, in part because this affection for beauty is an aid to obedience and submission to legal authority. As Burke put it,

> On the principles of this mechanic philosophy, our institutions can never be embodied, if I may use the expression, in persons; so as to create in us love, veneration, admiration, or attachment. But that sort of reason which banishes the affections is incapable of filling their place. These public affections, combined with manners, are required sometimes as supplements, sometimes as correctives, always as aids to law There ought to be a system of manners in every nation which a well-formed mind would be disposed to relish. To make us love our country, our country ought to be lovely.[114]

In a national populist vein he praises the good sense of the people of England, who understand that the

> spirit of innovation is generally the result of a selfish temper and confined views. People will not look forward to posterity, who never look backward to their ancestors. Besides, the people of England well know that the idea of inheritance furnishes a sure principle of conservation, and a sure principle of transmission, without at all excluding a principle of improvement. It leaves acquisition free; but it secures what it acquires. Whatever advantages are obtained by a state proceeding on these maxims are locked fast as in a sort of family settlement, grasped as in a kind of mortmain forever.[115]

Often associated with this is his well-known comment that

> to be attached to the subdivision, to love the little platoon we belong to in society, is the first principle (the germ, as it were) of public affections. It is the first link in the series by which we proceed towards a love to our country and to mankind.

Less frequently quoted is the opening of these ruminations, which consist of Burke chastising the "third estate" its insubordination, described as coming to "despise their own order." He also compares them to the revolutionaries more to his taste who sought to "ornament" their society and beautify it, unlike the French revolutionaries whom Burke compares to "Jew brokers contending with each other who could best remedy with fraudulent circulation and depreciated paper the wretchedness and ruin brought on their country by their degenerate councils."[116]

What we find here is very important, as it is one of the first instances of conservatives coming to praise to the common man and his traditions and practices in beatific terms. But notably only so long as the common man remains lovingly attached to his station and the little platoons to which he belongs. His submissive cooperation allows the harmonious continuation of society without posing a threat to its basic structure. This is because finding beauty and meaning in our little platoon, which we understand and exist within, is a precondition for the aesthetic appreciation of society and its hierarchies more generally. It is beautiful because it entails making one's contribution to the beautification of society without complaint, recognizing that each has a part to play but it is neither an equal or equally rewarded part. Moreover, much as Burke described beauty as a rather stultifying and complacent aesthetic effect, there is a tranquil boredom which is to emerge within these little platoons.

This is in stark contrast to the sublime power and splendor of the higher orders to which agency and creativity are aggregated, and which are the primary beneficiaries of Burke's defensive gestures. Equality is not simply a threat to political order, but to the possibility of sublime dynamism. At best equality is to be understood as strictly moral and never meaningful. Aspiration for anything more is a "monstrous" fiction which leads to bitterness toward an unchangeable social order which, Burke insists, benefits all, including the least fortunate. And besides, it's not like the well off are actually that much happier anyways, since there is contentment to be found in accepting one's place and not seeking to lodge complaints about what Burke thinks cannot be changed. As he puts it in one of the more purple (and that's saying something) paragraphs of the *Reflections*:

> You would have had a free Constitution, a potent monarchy, a disciplined army, a reformed and venerated clergy, a mitigated, but spirited nobility, to lead your virtue, not to overlay it; you would have had a liberal order of commons, to emulate and to recruit that nobility; you would have had a protected, satisfied, laborious, and obedient people, taught to seek and to recognize the happiness that is to be found by virtue in all conditions, in which consists the true moral equality of mankind, and not in that monstrous fiction which, by inspiring false ideas and vain expectations into men destined to travel in the obscure walk of laborious life, serves only to aggravate and embitter that real inequality which it never can remove, and which the order of civil life establishes as much for the benefit of those whom it must leave in an humble state as those whom it is able to exalt to a condition more splendid, but not more happy.[117]

Intriguingly Burke at various points seems to acknowledge the deliberately ideological dimension of his efforts, as when he describes the hammier appeals to the age of chivalry as

> all the pleasing illusions which made power gentle and obedience liberal, which harmonized the different shades of life, and which by a bland

assimilation incorporated into politics the sentiments which beautify and
soften private society, are to be dissolved by this new conquering empire
of light and reason.

In other words, perhaps the values of chivalry were simply illusory and irrational.
But who cares when they "without confounding ranks, had produced a noble
equality, and handed it down through all the gradations of social life."[118] An
equality in sentimentalized imagination without equality in fact is to Burke's
taste. This will not be the only place where these kinds of acknowledgments
occur, and they are even more explicit when Burke describes what institutions
are needed to not beatify, but to sublimate power to transform it into authority.

Burke's attempt to sublimate power into authority is an extraordinarily important gesture in the Enlightenment context, where critics like Paine
and Voltaire—the latter of whom united "blasphemy and obscenity so happily
together"[119]—took great pride in lampooning the powers that be with great
acumen. This had the clear effect of demythologizing and denaturalizing the
legitimacy of authority and situating it historically and contextually in a long
series of depravities, vulgarity, and violence brought about by the insulation of
power from accountability. This was a vital cultural complement to the emergence of egalitarian modernity.

In his more Whiggish moments, Burke himself had played a role in this historical process of desublimation circa his early yearning to constrain the English
monarchy and especially his chastisement of abstract appeals to national sovereignty to justify the imposition of undue taxation without representation on
the Americans. The residue of these sympathies may explain why his effort at
resublimating the authority of the French Ancien regime rarely reaches the levels of theoretical and philosophical bombast it will achieve with De Maistre.[120]
To be clear though, if Burke's temperament and fading Whiggish inclinations
wouldn't allow it, this wasn't for a lack of effort on his point. One of Burke's
most remarkably self-conscious moments is actually a rare programmatic sugges-
tion, where he describes the "august fabric of states" as the production of a "wise
architect" who sought to have it preserved "as a sacred temple." Those who work
in the administration of government should be attentive to the sacral quality of
their task, and therefore not pay attention to the "transient praise of the vulgar."
He then goes on to argue that individuals of high status and power need to be
sublimated directly, to better calcify respect for their authority and the social
structures they defend. Religion can here play an important role in buttressing
seemingly secular authorities, by functionally linking them to a transcendent
authority more powerful and beyond contestation than they are.

> Such sublime principles out to be infused into persons of exalted situation;
> and religious establishments provided, that may continually revive and
> enforce them. Every sort of moral, every sort of civil, every sort of politic
> institution, aiding the rational and natural ties that connect the human

understanding and affections to the divine, are not more than necessary, in order to build up that wonderful structure, Man; whose prerogative it is, to be in a great degree a creature of his own making, and who when made as he ought to be made, is destined to hold no trivial place in the creation. But whenever man is put over men, as the better nature ought ever to preside, in that case more particularly, he as nearly as possible be approximated to his perfection.[121]

Burke then immediately proceeds to describe how these efforts will in turn make the general population respond to the state and its leaders with "wholesome awe." This is especially key in an era where popular government seems to be the wave of the future, and the common people must be given "some determinate portion of power." The feeling that they are not in fact the masters of society, and so free to change it as they wish, but under the jurisdiction of God and his earthly lieutenants. Otherwise one has a "perfect democracy" which is the "most shameless thing in the world."[122]

Oddly Burke never seems fully confident that this form of sublimation through association with religion is sufficient, let alone that any of the sources of awe and transcendent majesty he word-associates with would conform to anything real or true. In a more famous passage Burke seems to hedge his bets by describing society as less the product of a divine architect and instead in the more worldly terms of a contract. But unlike the Enlightenment philosophers for whom the contract is either between the living or a mere heuristic device to capture something important about political legitimacy, Burke's contract is a Gothic compact between "those who are living, those who are dead, and those who are to be born."[123] This contract is itself sublime and imposes an obligation on subjects "infinitely superior" to their specific will. This means we are "not morally at liberty" to change society, because we are under a mysterious "supreme necessity" which is "not chosen" and which apparently can be asserted without admitting any need for "discussion, and demands no evidence."[124] To which the sensible follow Hitchens in saying that what can be asserted without evidence can be dismissed without evidence. Though perhaps not without laughter.

This last point is very much in keeping with Mary Wollstonecraft's assessment of Burke in *A Vindication of the Rights of Men* as having a

> "mortal antipathy to reason; but, if there is any thing like argument, or first principles, in your wild declamation, behold the result:—that we are to reverence the rust of antiquity, and term the unnatural customs, which ignorance and mistaken self-interest have consolidated, the sage fruit of experience: nay, that, if we do discover some errors, our *feelings* should lead us to excuse, with blind love, or unprincipled filial affection, the venerable vestiges of ancient days. These are gothic notions of beauty – the ivy is beautiful, but, when it insidiously destroys the trunk from which it receives support, who would not grub it up?

> Further, that we ought cautiously to remain for ever in frozen inactivity, because a thaw, whilst it nourishes the soil, spreads a temporary inundation; and the fear of risking any personal present convenience should prevent a struggle for the most estimable advantages. This is sound reasoning, I grant, in the mouth of the rich and short-sighted."[125]

Burke deploys his very considerable literary talents to give the semblance of argumentative weight to positions that are as deeply vague or even simply asserted as they are strongly felt. But saying this doesn't really account for why it is that Burke ascribes weight to those specific positions and not others. To put it another way, it doesn't tell us why Burke feels the way he does about political issues.

Burke on the "Swinish Multitude"

> Nothing is a due and adequate representation of a state that does not represent its ability as well as its property. But as ability is a vigorous and active principle, and as property is sluggish, inert, and timid, it never can be safe from the invasion of ability unless it be, out of all proportion, predominant in the representation. It must be represented, too, in great masses of accumulation, or it is not rightly protected. The characteristic essence of property, formed out of the combined principles of its acquisition and conservation, is to be unequal. The great masses, therefore, which excite envy and tempt rapacity must be put out of the possibility of danger.[126]

Understanding Burke's approach to politics as fundamentally aesthetic can help frame the more pertinent question of what, exactly, he thought was sublime and what he believed to be ugly. The last section contained plenty of suggestive remarks on these points but don't give us the full answer as to why Burke found himself supporting the Ancien regime—in spite of his gentle criticisms—and what he saw as fundamentally threatening it.

As Robin, Macpherson, and others have pointed out, the explanation lies in Burke's horror at the threat posed to private property and the ranks and divisions associated with it.[127] Indeed he regards respect for property and foundational hierarchies as the functional basis for the kind of beautiful and orderly societies Burke admires to perpetuate themselves. While he remained torn between supporting and sublimating the aristocracy as it was supposed to be, and criticizing its entrenched privileges in the name of a more mobile and meritocratic system, the constant in Burke's outlook was to sympathize with the cause of property and power against its expropriators.[128] Indeed late in his *Reflections* he even manages to harmonize these two inclinations by describing how the new meritocratic and the old aristocratic elite share much in common. Burke opines that the Revolution might not have happened if they'd been united rather than divided by the aristocrats desire to refuse to share some of their privileges with their brothers—a strange concession to the democratic character of the age which is self-serving in its willingness to accept redistribution where it benefits the new elite, but no more than that.[129] Interestingly this is true even in Burke's seemingly more radical moments; when describing why he sympathized with the American revolutionaries, he couches his defense as a critique of abstract notions of sovereignty being used to justify the expropriation of property in the colonies. He points out that the revolutionaries are property owners, much as the men trying to tax them are, and this should be the basis of empathy and understanding between the two groups.[130]

Like more liberal proponents of possessive individualism the notion that property, whether justified by genteel aristocratic aesthetics or meritocratic efficiency, is at least as abstract an idea as any he criticizes rarely features in Burke's writing. This isn't to say he doesn't provide arguments of a sort for respecting it—there are well over a 100 references to property in the *Reflections* alone, suggesting a mania of sorts. Burke will describe respect for property as the "root" of national prosperity, and will appeal to Smithian and other proto-utilitarian arguments on the role self-interested accumulation can play in contributing to economic growth in a natal capitalist society. At other points he defends property's role in securing order and stability. This includes in national assemblies, which are by no means to include representatives from every walk of life. For Burke, representatives "should be respectably composed, in point of condition in life, of permanent property, of education, and of such habits as enlarge and liberalize the understanding."[131]

This also suggests property can be defended for its role in elevating the quality of the individuals who possess it. Burke sometimes describes property in terms of liberty, as the ability to dispose of what one possesses as one likes. This links readily to his economic arguments, and one of the reasons Burke cautioned the government against directly providing relief to the poor was his confidence that it would compromise property and that unconstrained market freedom would be more likely to aid the least well off anyways.[132] There are references to property as a "right" which has emerged over thousands of years. Elsewhere Burke describes the yearning to protect what one happens to possess in terms of human nature which in turn contributes to the preservation of communities, depicting the

> strong struggle in every individual to preserve possession of what he has found to belong to him, and to distinguish him, is one of the securities against injustice and despotism implanted in our nature. It operates as an instinct to secure property, and to preserve communities in a settled state.[133]

Burke even opines that for men of property to be honored and even "privileged" by the law, a denial of liberal legal equality as sharp as any is nothing to get up in arms about.[134]

In the *Reflection* the gish galloping argumentation in favor of property that rapidly piles claims upon claims upon claims blunts their overall effect for readers who don't immediately share Burke's sensibilities. More effective are his arguments in the "Thoughts and Details on Scarcity" where he argues that the redistribution of wealth would very little improve the lot of the poor since there are so few rich. Burke also defends property by appealing to the self-interest of individuals and arguing that the allure of wealth can stimulate economic activity. In this respect demands for equality will only make the poor worse off, or at least not improve their lot, while also impoverishing the rich. He also expresses skepticism at the cost and effectiveness of the government providing goods to the general public.

However, even in these more sober and calculated ruminations, Burke cannot help ascribing sublimely magical and even divine properties to the market. And in a rather charming way. When responding to the hypothetical argument that without relief the poor will starve Burke observes that it is not the duty of government to

> supply to the poor, those necessaries which it has pleased the Divine Providence for a while to with-hold from them. We, the people, ought to be made sensible, that it is not in breaking the laws of commerce, which are the laws of nature, and consequently the laws of God, that we are to place our hope of softening the Divine displeasure to remove any calamity under which we suffer, or which hangs over us.[135]

Note how quickly and without argument Burke claims the laws of commerce are in fact the laws of nature and in fact more than that the laws of God. When this sublimating language fails to work, Burke turns to more beatific language, calling on the nation to be bound together "rich and poor together, against those wicked writers of the newspapers, who would inflame the poor against their friends, guardians, patrons, and protectors" and others willing to let them starve.[136] Because it is surely those damned newspapermen and not starvation which would motivate people to action.

Burke expresses skepticism that anyone actually dies from famine, opining that

> even now, I do not know of one man, woman, or child, that has perished from famine; fewer, if any, I believe, than in years of plenty, when such a thing may happen by accident. This is owing to a care and superintendence of the poor, far greater than any I remember.[137]

These kinds of passages make one wonder whether, for all Burke's shrill resolution in favor of priests, he ever bothered to pick up the Bible and read it. Admittedly passages like "blessed are the poor" and "that which you do unto the least of us, you do unto me" are a bit vague, but a man of Burke's erudition could likely piece the message together.

The effect of all this is to give the impression that property is a fetish or "sublime object"[138] of Burke's, which is aesthetically ramified as the foundation to the beautifully submissive societies he wants to see and which emerges from the sublime operations of providence and God in the world. He sees in property the means through which humanity is sorted into its proper organic divisions and associates men of property with genteel or meritocratic qualities which make them more sublime and require their authority to be entrenched in law and consciously aestheticized through ideological apparatuses like the Church's. Burke's political inclinations reflect this fetishization throughout and explain the surface shifts in his orientation. It also explains Burke's visceral reaction to democracy and even the extension of equal liberal rights to the masses, and his tendency to favor representational schemes which favor the political and class power of the rich and properties. Indeed he makes the rather innovative point that if one is to adopt the features of a republican government, it becomes more incumbent than before that the rich have "additional security" to protect them from the kinds of envy which will inevitably emerge.

> Now take it in the other point of view, and let us suppose their principle of representation according to contribution, that is according to riches, to be well imagined, and to be a necessary basis for their republic. In this their third basis they assume that riches ought to be respected, and that justice and policy require that they should entitle men, in some mode or other, to a larger share in the administration of public affairs; it is now to be seen how the Assembly provides for the preëminence, or even for the security of the rich, by conferring, in virtue of their opulence, that larger measure of power to their district which is denied to them personally. I readily admit (indeed, I should lay it down as a fundamental principle) that in a republican government, which has a democratic basis, the rich do require an additional security above what is necessary to them in monarchies. They are subject to envy, and through envy to oppression. On the present scheme it is impossible to divine what advantage they derive from the aristocratic preference upon which the unequal representation of the masses is founded. The rich cannot feel it, either as a support to dignity or as security to fortune: for the aristocratic mass is generated from purely democratic principles; and the prevalence given to it in the general representation has no sort of reference to or connection with the persons upon account of whose property this superiority of the mass is established. If the contrivers of this scheme meant any sort of favor to the rich, in consequence of their contribution, they ought to have conferred the privilege either on the individual rich, or on some class formed of rich persons (as historians represent Servius Tullius to have done in the early constitution of Rome); because the contest between the rich and the poor is not a struggle between corporation and corporation, but a contest between men and

men, —a competition, not between districts, but between descriptions. It would answer its purpose better, if the scheme were inverted: that the votes of the masses were rendered equal, and that the votes within each mass were proportioned to property.[139]

So the key takeaway from Burke's outlook is that while its central philosophical approach is aesthetic its key political program gradually comes to be, as MacPherson highlighted long ago, the protection of property and the hierarchical relations which emerge from unequal property regimes.[140] Burke is quite willing to entertain considerable and even revolutionary transformations in the settled traditions of a state, including circa the Glorious Revolution and the American Revolution, where these are conceived as a defense of property and its associated merit. In these contexts he will tend to aestheticize even so radical geopolitical transitions as the loss of an entire continent as a form of continuity. But in circumstances where property is threatened one sees the most apoplectic, apocalyptic, and even sentimental rhetoric since it is typically framed as the pivot around which most of the other beatific and effective institutions and traditions pivot.

So what we have with Burke is the creation of a very effective form of right-wing ideology, most notable above all for its plasticity in relation to the thrust of modernity. Since Burke's conception of property straddles the line between reverence for the genteel aristocracy and the more vulgar but potentially meritocratic ethos of possessive individualism, it is capable of shifting orientation in a variety of directions. It can move from upholding more right-liberal forms of ordered liberty conservatism to more traditionalist variants where necessary. Much of this will depend on which form of property is ascendant in a given society.[141] This can seem unprincipled on the surface until one recognizes that in fact it is exceptionally consistent on the key point that matters. So long as property is respected one can count on Burke as a stalwart, if cantankerous, ally.

What's deflating about this is that the fetish Burke makes of property is often so foundational and animates so many of his other convictions that they can appear of second-order importance at best. Many of the vacillations in his writing can be explained through it. His traditionalism and wariness of change can be bent where bourgeois or American property is threatened. Much as his partial embrace of Enlightenment will reach a hard limit when confronted with the French Revolution, after which he will retreat back into traditionalism and irrationalism. Burke will present himself as the wise statesman and proponent of common sense when defending the everyday person and the profits to be made through free trade, before turning into the chivalric defender of the aristocracy when the swinish multitude comes gunning for their land and their servants. Or he will beatify the little platoons of society, where each man is king of his own castle, so long as each man doesn't aspire to break the far more sublime contract between the living and the dead which stipulates that our poor monarchs need significant rights to influence what goes on beyond their front door. Seen from this standpoint Burkeanism looks less like an admirably pragmatic kind of disposition, and more like a thoroughly ideological set of movements arguing whatever is required to uphold the divine order ordained by God. Not the soft humanistic Christian God of course. The real one upon which it is written "In God we Trust."

Saying all that, this remarkably petit bourgeois sensibility did inoculate Burke against some of the more spectacular forms of right-wing animosity which emerged over time. Many of which would come to fetishize not property as a basis for the hierarchical division of society, but state power and even the grand capacity for violence on a titanic scale. One feature of Burke's work which is admirable is how he often found this disposition itself revolting. Too disconnected from the material prosperity which is proof of success, too willing to threaten market relations in its aspirations to forms of bigness and scale to which even Burke was allergic. In this Burke also contributed to the formation of a distinctly British form of conservatism, which prided itself on going just far enough and no further and which could compromise with certain aspects of egalitarian modernity so long as they could be cautiously managed. In this respect Edmund Fawcett is right that "Burke's writings gave conservatism in retrospect, particularly conservatism in Britain and the United States, a tone of balance, openness to facts, and all-round moderation that stood out in contrast to the blind zeal of conservatism in France and Germany."[142] The next figure we will look at had no such compunctions.

De Maistre, Violence, and Authority

Isaiah Berlin famously described Joseph de Maistre as the intellectual godfather of 20th-century fascism—an honor even he might have passed on for its extremist associations.[143] Nevertheless Fawcett is right that where Burke was willing to allow for "argument, and disagreement" De Maistre "wanted from politics authority and obedience" and that his "anti-rationalist legacy passed to authoritarian, illiberal conservatism."[144] Part of these differences can at least be accounted for by biography. It would be going too far to call Burke, an active politician, an armchair critic of the French Revolution and egalitarian modernity. But Burke got to view the Revolution with the kind of sardonic disdain indicating a degree of distance from events, which makes the occasional eruptions of shrill denunciation that creep into his work seem more like affective bloviation.

By contrast the French Revolution made De Maistre into an exile, as did two decades of invincible French troops who contemptuously swept aside the forces of every petty fiefdom he served. Eventually De Maistre was forced all the way from the sunny Mediterranean to decidedly less picturesque 19th-century Russia, where the man was occasionally so poor he was forced to eat his servant's soup.[145] Consequently if disdain ever does creep into his work it is always textured with a kind of demonic proximity—a deep and abiding allergy to a pollution which spreads without limit or cure. Much more common is a sense of existential dread in a full Kierkegaardian vein: the sense of being confronted with a dizzying new array of human possibilities and wanting nothing more than to be relieved of them through the restoration of a more firm world eternally lost. This reflects Corey Robin's superb statement that

> Forged in response to challenges from below, conservatism has none of the calm or composure that attends an enduring inheritance of power...Even Maistre's professions of divine providence cannot conceal or contain the turbulent democracy that generated them. Made and mobilized to counter the claims of emancipation, such statements do not disclose a dense ecology of deference; they open out onto a rapidly thinning forest.[146]

With De Maistre we do indeed see the final nail in the coffin of the old Aristotelian and even Filmerian calm which defined the early modern era. Despite his routine appeals to scholastic and Catholic authorities, there is none of the measure and dryness one would expect of a follower of Thomas Aquinas or Ignatius Loyola. Try though they might, the political right has never recovered this because a form of organic and stratified totality has never again become so hegemonic as to be beyond contestation.

But with De Maistre the political right purchased something extraordinary for their loss. Aesthetically it gained a capacity for excitement and daring, a transition from mere moralism toward a world illustrated with primary colors occasionally fusing into brilliant light contrasted with starkest blacks. Part of this was initially motivated by desperation in the face of the oncoming democratic nihilism, but it is an active and purposive aesthetic and not a defeated one. If anything the stakes being raised so high and the danger becoming so real dialectically animate the corpse-like values De Maistre defends and which Enlightenment reason had seemed to destroy even before the revolution. In other words his writing showed that the political right could posture as cool and even dangerously counter-cultural—something boring old Burke will never be described as. While the 60-year-old Burke contented himself with hoary denunciations of out-of-touch Enlightenment philosophers, De Maistre, 36 when the Revolution began, called it a fundamentally destructive force allegorically and maybe literally sent by Satan himself and defied anyone to say different.

While this was a concession of sorts to mass society—so prescient in its anticipation of the coming Romantic era De Maistre would profoundly influence—it was distinctly conservative in its ferocious elitism. But in this case an elitism in which ordinary people were invited to participate in aesthetically but not politically. It was to be through direct libidinal investment in sublimating the authorities which governed them to the highest degree rather than political agency. Sometimes this was a conscious effort on his part, as when he described "monarchy" as "without contradiction, the form of government that gives the most distinction to the greatest number of persons" because ordinary people can participate in its splendor "as a portion of sovereignty."[147]

But more importantly in De Maistre's work the political right gained a sense of conscious political agency with historical mission for the first time. As Robin claims

> once the old regime is threatened or toppled, the conservative is forced to realize that it is human agency, the willed imposition of intellect and imagination upon the world, that generates and maintains inequality across time…From the revolution, the conservative develops a particular attitude toward political time, a belief in the power of men and women to shape history, to propel it forward or backwards; and by virtue of that belief, he comes to adopt the future as his preferred taste.[148]

This is especially true where the future can be made to look less like an egalitarian present; conservatives will often look to the past for inegalitarian models, but the political right as a whole won't necessarily. Moreover as believers in the fundamental inequality of humankind it will turn out that this belief in the human capacity to change history and map that inequality onto society fits the political right quite well. While the political right will only ever be willing to endorse political agency parsimoniously, it will do so with relish and enthusiasm where that agency is allocated to the truly deserving who best understand how to use it. And just as importantly, who to use it against.

This is where the specter of violence comes in for De Maistre, which is the supreme marker of political agency calcified into authority. De Maistre's writings are littered with expressions of support for violence, of which his famous comment speculating on whether the executioner is "this sublime being" who is the "cornerstone of society" and "all order" is only the most famous.[149] In a more ambiguous moment De Maistre ruminates on the execution of Louis XVI and prophesizes that each "drop of Louis XVI's blood will cost France torrents; perhaps four million Frenchmen will pay with their lives for the great national crime of an antireligious and antisocial insurrection, crowned by a regicide." I say ambiguous since the passage compresses a huge number of different affects—including different mythological affects— into its foretelling of genocidal destruction. There is more than a smidge of the providential hand of God reaching against the Revolutionaries to bestow well-deserved divine justice. But there is also an aura of Grecian tragedy and the hubris of the French nation brings about its unwitting downfall—a clear example of the rhetoric of Hirschman's perversity thesis in action.[150] At a point it veers away from these lofty sentiments and de Maistre seems to check his violent impulses with a kind of political realism, lamenting that it is foolish to suppose France's internal problems won't impact Europe as a whole and that "terrible means" will be required to set her on course again. Of course this realism also implies a degree of artifice and human agency behind these "terrible means" which distinguishes these moments from those that flirt with divine or mythologized interventions which bring them the risk of culpability for demanding mass murder; perhaps one of the reasons de Maistre checked his inclinations.

Similar ambiguities pervade his comments on war. In a short chapter of the *St. Petersburg Dialogue* De Maistre begins by approving the gentleness of war between the 18th-century European monarchs. But De Maistre then moves quickly into a diatribe straight from the Judge in Cormac McCarthy's *Blood Meridian* when he declares that "war is divine in its very nature."[151] It is divine in its results, which always in the end work to advance the will of God. It is divine in the protection and fame it grants to great leaders. It is divine in the manner in which one is called to a sublime activity, where the souls of even great leaders become swept into the furor of the moment. De Maistre even hypothesizes that God uses war as a means of rectifying the inequities and injustices of the world. And above all wars are divine in the way they establish inequalities between nations, either debasing them or "perfecting them in every way."

In each of these circumstances we see the sublimation of violence being carried out at various levels, whether as an act of human agency by great men, divine intervention to bring about justice, or even the kind of tragic perversity which emerges when the underserving reach too far and bring on themselves blood and ashes. To invoke Foucault,[152] there is an awareness for the first time with De Maistre of the way the spectacular qualities of violence imposed upon the bodies of men and women can serve to entrench the grandeur and legitimacy of sovereign power.[153] But beneath these rhetorical sublimations is something more disturbing: an understanding of how inorganic the Ancien regime actually was and how illegitimate it now looks. With De Maistre the political right comes to itself as potentially on the losing end of history, confronted by rivals of vast means and intelligence who will not stop until up is down and King is *citoyen*. He is consequently aware of how intense and overwhelming the forms of power and violence will be if one wants to put Humpty Dumpty together again. Many of the seeming tensions within De Maistre's work, between its moments of hard-boiled realism and rhapsodic transcendence, can be understood as an endless search for just which kind of power will do the trick.

The Luciferian Peril of Revolution

> There is a Satanic quality to the French Revolution that distinguishes it from everything we have seen or anything we are ever likely to see in the future.
>
> (Joseph De Maistre, *Considérations on France*)

In lesser hands, one might consider de Maistre's comparison of the French Revolutionaries to Satan as mere rhetorical exaggeration. Part of a long line of manic hyperbole which climaxes in our time with more or less every word Tucker Carlson and Laura Ingraham say. But De Maistre means the references to Satanic rebellion quite literally, becoming one of the first conservative theorists to frame political insurrection as a more fundamental kind of onto-theological rebellion. There are of course hints of this in the more purple passages of Burke's writings, but nothing that rises to the hoarse pitch of describing a "fight to the death between Christianity and philosophism"—a fundamentally destructive force that corrodes the "cement" which holds society together precisely through its not being questioned. This also testifies to the fundamental idealism of his work-a philosophical idealism that will be an addiction of many reactionary thinkers going forward. De Maistre's religious idealism stressed the divine nature of existent power, which meant that political antagonisms could not blamed on the social form itself without inadvertently blaming God. Conveniently De Maistre then redirects blame for political antagonisms on the influence of corrupting ideas. In the future this tactic will be a very familiar tool in the reactionary tool kit: explain away the origins of social dissatisfaction by redirecting attention from the substance of criticism to the critics themselves. The critics can be condemned for agitating the normally contended masses against their sublime leaders by stripping away what Burke called "all the pleasing illusions" that made submission easier.

This brings us to one of the great paradoxes in De Maistre's work, which is how he squares his condemnation of the Luciferian pride of the people as a whole who would be king with a full-throated defense of actual men imaginative enough to believe themselves king. Consider that Milton was a favorite of Edmund Burke's and that both major conservative thinkers affirm that Lucifer's great sin was indeed pride. In their hands this is deeply connected with the speculative thinking of the Enlightenment philosophers, who wish to create whole societies and moralities of their own independent powers of reasoning. De Maistre emphatically denies that anyone actually has such a gift; though as we will see he is not entirely consistent on this point. In his *Considerations on France* he makes the distinctly Augustinian claim that "man can modify everything within the sphere of his activity, but he creates nothing."[154] The creative power for authentic generation lies only with God, generating the anger and ressentiment of those philosophers who wish to be like God. Lacking the power to do so independently they defy the sublime "natural constitution" which God has imposed on his creation and stoke the worst impulses of the mass of people as a whole. Directing them against the divine and natural sovereign constitutions and those leaders whom God has providentially ordained to rule over his creation.

Beyond just relying on an immense array of theological suppositions—a point which De Maistre seems worried about when he tries to defend the claim that his conservative Christianity has certain privileged access to the truth which comparable faith traditions don't—this is open to a far more lethal and immanent objection. Why, if it is the case that man is not to usurp the creative or political power of God, is it legitimate to support a monarchial regime which transparently apes the majesty of the divine in its pomp and authority? How can one declare that "no constitution is the result of deliberation"[155] since it is the duty of subjects to obey and that the rights of people "proceed from the concessions of sovereigns," while still lecturing the Enlightenment philosophes about a lack of humility toward their own reasoning powers? De Maistre squares the problems in an ingenious way. He attaches spectacular power, authority, and creative capacities to the monarch throughout his work. But these are always a fiduciary grant by divine authority, which in effect marks the truly special individual as the founder of a constitution or kingdom. In his *Essay on the Generative Principle of Political Constitutions* he proudly declares:

> It is always an oracle, which founds cities; it is always an oracle, which announces the Divine protection, and successes of the heroic founder. Kings, especially, the chiefs of rising empires, are constantly designated, and, as it were, marked, by Heaven, in some extraordinary manner. How many thoughtless men have ridiculed the Saint-Ampoule [holy oil] without ever dreaming that the Saint-Ampoule is a hieroglyph, and that it is only necessary to understand it.[156]

Only the sovereign lawgiver truly understands what is required, which means he is to be obeyed and not questioned. He goes out of the way to stress their distinctive qualities through many works, including multiple times in the same essay:

> Lawgivers, strictly speaking, are extraordinary men, belonging perhaps only to the ancient world and to the youth of nations. Providence has decreed the more rapid formation of a political constitution, there appears a man clothed with an indefinable power; he speaks, and he makes himself to be obeyed. These lawgivers par excellence possess one distinctive characteristic: they are kings, or eminently noble; on this point, there is and can be no exception.[157]

What makes these lawgivers special is their distinctive understanding of the socio-political aims required by providence, which De Maistre insists pre-exist codification and consequently cannot be fully deliberated upon by the mass of men. Indeed De Maistre even warns against such forms of codification, and indeed warns against anyone asking him to explain his own reasoning, claiming that it is

> "…only when society finds itself already constituted, without being able to say how, that it is possible to make known [its fundamental laws], or explain, in writing, certain special articles; but in almost every case these declarations or explanations are effect or cause of very great evils, and always cost the people more than they are worth."[158]

As we will see this is another feature of conservative rhetoric which will have a long history: the affirmation of contradiction as a signifier of profound depths. Here I am not talking about a Hegelian overcoming (more on that later) which is something else entirely. Instead what we see is De Maistre consciously espousing contradictions by presenting them as paradoxes, and so giving them a kind of mysterious glamor, a surface profundity, and even an exclusionary danger which entitles only the rarefied few to tangle with them. In this case we can only know after society is made what its fundamental laws were even before it came into existence, which itself is a topic the wise don't inquire too deeply into. Perhaps because ruminating on how the internal melodramas of the Frankish court led to all kinds of violent conflicts might make them look rather less impressive. More-over while we can only begin to understand the fundamental laws which govern society when they are written down, the basis of their being laws remains an ambiguous and threatening mystery. A mystery which should be treated as a kind of hidden knowledge is ironically known only to those with minds so untroubled by critical dispositions that they could sleep easy even after encountering the profane (read: shameful) origins of Ancien power.

This obviously has rabidly anti-democratic and anti-liberal implications the whole way down, condemning everything from the transparent rule of law to deliberative and participatory political mechanisms. What makes De Mais-tre intriguing, and in many ways the founder of far-right discourse, if not fas-cism,[159] isn't his hyperbole. We've seen Burke was plenty capable of that. It isn't even De Maistre's anti-rationalism, with which Burke would have sympathized. It is his radical rejection of any concession to egalitarianism—even Christian egalitarianism!—coupled with his unparalleled ability to dramatize and subli-mate stark inequality.

This takes on a huge number of different rhetorical forms in his work. They include characterizing the sovereign as providentially called by God to a special task, to the deliberate affirmation of contradiction as a paradox which only a rarefied few are invited to understand. Even where De Maistre offers a quasi-concession to the Enlightenment it is by inverting its contractarian mythologies and insisting that it is in fact submitting to monarchy and participating in its projects without any power of their own which elevates the masses and puts them in touch with the transcendent. When all such appeals to transcendence fail, De Maistre can always resort to the materiality of violence, but a violence which itself takes on a vividly performative dimension.

Generations of the most exciting conservative thinkers from Dostoevsky through Schmitt would pay attention. Compared to De Maistre's titanic portray-als of power and violence, Burke's petit-bourgeois fetishism of property can only appear a bit dull and even conventional. With De Maistre the political right learned to be interesting. And what we've seen is that being interesting needn't entail, and in a fight between organic intellectuals we might actually benefit from, not being intellectually consistent or even plausible. If one takes seriously De Maistre's belief in the agency of lawgivers, bound only by the need to interpret the will of prov-idence or God as revealed only to them, one might go even further and see the rationalistic demand for consistency or explication as vulgar, banal, and inhibiting the right to limitless agency to which the gilded few are entitled.

Conclusion

This was a long chapter by necessity since it told a vital story about understanding the political right. It has never ceased to yearn for something like the good old fashioned Aristotelian universe and the ideology of society as an unequal organic unity in which each had their necessary place but by no means required equal rights or powers. By the time we get to Filmer's rather deflated natural law response to the egalitarian rationalism of the Enlightenment it becomes rather clear that simply appealing to these kinds of tropes to uphold hierarchical forms of socio-political organization is not going to cut it any longer. It was a time when revolutionary liberal and more radical than liberal movements were on the march, but right-wing intellectuals have almost always produced their best work in moments of crisis and response. With Burke and De Maistre we see the modern political right becoming intellectually self-conscious and updating itself for the first time, sometimes developing its own mirror concepts through a symbiotic antagonism with the left[160] and, in more creative moments, generating distinct conceptual idealizations of its own. While few of the forthcoming authors we look at would follow either with the zeal of disciples, their lighting of this creative spark ensured that modern egalitarians would no longer possess the intellectual monopoly they'd enjoyed since at least the early 17th century. It was a watershed moment and one whose varied consequences we continue to live with now.

Notes

1 Edmund Burke. *Reflections on the Revolution in France*. (Oxford, UK: Oxford University Press, 2009) at p. 79
2 Roger Scruton. *A Political Philosophy: Arguments for Conservatism*. (London, UK: Bloomsbury, 2006)
3 See Jordan Peterson. "Open The Damn Country Back Up, Before Canadians Wreck Something We Can't Fix." *National Post*, January 10th, 2022
4 This point is stressed by Corey Robin. See Corey Robin. *The Reactionary Mind Second Edition: Conservatism from Edmund Burke to Donald Trump*. (Oxford, UK: Oxford University Press, 2018)
5 Edmund Burke. *Reflections on the Revolution in France*. (Oxford, UK: Oxford University Press, 2009) at p. 86
6 See Roger Scruton. "Eliot and Conservatism" in *A Political Philosophy: Arguments for Conservatism*. (London, UK: Bloomsbury, 2006)
7 Most prominently Martha Nussbaum. *Political Emotions: Why Love Matters for Justice*. (Cambridge, MA: Belknap Press of Harvard University Press, 2015)
8 The importance of Aristotle for revolutionary authors like Marx has been well established. This includes both philosophically and politically. Philosophically, authors like Meikle have made a compelling case that Marx draws heavily on Aristotle's metaphysics of substance and much of his naturalized anthropology. Politically the conception of human flourishing discussed by Marx, particularly in *Capital Volume Three*, is more than a little stamped by Aristotle. Particularly in comments about how in an ideal society one would see the "development of human powers as an end in itself." Of course Marx is a thoroughly modern thinker in other respects, and doesn't follow Aristotle in linking the development of human powers to a larger

process of immanent ontological development. See Karl Marx. *Capital Volume Three: A Critique of Political Economy*, trans. Ernest Mandel. (London, UK: Penguin Books, 1993) at p. 959. For the point on Aristotle's influence on Marx's metaphysics see Scott Meikle. "History of Philosophy: The Metaphysics of Substance in Marx." in Terrell Carver. *The Cambridge Companion to Marx*. (Cambridge, UK: Cambridge University Press, 1991)

9 Ayn Rand's famously and uncharacteristically high appraisal of Aristotle is a good example. See Jennifer Burns. *Goddess of the Market: Ayn Rand and the American Right* (Oxford, UK: Oxford University Press, 2009)

10 Leo Strauss. *The City and Man*. (Chicago, IL: The University of Chicago Press, 1978) at p. 38

11 See Charles Taylor. *Modern Social Imaginaries*. (Durham, NC: Duke University Press, 2004) at p. 11

12 Aristotle. "Metaphysics" in *The Basic Works of Aristotle*. (New York, NY: The Modern Library, 2001) at p. 755

13 Some have inferred from this the unusual conclusion that in a teleological account of nature the future state of a being in effect dictates what it is to become. This is a complex point where Aristotle would seem to emulate the teachings of Plato on the relation of the temporalized form of objects and how they wish to approximate the eternal form. While an interesting topic, I will not discuss it here.

14 Aristotle. "Parts of Animals" in *The Basic Works of Aristotle*. (New York, NY: The Modern Library, 2001) at p. 656

15 See Alasdair MacIntyre. *After Virtue: A Study in Moral Theory: Third Edition*. (Notre Dame, IN: University of Notre-Dame Press, 2007)

16 Aristotle. "Nichomachean Ethics" in *The Basic Works of Aristotle*. (New York, NY: The Modern Library, 2001) at p. 950

17 The depth of Aristotle's understanding of these ambiguities and what we would now call "moral luck" is stressed by Hall. See Edith Hall *Aristotle's Way: How Ancient Wisdom Can Change Your Life*. (London, UK: Penguin Press, 2018)

18 He does conclude that it would be "absurd" to claim they have no virtues, but goes on to say that while "clearly" moral virtues belong to them all, the temperance "of a man and of a woman, or the courage and justice of a man and of a woman, are not, as Socrates maintained, the same; the courage of a man is shown in commanding, of a woman in obeying." See Aristotle. "Politics" in *The Basic Works of Aristotle*. (New York, NY: The Modern Library, 2001) at pp. 1143, 1144

19 He is criticized for this position by Nussbaum. See Martha Nussbaum. *Political Emotions: Why Love Matters for Justice*. (Cambridge, MA: Belknap Press of Harvard University Press, 2015)

20 Aristotle. "Nichomachean Ethics" in *The Basic Works of Aristotle*. (New York, NY: The Modern Library, 2001) at p. 936

21 See Sheldon Wolin. *Politics and Vision: Continuity and Change in Western Political Thought-Expanded Edition*. (Princeton, NJ: Princeton University Press, 2016) at p. 55

22 This raises substantial problems highlighted by modern philosophers which will be important later on, not least of which is that if it is true that nature in the most holistic sense is determinative of the content of our soul, doesn't that suggest our character is not our own doing since it is the result of morally arbitrary factors? If it is not nature, then there is a substantial gap in Aristotle's oeuvre as he doesn't foreground the human power of will which would be a precondition of choice, as at least someone like Augustine later did.

23 See Aristotle. "Politics" in *The Basic Works of Aristotle*. (New York, NY: The Modern Library, 2001) at p. 1127

24 Aristotle. "Politics" in *The Basic Works of Aristotle*. (New York, NY: The Modern Library, 2001) at pp.. 1184–1185

25 Aristotle. "Politics" in *The Basic Works of Aristotle*. (New York, NY: The Modern Library, 2001) at pp. 1186

26 Aristotle. "Politics" in *The Basic Works of Aristotle*. (New York, NY: The Modern Library, 2001) at p. 1190

27 Aristotle. "Politics" in *The Basic Works of Aristotle*. (New York, NY: The Modern Library, 2001) at p. 1196

28 Aristotle. "Politics" in *The Basic Works of Aristotle*. (New York, NY: The Modern Library, 2001) at p. 1204

29 This included Robert Filmer, as we will see in the next section. He complained about the parliamentary supporters and levelers who appealed to the more democratic arguments in Aristotle's work and rather tediously rolled out the counter-statements to try and balance the ledger in his direction instead.

30 Aristotle. "Parts of Animals" in *The Basic Works of Aristotle*. (New York, NY: The Modern Library, 2001) at p. 657

31 This is obviously Marx's point at the conclusion of *Capital Volume Three*, where he discusses how the development of each person's human powers should become an end for the socialist politics of the future. See Karl Marx. *Capital Volume Three: A Critique of Political Economy,* trans. Ernest Mandel. (London, UK: Penguin Books, 1993). Martha Nussbaum raises a similar objection from within the liberal egalitarian tradition. See Nussbaum, Martha. *Creating Capabilities: The Human Development Approach*. (Cambridge, MA: Belknap Press of Harvard University Press, 2011)

32 See Alan Ryan. *On Aristotle: Saving Politics from Philosophy*. (New York, NY: Liveright, 2014) at p. 62

33 Consider Russell Kirk's claim that the first principle of conservatism is "the conservative believes that there exists an enduring moral order. That order is made for man, and man is made for it: human nature is a constant, and moral truths are permanent." See Russell Kirk. "Ten Conservative Principles." *The Russell Kirk Center*, https://kirkcenter.org/conservatism/ten-conservative-principles/

34 John Milbank. *Theology and Social Theory: Second Edition*. (Oxford, UK: Blackwell Publishing, 2006) at p. 10

35 There are many different flavors of this at almost every theoretical level. For a natural law which endorses many socially conservative positions, see John Finnis. *Natural Law and Natural Rights: Second Edition* (Oxford, UK: Oxford University Press, 2011) and especially his rather eye rolling take on homosexuality in John Finnis. "Law, Morality, and Sexual Orientation." In John Corvino. *Same Sex: Debating the Ethics, Science, and Culture of Homosexuality*. (Lanham, NY: Rowman and Littlefield 1997). For a defense of scholastic metaphysics and aesthetics in the service of conservatism, see James Matthew Wilson. *The Vision of the Soul: Truth, Goodness and Beauty in the Western Tradition*. (Washington, DC: The Catholic University of America Press, 2017)

36 See Peter Augustine Lawler. *Postmodernism Rightly Understood: The Return to Realism in American Thought*. (Lanham, MA: Rowman and Littlefield, 1992)

37 See St. Augustine. *On Free Choice of the Will*, trans. Thomas Williams. (Indianapolis, IN: Hackett Publishing, 1993)

38 St. Thomas Aquinas. *Introduction to St. Thomas Aquinas,* ed. Anton C. Pegis. (Toronto, ON: Random House, 1948) at p. 442

39 St. Thomas Aquinas. *Introduction to St. Thomas Aquinas,* ed. Anton C. Pegis. (Toronto, ON: Random House, 1948) at pp. 267–271

40 See Saint Augustine. *City of God*. (London, UK: Penguin Books, 2004). For a helpful guide see Alan Ryan. *On Augustine: The Two Cities*. (New York, NY: Liveright, 2016)

41 For an early expression of this see Augustine. *Confessions of Saint Augustine*. (London, UK: Duncan Baird Publishers, 2006)

42 See Paul Tillich. *The Socialist Decision*. (Eugene, OR: WIPF and Stock Publishers, 1977)

43 See Obery Hendricks. *Christians against Christianity: How Right-Wing Evangelicals Are Destroying Our Nation and Our Faith*. (Boston, MA: Beacon Press, 2021)

44 See Barry Goldwater. *The Conscience of a Conservative*. (Mansfield Centre, CT: Victor Publishing Company, 2011) at p. 62

45 For instance one of the political right's recent fixations is with trans activism, which is presented as representative of the decay modernity. Sometimes this is described in terms of the rise of nominalism, framed as the belief that there are no essential characteristics in nature. It is simply matter in motion that can be infinitely manipulated in line with human desire. This extends down to the flesh of our bodies, and even our gender identity. See Peter Augustine Lawler. *American Heresies and Higher Education*. (South Bend, IN: St Augustine Press, 2016)

46 This is no exaggeration, as we will see when we get to Joseph de Maistre.

47 The analogical appeal of this rhetoric persists to the present day. For instance Roger Scruton's defenses of the British monarchy and hierarchy often appeal to familiar and even parochial tropes. See Roger Scruton. *On Human Nature*. (Princeton, NJ: Princeton University Press, 2017) and Roger Scruton. *The Meaning of Conservatism: Third Edition*. (South Bend, IN: St Augustine's Press, 2002) and Roger Scruton. *The Soul of the World*. (Princeton, NJ: Princeton University Press, 2014). Nationalist conservatives will also describe their idealization of the nation and its members over others in terms that echo familiar attachments and preferences. See Yoram Hazony. *The Virtue of Nationalism*. (New York, NY: Basic Books, 2018)

48 Robert Filmer. *Patriarcha*. (Published by Daniel M. Bring, 2019) at p. 9

49 Robert Filmer. *Patriarcha*. (Published by Daniel M. Bring, 2019) at p. 12

50 Robert Filmer. *Patriarcha*. (Published by Daniel M. Bring, 2019) at p. 13

51 Robert Filmer. *Patriarcha*. (Published by Daniel M. Bring, 2019) at p. 15

52 Robert Filmer. *Patriarcha*. (Published by Daniel M. Bring, 2019) at p. 46

53 Robert Filmer. *Patriarcha*. (Published by Daniel M. Bring, 2019) at p. 46

54 Robert Filmer. *Patriarcha*. (Published by Daniel M. Bring, 2019) at p. 14

55 Robert Filmer. *Patriarcha*. (Published by Daniel M. Bring, 2019) at p. 27

56 Schmitt will later make much of the same reasoning.

57 Robert Filmer. *Patriarcha*. (Published by Daniel M. Bring, 2019) at p. 29

58 Robert Filmer. *Patriarcha*. (Published by Daniel M. Bring, 2019) at p. 42

59 The argument was made more powerfully by Carl Schmitt centuries later, and I will come back to his claims further in this book.

60 Robert Filmer. *Patriarcha*. (Published by Daniel M. Bring, 2019) at p. 4

61 Robert Filmer. *Patriarcha*. (Published by Daniel M. Bring, 2019) at p. 9

62 Some grant the title to Richard Hooker, another English author who wrote a far more extensive tract arguing for a kind of proto-nationalist religiosity and expressing skepticism about voluntarism as opposed to implicit theories of political legitimacy. He was also responding to a comparatively tumultuous time in English history which had been settled by the sensible and moderate government of Elizabeth I. The problem is that Hooker's work still takes for granted the broad legitimacy of his claims to general readers, and seeks to persuade a few outliers. Filmer's is more indicative of the tone modern conservatism would take, in the sense of being simultaneously convinced of the self-evidence of his claims and befuddled that their credibility is increasingly questioned by arrogant and dangerous democrats. See Brad Little John. "Richard Hooker: A Forgotten Father of National Conservatism" *The American Conservative*, September 23rd, 2020

63 Interested readers can peruse my books Matthew McManus. *A Critical Legal Examination of Liberalism and Liberal Rights*. (Gewerbestrasse, Switzerland: Palgrave MacMillan, 2020) and Matthew McManus. *Liberalism and Socialism: Mortal Enemies or Embittered Kin?* (Cham, Switzerland: Palgrave MacMillan, 2021)

64 For a modern take on this last point see Yoram Hazony's comments on the "dance" of liberalism and Marxism in Yoram Hazony. "The Challenge of Marxism." *Quillette*, August 16th, 2020

65 See John Locke. *First Treatise of Government*. Johnlocke.net. https://www.johnlocke.net/major-works/two-treatises-of-government-book-i

66 Sometimes not even unwritten. Russell Kirk wrote his most famous work with the express intent of rebutting the Millsian challenge. See Russell Kirk. *The Conservative Mind: From Burke to Eliot.* (Washington, DC: Gateway Editions, 2016)

67 For this reference to beliefs making the world in a "more than metaphysical" sense, see Jordan Peterson. *Maps of Meaning: The Architecture of Belief.* (New York, NY: Routledge Press, 1999) at p. 13

68 C.B. Macpherson. *The Political Theory of Possessive Individualism: Hobbes to Locke.* (Don Mills, ON: Oxford University Press, 1962)

69 I say "rational" individuals because even mature liberal theorists were often willing to deny the extension of basic rights to most of the human race on the basis that they lacked a sufficient capacity for reason. This helps explain the ideological justifications appealed to during the imperial age, where liberals proclaim themselves partisans of freedom and equality and Bentham for all put much of humanity in chains. For their own good of course. For a probing take on this complex history, see Domenico Losurdo. *Liberalism: A Counter-History*, trans. Gregory Elliot. (London, UK: Verso Press, 2014). On the often very racist dimensions of this reasoning, see Charles W. Mills. *Black Rights/White Wrongs: A Critique of Racial Liberalism.* (Oxford, UK: Oxford University Press, 2017)

70 For the moral developments in this field see J.B. Schneewind. *The Invention of Autonomy: A History of Modern Moral Philosophy.* (Cambridge, UK: Cambridge University Press, 1998)

71 For a one-sided, but readable contemporary defense of the Enlightenment as a brand see Steven Pinker. *Enlightenment Now: The Case for Reason, Science, Humanism, and Progress.* (London, UK: Penguin Books, 2019)

72 See Immanuel Kant. *On History*, trans. Lewis White Beck, Robert E. Anchor, and Emil. L Fackenheim. (United States: The Library of Liberal Arts, 1957)

73 Hobbes' criticisms of Aristotle can be understood to anticipate the logical positivists in arguing that much of his and the scholastics views of nature and morality were literally nonsensical, meaning incapable of being validated by reference to empirical objects. Consider his claim early in *Leviathan* that "...seeing all names are imposed to signify our conceptions; and all our affections are but conceptions; when we conceive the same things differently, we can hardly avoid different naming of them. For though the nature of that we conceive, be the same; yet the diversity of our reception of it, in respect of different constitutions of body, and prejudices of opinion, gives everything a tincture of our different passions. And therefore in reasoning, a man must take heed of words; which besides the signification of what we imagine of their nature, disposition, and interest of the speaker; such as are the names of Vertues, and Vices; For one man calleth Wisdome, what another calleth Feare; and one Cruelty, what another Justice; one Prodigality, what another Magnanimity; one Gravity, what another Stupidity, &c. And therefore such names can never be true grounds of any ratiocination. No more can Metaphors, and Tropes of speech: but these are less dangerous, because they profess their inconstancy; which the other do not." See Thomas Hobbes. *Leviathan.* (London, UK: Penguin Books, 2017) at p. 33

74 Immanuel Kant. *Critique of Pure Reason*, trans. Abbott Thomas Kingsmill. (Mineola, NY: Dover Classics, 2004)

75 Later critics made peace with and were even willing to appropriate Enlightenment for right purposes.

76 On occasion one sees grazing attacks launched against the edges and weak points, though these are atypically cautious even when launched by the more strident conservative thinkers. See Roger Scruton. *The Soul of the World.* (Princeton, NJ: Princeton University Press, 2014) and James Matthew Wilson. *The Vision of the Soul: Truth, Goodness and Beauty in the Western Tradition.* (Washington, DC: The Catholic University of America Press, 2017) for some recent examples.

77 Roger Scruton. *Conservatism: An Invitation to the Great Tradition.* (New York, NY: All Points Books, 2017)

78 Russell Kirk. *The Conservative Mind: From Burke to Eliot.* (Washington, DC: Gateway Editions, 2016)

79 See Edmund Neill. *Conservatism.* (Cambridge, UK: Polity Press, 2021) at p. 47

80 See David Hume. *A Treatise of Human Nature.* (Mineola, NY: Dover Press, 2003)

81 See David Hume. "Idea of a Perfect Commonwealth." *Liberty Fund,* https://oll.lib-ertyfund.org/page/oll-reader-70

82 MacIntyre himself, while supporting a kind of traditionalism and a huge influence on the intellectual right, is only uncomfortably lodged at that edge of the political spectrum given he has many good things to say about Marx and many bad things to say about capitalism. I will discuss this more later on.

83 See Alasdair MacIntyre. *Whose Justice, Which Rationality?* (Notre Dame, IN: University of Notre-Dame Press, 1989) at pp. 281–325

84 Alasdair MacIntyre. *Whose Justice, Which Rationality?* (Notre Dame, IN: University of Notre-Dame Press, 1989) at p. 324

85 See David Hume. "Of The First Principles of Government." https://davidhume.org/texts/emp/fp

86 See David Hume. "Of the Original Contract." https://cpb-us-w2.wpmucdn.com/blogs.cofc.edu/dist/8/406/files/2014/09/David-Hume-Of-the-Original-Contract-1kif9ud.pdf

87 See David Hume. *An Enquiry Concerning the Principles of Morals.* (Indianapolis, IN: Hackett Publishing, 1983) at p. 27

88 Russell Kirk. *The Conservative Mind: From Burke to Eliot.* (Washington, DC: Gateway Editions, 2016)

89 See Roger Scruton. "Why I Became a Conservative." *The New Criterion,* September 2003

90 See Jesse Norman. *Edmund Burke: The Visionary Who Invented Modern Politics.* (London, UK: William Collins, 2013) at p. 1

91 C.B. Macpherson. *Burke.* (Oxford, UK: Oxford University Press, 1980) at p. 1

92 C.B. Macpherson *Burke.* (Oxford, UK: Oxford University Press, 1980) at pp. 42–43

93 Ted Honderich. *Conservatism: Burke, Nozick, Bush, Blair?* (London, UK: Pluto Press, 2005) at p. 11

94 Corey Robin. *The Reactionary Mind Second Edition: Conservatism from Edmund Burke to Donald Trump.* (Oxford, UK: Oxford University Press, 2018) at pp. 105–132

95 C.B. Macpherson *Burke.* (Oxford, UK: Oxford University Press, 1980)

96 See Uday Singh Mehta. *Liberalism and Empire: A Study in 19th Century British Liberal Thought.* (Chicago, IL: University of Chicago Press, 1999)

97 Russell Kirk. *The Conservative Mind: From Burke to Eliot.* (Washington, DC: Gateway Editions, 2016)

98 Ian Shapiro also supports this reading. See Ian Shapiro, *The Moral Foundations of Politics* (New Haven, CT: Yale University Press, 2003) at Ch 6.

99 Edmund Neill. *Conservatism.* (Cambridge, UK: Polity Press, 2021) at p. 25

100 James Matthew Wilson. *The Vision of the Soul: Truth, Goodness and Beauty in the Western Tradition.* (Washington, DC: The Catholic University of America Press, 2017) at p. 26

101 James Matthew Wilson. *The Vision of the Soul: Truth, Goodness and Beauty in the Western Tradition.* (Washington, DC: The Catholic University of America Press, 2017) at pp. 126, 127

102 This sense comes especially through in his book Roger Scruton. *Conservatism: An Invitation to the Great Tradition.* (New York, NY: All Points Books, 2017) where he describes Hegel as giving the most "systematic" account of the conservative worldview.

103 This outlook comes through most prominently in Roger Scruton. *The Meaning of Conservatism: Third Edition.* (South Bend, IN: St Augustine's Press, 2002)

104 Levin rather briskly rushes over his account of Burke's discussion of obligation, highlighting how one is granted certain privileges and protections he has done

"nothing to earn" but to which he is nevertheless entitled. What Yuval doesn't highlight is how profoundly this undercuts the arguments for inequality. If it is the case that rich and poor children alike have done "nothing to earn" the circumstances of their birth, we might immediately ask why such gross disparities might exist between them so that so many are afforded so little while a few can attend 60K a year schools? This goes doubly so when the number of demands made of the poor is often so much greater than those demanded of the rich, yet their reward is so much more meager? As we will see Burke develops many truly beautiful streams of prose to tell dissenters in no uncertain terms: shut up and deal with it.

105 See Yuval Levin. *The Great Debate: Edmund Burke, Thomas Paine and the Birth of Right and Left.* (New York, NY; Basic Books, 2014) at p. 101

106 Ted Honderich. *Conservatism: Burke, Nozick, Bush, Blair?* (London, UK: Pluto Press, 2005)

107 Jesse Norman characterizes the *Equiry* as "not a deeply philosophical work" and one that bears the marks of its author's tender age, but acknowledges that it develops themes that last in Burke's work for some time. See *Edmund Burke: The Visionary Who Invented Modern Politics.* (London, UK: William Collins, 2013) at p. 28

108 Edmund Burke. *A Philosophical Enquiry in the Sublime and Beautiful.* (London, UK: Penguin Books, 1998) at Chapter "Sympathy"

109 Jesse Norman. *Edmund Burke: The Visionary Who Invented Modern Politics.* (London, UK: William Collins, 2013) at p. 201

110 Edmund Burke. *A Philosophical Enquiry in the Sublime and Beautiful.* (London, UK: Penguin Books, 1998) at Chapter "Beautiful Objects, Small"

111 Edmund Burke. *A Philosophical Enquiry in the Sublime and Beautiful.* (London, UK: Penguin Books, 1998) at Chapter "Grace"

112 Edmund Burke. *A Philosophical Enquiry in the Sublime and Beautiful.* (London, UK: Penguin Books, 1998) at Chapter "The Beautiful in Sounds"

113 Even Levin, who treats Burke on the whole admiringly, points out that his editor thought the passage was a bit much. Yuval Levin. *The Great Debate: Edmund Burke, Thomas Paine and the Birth of Right and Left.* (New York, NY; Basic Books, 2014) at pp. 61–64

114 Edmund Burke. *Reflections on the Revolution in France.* (Oxford, UK: Oxford University Press, 2009) at pp. 77, 78

115 Edmund Burke. *Reflections on the Revolution in France.* (Oxford, UK: Oxford University Press, 2009) at p. 33

116 Edmund Burke. *Reflections on the Revolution in France.* (Oxford, UK: Oxford University Press, 2009) at p. 47

117 Edmund Burke. *Reflections on the Revolution in France.* (Oxford, UK: Oxford University Press, 2009) at pp. 36, 37.

118 Edmund Burke. *Reflections on the Revolution in France.* (Oxford, UK: Oxford University Press, 2009) at pp. 76, 77

119 Edmund Burke. *Selected Letters of Edmund Burke.* (Chicago, IL: University of Chicago Press, 1983) at p. 268

120 See Yuval Levin. *The Great Debate: Edmund Burke, Thomas Paine and the Birth of Right and Left.* (New York, NY; Basic Books, 2014) for some accounts of these histories.

121 Edmund Burke. *Reflections on the Revolution in France.* (Oxford, UK: Oxford University Press, 2009) at p. 92

122 Edmund Burke. *Reflections on the Revolution in France.* (Oxford, UK: Oxford University Press, 2009) at pp. 92, 93

123 To be clear, this isn't to preclude the possibility that we do in fact owe moral obligations to either future generations and even to the dead. Subtle work on these points has been done by contemporary analytical philosophers like Derek Parfit and Frances Kamm. The point is that Burke's dramatic insistence on this point is not itself an argument for obligations to future generations and to the dead, let alone an

argument for the very robust duties he assigns to people. See Derek Parfit. *Reasons and Persons*. (Oxford, UK. Oxford University Press, 1986) and Frances Kamm. *Morality, Mortality: Death and Who to Save from It Vol I*. (Oxford, UK. Oxford University Press, 1992)

124 Edmund Burke. *Reflections on the Revolution in France*. (Oxford, UK: Oxford University Press, 2009) at p. 97

125 Mary Wollstonecraft. A Vindication of the Rights of Men. https://oll.libertyfund.org/title/wollstonecraft-a-vindication-of-the-rights-of-men

126 Edmund Burke. *Reflections on the Revolution in France*. (Oxford, UK: Oxford University Press, 2009) at p. 51

127 See C.B. Macpherson. *Burke*. (Oxford, UK: Oxford University Press, 1980) and Corey Robin. *The Reactionary Mind Second Edition: Conservatism from Edmund Burke to Donald Trump*. (Oxford, UK: Oxford University Press, 2018)

128 Norman points out that Burke undoubtedly had good things to say about the aristocracy, but these were usually couched in qualified terms. For instance, he would insist on the necessary role of the aristocracy so long as its members did in fact live up the chivalric and gentlemanly virtues they espoused. The fact that Burke himself witnessed repeated evidence through a long political career that they did not does not seem to have dissuaded him. Jesse Norman. *Edmund Burke: The Visionary Who Invented Modern Politics*. (London, UK: William Collins, 2013)

129 Edmund Burke. *Reflections on the Revolution in France*. (Oxford, UK: Oxford University Press, 2009) at p. 139

130 See "Speech on American Taxation" in Edmund Burke. *A Philosophical Enquiry into the Origins of the Sublime and Beautiful: And Other Pre-Revolutionary Writings*. (London, UK: Penguin Books, 1999)

131 Edmund Burke. *Reflections on the Revolution in France*. (Oxford, UK: Oxford University Press, 2009) at p. 41

132 Edmund Burke. "Thoughts and Details on Scarcity." *Select Works of Edmund Burke, Vol IV*. Online Library of Liberty, https://oll.libertyfund.org/title/canavan-select-works-of-edmund-burke-vol-4#lf0005-04_head_011

133 Edmund Burke. *Reflections on the Revolution in France*. (Oxford, UK: Oxford University Press, 2009) at p. 131

134 Edmund Burke. *Reflections on the Revolution in France*. (Oxford, UK: Oxford University Press, 2009) at p. 131

135 Edmund Burke. "Thoughts and Details on Scarcity." *Select Works of Edmund Burke, Vol IV*. Online Library of Liberty, https://oll.libertyfund.org/title/canavan-select-works-of-edmund-burke-vol-4#lf0005-04_head_011

136 Edmund Burke. "Thoughts and Details on Scarcity." *Select Works of Edmund Burke, Vol IV*. Online Library of Liberty, https://oll.libertyfund.org/title/canavan-select-works-of-edmund-burke-vol-4#lf0005-04_head_011

137 Edmund Burke. "Thoughts and Details on Scarcity." *Select Works of Edmund Burke, Vol IV*. Online Library of Liberty, https://oll.libertyfund.org/title/canavan-select-works-of-edmund-burke-vol-4#lf0005-04_head_011

138 Slavoj Zizek. *The Sublime Object of Ideology*. (London, UK: Verso Press, 2009)

139 Edmund Burke. *Reflections on the Revolution in France*. (Oxford, UK: Oxford University Press, 2009) at pp. 177, 178

140 C.B MacPherson. *Burke*. (Oxford, UK: Oxford University Press, 1980)

141 In the 20th and 21st centuries we saw commentators like Yuval Levin argue for the liberal take and Russell Kirk argue for the illiberal one, with someone like Roger Scruton arguably straddling the line between the two depending on context and inclination.

142 Edmund Fawcett. *Conservatism: The Fight for a Tradition*. (Princeton, NJ: Princeton University Press, 2020) at p. 3

143 Isaiah Berlin. "Joseph de Maistre and the Origins of Fascism." *The New York Review of Books,* September 1990

144 Edmund Fawcett. *Conservatism: The Fight for a Tradition.* (Princeton, NJ: Princeton University Press, 2020) at p. 7

145 See Edmund Fawcett. *Conservatism: The Fight for a Tradition.* (Princeton, NJ: Princeton University Press, 2020) at p. 8

146 See Corey Robin. *The Reactionary Mind Second Edition: Conservatism from Edmund Burke to Donald Trump.* (Oxford, UK: Oxford University Press, 2018) at p. 33

147 See Joseph de Maistre *Considerations on France,* trans. Richard A. Lebrun. (New York, NY: Cambridge University Press, 1994) at p. 89

148 See Corey Robin. *The Reactionary Mind Second Edition: Conservatism from Edmund Burke to Donald Trump.* (Oxford, UK: Oxford University Press, 2018) at p. 51

149 He goes on to reject the idea while holding that he nevertheless approximates the soldier, but in the way a circle curves round to the same point. See Joseph De Maistre. *St. Petersburg Dialogues,* trans. Richard A. Lebrun. (Montreal, QC: McGill-Queens University Press, 1993) at p. 207

150 See Albert O. Hirschman *The Rhetoric of Reaction: Perversity, Futility, Jeopardy.* (Cambridge, MA: The Belknap Press of Harvard University Press, 1991)

151 See Joseph De Maistre. *St. Petersburg Dialogues,* trans. Richard A. Lebrun. (Montreal, QC: McGill-Queens University Press, 1993) at pp. 218, 219

152 Though of course if one was a consistent Foucauldian, we'd have to note the irony that this self-consciousness concerning the need for spectacular displays of sovereign power came just as the world began to move toward a new model of disciplinary power directed toward the soul rather than the body. Not blood but banalization was to be its signature.

153 See Michel Foucault. *Discipline and Punish: The Birth of the Prison.* (New York, NY: Vintage Books, 1995)

154 Joseph de Maistre *Considerations on France*, trans. Richard A. Lebrun. (New York, NY: Cambridge University Press, 1974) p. 91

155 At points he begrudgingly admits that the American constitution might be thrown up as a counter-example but dismisses that by predicting the new Republic doesn't have long to live.

156 Joseph De Maistre. *Essay on the Generative Principle of Political Constitutions*, trans. (Krakow, Poland: New Direction, 2019) at p. 69

157 Joseph De Maistre. *Essay on the Generative Principle of Political Constitutions*, trans. (Krakow, Poland: New Direction, 2019) at pp 37, 38

158 Joseph De Maistre. *Essay on the Generative Principle of Political Constitutions*, trans. (Krakow, Poland: New Direction, 2019) at p. 67

159 See Isaiah Berlin. "Joseph de Maistre and the Origins of Fascism" *The New York Review of Books,* September 1990

160 See Edmund Neill. *Conservatism.* (Cambridge, UK: Polity Press, 2021)

2

PRESERVING THE SOUL
OF THE WORLD

Conservatism's Pluralistic Nostalgia

Hirschman points out that if the political right leans very heavily on mechanical rhetorical appeals to perversity, futility, and jeopardy, one could say something analogous about the political left's equally hokey love of presenting itself as "on the right side of history."[1] The implication is that there is a progressive teleological direction to history and conservatives are on the wrong side of it. Their defeat is consequently inevitable, bordering on ordained. Marx's sometimes confident declaration that one day the "knell" of capitalist private property would sound and Mill's belief in the edifying spread of civilization are just two examples of this.

Whatever the theoretical basis for this optimism, Hirschman was undoubtedly right that it has produced an unhealthy stridency among liberals and progressives. And more importantly it has led to a deep underestimation of both the power and appeal of the modern right. As we saw, even with Burke and De Maistre, conservatives got over their initial shock at the revolution against Europe's most luxurious monarchy and quickly developed highly novel intellectual weapons to push back. So successful were they that by 1815 the Republic was no more, a discount Bourbon monarchy was temporarily restored, and everywhere except for a few qualified experiments in the United Kingdom and the United States, liberalism and democracy seemed to have been routed.[2] Even Joseph de Maistre was in a more relaxed and forgiving mood. Reflecting on the fall of Napoleon, who had led the armies of France from victory to victory for 20 years, he asked who had ever

> concentrated in himself more of [splendid appearances] than the extraordinary personage whose fall still resounds throughout Europe? Has there

DOI: 10.4324/9781003307952-4

ever been a sovereignty outwardly so well fortified, a greater consolidation of means, a man more powerful, more active, more formidable? For a long time, we saw him trample under foot twenty nations silent and frozen with dread; and his power at length had struck certain roots which might have led even hope to despair. Yet he is fallen, and so low, that Pity while contemplating him, draws back for fear of being touched by him.[3]

Many pensive conservatives might have thought the same about the egalitarian ethos as a whole: utterly discredited by the Terror, imperialism, and defeat on battlefields from Russia to Waterloo.

And yet within a decade Europe's oldest and most Catholic Spanish empire crumbled in the face of liberatory movements—mostly establishing unstable republics—throughout North America and the United Kingdom began its lurching march toward universal male suffrage. The restored Bourbon monarch farcically playacted its former glories until 1830, leading the monarchist Chateaubriand to describe the sacre of its final king Charles X as "not a sacre, but a representation of one."[4] By 1848 even the most zealous of reactionaries could recognize that the pressures for liberalization were becoming all but overwhelming, while a handful of more audacious conservatives began to experiment with reforming themselves into an ideology with legitimately mass appeal. Perhaps most dangerous of all, and less commented on by right-liberal hagiographers,[5] it became apparent to the political right that there were far more frightening things than liberalism which could emerge from the abyss of egalitarian modernity. While it took a little while to get the major prongs in place, by the mid-century Marx and Engels could already gleefully troll that the specter of communism was haunting Europe. And its time was coming.

What we see through much of the 19th century is a cyclical tug-of-war, with liberals and other progressives winning considerable victories before facing reaction and even regression. But where liberalism radicalized, toured, and was violently imposed while remaining recognizably itself, the political right's response was far more varied. To the extent that the political right can be understood as an effort to maintain traditional hierarchies and power structures against egalitarian pressures, the intellectual response to liberalism depended very much on what kind of traditionalist hierarchies one was defending and why. It is difficult to imagine Thomas Carlyle appearing in mid-19th-century Germany, since so much of his political thinking turns on responding to the perceived or real vulgarities of British economic liberalism. Where else but in a Russian Empire, nominally the iron cornerstone on which the reactionary Metternichian system was built, but in reality ideologically fracturing, could Dostoevsky have appeared?

So it was during the 19th century that intellectual conservatism truly assumed the eclecticism for which it is now known, responding to the egalitarian thrust of modernization with everything from compromised acceptance to downright hostility. This disunity would prove both a weakness and a strength. A weakness because, for all the statesmen and intellectuals like Metternich and De Maistre who tried to unify European and Anglo elites against their common foe, a combination of geopolitical and ideological differences, along with pure ego, stupidity, and greed, kept them divided (a shame since these vices were so uncommon among the genteel class before it was driven to them by the insurrectionary masses). However, the political right also found strength in diversity because variety contributed to the endless adaptability of the tradition in response to its foes. Far from being straightjacketed by myopia reactionaries came into contact with one another, learned from one another, and discovered that they could be strong.

Hegel—Between Radicalism, Liberalism, and Conservatism

The criticism of the German philosophy of state and right, which attained its most consistent, richest, and last formulation through Hegel, is both a critical analysis of the modern state and of the reality connected with it, and the resolute negation of the whole manner of the German consciousness in politics and right as practiced hereto, the most distinguished, most universal expression of which, raised to the level of science, is the speculative philosophy of right itself. If the speculative philosophy of right, that abstract extravagant thinking on the modern state, the reality of which remains a thing of the beyond, if only beyond the Rhine, was possible only in Germany, inversely the German thought-image of the modern state which makes abstraction of real man was possible only because and insofar as the modern state itself makes abstraction of real man, or satisfies the whole of man only in imagination. In politics, the Germans thought what other nations did. Germany was their theoretical conscience. The abstraction and presumption of its thought was always in step with the one-sidedness and lowliness of its reality. If, therefore, the status quo of German statehood expresses the completion of the Ancien regime, the completion of the thorn in the flesh of the modern state, the status quo of German state science expresses the incompletion of the modern state, the defectiveness of its flesh itself. Already as the resolute opponent of the previous form of German political consciousness the criticism of speculative philosophy of right strays, not into itself, but into problems which there is only one means of solving – practice.

(Karl Marx, *Critique of Hegel's Philosophy of Right*)

There are many people, plenty of whom I know personally, who would object loudly to Hegel appearing in a book on the political right. After all, for plenty of contemporary commentators like Fredric Jameson[6] and Slavoj Zizek,[7] Hegel pioneered and perhaps even perfected the dialectical method which has scandalized reactionaries from the beginning. Those who admit that there might have been a conservative turn later in Hegel's work highlight his early zeal for the French Revolution and stress how it never fully left him; didn't he after all toast the anniversary of Bastille Day until his death?[8] Even Marx, who rarely had anything good to say about anyone, described himself as a pupil or disciple of "that mighty thinker."[9] Ergo implicating Hegelianism in one of the most self-consciously radical (and violent) political projects in modern history.

For many conservatives and right-wing liberals—particularly in the Anglosphere—this guilt by association with Marxism is so damning that they've condemned Hegel as the root of all evil from the 19th century forward. Beyond the already sufficient Marx connection, Hegel is simply too obscure, too German, too remote from good ol' fashioned Anglo common sense, and worst of all too much of an emblematic university professor. Paul Gottfried may be a bad man, but he was undoubtedly right to point out that—even with unimpeachable credentials as both a partisan for Western civilization and an "I'm not a racist but..." style commentator—Hegel was a hard sell to many through the mid- to late-century American right.[10] On the right-liberal end of things, Popper's simultaneously mocking and damning characterization of Hegel as a magician for whom it was "child's play" to "draw real physical rabbits out of purely metaphysical silk hats" while agitating a dangerously statist tribalism has been very influential on the liberal and libertarian right.[11] This was echoed by Ludwig von Mises who argues that for Hegel, the "Sates is Divine Will" and argues that liberalism rejects "the Hegelian Marx and his school who have replaced the cult of 'State' with the cult of Society."[12] Even those with one eye away from the liberal tradition, notably Strauss, preferred to take their cues from a less historicist and more natural law-oriented approach.[13] Many of these commentators were second to no Anglo-liberals in racing to slam the Prussian polymath. This could even trickle down to pop commentators like Ben Shapiro, as when he claimed that "Hitler claimed ideological forebears in Kant, Hegel, and Nietzsche."[14] Absurd of course, but undoubtedly revealing.

And yet the positive, and not merely negative (how Hegelian!), influence of Hegel on the history of the political right can hardly be doubted. This is true even in the modern Anglo-world, which for a long time seemed determined to resist Hegel for as long as dialectically possible. For Roger Scruton, Hegel captures the

> starting point of conservative philosophy...in his *Phenomenology of Spirit* (1806), which shows how relations of conflict and domination are overcome by the recognition of mutual duties, and how, in the course of this, individuals achieve not only freedom of action, but also social membership.[15]

Here Scruton follows in the footsteps of a long and provocative tradition of conservative British idealism deeply inspired be Hegel, ranging from Bradley through Michael Oakeshott. Hegel was also an important influence on neo-conservatives in the United States like Francis Fukuyama. And of course his influence on European and world conservatism, always less wary of Hegel's deific language toward the state and community than many Anglos, has been profound. In between the enigmatic pages celebrating the ethical reconciliation of the individual to the state as an expression of her freedom and the lengthy descriptions of European civilization as the apex of world spirit, plenty of conservatives found ammunition for their favored positions. As Fawcett put it, "between the left-socialist Hegel and the right-liberal Hegel of person-blind unity to state sanctioned law, loomed a third Hegel, that of appeal to ethical conservatives as a source for their belief in the social roots of moral norms."[16]

To be clear, my intention in this section isn't to imply that this conservative Hegel is more real than his left-socialist or right-liberal doppelgangers, or even less that there was a transition (or maturation if you approve) in his thought from revolutionary radicalism to conservatism. There are plenty of ways to say usefully radical and left things with Hegelian philosophy, and I have done so plenty of times myself.[17] What I intend to do is to self-consciously give an interpretation which foregrounds the conservative and right-leaning features of Hegel's work to explain his attraction to the political right and why they claim him as one of their own. Whether such an interpretation is in fact truthful to what Hegel himself thought and indeed whether it is even possible to give an entirely accurate interpretation of an often-mystical-sounding thinker who was admirably polymorphic and elevated argumentative charity to a philosophical method are questions I put aside here.

A Conservative Approach to Hegel

At the normative core of Hegel's project is a commitment to freedom, though understood in a very distinct way. This point is made consistently from the sections on self-consciousness in the *Phenomenology of Spirit onward*. For all the labyrinthine turns Hegel's thought will go through, he will remain eminently committed to freedom, indeed even becoming a somewhat chauvinistic partisan for its cause. As he put it in his *Lectures on the Philosophy of History*:

> The History of the World travels from East to West, for Europe is absolutely the end of History, Asia the beginning. The History of the World has an East kat xochn; (the term East in itself is entirely relative), for although the Earth forms a sphere, History performs no circle round it, but has on the contrary a determinate East, viz., Asia. Here rises the outward physical Sun, and in the West it sinks down: here consentaneously rises the Sun of self-consciousness, which diffuses a nobler brilliance. The History of the World is the discipline of the uncontrolled natural will, bringing it into obedience to a Universal principle and conferring subjective freedom. The East knew and to the present day knows only that *One* is Free; the Greek and Roman world, that *some* are free; the German World knows that *All* are free. The first political form therefore which we observe in History, is *Despotism*, the second democracy and aristocracy, and the third monarchy.[18]

But in case the fact that Hegel's philosophy of freedom can't be reduced down to a bumper sticker slogan like "Live Free or Die" didn't provide a clue, things are never simple in the Hegelian universe. For Hegel, freedom is not mere license to do whatever one wishes, since this would entail a self-conscious individual becoming a slave to their appetites. In this Hegel agrees not only with many of the Greek authors who were a major influence on his early work, but also to an extent with Kant, who held that there was an intrinsic connection between the autonomy of the will and a willingness to do one's duty through submitting to the moral laws we gave ourselves. But where for Kant this is an eminently individualistic enterprise, for Hegel the singular autonomous lawgiver idealized in the *Groundwork to the Metaphysics of Morals* is engaged in a kind of empty formalism.[19] Lacking any concrete content the kinds of imperatives willed by the moral lawgivers can only be impotent at best, or end in violence at worst. The latter isn't overstating things; at various points in the *Philosophy of Right* Hegel describes the excesses of the Jacobin terror as stemming from an egalitarian universalism which approximates Kantian philosophy; he describes the

> terrible epoch of the French Revolution, by which all distinctions in talent and authority were to have been superseded. In this time of upheaval and commotion any specific thing was intolerable. Fanaticism wills an abstraction and not an articulate association. It finds all distinctions antagonistic to its indefiniteness, and supersedes them. Hence in the French Revolution the people abolished the institutions which they themselves had set up, since every institution is inimical to the abstract self-consciousness of equality.[20]

However, one cannot read into this the kind of counter-revolutionary impetus found without qualification in De Maistre or Burke. This is in part because Hegel's philosophy of history requires each moment of transition to follow a deeper necessity. Consequently simple condemnation of the French Revolution as "Satanic" misses the point. Hegel also admits that the authoritarian etatism of the Ancien regime was doomed to fail because, while the people themselves had indeed created the institutions which governed them, they could no longer recognize themselves and their freedom within them. They'd been alienated from the world they created through the domination of a political system in which the singular, abstract will of a single individual—the King—was intended to express the freedom of the people as a whole. This led to a tension wherein a radically particular will came to stand in for the self-determination of the radically universalistic will of the people as a whole, leading to the eruption of forces which neither revolutionaries nor conservatives could understand or control. Hegel came to argue that the monarchy can avoid the dangers of both an alienated particularism and a radically leveling universalism[21] through expressing the self-determination of the people in an orderly manner. In other words the mass of people will be asked to identify their freedom with the authorities which govern them.

Another example of these shifts can be seen in Hegel's treatment of nationalism, which again is formulated in stark contrast to Kant's egalitarian universalism. Late in his life Kant famously ruminated about a transition away from the Westphalian model of near-absolute national sovereign toward a cosmopolitan order of republican states ordered by a league of nations.[22] Hegel is immediately skeptical of this claim, in a way that would be intimately familiar to generations of right-wing nationalists.[23] He emphasizes that the "nation as state is the spirit substantively realized and directly real. Hence, it is the absolute power on earth."[24] Hegel then goes on to qualify his argument by acknowledging that this existence is only formal insofar as a state is not recognized by other states, and even goes on to compare this to the "individual person" who is "not real unless related to others."[25] Hegel then asserts that conflict between nations is inevitable, and can never be conciliated by the kind of world system Kant wishes. Indeed he goes on to say that "when the particular wills of states can come to no agreement, the controversy can be settled only by war."[26] Paradoxically, this kind of conservative international realism seems to express the same kinds of agonistic relations at the global level that Hegel once detected interpersonally and even within the domestic sphere. The pacific harmony he now reads into the relations of the nation-state cannot be emulated internationally, where the state of nature and consequently war persist. Hegel even goes on to make a distinctly Eurocentric division between civilized states, which may go to war with one another but whose sovereignty remains intact, and "barbarians," the mere "herdsmen, and tillers of the soil," who are "inferior" and consequently whose independence is "merely formal."[27] This ethno-chauvinist elitism links uncomfortably with Hegel's prescient and very materialist sounding observation that the dynamic but contradictory forces of the capitalist market may compel states to seek resolution for population and economic woes through imperialism and colonization.[28]

Nevertheless despite the bloody quality of these enterprises, Hegel does reconcile the agonistic tensions at a higher level since even war between states has its role in the movement of history. But unlike earlier books like the *Phenomenology*, where irreconcilable conflicts pre-empted the necessary transition to a new form of relations and a consequent new set of appearances, Hegel's response to national conflict in *The Philosophy of Right* is to appeal to the cunning of world history to describe and partially defend the bloody concert of Europe and its imperialism.[29] In the end the slaughter bench Hegel witnessed can be justified since the competition between nation-states and their drive for power leads those who are the current "bearers" of world spirit to become dominant for the epoch. Their exercise of global hegemony thereby serves a higher purpose than what most participants can glean, though the Hegelian philosopher can see into their inner necessity.[30]

Understood this way it is very hard to not see Hegel as offering an ideological apologia for the worst impulses of European power at the beginning of the 19th century. By sublimating the interventions of power at the international level and arguing they only immediately flow from the self-interestedness of states (and the elites that govern them) while in fact serving a higher purpose in spite of themselves. One might defend him by pointing out his consistent insistence that the job of the philosopher is only to understand her own time in thought, and that this was the world-historical horizon in which Hegel was embedded at the beginning of the 19th century. But in this Hegel seems to have betrayed his earlier position, which is that the presence of conflict in any situation always indicates the birth pangs of the new. Instead the language of the *Philosophy of Right* largely precludes the possibility of novel historical developments which would break the back of the nationalist and imperialist world order he is describing.

These arguments have been deeply comforting for many conservatives, who could immediately appeal to him to defend the historical violence of their own nation-states as a necessary stage of transition while vindicating their ongoing hegemony as serving a world historical function. As we will see cruder iterations of these dogmas weren't foreign to various neoconservative intellectuals. But is this in fact the proper way to understand Hegel?

Is Hegel a Conservative Thinker?

Hegel's thought has a rather onion-like quality. Rather than seeing society as a pyramid and moving hierarchically from bottom to top, one finds human subjects incorporated into ever broader ethical spheres and historical periods—while spirit simultaneously becomes more self-conscious about how each sphere is the product of its own self-determination as history progresses.[31] Right-Hegelians past and present tend to conceive of ethical idealism in an affirmative sense. Human beings come to recognize themselves in the various ethical spheres as they exist in the present, seeing them as the product of a history whose necessity they now recognize and consequently redeem of its crimes. They are consequently reconciled to past and present, legitimating the various forms of power that have come to exist because individuals conceive of that power as ultimately flowing from them and so in no way an alienating force of domination. In this way power ceases to appear as power and becomes authority. This includes the authority of state power to pursue self-interested goals wherever it needs to around the globe, prioritizing its own national ambitions over the crudely formal universalism embodied in international institutions. Read in this way, as Roger Scruton notes, Hegel seems to have accomplished the magnificent task of effectively systematizing the proudly unsystematic social ruminations of everyone from Burke to the Brexiters.[32] This consequently entitles him to the honor of the most profound and sophisticated conservative thinker.

But there is another side to this story, which is that Hegel can be given a liberal and even radical interpretation.[33] And indeed this is exactly what Marx will achieve almost immediately in his critique of right-Hegelianism. In his youthful *Critique of Hegel's Philosophy of Right* Marx is already critical of the kind of banal positivism which emerges from right-Hegelianism, a thoughtless affirmation of what is that only achieves its banal grandeur by abstracting away from the real conditions of domination which still pervade so much of the world.[34] This would later be sharpened in his mature materialist critique, as Marx would point out that Hegelianism is only able to achieve these moments of reconciled affirmation in thought rather than practice. This is in part a consequence of a deep deficiency in Hegel's method, which conceives of contradictions according to its idealist "logic" of (semantic) self-reflection and so sets itself the task of demonstrating how they can be overcome within the thought of the philosopher and through aesthetics and religion for the everyday person.[35] Hegel fails to see that the contradictions within history and society are not idealist abstractions that can be thought past. They are real contradictions emerging from the material conditions of the social form, and consequently can and will only be overcome through revolutionary praxis. Consequently right-Hegelianism is an eminently ideological exercise because it seeks to defend as ethical and rational an alienated and reified lifeworld still riven with tensions brought about by technological transformation and changes in relations of power.[36]

The parameters of this Marxist critique are well known and I won't rehearse them here. But it is worth noting that many increasingly think that Marx was excessively harsh in reading into Hegel what was actually only present in his conservative interpreters.[37] While it would be hard to make the late Hegel into a kind of radical, there is a more corrosive sense in which even the aged and revered Prussian lecturer takes away what he seems to be happily giving. This can be seen when we recognize that the sublime qualities attached to power which make it authority in the ethical Hegelian state are only those which the people themselves associate with their leaders. They are cognitively ascribed sublime qualities, not sublime qualities intrinsic to the state and its institutions themselves. Power and those who wield it become sublime as a result of their fulfilling their ethical duty, but this aura is attached to them not due to any specific features the individuals in positions of power have. In Lacanian terms, the King is no longer to be exalted by the people because his majesty is the King.[38] He is only the King because he is recognized as such and exalted by the will of the people, who may well change their mind. The King's majesty flows from the people upward, not the other way around. Through this the people would come to see the concrete power (and privileges) of those in positions of domination as justified by an inner necessity which simultaneously exalts their position while so deindividualizing it that they cannot be the subject of ressentiment or anger. Indeed in the more liberal and radical moments of the *Philosophy of Right* Hegel almost risks (or perhaps that was the subversive intention) undermining whatever residual grandeur the monarchy possesses by describing the King as an almost impotent vessel merely embodying and then signing off on the will of the nation. Indeed there is an almost Kafkaesque quality to the Hegelian monarch, who never gets to become Carlyle's "great man" or even the young Hegel's

Napoleonic "world spirit" conquering the world from horseback. Instead he's an effective pencil pusher. As Hegel puts it:

> It is often maintained that the position of monarch gives to the affair of state a haphazard character. It is said that the monarch may be ill-educated, and unworthy to stand at the helm of state, and that it is absurd for such a condition of things to exist under the name of reason. It must be replied that the assumption on which these objections proceed is of no value, since there is here no reference to particularity of character. In a completed organization we have to do with nothing but the extreme of formal decision, and that for this office is needed only a man who says "Yes" and so puts the dot upon the "I." The pinnacle of state must be such that the private character of the occupant shall be of no significance.[39]

In passages like these Hegel seems to be almost humorously subversive by presenting the powers that be as effectively impotent relics, inviting and almost demanding their criticism and lampooning. Whether this is true—perhaps Hegel was trying to sneak in corrosive views through the back door given the authoritarian conditions of the post-Napoleonic Prussian state—we cannot know for sure. But we can say for certain that in these moments Hegel demonstrates an aptitude for disassembling (dare I say deconstructing?) and ideologically unmasking the reified forms power takes when it presents itself as authority. Something very similar occurs in the aforementioned descriptions of colonialism and imperialism. While in passages like those discussed earlier he seems to be defending it uncritically, in the same paragraphs Hegel dryly observes how European states failed to grant their colonies the same rights as the mother countries, much as masters mistreated their slaves. The result was wars for independence, which cost many lives before it turned out that independence and freedom were to the "greatest advantage to the motherland, just as the liberation of the slaves was to the greatest advantage of the slaves."[40] Here we see the authority claimed over peoples unmasked as the mere stupidity of power wasting itself in maintaining privileges and status which were not in the material interests of anyone anyways. It is hard to think of a more amusing, if dark, condemnation of the right-wing elevation of power over equality and freedom.

So it is very possible, given the open-endedness of Hegel's system, that the more conservative moments in his late writings are intended to present the appearances reactionary ideology assumes to the critical philosophical consciousness before he immediately undermines it. Rather like the old joke describing the wealthy man's auspicious appearance in resplendent detail before describing how he slipped on a banana peel and fell on his ass with a thud. Consequently authors like Scruton who focus only on the first part are missing the point entirely, offering one-sided and ultimately undialectical appraisals of Hegel that do an injustice to the emancipatory thrust of his thought.

We may never know for certain, and perhaps that's besides the point. Hegel's thinking was nothing if not an engine for further thought by countless interpreters—a testament above all else to his eternal greatness as a political thinker. What is undeniable is that Hegel does and has offered reactionaries what appear to be lethal weapons. Whether they're in fact nothing but toy swords is an open matter.

Thomas Carlyle and Romantic Reaction I

> This mad state of matters will of course before long allay itself, as it has elsewhere begun to do; the ordinary necessities of men's daily existence cannot comport with it, and these, whatever else is cast aside, will have their way. Some remounting-very temporary remounting-of the old machine, under new colors and altered forms, will probably ensue in most countries: the old historonic Kings will be admitted back under conditions, under 'Constitutions' with national Parliaments, or the like fashionable adjuncts; and everywhere the old daily life will try to begin again. But there is now no hope that such arrangements can be permanent that they can be other than poor temporary makeshifts, which, if they try to fancy and make themselves permanent, will be displaced by new explosions recurring more speedily than last time....For universal democracy, whatever we may think of it, has declared itself as an inevitable fact of the days in which we live; and he who has any chance to instruct, or lead, in his days, must begin by admitting that: new street barricades, new anarchies, still more scandalous if less sanguinary, must return and again return, till governing persons everywhere know and admit that. Democracy, it may be said everywhere, is here.[41]
>
> (Thomas Carlyle, "The Present Time")

With Thomas Carlyle a very recognizable and modern[42] conservative intellectual comes onto the scene. That is, the conservative as a loser: bitter but not entirely resigned, hardened by defeat but still hoping for final vindication, and no longer prophesizing apocalypse because it is already here. Unlike the other authors analyzed in this chapter, Carlyle was not a great original thinker or artist. At his worst, he's all but insufferable. Nietzsche's more overwrought moments at least see him marching to the relentless pounding of his own drum. Carlyle lacks even that, and his weakest writings find him vacillating between a yearning for greatness and supplication all at once.[43]

However, Carlyle was a powerful public intellectual with a talent for coupling theoretical observation with grim humor and a kind of solemn gravity. In this respect he prepared an important archetype which would be followed by everyone from Russell Kirk to Roger Scruton. More importantly Carlyle was also one of the first major conservatives to assume the victory of democratic egalitarianism was all but inevitable, but not seek to reconcile with it like the right-Hegelians or withdraw into mere defeated contemplation. Indeed Carlyle's most significant theoretical contribution is his emphasis on heroic personalities and greatness, which are seen as playing the defining role in world history. This occasionally gives his work a Homeric quality, but Carlyle's major heroes are very unlike indifferent and aloof Achilles. Living through a popular era, Carlyle's major heroic figures are men like Oliver Cromwell, who can simultaneously surf the tides of insurrection and bring them to heel.[44]

Carlyle's work is one of the major instances of conservatism developing symbiotic opposites to the prevailing progressive mores which stamp their context. In this case his romantic heroism comes across as the distorted mirror of the utilitarian and liberal individualism which was becoming ascendant in the United Kingdom, something J.S. Mill himself seems to have responded to with his own brilliant reinterpretation of Carlyle and Coleridge's romanticism into an expressive individualist version of liberal socialism. Carlyle was willing to accept and even defend considerable political liberty and creativity so long as it was licensed by the presence of genius. Unsurprisingly given Carlyle's own modest background[45] he was even willing to detect and applaud the presence of genius in many figures of modest backgrounds. His seminal essay on Hero-Worship holds that the history of humankind has been the biography, or at least the actions, of great men. To an extent Carlyle locates the strength and character of "great" men like Mohammed, Martin Luther, Robbie Burns, and (more problematically) Napoleon in the modesty and trial of their upbringing. In this sense Carlyle's individualism can even have a whiff of the democratic about it. At least in the sense that nature or God ensures men of genius to emerge across the social body, and it is a good and just society which allows them to rise to even the highest auspices of power. Some of the most intelligent internal criticisms Carlyle makes of the conservative movement are directed against the pedantic and soft aristocracy and monarchies of 1848. These groups were unable or unwilling to do what was needed and consequently brought about their own tragic fall before the "dumb masses" who would never have been capable of such a feat unless faced with such mediocre opponents.

> What can be more miserable than this universal hunting out of the high dignitaries, solemn functionaries, and potent, grave and reverend signiors of the world; this stormful rising-up of the inarticulate dumb masses everywhere, against those who pretended to be speaking for them and guiding them? These guides, then, were mere blind men only pretending to see? These rulers were not ruling at all; they had merely got on the attributes and clothes or rulers and were superstitiously drawing the wages, while the work remained undone? The Kings were Sham-Kings, play-acting as at Drury Lane; and what were the people withal that took them for real? It is probably the hugest disclosure of falsity in human things that was ever at one time made...Such a spectacle, can we call it joyful? There is a joy in it, to the wise man too; yes, but a joy full of awe, and as it were sadder than any sorrow, -like the vision of immortality, unattainable except through death and the grave![46]

But it is important to make a major qualification here. Carlyle's concessions to individualism, and his own creative theorizing on it, are less original than one might expect. He consistently stresses that the creative artist or political maverick doesn't receive their genius from their own powers or even from the environment they're surrounded by. Instead Carlyle continuously stresses that genius lies in the ability to apprehend, immediately in the case of the less educated and through layers of conceptual insight in the case of the polymath, the providential and transcendental order and imperatives of God within nature. Technical questions such as what this transcendent order is and how we are to know it are not questions Carlyle usually takes much interest in. Indeed, one suspects he'd argue that the very effort to systematize an answer to technical philosophical questions was reflective of the spirit of Benthamite calculators and sophisticates Carlyle despises above all else. Yet his answers to these very basic philosophical questions are not only unconvincing, but routinely arrogant and even farcically amusing. Indeed on these points where his reach transparently exceeds his grasp, Carlyle comes very close to pioneering an ironically pedestrian form of conservative commentary familiar to millions: the blowhard rant.

A rib-splitting example of this is in Carlyle's rambling pamphlet on prison reform, where he takes profound issue with the efforts to make the lives of prisoners more humane. Intriguingly, his greatest outrage is reserved for those who (correctly) point out that much of the Christian religion weighs in the direction of showing compassion and forgiveness toward sinners. At times Carlyle's outrage seems choked by a deep fear that these critics are correct, as when he claims that if indeed the Christian religion prescribes a "healthy love of scoundrels," otherwise "what am I, in heaven's name, to make of it? Me for one, it will not serve as a religion on these strange terms."[47] Here a more insightful and daring critic might raise the question Nietzsche was galling enough to ask: whether it may actually be that these "sugary" egalitarian humanists had roots in a Christian faith badly perverted to uphold rank and punishment. But Carlyle would never go that far in challenging Christendom. Instead he conceives Christianity along the lines of petit bourgeois fire and brimstone which justifies the hatred of sinners as "divine hatred." We also get one of his efforts to defend this as a kind of transcendent religious law mysteriously imprinted into the heart by God, even if many intelligent men and a growing plurality (and eventual majority) reject it.

> What this Law of the Universe, or Law made by God, is? Men at one time read it in their Bible. In many Bibles, Books, and authentic symbols and monitions of Nature and the World (of Fact, that is, and of Human Speech, or Wise Interpretation of Fact), there are still clear indications towards it. Most important it is, for this and or some other reasons, that men do, in some saw, get to see it a little. And if no man could now see it by any Bible, there is written in the heart of every man an authentic copy of it direct from Heaven itself; there, if he has learnt to decipher Heaven's writing, and can read the sacred oracles (a sad case for him if he altogether cannot), ever

born man may still find some copy of it. 'Revenge' my friends! Revenge
and the natural hatred of scoundrels, and the ineradicable tendency to
revancher oneself upon them, and pay them what they have merited: this is
forever more intrinsically a correct, and even a divine feeling in the mind
of every man.[48]

Calling this a terrible argument seems unfair to the notion of argument. It's
not even a consistent set of bare assertions. In the time it takes to send a text
message Carlyle appeals to the "Law of the Universe," the "Law Made by God,"
"many bible Books, and authentic symbols and monitions of Nature and the
world," "sacred oracles," and "heaven's writing." Anything other than simply
acknowledging the hard truth that all Carlyle is really standing on is that he
really, really feels this is the right thing to do but can't just assert that plainly.
Ironically, Carlyle has to give his feelings but with a sublimated and demotic
twist by insisting they have both been "written in the heart of every man" and
flow from "divine feelings." This is conservative irrationalism at its most mili-
tantly irrational, flailing about to glamorize the more vicious kinds of prejudice
and proudly hateful affects in the face of religious and utilitarian objections of a
higher order of sophistication.[49]

But more importantly they reflect how thin Carlyle's heroic individualism
really is, even compared to right-wing counterparts. It is a heroic individualism
that nevertheless requires the hero's subordination to a higher order, which he
is unable to defend or define but whose existence Carlyle confidently proclaims
and which conveniently accords with all the sentiments and pre-theoretical convictions "written" into his heart. Carlyle's individualism therefore lacks either
the genuinely self-creating and legislating majesty of Nietzsche's ubermensch
or Dostoevsky's more consistent form of Christian existentialism which at least
stresses the need to put aside egoism to achieve the freedom made possible by
universal love and forgiveness. In some respects it exists at a halfway point.
Carlyle is on somewhat safer waters when defending his conception of a more
mobile—but still highly stratified—social hierarchy.

Thomas Carlyle and Romantic Reaction II

One of the best-known features of Carlyle's work is its critical response to capitalism and ontological and ethical materialism (what we would probably now
call consumerism). This applies both at the individual and cultural level, as his
work is replete with criticism of "calculators," unbridled laissez faire, the bald
assertions that "society" merely "exists for the protection of property," and so
on.[50] There is undeniably a purely elitist dimension to this, as Carlyle often
bemoans how the spread of plebian materialism has undermined the heroic and
transcendent pursuits of humankind. Everything becomes reduced and banalized into pursuit of the almighty pound sterling. At various points Carlyle even
infers a proto-Hayekian conception of the market as having a deep elective

affinity to the leveling effected by democracy, in the sense that higher order pursuits are abandoned for the venal. But he was admirably even handed in his approach.[51] Carlyle's elitism is complemented by the conviction that the ugliness of 19th-century laissez faire is compounded by the failure of the new captains of industry[52] to take seriously the noblesse oblige duties toward the lower classes so integral to the old aristocracy's legitimacy.[53] And as mentioned Carlyle does defend a kind of reconfiguration of the democratic ethos in terms of merito-cratic social mobility. Indeed one of his soft criticisms of market society is pre-cisely that it constrains the various paths available to the "gifted soul" and "born genius." Options are reduced to the "unlearned career of the Industrialisms" or the "learned career of the three professions, Medicine, Law (under which we may include politics), and the Church."[54]

These anti-capitalist points made it possible for figures like J.S. Mill, Friedrich Engels, and Karl Marx to find redeeming attributes to Carlyle's work. Carlyle himself was occasionally willing to flirt with patriarchal forms of modest redis-tribution, though even his most admiring left analysts never denied his reac-tionary core.[55] And it is undoubtedly reactionary. At a superficial level Carlyle's concern for the working classes, even at the level of their material well-being, was always relentlessly cultural and idealist in its orientation. Their character, and especially the extent to which that bleeds into the character of the nation, is what matters first and foremost and not their material well-being or flourishing. Let alone their entitlements to mass participation. In moments Carlyle can express these views as a kind of parochial concern for the lower order's education, care, and community.

But in others it takes on a far more stridently disciplinary form in the full Foucauldian sense. Carlyle is scathingly critical of the unwillingness of the state to intervene in the face of unemployment brought about by market forces. But that is not chiefly out of a pronounced empathy, but because the idleness and im-moralism of the poverty strikes him as disorderly and unmanly. This means the unemployed can be rightfully coopted into what can only be described as chain gangs and borderline (perhaps not even borderline) slavery, for their own good and the good of the more industrious people they would prey upon. This last is something Carlyle doesn't shy away from describing in the most condescend-ing terms. When conceiving a hypothetical speech by a British prime minister addressed to the "floods of Irish and other Beggars, the able-bodied Lackalls, nomadic or stationary, and the general assembly, outdoor and indoor, of the Paper relations of these Realms" brought into being by the Irish potato famine Carlyle condemns the industrialist for letting them fall into nomadism and beer. But the prime minister then mocks the indolent for cherishing the freedom to move and sell their labor when that results in nothing but idleness, beggary, and thieving. The solution is forced labor. Coerced, if need be, at gun point:

> To each of you I will then say: Here is work for you; strike into it with manlike, soldier-like obedience and heartiness, according to the methods

here prescribed-wages follow for you without difficulty; all manner of just remuneration, and at length emancipation itself follow. Refuse to strike into it; shirk the heavy labor, disobey the rules-I will admonish and endeavor to incite you, if in vain, I will flog you; if still in vain, I will at last shoot you-and make God's earth, and the forlorn-hope in God's Battle, free of you.[56]

One might say Carlyle's philosophy boils down to: that unburdened compassion which you show unto the least in Britain you also show unto the Devil. At least "let them eat cake" had some redeeming literary virtues through understanding that brevity is the soul of even haughty wit. What is remarkable about the whole speech is not just how pitiless its tone of condemnation is—and pitiless is the only way to describe a response to the Great Potato famine in which a million and more people died—but how unwilling it is to acknowledge the historical and material determinants of their circumstance and human powerlessness in the face of catastrophe.[57] In this context Carlyle's petit bourgeois wrath directed against the powerless precisely for their powerlessness seems not only pathetic but rather small. The bellicosity of its rhetoric doesn't shield but reveals a poverty of analysis and a kind of abstraction from human life into a world where the tactile becomes less interesting than a transcendent universe of simple primary colors and easy authoritarian solutions to structural problems.

But more importantly we can see how the kind of meritocratic dynamism underpinning Carlyle's outlook is in no ways legitimately democratic or egalitarian. The rarefied few need to be given opportunities for advancement, which the old aristocracy precluded. And their latitude for action should be broader than what is permitted by laissez faire economics. But robust political agency and even liberal individual freedoms by no means need to be granted to everyone. In his pamphlet *Past and Present*, Carlyle echoes Aristotle in describing man as not just a social animal, but social precisely because of a willingness of most of us to submit. This admiration for the man of submission mixed with a degree of contempt. At the same time Carlyle's despair over mass demands for participation and power is complicated by an admiration for those heroic figures who refuse to submit to strictures and are entitled to do so because of their alignment with a higher kind of order. In this respect Carlyle's conservatism defends subordination as proper, if still scornful, for the many while defending agency for the rarefied few. Moreover despite routinely describing submission as natural for most of us, Carlyle seems anxious about the self-evidence of this very claim. He indexes and approves those ideological institutions which calcify this propensity.

Aristocracy and Priesthood, a governing class and a Teaching Class: these two, sometimes separate, and endeavouring to harmonise themselves, sometimes conjoined as one, and the King a Pontiff-King-there did no society exist without these two vital elements, there will none exist. It lies in the very nature of man: you will visit no remotest village in the most republican country of the world, where virtually or actually you do not find these two powers at work. Man, little as he may suppose it, is necessitated to obey superiors. He is a social being in virtue of this necessity; nay he could not be gregarious otherwise. He obeys those whom he esteems better than himself, wiser, braver; and will forever obey such; and even be ready and delighted to do it.[58]

As an argument this passage, despite being confidently asserted, is very strange. It begins with a universalistic assertion about bifurcated authority structures, which is then naturalized as part of our character. No historical evidence is given for this, and the descriptive claim quickly transforms into a moral argument about the necessity to obey superiors. So we have an argument where Carlyle claims submission (1) is a part of our nature while immediately acknowledging that (2) many of us don't feel it is in our nature which is to our moral detriment. Carlyle then drops this line of reasoning to move back to social and psychological analysis, highlighting that we will always obey those we deem better than ourselves, and happily so. Though of course the entire theme of *Past and Present* is essentially whinging that too many of us deem the capitalists better than us and regard them as the proper aristocracy, when that is not in fact true.

This bad argumentation might be easier to swallow if it weren't coupled with a rhetoric of dehumanization and instrumentalization that is ironically even more brutal than what was normal (at least domestically)[59] in 19th-century bourgeois society. True, Carlyle does sometimes side with the working and impoverished man, stressing that there is something deeply fair about the claim that one should receive a fair day's wages for a fair day's work. But this by no means entitles the mass of people to political participation or even the standard liberal liberties, since the

> liberty of not being oppressed by your fellow man' is an indispensable, yet one of the most insignificant fractional parts of Human Liberty...Of all the paths a man could strike into, there is, at any given moment, a best path for every man; a thing which, here and now, it were of all things wisest for him to do...Whatsoever forwards him in that, let it come to him even in the shape of blows and spurnings, it liberty.[60]

Such an outlook is the basis of Carlyle's aloofness to the agency and suffering of the starving Irish next door, whom he elsewhere chastises for not possessing the manly independence of Scots who fought for their equality against the British.[61] The fact that this is justified as flowing from a kind of higher ethos than the calculative psychological hedonism prominent among capitalist utilitarians at the time doesn't make it more impressive, but more vulgar and disciplinary. It operates not just at the mere surface of freely negotiated contracts based on need but is implemented so the worthy can govern the souls of the unworthy for their own betterment[62] by disciplining the laboring body of the starving.[63]

It isn't difficult to see what the appeal of such a philosophy might be to those who are convinced they are Carlyle's heroic figures or men of genius. That his arguments are often specious, irrationalist, self-contradicting, transparently self-aggrandizing, and often long on moralism and short on moral impartiality is part of their literary charm. They speak to the real force of Carlyle's personality. But these weaknesses also insulate his readers from the responsibility for any kind of consistency, in part because they permit exceptions and agency for those chauvinistically attracted to their peaks while largely requiring submission and obedience from those at the bottom if they are confronted by those Carlyle and his followers deem to be genuinely great men. But for those of us who agree with Tolstoy that history is little charmed by claims to personal greatness there isn't much to be impressed with.

Dostoevsky's *Devils* and the Dangers of Liberalism and Socialism

Then—this is all what you say—new economic relations will be estab-lished, all ready-made and worked out with mathematical exactitude, so that every possible question will vanish in the twinkling of an eye, simply because every possible answer to it will be provided. Then the "Palace of Crystal" will be built. Then... In fact, those will be halcyon days. Of course there is no guaranteeing (this is my comment) that it will not be, for instance, frightfully dull then (for what will one have to do when everything will be calculated and tabulated), but on the other hand everything will be extraordinarily rational. Of course boredom may lead you to anything. It is boredom sets one sticking golden pins into people, but all that would not matter. What is bad (this is my comment again) is that I dare say people will be thankful for the gold pins then. Man is stupid, you know, phenomenally stupid; or rather he is not at all stupid, but he is so ungrateful that you could not find another like him in all creation. I, for instance, would not be in the least surprised if all of a sudden, *à propos* of nothing, in the midst of general prosperity a gentleman with an ignoble, or rather with a reactionary and ironical, countenance were to arise and, putting his arms akimbo, say to us all: "I say, gentleman, hadn't we better kick over the whole show and scatter rationalism to the winds, simply to send these logarithms to the devil, and to enable us to live once more at our own sweet foolish will!" That again would not matter, but what is annoying is that he would be sure to find followers—such is the nature of man. And all that for the most foolish reason, which, one would think, was hardly worth mentioning: that is, that man everywhere and at all times, whoever he may be, has preferred to act as he chose and not in the least as his reason and advantage dictated. And one may choose what is contrary to one's own interests, and sometimes one *positively ought* (that is my idea). One's own free unfettered choice, one's own caprice, however wild it may be, one's own fancy worked up at times to frenzy—is that very "most advantageous advantage" which we have overlooked, which comes under no classification and against which all systems and theories are continually being shattered to atoms.

(Dostoevsky, *Notes from Underground*)

With Nietzsche, Dostoevsky is the greatest reactionary critic of the 19th century. Dostoevsky's genius and influence are beyond contestation by anyone who has helplessly turned the pages of any one of his great novels. Most literary talents would settle happily for a legacy that included *Poor Folk* and *Notes from Underground*, assured of a minor but permanent place in the world canon. But these were just warm-ups for the four great novels which, with *War and Peace*, *Ulysses*, and *Beloved*, come very close to the Platonic ideal of the form.[64] That Dostoevsky was able to accomplish this despite, or perhaps because of, the enormous challenges imposed by imprisonment, sickness, and vice is not just impressive but even heroic.

Dostoevsky's influence on the political right has been extraordinary. Nietzsche, who rarely had a kind word for anyone—let alone a believing Christian—was euphoric about his work. In *Twilight of the Idols* he described Dostoevsky as

> the only psychologist...from which I have anything to learn: he is one of the happiest accidents of my life, even more so than my discovery of Stendhal. This profound human being, who was ten times justified in despising the superficial Germans, found the Siberian convicts in whose midst he lived for a long time, nothing but the worst criminal for whom no return to society was possible, very different from what he himself had expected-he found the to be carved out of about the best, hardest, and most valuable timber growing anywhere on Russian soil.[65]

Ayn Rand regarded Dostoevsky as a tremendous novelist, on par with Victor Hugo (though naturally not herself).[66] Beyond Rand exploiting the eminently Dostoevskyean technique of having characters stand in for philosophical positions within her own novels, her celebration of the long-hard triumph of capitalist reason over collectivist irrationalism can be seen as both refuting his anti-modernism and affirming Dostoevsky's conviction that the average person wasn't very much interested in or driven by reason. More recently Jordan Peterson has routinely appealed to Dostoevsky in his characterizations of left-wing activists and intellectuals. Often writing in a rather shrill manner, his pop-psychological portraits undeniably owe a lot to Dostoevsky's grim satire on socialists and anarchists in works like *Devils*. As he put it in his recent *Beyond Order: 12 More Rules for Life*:

> The incomparable Russian novelist Fyodor Dostoevsky addressed the same question as Nietzsche-at about the same time-in his masterwork *The Possessed* (alternative known as *Demons* or *The Evils*). The protagonist in that novel, Nikolai Stavrogin, is wed to the same ideals that eventually birthed

revolutionary communism, although he lives his fictional life decades before the full-fledged turmoil began in what became the Soviet Union. The appearance of these ideals was not a positive development, in Dostoevsky's view. He could see that the adoption of a rigid, comprehensive utopian ideology, predicated on a few apparently self-evident axioms, presented a political and spiritual danger with the potential to far exceed in brutality all that had occurred in the religious, monarchial, or even pagan past. Dostoevsky, like Nietzsche, foresaw that all of this was coming almost fifty years (!) before the Leninist Revolution in Russia. That incomprehensible level of prophetic capacity remains a stellar example of how the artist and his intuition brings to light the future far before others see it.[67]

(High praise)

All this makes critically assessing the reactionary bent of Dostoevsky's thought necessary and problematic. Compounding the difficulty is the fact that he is less known for writing directly about political issues in his own authorial voice.[68] Instead his major positions are best staked out in works of fiction, which bring with them major interpretive difficulties.[69] A political theorist has to completely reconstruct Dostoevsky's argument for him before critiquing it. This obviously leaves one open to the immediate accusation that a critical commentator can by no means do justice to the embedded insights of the art. One could also point out that as an artist, such a reconstruction invariably sacrifices many of the aesthetic and rhetorical affects which are crucial to the themes and arguments the book is making. This is especially true for an author like Dostoevsky where his characters—unlike the far more rote caricatures of second handers like Rand—are very much flesh and blood beings with vastly complex internal lives. Conveying that confusion in the powerful way he does is crucial to appreciating much of Dostoevsky's condemnation of the modern world. Modernity is portrayed as producing often nihilistic and violence pathological responses which must be understood psychologically rather than rationally or argumentatively. In a word one must "feel" how the philosophical convictions of the characters are lived, not just assess them based on their logical or empirical merits.

Because of these interpretive difficulties I am not going to be presenting Dostoevsky's positions according to some artificial chronology, let alone break them up and respond to them point by point. Instead I am going to approach his critical literary techniques as one would internally tangent circles, starting from his broadest and most surface criticisms down to his most profound, while highlighting the intersections between each. Seen this way we can see three different literary techniques used by Dostoevsky to condemn modernity. The first is satirical. One sees this technique used most effectively in *Devils*, though his skills were well honed within *Notes from the Underground* and even *Crime and Punishment*. The second literary technique is psychological, which is where Dostoevsky is at his most masterful and innovative. Here *Crime and Punishment* is undoubtedly the gold standard. Rashkolnikov's inner spiritual conflict as he endeavors to synthesize and live by the impossible and contradictory ideals imposed by foreign modernity doctrines is masterfully displayed. As are the consequences to his well-being and tragically those of his victims. Finally the third literary technique Dostoevsky deploys are philosophical dialogues and antagonisms, usually personified in the vivid conflicts and relationships between his characters. This reaches its apex in *The Brothers Karamazov*, particularly in the well-known chapters on "The Grand Inquisitor," and the complex relationships which emerge between Ivan Karamazov, his brother Alyosha, and Father Zosima.

I will begin by discussing his satirical technique. The satirizing of the left, which takes up much of the *Devils*, gains much of its power from familiarity. The young Dostoevsky was a member of various radical groups, beginning with the Petrahevsky circles and eventually descending into revolutionary agitation. While Dostoevsky was always an idiosyncratic leftist in rejecting the atheism and materialism of his comrades, his commitment seems to have been sincere. Joseph Frank maintains that Dostoevsky's primary aspiration was the liberation of the serfs—at the time little more than slaves—and that he could be understood as a kind of "Christian Socialist."[70] This comes hauntingly through in early epistolary novels like *Poor Folk*. The book pales psychologically and philosophically next to the four great novels of his maturity, and it must be said that it lacks the social rawness and materialist sensibility of a Dickens or Orwell at their best.[71] But its sentiments and humanistic affect for the urban lower classes, coupled with the typical Dostoevskyean flourish of a love affair doomed largely by economic precarity, make *Poor Folk* a worthy effort.[72] One can see why many progressives and socialists were excited and delighted to welcome the talented up and comer to their ranks.

What catalyzed his conversion is a matter of considerable debate, with Frank arguing the best clues can be found in Dostoevsky's novel *The House of the Dead*.[73] Dostoevsky's dalliances with socialist radicalism eventually got him arrested, where after a moderately comfortable stay in the Peter and Paul Fortress as a result of his middle-class status, he was brought out to be executed. Having made whatever peace he could with God and death—and for Dostoevsky the two are never far apart[74]—he was no doubt stunned at having his sentence commuted to a lengthy prison term in Siberia followed by military service. There Dostoevsky was exposed to depths of cruelty on the part of the guards and fellow inmates which few of us can fully comprehend. But more importantly Dostoevsky became aware of both the sinfulness of many of the working-class inmates that surrounded him and, more importantly, their intense disdain for the educated middle-class prisoners who presented themselves as their saviors. As Frank puts it:

> In the first letter he wrote to his brother after leaving the prison camp, Dostoevsky said that the peasant convicts would have eaten him and the other upper-class prisoners alive if they had had the chance, so much were they alien and resented. You may, he tells his readers, have had friendly

and even fatherly relations with peasants all our lives, but you never really know them. All that is only an 'optical illusion.' The truth only appears when a nobleman is place in the situation of Dostoevsky himself–when he is forced to become one of the common people.[75]

In lesser figures this might have instilled a mere crude and Carlyean disdain for the lower orders brought about by disappointment in their failure to abide by his expectations. But Dostoevsky was made of deeper stuff. His political response to the twinned experiences of persecution by the Tsarist regime on the one hand, and exposure to both the real hardship and disdain of the lower orders, is complex. Dostoevsky doesn't transition to crude elitist reaction, suppliantly identifying himself with the superior power of the Tsar and coming to disdain the lower orders as a kind of ex post facto Nietzschean vengeance. On the other hand his socialist politics are rapidly dropped even as his affiliation with the lower orders deepens. Dostoevsky became a kind of conservative populist before his time. He continued to express disdain for the spiritual detachment of wealthy, as in *The Idiot* (one of his few works that focuses on the upper echelons of society).[76] But their power isn't begrudged or coveted by or for the lower orders, in no small part because it is the possession of power and affluence which corrupts the rich. It is the possession of some small privileges or aptitudes, rather than abject destitution, which are frequently a catalyst for a descent into evil throughout Dostoevsky's novels. The comparative proximity of the lower middle and upper middle classes to greater power and affluence stirs in them an envious desire for more and ressentiment of those who have it.[77] At the same time Dostoevsky will often idolize the peasant classes for retaining a kind of spiritual and moral integrity in the face of sin, not in spite of but in part because of their destitution. Why he did so having experienced the opposite one can only guess at. In so doing Dostoevsky provides a novel portrait—and it must be said defense—of the social stratification of society.

But more importantly Dostoevsky's novels offered the political right a powerful way of simultaneously mobilizing anti-elitist sentiments against both the rich *and* radical intellectuals, while lauding and even sublimating the working class, all while maintaining the hierarchical structure of society largely as is. Or indeed even being able to characterize any radical transition away from the status quo as in fact hurting the very lower classes it was intended to benefit. Dostoevsky was a master of portraying the "perversity thesis" as a form of literary satire, wherein the well-meaning but violent efforts of progressives and revolutionaries inevitably backfire by producing negative results for those they aspired to help.[78] But this is given a remarkable Christian thrust by Dostoevsky which goes beyond merely this world. His radicals aren't merely harming the serfs in this life, but perverting their spiritual purity. Often times Dostoevsky's most saintly and poor characters are defined by a lack of expectations for this life.[79] This means they focus highly on the next life, ensuring the poor possess a spiritual endowment which could only be lost through exposure to the radicalism of egalitarian and materialist modernity.

Here Dostoevsky vacillates considerably throughout his novels on the potential appeal of modernist and foreign doctrines to the working classes. As we will see, in his more psychological and philosophical moments, Dostoevsky seems anxious and even expectant that radicals will eventually succeed in corrupting the working class. The result would be the rise of a new kind of tyranny. For this he is often rightly lauded for having predicted the eventual success of Lenin and the Bolsheviks decades before the October Revolution. These prophetic anxieties about inexorable left-wing totalitarianism sit uncomfortably next to his frequent portraits of the nigh incorruptible peasantry and his savage portrayal of the political left as a collection of out-of-touch boobs and narcissists incapable of even successfully organizing small-scale troubles in a backwater Russian village.

At Dostoevsky's peak all of these contrary responses come together in an artistically masterful way, as in his amusing portrayal of a meeting of radicals in *Devils*. Anyone who has spent anytime with leftists at their very worst will recognize some of the tropes: the incessant pedantry over titles and proper names, superficial egalitarianism occluding a desperate and narcissistic desire for affirmation, and a puritanical moralism thinly masking a lack of genuine human pity and empathy. In the *Devils* the radical's chief philosopher Shigalyov, a clever but superficial and calculating man, rises to speak. He proclaims to have devised a system which is the "only solution to the social problem." There is only one catch:

> Plato, Rousseau, Fourier, aluminum columns—all that is good only for sparrows, not human society. But since the future form of human society is needed right now, when we're finally ready to take action, in order to forestall any further thought on the subject, I'm proposing my own system of world organization. Here it is!' he said, tapping his notebook. 'I wanted to expatiate on my book to this meeting as briefly as possible, but I see it's necessary to provide a great deal of verbal clarification; therefore my entire explication will take at least ten evenings, corresponding to the number of chapters in my book.' (More laughter was heard) 'Moreover I must declare in advance that my system is not yet complete.' (Laughter again). 'I became lost in my own data and my conclusion contradicts the original premise from which I started. Beginning with unlimited freedom, I end with unlimited despotism. I must add, however, there can be no other solution to the social problem except mine.[80]

Dostoevsky's Underground Man

Funny stuff. This is not the only place where Dostoevsky engages in a satirical upending at the expense of the left and progressive movements generally. A more complex example is found in *Notes from the Underground*, which at one level can be understood as the psychological examination of a man who has so internal-ized the contradictory impulses of modernist doctrines of freedom, equality, and materialism that he is no longer able to value anything above anything else. As Julia Kristeva put it, the *Notes*

> plot the provisional position in a violent recovery of the self that, beyond some neurotic affairs, accedes to the splitting of the antihero; edge-to edge lie drives and sense, there were arises-or collapses-the speaking being, the parletre. He palpates the living plasma, that probiotic constituent that is nothing other than the distinctive capacity of the unhappy consciousness, the insect, the 'mouse' or the 'ant' to mutate.[81]

This plastic quality is of course emblematic of the freedom also promised by modernity which turns out to be a poisoned chalice. In another ironic perver-sion of modernity's emancipatory rhetoric, the Underground Man longing to be completely free comes to feel himself incapable of action. This immanent per-versity of liberal and socialist materialism's political emphasis on freedom is seen in how they epistemically legitimatize their views by appealing to the authority of an absolutely deterministic science. Taking both prongs of this literally we have a doctrine which argues we should be limitlessly free because the absolutely rigid laws of nature or history dictate that we must be. In the pathology of the Underground Man we see the transition of unlimited freedom into unlimited despotism carried out again, but this time at the level of natural ontology. So deep are the natural constraints on freedom that it breeds comically nihilistic efforts to break out of it. As Frank highlights:

> How, for example, can you live in a world in which nobody is morally responsible for anything because you know that there is no such thing as free will and everything happens according to the laws of nature? Dostoev-sky tries to imagine such a world, and the example he uses is of somebody being slapped in the face. The person feels insulted and outraged because his dignity as a human being has been violated. But then his reason tells him that it is ridiculous to have such feelings because whoever did the slap-ping is not responsible for it. The offender was only acting as an instrument of the laws of nature. Or suppose that, after the slap, you feel generous and want to forgive the person who insulted you. But this is equally ridiculous: you can't forgive a law of nature, and the notion of forgiveness implies that you as well as your adversary are both morally responsible...Since, as a follower of Chernyshevsky, you know this is absurd, what you are left with is the inertia, the inability to do anything, that the Underground Man says is the result of his acute intelligence and self-consciousness....The prob-lem is that even though the Underground Man is convinced that all this is rationally true, he finds it very hard to live with.[82]

This is very, if grimly, funny stuff. Its power comes in part from the acuity of its satirical portrait of modern egalitarians. Dostoevsky not only spent time with these kinds of radicals but identified with them for a long period of time. Consequently there is a degree of familiarity with their mannerisms and tics which contributes to the accuracy of Dostoevsky's portrayal. Undoubtedly his portraits are exaggerations. But like all effective satire they bite through exploiting the minimal aesthetic gap between art which we and the author knows to be unreal, and reality which is supposed to be exemplarily real. More than that Dostoevsky exposes the personal limitations of liberals and socialists and condemns them in a dialectically entwined manner. He simultaneously condemns the radicals for becoming corrupted by the ideologies they espouse while also heavily implying that the ideologies themselves were always corrupt given they appeal to the instinctively decadent and authoritarian. Rather than a chicken or egg scenario, we're left with a spiraling circle of decadence which threatens to widen and consume Russia and eventually the world if left unchecked.[83]

As art this is all very well and good, though one should immediately question its wholesale extension to the left and liberals. One of the dangers of great art is that its portrait of a movement overwhelms our ability to appreciate the differences and variation found among real people and movement. Reactionaries who take Dostoevsky's satirical pathologizations of the left at face value seriously risk falling into the trap of *a priori* psychologism, much as the Jacobins were roused by Rousseau's affecting condemnation of corrupted bourgeois urbanites or socialists found consolation in Tolstoy's lacerations of the Russian aristocracy. To put it bluntly, reactionaries risk the joke going over their head in their enthusiasm to take damning portraits literally. But more importantly the consciously exaggerated quality of Dostoevsky's portraits gives them a clear one-sidedness that threatens to turn into self-contradiction at points. The price for not taking the radical's views seriously, describing them as the narcissistic product of an out-of-touch minority, impotent to act in the case of the Underground Man or impotent to have an effect in the case of *Devil*'s radicals, is that it deflates the whole weight of Dostoevsky's critique. If it turns out these people are all a bunch of idlers, grifters, and minor terrorists, what danger do they really pose to society and how elevated could art which dedicates hundreds of pages to satirizing them be?

This will be a recurrent problem for many on the political right, who will vacillate between the temptation to mock the left into insignificance one day while presenting it as an existential threat the next. Often they will try to do both simultaneously despite the clear contradiction between these dispositions, much as Hirschman points out plenty of conservatives will simultaneously describe the left as transformatively perverting society while in the same breath mocking them for being powerless to change society's iron laws.[84] It is too his great credit that Dostoevsky is unusually sensitive to this problem, and while his work does sometimes straddle uncomfortably between them (as with *Devils*) his most effective criticisms of modernity are in situations where he powerfully depicts the allure of the ideas he once embraced only to reject.

More effective are Dostoevsky's equally pathological portraits of those warped by modern ideas, but which take their infectious appeal seriously. *Notes from the Underground* toys with this prospect, especially in its concluding sections where the Underground Man becomes less of a tragicomic guide to his inner life and goes into the world to experience real suffering as a consequence of his malady.[85] There we see how Dostoevsky feels not only contempt but real empathy and pity for the Underground Man in his short relationship with Liza. Here the Underground Man desperately wants to form genuine human connection with Liza, understood on the Christian lines of two souls entering into loving relation together. But he cannot, due to the perverting impact of the philosophies which so dominate Underground Man's intellect. This leads to his famous declaration that an ambiguous "they" will not let him be good.[86] Here we see clearly Dostoevsky's thesis that it is not material, but spiritual, deprivation and mutilation which are at the core of the middle-class Underground Man's pain. Indeed the expressions of pity deeply impoverished Liza show him invert the modernist claim that material flourishing is conducive to happiness. Despite being far less wretched the Underground Man is clearly the more destitute of the pair.

Dostoevsky on the Need for Crime and Punishment

This thematic point is expressed through almost exactly the same love affair in *Crime and Punishment*, which is the main book where his psychologically critique of modernity is unpacked. Undoubtedly Dostoevsky's most famous novel, *Crime and Punishment*, is also his most entertaining. Doubtless this was partly out of necessity, as Dostoevsky (like many of us, never quite able to live up to his own ideals) owed large sums of money to many people and needed a big hit. Surprisingly the pulpier frames of the novel—its youthful hero, murders and detectives, noble prostitutes, forced loveless marriages—work brilliantly as both spectacle and scaffolding to support one of the great psychodramas in literature.

The main plot is deceptively simple. The protagonist is a young, upwardly mobile law student named Rodion Raskolnikov. Initially successful, and having written an enthusiastically received article on crime and the teleological suspension of the ethical enjoyed by great men, things have since taken a sour turn. Raskolnikov lives in a filthy hovel and is routinely subjected to abuse by an exploitative pawnbroker to whom he hawks meager possessions. Being too poor to continue his education, and with a mother and sister to support, Raskolnikov decides to rob and kill the pawnbroker to finance his education and support his family. Things don't go well at first and he winds up having to kill both the pawnbroker and her sister. Still, at various points in the novel Raskolnikov either seems to have gotten away with his crime or tries to outwit a stubbornly suspicious detective. In the end his conscience leads him to confess to the double murders when someone else already had, leading to him being sentenced to a modest eight years in prison accompanied by his lover, another prostitute, Sonya.[87]

As a Dostoevskyean text, *Crime and Punishment* doesn't really live at the level of its plot, which is enjoyably suspenseful but hardly ground-breaking.[88] Most of the novel takes place in Raskolnikov's head and in his interactions with the colorful and often corrupt personnel of lower-middle- to working-class St. Petersburg. The central drama is his, and by extension urban Russia's, deep attraction to and infection by the scientific ideas and both the egalitarian and anti-egalitarian political programs of the West. These include liberalism, socialism, materialism, scientific rationalism, and, somewhat more idiosyncratically, a kind of Carlylean or even proto-Nietzschean belief in "Great men" as the motor of history. The modern ideas spreading from West to east continuously run up against the seemingly more primitive and superstitious beliefs of Christian Orthodoxy which are seemingly embedded—however remotely—in the collective unconscious psyche of the major characters and which stubbornly resist surrender or assimilation by both the more thoughtful and simple characters.[89]

Presented in this way one might suspect Dostoevsky is merely using different characters as mouthpieces for ideological debates, and there is certainly an element of that which will become more formalized in *Devils* and *The Brothers Karamazov*. Unfortunately this technique will generate many inferior emulators. But suggesting that multilayered personalities like Raskolnikov, Porfiry, or Sonya are merely bipedal soapboxes would do a disservice to the remarkable artistry shown in *Crime and Punishment*. It would also miss the key innovation that makes Dostoevsky the novelist such an important artistic figure for the political right. His focus is not simply on the philosophical stakes at play in the debate between ideas but how their impact is felt, lived, and warped by the psychological dispositions and histories of his central players.

This not only adds layers of complexity and humanity to the story but more importantly highlights a central Dostoevskyean conviction that ideas cannot be judged on a purely rational basis. This ignores the way they are internalized and impact the concrete lives of real human beings, which is where the real gravity of moral and spiritual life is to be found. This is an extraordinary shift in emphasis, as Dostoevsky moves the political and philosophical battlefield from reason—where it seemed like egalitarian modernity must everywhere triumph—to the soul, where it turned out conservative authors could not only compete but thrive with their competitors. Through short-circuiting reason and appealing directly to the deepest spiritual yearnings of the human heart, authors like Dostoevsky profoundly undercut the appeal of modernity by presenting it as an ideology no one could possibly live by. However, it also opened the door wide open to legitimizing the most dangerous forms of irrationalism and authoritarianism which—however much Dostoevsky tried to keep a lid on them—were bursting at the seams to come out.

Patient Zero of Dostoevsky's analysis is undoubtedly Raskolnikov, to whom more attention is directed than either the Underground Man or Ivan Karamazov, his two other complex portraits of men corrupted by modern ideas. The decision to make Raskolnikov young, intelligent, urban, and a law student is by no means coincidental. Dostoevsky is framing the transition to egalitarian modernity partly as a generational issue, but more significantly as the result of a small but vocal class of bourgeois-educated Russians increasingly aspiring to middle-class status and power respectable in an increasingly interconnected world. In this context the stern aristocratic hierarchies of Tsarist Russia, backed by the Orthodox clergy and police force, lose their charm and seem increasingly anachronistic and backward. This simultaneous—and very middle class—envy and even ressentiment toward both the powerful within Russia and the West without sits uneasily with Raskolnikov's sense of superiority toward the traditions and ordinary people of Holy Russia.

These kinds of resentments are almost always personalized by Dostoevsky as form of individuated self-hatred which actuates much of his character's behaviors. Before Nietzsche, Dostoevsky was acutely aware of the self-reinforcing psychodynamic that exists between feelings of inferiority and superiority. How the inability to live with feelings of inferiority for so long eventually bursts out in radical assertions of will and domination. His corrupted characters internalize a belief in the backwardness of their own country, and consequently their own deeply felt religious heritage, and come to disdain them. In some moments his characters express these feelings through a sense of pity and socialist progressivism toward those disadvantaged by Russia's backwardness, though these feelings are always formulated with an air of intellectualized remove. In other moments their feelings of inferiority and pity toward the needy become disdain. The dumb peasantry are conceived as being in the thrall of the very traditions and religious illusions which victimize and hold them back and from which the modern intelligentsia has freed itself. In these moments the egalitarian ethos which animates the modernizer, which has a superficial resemblance to Christian compassion, is exposed as another kind of authoritarian elitism. The modernizers may even come to reconcile the twinned sentiments of egalitarian schmaltz and elitist aping together, however inauthentically, as the characters in *Devils* do. That is by suggesting that for the good of the peasantry and common people the elite must take control and apply their science without limitation or compunction to reinventing society.

Rashkolnikov is a paradigmatic character who runs the circuit of these psychodynamics, living out in microcosm the psychological agony of modernity. His main quest in *Crime and Punishment* is finding a way to subdue the guilty conscience which insists that his murder was wrong. All of his intellectual and practical efforts can be given a political and philosophical interpretation. What is interesting about the psychodrama is how each of Rashkolnikov's efforts proves inadequate, and consequently mutates organically into another to which it is seemingly opposed, but is in fact tethered by complex psychological links. It is important to note that, although Raskolnikov runs through these different arguments at great length in his head, he never engages in anything like an internalized Socratic dialogue measuring them dispassionately. At no point is he capable of simply reasoning himself into or out of the right mindset, as the Enlightenment philosophers may have wanted. Instead it is Raskolnikov's Kierkegaardian inability to psychologically affirm the viewpoint, act on it, and live with himself that catalyzes his psychological changes and actions.

At some points in *Crime and Punishment* Raskolnikov appeals to a crude utilitarian egotism to defend his murder, conceiving himself as young, full of potential and desire while the pawnbroker is old, unhappy, and contemptuous of all. There is a kind of simple meritocratic logic linked to the narrowest psychological hedonism in these moments, but it quickly proves unsustainable in the face of corrosive guilt.[90] Elsewhere Rahkolnikov generalizes his psychological hedonism into an ethical hedonism. If it turns out the pawnbroker was bringing suffering into the world by her miserable disposition, and Raskolnikov will bring great happiness through the pursuit of an education and self-development funded by money she wasn't even using, isn't it the case that the utility scales are balanced in his favor? This is a more recurring argument Raskolnikov tells himself, but it doesn't work for very long either. In both of these cases the effort to reduce the pawnbroker's (and by extension Raskolnikov's own) life to a mere set of utility metrics, not to mention the transparently self-serving basis of the entire argument, led it to fall apart.

Finally Rashkolnikov will turn to his most infamous argument, which is that great men are not required to adhere to the moral strictures of society. Instead they create a law unto themselves through a teleological suspension of the ethical by mere human will, much like Napoleon did. Here hedonistic calculus turns smoothly into pure decisionism. This is undoubtedly the position closest to Rashkolnikov's heart; it was the basis of his initial paper on crime and is echoed in his first confession to Sonya late in the novel.

"What if it were really that?" he said, as though reaching a conclusion. "Yes, that's what it was! I wanted to become a Napoleon, that is why I killed her... Do you understand now?"

"N-no," Sonia whispered naïvely and timidly. "Only speak, speak, I shall understand, I shall understand *in myself*!" she kept begging him.

"You'll understand? Very well, we shall see!" He paused and was for some time lost in meditation.

It was like this: I asked myself one day this question—what if Napoleon, for instance, had happened to be in my place, and if he had not had Toulon nor Egypt nor the passage of Mont Blanc to begin his career with, but instead of all those picturesque and monumental things, there had simply been some ridiculous old hag, a pawnbroker, who had to be murdered too to get money from her trunk (for his career, you understand). Well, would he have brought himself to that if there had been no other means?

Wouldn't he have felt a pang at its being so far from monumental and… and sinful, too? Well, I must tell you that I worried myself fearfully over that 'question' so that I was awfully ashamed when I guessed at last (all of a sudden, somehow) that it would not have given him the least pang, that it would not even have struck him that it was not monumental… that he would not have seen that there was anything in it to pause over, and that, if he had had no other way, he would have strangled her in a minute without thinking about it! Well, I too… left off thinking about it… murdered her, following his example. And that's exactly how it was! Do you think it funny? Yes, Sonia, the funniest thing of all is that perhaps that's just how it was.[91]

This is the apex of the hedonistic philosophies Raskolnikov has been playing with the whole time. This is a point expressed even more vividly in Ivan's famous axiom in *The Brothers Karamazov* that in the absence of God "everything is permitted." Now one might point out that the reconstruction of Dostoevsky's positions as I've framed them here is artificial and contrary to his own aesthetic intentions. But I would argue that reconstructing the argument as I have helps Dostoevsky's political thinking gain a kind of immanent traction. It can almost be seen as expressing in literary and psychological form the broader historical and intellectual narrative later articulated in Alasdair Macintyre's *After Virtue*. In this book MacIntyre chronicles the efforts of modern thinkers to ground morality in various forms of anti-religious and anti-teleological argumentation.[92] One of the developments is it passes back and from psychological to a more grandiose ethical hedonism that tries to calculate the good for the whole world. And finally one ends up believing in no good at all, and winds up being convinced that one is simply an atomized end in one's self. At its climax modernity finds itself moving from universal rights and well-being for all to a Nietzschean will to power which tyrannizes everyone—including even the modern superman, who is left to will values into being which glitter but disappoint in having no other basis but his will.

However, as with Macintyre's book, there is undoubtedly a sense in which the complex narrative movements gain their power through aestheticization and their situatedness in a bigger and grander story. One which has a symbiotic association with a kind of traditionalism and a homely counterpoint which coexists in a strangely liminal space with the projection of more transcendent ideals. A typical feature in many of Dostoevsky's most political works is the full or partial redemption of one of the male protagonists or anti-heroes through an encounter with a member of the working class, typically a woman and sometimes a member of their family.[93] In these circumstances we see the kind of erotic or familial love felt for these women sublimated into a less intellectualized and more immediate form of Christian love which then generalizes authentically to the rest of humanity. This love is ultimately portrayed as both extending to, and having its ultimate root in God.

By doing this Dostoevsky accomplishes an important and direct aesthetic synthesis between the homely and the transcendent, but one which intentionally short circuits all the other layers of social and metaphysical reality which are of interest. This has the effect of depoliticizing them by relegating all intermediary issues from individuated love to God a second tier. And not coincidentally it is within these layers that the realm of the most contestable human politics with which Dostoevsky would be familiar exists. From a modern feminist standpoint we should go even further and regard Dostoevsky's fetishization of female purity and her subordination to male needs within the family as an already fatal flaw. This politically motivated depoliticization is a serious problem with Dostoevsky's analysis. And one that, as I shall point out drawing on Tolstoy, isn't even consistent with his own Christian disposition. In his effort to bypass the corrupt classes and struggles of the world to directly access the meaning provided by God, Dostoevsky ends up drawing a clear line between the peasantry and the divine which expels much of the world within which questions of meaning and morality are negotiated and fought over.

For now, I will simply say that there is no juncture at which any of Dostoevsky's heroes or villains ever actually refute the modernist doctrines they variably identify with and reject. Instead they find them psychologically difficult to maintain, and consequently abandon them for a philosophy which is easier to live by. But it has to be said that in the end this proves far less than Dostoevsky hopes. Appeals to our psychological dispositions is undoubtedly, as everyone from Aristotle to Rawls knew, an important feature of a metaphysics and certainly a political philosophy. But it is by no means the singular or even most important feature to consider; the truth comes immediately to mind as one that might be more important than our feelings about the truth. On that front Dostoevsky's argument looks far weaker. One doesn't refute materialism by showing that materialism is unpalatable, but by showing it is wrong. Even if Dostoevsky were correct that it was impossible for the human mind to accept the implications of materialism and live with them, that might simply indicate a limitation to human consciousness and imagination rather than the doctrine itself. There is no guarantee that the best metaphysical theory will conform to our moral or aesthetic convictions or wishes, any more than an accurate cancer diagnosis conforms to our wishes about our health. The same problem applies with Dostoevsky's treatment of the political doctrines of modernity. To the extent these constitute a twinned effort to accept scientific materialism and/or rationalism as a metaphysic and maintain a sense of moral value in a secular universe they are all undoubtedly flawed. Dostoevsky himself was aware of some of the more serious philosophical flaws, as indicated by Raskolnikov's drifting through many different flavors of utilitarianism and ending with decisionism. But on the matter of whether they are more seriously flawed than an Orthodox Christianity predicated on a very questionable anti-materialist metaphysics, things are far more questionable.

One can even take a more radical position still, following Nietzsche and Tolstoy on different sides, and ask whether Dostoevsky's Christian traditionalism is in fact true to its own principles. If Christianity is, as Nietzsche claims, defined by a relentless spiritual quest for the truth then Dostoevsky's irrationalist psychologizing may very well appear as a kind of spiritual limitation: an unwillingness to go all the way in not simply asking but faithfully enduring the most fundamental question a Christian can ask, the question against Christianity itself. However if Christianity is truly the faith of the wretched of the earth, as Dostoevsky seems to think, it is very questionable whether one can adopt the abridged conservative universe defended in his novels. Indeed it would seem very plausible that Tolstoy's condemnation of the violence underpinning imperialist Russia and all class societies in the emphatically Christian terms set out within *The Kingdom of God Is within You* would be a more authentic expression of Dostoevsky's own faith.[94] To dive into these issues we must turn from Dostoevsky's psychological ruminations to his more directly philosophical ones. Especially those presented in the great work of his maturity *The Brothers Karamazov*.

Dostoevsky's Influence on the Political Right

Dostoevsky's greatest novel is undoubtedly *The Brothers Karamazov*.[95] It is also his most philosophically complex, even if the plot is perhaps his most straightforward since the early novels. *Brothers* abandons some of the partisan inclinations of *Crime and Punishment* and especially *Devils*, where attractive characters could undoubtedly espouse views contrary to Dostoevsky's own but where the presentation leaves little doubt what will come out on top. In *The Brothers Karamazov* one is presented with three potentially admirable but flawed mouthpieces who have psychologically responded to the changing of their country and the abuse of a deadbeat father in various ways. This includes in the formulation of their distinctive philosophies, which each bear the stamp of their upbringing and personality even if only Ivan's evolves into an intellectually defensible system.

Dmitri is a sensualist and romantic, who is always searching for highs of experience and pleasure. While this notably includes the crasser forms of hedonistic pleasure available at the time—(too) much of the center of the novel is taken up with planning a fantastically decadent snuff party—Dmitri's intelligence and personal daring means he aspired to higher levels of sensuality as well. This includes finding a degree of resonance in violence and in the pursuit of erotic infatuation initially mistaken as a kind of love. Initially Ivan comes across as a strict contrast to Dmitri: icy and analytical. Ivan is the upwardly mobile free thinker in the family who carefully conceals his own longings within layers of intellectualized argumentation, allegory, and withdrawal. However, there is a sense in which his often-self-contradicting intellectual pursuits echo the kind of hedonistic variety and lack of focus found in Dmitri.[96]

It can be tempting to follow Kristeva and claim that all the Karmazov's are "sensualists. The word naslazhdenie (sensual pleasure) peppers Dostoevsky's writing, but Alyosha turns his ecstasies back into pedagogical plans and only Dmitri's purifying torture gives him full voice without killing him."[97] But this goes too far. Ivan's intellectual sensualism is invariably compromised by the twinned failing of the world to live up to his ideals and his own inability to believe in them. In psychoanalytic terms this is expressed through an Oedipal ressentiment of the father then internalized as profoundly individuated guilt over his death. This is even projected through a psychic fantasy of Satan arriving to chat.

Finally there is Alyosha, the youngest legitimate Karamazov brother. Not quite a Christ figure in the vein of *The Idiot*'s Prince Myshkin, Alyosha is the Christian hero at the center of the novel.[98] He initially lacks the energy and charisma of Dmitri and the intelligence and intellectual honesty of Ivan, but ends up being the most admirable character next to Zosima. To the extent Alyosha could be uncharitably called a sensualist, it could only be achieved at either a Nietzschean or Lacanian level where his disavowed desires become religiously sublimated using the symbolic material of religion, either as an object of revenge or fetishistic attachment. Such a reading may be possible for Zosima, but it seems implausible for Alyosha—who for the most part lacks these psychic complications. Indeed there is a strange sense in which his lack of psychodynamic dramas is part of the appeal of both Alyosha and the doctrine he represents. He isn't free from guilt over doing the wrong thing, but Alyosha is free from the worst kind of guilt: the guilt that appears when one is tempted to believe there is nothing good and evil, even thinking cannot make it so. And worse, finding that liberating.

All three characters have a dark mirror in their rumored bastard brother Pavel Smerdyakov. Consciously one of Dostoevsky's most simply defined characters, Smerdyakov approximates what Zizek would call the "excremental remainder" of the symbolic tensions embodied in the three major brothers.[99] He is the displaced psychic rot which one can find in all the members of the Karamazov family, coagulated as a literally bastardized embodiment of their sins and familial conflicts. Like his father Fyodor and half-brother Dmitri, Smerdyakov is a sensualist and a hedonist, but knows no limitations—he is even willing to contemplate and enact murder and torture to experience the upper echelons of experience. Like Ivan, he possesses a kind of intelligence which borders on cunning, but has none of Ivan's philosophical depth or curiosity about the lived reality of others. Like Alyosha, Smerdyakov is at times eager to belong to the family, but is not motivated by love or even a desire for communion. His familiar yearnings are purely egoistic and driven by resentment and anger at his displacement. In the end Smerdyakov is primarily responsible for the patricide which puts the novel's main murder plot into motion.[100]

While the contrasts between all three/four brothers are interesting and important for generating the novel's tension, we need only concern ourselves with the primary philosophical conflict here. This is best embodied in the divide between Ivan, Alyosha, and Father Zosima, especially as chronicled in books Five and Six.[101] What is interesting here is that the main dialogue between Ivan and Alyosha is actually much more of an internal dispute. At all points Ivan is the primary discussant, and it is not Alyosha who presents the pro or con of the argument so beautifully presented in the parable of the Grand Inquisitor.

Indeed Alyosha is for the most part a passive listener through much of these chapters. Perhaps he is overawed by Ivan's rational intelligence and aesthetic power. Or perhaps Alyosha intuitively recognized that the intellectual arguments Ivan puts forward are in fact the husk concealing a deeper emotional wound that strives to be healed but which his own critical intelligence opens anew. This last point is important since there is no denying Ivan's intelligence or the force of his arguments through books Five and Six. But taken together it becomes clear that Ivan's analytical approach wants to put forward self-evident propositions which always threaten to become dialectical and turn into their opposite. This becomes religiously dramatized late in the book when Ivan hallucinates and sees Satan himself before succumbing to madness.

The major dialogue of the novel opens with Ivan and Alyosha meeting for soup, during which Ivan (characteristically) engages in highly abstract but self-swallowing ruminations that blur the lines between philosophical argument and self-examination. This includes stressing Ivan's own "Euclidean" frame of mind, which he wishes to project onto God for the sake of making the world intelligible to human consciousness even if he doubts it can actually be reduced as such. This is of course a rather Kantian problem as Ivan ponders whether the world in itself is in fact conformable to the transcendental Euclidean structure of consciousness. And, like Kant, Ivan goes back and forth between musing on whether God exists or was created by humankind. Observing that it seems unlikely so amoral a being as man could create such a sublime object as God, Ivan suggests that this moral grandeur may be enough to accept God "simply" as a kind of transcendental postulate of practical reason. But he then acknowledges with Schopenhauer that the suffering and imperfection of the world immediately contradicts even the practical ideal that a benevolent God looks over us.

This last transition is crucial, since it indicates that for Dostoevsky it is the affective ability of religion to answer our most pressing moral, political, and spiritual questions which count most stringently in religion's favor. This is even true for someone like Ivan, whose initial wrestling with metaphysics, social theory, and more generally the truths of reason resembles Goethe's Faust and his own corruption by the allure of modern science. As Faust put it:

> And so I sit, poor silly man, no wiser now than when I began. They call me Professor and Doctor, forsooth, for misleading many any innocent youth. These last ten years no, I suppose, pulling them to and fro by the nose; and I see all our search for knowledge is vain, and this burns my heart with bitter pain...Yet I take no pleasure in anything now for I know I know nothing, [102] I wonder how I can still keep up the pretence of teaching or bettering mankind with my empty preaching.[103]

In this sense Ivan is a quintessential 19th-century man. Initially confident that the propositions of reason will get us closer to the truth of the world, he sees how the propositions of reason only immediately lead to more questions or twist cruelly into their opposites without the possibility of synthesis or advancement. The Euclidean quest for certainty leads to Kantian skepticism of the world in itself. The attempt to historically explain away God through benign anthropomorphism and social theorizing turns religion into an opiate of the masses and immediately exposes how sharp the contrast is between humanity and its own projected ideals. Far from describing God as a kind of moral relaxant, Ivan realizes how the idea of God only generates more psychological difficulties as humankind raises impossible standards it can never abide by and, in so doing, comes to cruelly and relentlessly punish itself.

This brings us to the heart of Ivan's discussion with Alyosha, which includes a lengthy and deeply moving admission that it is in fact the moral problems of theodicy rather than their strictly metaphysical or onto-theological questions about God's existence which are ultimately at the base of Ivan's existential problems. This is a striking acknowledgment, since it seems to cut against the very positions Dostoevsky wants to defend. Even if reason could dissolve the riddles of existence to bring us to a Christian conclusion, or worse even if faith could transcend questions about God's existence, neither would be enough. Ivan delivers a devastating account of how this world, the creation of a so-called benevolent God, includes parents who are willing and perhaps even enjoy the experience of seeing their children freeze to death in a latrine. Ivan asks whether this could possibly be redeemed by locating it in some divine plan which justifies it in the last instance, or if it can be explained away in secular terms as the mere consequence of deterministic laws (perhaps set by a theistic God) playing themselves out. Ivan reaches the remarkable conclusion that even if the suffering of the child could be justified or evaluated in those consequentialist terms, he wouldn't accept it. Ivan would rather remain indignant in the face of any kind of reason or faith that neutralizes our horror toward the injustice of world, even if he cannot disprove it.

Here we can see how Dostoevsky is in fact very much entitled to his observation that, far from being a hoary apologist for reactionary Christianity, he in fact states the problems with his positions in very strong terms.[104] This is carried out so successfully that even many of Dostoevsky's reactionary fans don't acknowledge how deeply Ivan's dilemma cuts into the efforts of conservatives to defend, say, orthodox (or Orthodox) Christian apologias. Dostoevsky generalizes the problems posed by lives lived through reason and lives lived through faith so far that it comes to invalidate not only the moral doctrines of modernity but even the kind of Christian scholasticism which might seek to mount a rational apologia of theodicy, since theodicy becomes morally and spiritually indefensible. This brings up a startling prospect: if Ivan is right and God or nature is unable or unwilling to fix the world, that leaves the task up to humankind. This brings us to the "Legend of the Grand Inquisitor" which is the heart of *The Brothers Karamazov*.[105]

The "Legend" microcosms the unusual argumentative design of *The Brothers Karamazov*. While Alyosha and Zosima are rightly taken to be the chief ideal figures of the novel, it is "Ivan, and not Dostoevsky or another character who wrote the legend."[106] This is remarkable since not only does the Legend include Jesus as the main (albeit a silent) character, but Christ is also undeniably presented as its most admirable and powerful force. This is in spite of Ivan's previous ruminations about humankind becoming responsible for its profane salvation. In some respects Frank is correct to argue that the

> aim of the legend is to undermine the rational arguments of Ivan by showing that they are really based on his contempt for mankind, as was mentioned earlier. It is contempt mixed with love, but contempt all the same. Since Ivan is the author of the poem, it reflects all the conflicts of his personality.[107]

The plot of the "Legend" is rather simple. Jesus returns in the 16th century and begins to perform miracles in Seville. He is quickly arrested by the forces of the Inquisition and sentenced to be burned at the stake. The Grand Inquisitor visits Christ in his cell and intelligently, if desperately, spells out his arguments for why the Church no longer needs Christ. This includes the Inquisitor's confession that he and the Church now consciously follow Satan, not just for worldly power but because they feel the burden of freedom Christ imposes upon mankind is too much for it to bear. By contrast Satan offers a way to placate immediate human needs while so liquifying the distinction between goodness and sin through his scientific materialism that he inadvertently mutilates humankind through the removal of choice. What is striking here is how subtly Dostoevsky demonstrates that an initially sincere Christian love can be perverted into evil and totalitarianism when good intentions are removed from spiritual humility. The Catholic Church here stands in for all the great self-secularizing variants of Christianity which emerge down to the present day, including liberalism and socialism. In the end Christ forgives the Inquisitor with a kiss, which awakens something of an older and more authentic love in the wretched old man. He lets Christ go, but remains committed to his idea.

The "Legend of the Grand Inquisitor" consciously repeats the dialogue between Ivan and Alyosha via a parable conceived by Ivan himself and reflecting the inner conflict within him. It displays Dostoevsky's mature conviction that the proper form Christianity should take is as a kind of interiority which reveals itself only through immediate praxis. Moreover it reveals its truth precisely through this praxis and not by an appeal to reason. It can never be articulated or defended through rationalistic philosophy or dialectics, which is one of the reasons the Legend ends with Christ forgiving the Inquisitor without ever resorting even to the scriptural apologias or parables that are his usual weapons in the New Testament. The paradox is how one can ever explain or enter into such an existence without it being intellectually explicated. This point is central to Father Zosima's later discussion with Ivan where the saintly Priest tries to articulate how a life lived in and for Christian love makes the truth of its teaching practically apparent to its adherents.

Unfortunately the sections with Zosima are among the weakest of the novel, despite their centrality in expressing Dostoevsky's own perspective. From a dramatic standpoint the Priest's death is undoubtedly a moving and a tragic moment for Alyosha, and indeed for the entire town. But the philosophical argument accompanying it is unconvincing. Part of the problem lies simply in trying to explicate a doctrine which is best perceived and understood through praxis, since any intellectual explication that wants to defend the dogmatics of Christianity without reason often winds up appealing to sentiments at best and ressentiment and even calculative reasons at worst. At various points Zosima simply appeals rather brutally to the existence of heaven and fear of hell as a dogmatic reason for belief. He wants to live forever, but in comfort and not in suffering. This sits uncomfortably, in the full Nietzschean sense, with Zosima's claim that we must try to develop enough love to encompass the entire world. A feeling reinforced by the implication that those Zosima doesn't approve of will deservingly end up in Hell. It is also not clear how his faith in the praxis of Christianity is less rigid than his rationalistic counterparts, or even less self-motivated in some respects. As put by Rob Srigley:

> While Zosima advocates humility, counsels against the desire for rewards, and repudiates vengeance, he also says that humble love will 'subdue the entire world,' that 'paradise' awaits the righteous, and that those who reject the Christian teaching will be punished eternally without hope of betterment Zosima's anticipation of these outcomes does not merely raise the problem of hypocrisy, but compromises the moral value of his teaching fundamentally. To state the matter straightforwardly, humble love employed for the purpose of conquest is not humble, the refusal of some rewards in anticipation of receiving even greater ones is not noble; and forgoing vengeance while receiving assurances that one's enemies will suffer eternally for their wrongdoing is not magnanimous. None of these are real wisdom, because real wisdom is character acquired through engagement with the permanence of the real world. Zosima's wisdom is a temporary disposition based on faith and is designed to hold down the baser desires in anticipation of a future when they will be satisfied more completely.[108]

These Nietzschean observations constitute significant external objections to Zosima and so Dostoevsky Christianity. But there is a deeper and more disquieting problem, which is that from an immanent standpoint, the Christian teachings in *The Brothers Karamazov* sit very problematically next to Dostoevsky's political conservatism. It isn't at all clear why a radical kind of Christian love should express itself through inwardness first and foremost and a narrow ethical immediacy at best. Zosima, and by extension Dostoevsky's God, is presented as a rather "beautiful" figure, notably free of the sublime but dehumanizing qualities attached to him by Burke and De Maistre. But he loses a great deal from this; indeed Dostoevsky's God is a rather small deity and the love he feels is also rather small. He is a Christian deity whose relation to his creation is reduced down almost purely to existential interiority,[109] or at best "ethical" immediacy.[110] Ironically, one could say for all his contempt for modernity in this respect, Dostoevsky is not only captured by but doubles down on the most skeptical modernist doctrines that "truth is subjectivity" in the sense of truth only having meaning in relation to the needs of the living, rather than by reference to either a transcendent reality or even the external world. In this respect his work doesn't escape the conservative tendency to appropriate symbiotically what he is trying to oppose, before reconfiguring it in reactionary ways.

But there is a more fundamental and immanent problem still, which flows from the narrowness of the Christian vision defended in *The Brothers Karamazov*. For all his pieties, Zosima can't realistically claim to have even shown to have brought as much love into the world as many of the reformers criticized in the novel. His care only ever extended to those easily within reach, never those far away or impacted by institutions and forces too big and too powerful to permit immediate—or at least obvious—resolution. This is in sharp contrast to Christ himself, who, contra some depictions, was hardly disinterested in socio-political agitation on behalf of the wretched of the earth.[111] Jesus was not just an amiable and tender deity who healed the sick and spoke kindly to prostitutes. The New Testament is replete with Christ criticizing the High Priests, trashing the moneylenders and idolators, calling for a global brotherhood where the poor and suffering would be honored and cared for, condemning nationalist chauvinism in the name of universal Samaritanism, and predicting the end of kingdoms defined by domination and exploitation. Christ's defining prayer calls for this will to be enacted on earth, as it is in heaven—not to await eternity where all will be fixed by divine command. Seen from this standpoint the Tsarist Russia, and indeed much of the world at the time, could only be seen as a fundamentally unjust society. One in which, as Kierkegaard might have said, there are millions of people in idolatrous Christendom, but hardly a single real Christian.[112] This was something far better understood by Dostoevsky's contemporary Leo Tolstoy, who was aware of the sharp contradictions between Christianity and the Christian idolatry and classism of Tsarist Russia. As he put it in his classic *The Kingdom of God Is within You*:

> We are all brothers—yet every morning a brother or sister must empty the bedroom slops for me. We are all brothers, but every morning I must have a cigar, a sweetmeat, an ice, and such things, which my brothers and sisters have been wasting their health in manufacturing, and I enjoy these things and demand them...We are all brothers, but I take a stipend for preaching a false Christian religion, which I do not myself belief in, and which only serves to hinder men from understanding true Christianity...The whole life of the upper classes is a constant inconsistency. The more delicate a man's conscience is, the more painful this contradiction is to him.

Tolstoy's Christianity is vastly more demanding, and in this sense far more authentically aligned with Jesus, than Dostoevsky's winds up being in *The Brothers Karamazov* if Zosima is meant to be our model. Tolstoyan Christianity commands us not simply to love one another in some abstract sense but to actively create a world where we treat each other as brothers and where the barriers to achieving that are overthrown. This includes the class society through which some are profoundly elevated above others, who are left to starve and die in ditches near gilded Churches. It recognizes that a society which professes to be Christian but which commits itself to abstract idols like the nation for which millions are sent to die can only be rightly seen as a mockery of God's intention.

> ...In the name of Christian love Russians were killing their brothers. There was no way to avoid thinking about this. There was no way to ignore the fact that murder was evil and contrary to the most fundamental tenets of any faith. Nonetheless, in the churches they were praying for the success of our weapons, and the teachers of faith looked upon this murder as the outcome of faith. And not only was the murder that came with the war sanctioned, but during the disturbances that followed the war I saw members of the Church, its teachers, monks, and ascetics, condoning the murder of straying, helpless youths. I turned my attention to everything that was done by people who claimed to be Christians, I was horrified.

From a Tolstoyan perspective, the kind of interiority and ethical immediacy of Dostoevsky is not nearly ambitious or radical enough to constitute a genuine Christianity. Dostoevsky's Christianity is an unbalanced one, demanding at the level of psychology but requiring no actions which would threaten or upset the established order. Astonishingly, Dostoevsky is able to achieve this in part through a hagiography of the peasant classes, who are admirable not just for the spiritual acuity but their political docility. Indeed they maintain their purity for Dostoevsky in part because, in his fiction at least, the very poverty and simplicity of peasant life means they have the potential to be uncorrupted by the materialist avarice of the higher orders.

In this respect it is easy to see why Dostoevsky has had such an influence on the political right, and indeed belongs at the very front rank of conservative writers. His fiction inverts the accusations of elitism which so often dog the political right by foregrounding the political quiescence of the peasants and transforming that into a virtue, sharply contrasted with the confused and often corrupted sensibilities of radicals and intellectuals. This would become a recurring motif in the history of the political right which profoundly assisted it in framing reaction in appealingly rural and populist terms without requiring any substantial transformation in the relations of power and domination which define much of society. More importantly Dostoevsky's aesthetics so affectively married undeniable spiritual depth and even profundity with quiescence before systemic injustices that it became possible to even assert that the two are intrinsically connected. In his novels political activism becomes symptomatic of confusion and even super-ficiality, no matter how intelligently defended and carried out. This would have an enduring impact on the political right, which has long tried to compensate for a thinly hidden sense of intellectual inferiority with assertions of spiritual depth relative to radicals and progressives. But in fact very few conservatives have ever managed to even approximate the depths of Dostoevsky, and most of their efforts to emulate it have been embarrassing parodies.

There is no feigning profundity, and much of Dostoevsky's came from an ability to understand and pathologize his opponents borne of deep experience and raw talent. If it is true, as Frank says, that *The Brothers Karamazov* constitutes Dostoevsky's kiss of forgiveness to the radical tradition it is a patronizing, then it is a pitying forgiveness coupled with deep anxiety over the prospect of the fools actually getting the real power they crave and do not deserve.[113] The way for progressives to prove him wrong is to be, like Tolstoy, better human beings than Dostoevsky thought we were.

Conclusion

The early to mid-19th century was one of intellectual resignation and even melancholy for the political right, with its great figures up to Nietzsche largely seeing the triumph of egalitarianism as inevitable. Indeed many of them watched with horror as liberalism gave way to socialism and mass democracy as even more energize and radical challenges to the status quo, and sought to respond and mollify as best they could. However, in the late 19th and early 20th cen-turies, we will see the political right move in two separate directions. The first is a continuation of this resigned conservatism, which engages in an ongoing struggle to preserve what it can by conceding what it must. But the other is a move toward radicalization and counter-attack, which will ultimately lead to the emergence of a systematic and organized far right which poses a threat to much of humanity.

Notes

1 See Albert O. Hirschman. *The Rhetoric of Reaction: Perversity, Futility, Jeopardy.* (Cambridge, MA: The Belknap Press of Harvard University Press, 1991)

2 Eric Hobsbawm. *The Age of Revolution 1789–1848.* (New York, NY: Vintage Books, 1996)

3 See Joseph De Maistre. *Essay on the Generative Principle of Political Constitutions*, trans. (Krakow, Poland: New Direction, 2019) at p. 40

4 Cited in Edmund Fawcett. *Conservatism: The Fight for a Tradition.* (Princeton, NJ: Princeton University Press, 2020) at p. 20

5 See for instance Jonah Goldberg. *Suicide of the West: How the Rebirth of Tribalism, Nationalism and Socialism Is Destroying American Democracy.* (New York, NY: Crown Forum, 2020)

6 See Fredrich Jameson. *Valences of the Dialectic.* (London, UK: Verso Press, 2010)

7 See Slavoj Zizek. *Less than Nothing: Hegel and the Shadow of Dialectical Materialism.* (London, UK: Verso Press, 2012)

8 See Peter Singer. *Hegel: A Very Short Introduction.* (Oxford, UK: Oxford University Press, 2001) at pp. 28, 29

9 Karl Marx. *Capital Volume One: A Critique of Political Economy,* trans. Ernest Mandel (London, UK: Penguin Books, 1990) at p. 103

10 Paul Edward Gottfried. *The Search for Historical Meaning: Hegel and the Postwar American Right.* (Dekalb: North Illinois University Press, 2010)

11 See Karl Popper. *The Open Society and Its Enemies: New One Volume Edition.* (Princeton, NJ: Princeton University Press, 2013) at p. 224

12 Ludwig Von Mises. *Socialism: An Economic and Sociological Analysis.* (Mansfield Center, CT: Martino Publishing, 2012) at p. 398

13 For a seminal example see the critique of historicism in Leo Straus. *Natural Right and History.* (Chicago: University of Chicago Press, 1953). This is well unpacked in Ted V. McAllister. *Revolt Against Modernity: Leo Strauss, Eric Voegelin, and the Search for a Postliberal Order.* (Lawrence: University of Kansas Press, 1995)

14 Ben Shapiro. *The Right Side of History: How Reason and Moral Purpose Made the West Great.* (New York, NY: Broadside Books, 2019) at p. 159

15 Roger Scruton. *Conservatism: An Invitation to the Great Tradition.* (New York, NY: All Points Books, 2017) at p. 55

16 Edmund Fawcett. *Conservatism: The Fight for a Tradition.* (Princeton, NJ: Princeton University Press, 2020) at p. 426

17 See Matthew McManus. "The Politics of Dialectics." Historical Materialism. Online, 2020. https://www.historicalmaterialism.org/book-review/politics-dialectics

18 Georg Hegel. *The Philosophy of History, trans.* J. Sibree. (Amherst, NY: Prometheus Books, 1991) at pp. 103, 104

19 Interestingly this point can be expressed in a less opaque form using the resources of analytical philosophy. Brandom, for instance, points out how the Kantian project as a whole, both in its pure and practical forms, runs into serious difficulties in accounting for the formation of semantic meaning with its strict cognitivist emphasis. His Hegel pragmatism aims to account for this without sacrificing the key Kantian emphasis on sapience as a precondition for both comprehending semantics and engaging in the logical task of semantic self-reflection. While brilliant as a reconstruction of the more theoretically high minded parts of Hegel's project, politically Brandom doesn't have much to say beyond an endorsement of a fairly vanilla liberalism. See Robert Brandom. *A Spirit of Trust: A Reading of Hegel's Phenomenology of Spirit.* (Cambridge, MA: Belknap Press of Harvard University Press, 2019). For my critical reading of the book see Matthew McManus. "The Politics of Dialectics." *Historical Materialism.* Online, 2020. https://www.historicalmaterialism.org/book-review/politics-dialectics

20 Georg Hegel. *The Philosophy of Right,* trans. S.W. Dyde. (Mineola, NY: Dover Classics, 2005) at p. xxxiii

21 Not long after Hegel produced his mature political writings, France underwent another of its routine political transitions with the rise of the Orleanist July Monarchy, where Louis Phillipe styled himself "King of the French" rather than the traditional "King of France"—a reflection of the practical wisdom of Hegel's observations.

22 Immanuel Kant. *Toward Perpetual Peace and Other Essays on Politics, Peace, and History,* trans. David Colclasure. (New Haven, CT: Yale University Press, 2006)

23 See Yoram Hazony. *The Virtue of Nationalism.* (New York, NY: Basic Books, 2018)

24 Georg Hegel. *The Philosophy of Right,* trans. S.W. Dyde. (Mineola, NY: Dover Classics, 2005) at p. 196

25 Georg Hegel. *The Philosophy of Right,* trans. S.W. Dyde. (Mineola, NY: Dover Classics, 2005) at p. 197

26 Georg Hegel. *The Philosophy of Right*, trans. S.W. Dyde. (Mineola, NY: Dover Classics, 2005) at p. 198

27 Georg Hegel. *The Philosophy of Right*, trans. S.W. Dyde. (Mineola, NY: Dover Classics, 2005) at p. 202

28 Georg Hegel. *The Philosophy of Right,* trans. S.W. Dyde. (Mineola, NY: Dover Classics, 2005) at pp. 128, 129

29 Georg. W.F. Hegel. *The Phenomenology of Spirit*, trans. J.N. Findlay. (Oxford, UK: Oxford University Press, 1977)

30 Georg Hegel. *The Philosophy of Right*, trans. S.W. Dyde. (Mineola, NY: Dover Classics, 2005) at p. 201

31 My reading here is partly inspired by Taylor's. Though Taylor's communitarian critique of liberalism has many facets that could be read in a conservative direction, he himself tends to take a left-Hegelian approach. See Charles Taylor. *Hegel and Modern Society*. (Cambridge, UK: Cambridge University Press, 2015)

32 See Roger Scruton. *Conservatism: An Invitation to the Great Tradition*. (New York, NY: All Points Books, 2017)

33 Even Gottfried acknowledges how easy it has proven for leftists to appropriate the dialectical method. See Paul Edward Gottfried. *The Search for Historical Meaning: Hegel and the Postwar American Right*. (Dekalb: North Illinois University Press, 2010)

34 Karl Marx. *Early Writings*, trans. Rodney Livingstone. (London, UK: Penguin Classics, 1992)

35 Robert Brandom. *A Spirit of Trust: A Reading of Hegel's Phenomenology of Spirit*. (Cambridge, MA: Belknap Press of Harvard University Press, 2019)

36 Karl Marx and Friedrich Engels. *The German Ideology*. (Amherst, NY: Prometheus Books, 1998)

37 My friend Borna Radnik has even claimed that Marx is best understood as offering the most profound misreading of Hegel ever given.

38 My interpretation here is guided by Slavoj Zizek. *Less than Nothing: Hegel and the Shadow of Dialectical Materialism*. (London, UK: Verso Press, 2012)

39 Georg Hegel. *The Philosophy of Right*, trans. S.W. Dyde. (Mineola, NY: Dover Classics, 2005) at p. 167

40 Georg Hegel. *The Philosophy of Right*, trans. S.W. Dyde. (Mineola, NY: Dover Classics, 2005) at p. 129

41 Thomas Carlyle. *The Essential Thomas Carlyle*, ed. Kasey James Elliott. (United States: Anarch Books, 2021) at p. 330

42 Even post-modern. The far-right intellectual Curtis Yarvin wrote an online book on Carlyle in which he proudly declared, "I am a *Carlylean*. I'm a Carlylean more or less the way a Marxist is a Marxist. My worship of Thomas Carlyle, the Victorian Jesus, is no adolescent passion—but the conscious choice of a mature adult. I will always be a Carlylean, just the way a Marxist will always be a Marxist." See Curtis Yarvin. *Moldbug on Carlyle*. February 4th, 2010

43 Erich Fromm would undoubtedly have found him a frustrating subject.

44 See Thomas Carlyle. "On Heroes, Hero-Worship, and the Heroic in History" in *The Essential Thomas Carlyle*, ed. Kasey James Elliott. (United States: Anarch Books, 2021)

45 Carlyle was born into a lower- or lower-middle-class family in Southern Scotland, whose talents were recognized early and fortunately cultivated by a complicated and supportive family. This undoubtedly shaped his convictions about the necessity for hard work, coupled with a kind of disdain or mass politicians who wanted to elevate the ordinary person without requiring them to work for it. Or at least work for it in the way someone like Carlyle would value.

46 Thomas Carlyle. "On Heroes, Hero-Worship, and the Heroic in History" in *The Essential Thomas Carlyle*, ed. Kasey James Elliott. (United States: Anarch Books, 2021) at pp. 332–334

47 Thomas Carlyle. "Model Prisons" in *The Essential Thomas Carlyle*, ed. Kasey James Elliott. (United States: Anarch Books, 2021) at p. 384

48 Thomas Carlyle. "Model Prisons" in *The Essential Thomas Carlyle*, ed. Kasey James Elliott. (United States: Anarch Books, 2021) at p. 391

49 Bentham, for instance, was well known for his work on prison reform.

50 Thomas Carlyle. "Chartism" in *The Essential Thomas Carlyle*, ed. Kasey James Elliott. (United States: Anarch Books, 2021) at p. 67

51 F.A. Hayek. *The Constitution of Liberty: The Definitive Edition*. (Chicago, IL: University of Chicago Press, 2011)

52 See the Villanova Center for Liberal Education. "Thomas Carlyle Resartus: Reappraising Carlyle for our Times" November 15th, 2010, https://www.youtube.com/watch?v=QbAlSqGouwY&t=20s

53 This isn't to contemporaneously defend ethical or woke capitalism, but merely to admire Carlyle's ability to see different sides of an argument which is far too frequently grasped from merely one point of view.

54 Thomas Carlyle. "Stump Orator" in *The Essential Thomas Carlyle*, ed. Kasey James Elliott. (United States: Anarch Books, 2021) at p. 484

55 In his review of *Past and Present* Engels claimed, "This is the condition of England," according to Carlyle. An idle landowning aristocracy which "have not yet learned even to sit still and do no mischief," a working aristocracy submerged in Mammonism, who, when they ought to be collectively the leaders of labor, "captains of industry," are just a gang of industrial buccaneers and pirates. A parliament elected by bribery, a philosophy of simply looking on, of doing nothing, of *laissez faire*, a worn-out, crumbling religion, a total disappearance of all general human interests, a universal despair of truth and humanity, and in consequence a universal isolation of men in their own "brute individuality," a chaotic, savage confusion of all aspects of life, a war of all against all, a general death of the spirit, a dearth of "soul," that is, of truly human consciousness: a disproportionately strong working class, in intolerable oppression and wretchedness, in furious discontent and rebellion against the old social order, and hence a threatening, irresistibly advancing democracy—everywhere chaos, disorder, anarchy, dissolution of the old ties of society, everywhere intellectual insipidity, frivolity, and debility. That is the condition of England. Thus far, if we discount a few expressions that have derived from Carlyle's particular standpoint, we must allow the truth of all he says. He, alone of the "respectable" class, has kept his eyes open at least toward the facts, he has at least correctly apprehended the immediate present, and that is indeed a very great deal for an "educated Englishman." Given the acidic words Engels almost invariably reserved for most non-socialist writers, this is high praise indeed. See Friedrich Engels. "A Review of *Past and Present* by Thomas Carlyle." Marxists.Org https://www.marxists.org/archive/marx/works/1844/df-jahrbucher/carlyle.htm

56 Thomas Carlyle. "The Present Time" in *The Essential Thomas Carlyle*, ed. Kasey James Elliott. (United States: Anarch Books, 2021) at p. 363

57 Marx made exactly this objection in his condemnation of Carlyle's pamphlet and he was entirely correct.

58 Thomas Carlyle. *Past and Present*. (Bolton, ON: Anodos Books, 2019) at pp. 93, 94

59 The colonies were a very different matter. See Domenico Losurdo. *Liberalism: A Counter-History,* trans. Gregory Elliot. (London, UK: Verso Press, 2014)

60 Thomas Carlyle. *Past and Present*. (Bolton, ON: Anodos Books, 2019) at pp. 84, 85

61 As with so many of Carlyle's predictions, this one turned out to be incorrect.

62 One could also make a feminist critique of its masculist dynamics. While Carlyle often asserts the need for a kind of macho self-possession and dignity which grant an entitlement to male freedom, this can very easily be lost through dispossession and being reduced to the pursuit of the most basic human needs through any means

necessary. In this case the autonomy granted is lost and one can be treated as a means to another's end.

63 Michel Foucault. *Discipline and Punish: The Birth of the Prison.* (New York, NY: Vintage Books, 1995)

64 See Gordon Marino. *Basic Writings of Existentialism.* (New York, NY: Random House, 2004)

65 See Friedrich Nietzsche. *Twilight of the Idols and the Anti-Christy,* trans. Walter Kaufmann. (London, UK: Penguin Books, 1990) at p. 110

66 Jennifer Burns. *Goddess of the Market: Ayn Rand and the American Right.* (Oxford, UK: Oxford University Press, 2009)

67 See Jordan Peterson. *Beyond Order: 12 More Rules for Life.* (Toronto, ON: Penguin Random House, 2021) at pp. 162, 163

68 The *Diary of a Writer* is a notable exception.

69 This was true even before the post-structuralist "death of the author" which relegates even authorial intention to a secondary concern.

70 See Joseph Frank. *Lectures on Dostoevsky.* (Princeton, NJ: Princeton University Press, 2020) at p. 47

71 See Fyodor Dostoevsky. *Poor Folk,* trans. Constance Garnett (Mineola, NY: Dover Thrift Editions, 2007)

72 See Fyodor Dostoevsky. *Poor Folk,* trans. Constance Garnett. (Mineola, NY: Dover Publications, 2007)

73 See Joseph Frank. *Lectures on Dostoevsky.* (Princeton, NJ: Princeton University Press, 2020)

74 As I shall discuss, one of the criticisms that can be made of his philosophy is its constant affirmation of the Christian viewpoint because of its promise of eternal life. This is never expressed in the crudely egoistic terms of longing for personal survival, though there is undoubtedly a twinge of that, but as a yearning for various forms of love to continue into the future. This is of course a haunting possibility that many have understood as the Christian tradition at its most beautiful; consider Dante's reunification with Beatrice in paradise at the close of his own epic. Or Jesus' reunion with the disciples after his resurrection. But it is very vulnerable to the critique that, through positing the enjoyment of transcendent love and reunification as an eternal reward for moral behavior, Christianity inevitably pollutes its own status as morally superior to the egotistical doctrines of modernity. Indeed in some respects even the profound gentleness and restraint of Zosima are given force in part because of his conviction that he will be rewarded many times over for refraining in this life, giving his spiritual ruminations a kind of crypto-calculative dimension. This isn't to even address the more directly Nietzschean critique that the obverse of this calculus of eternal bliss is the omnipresent threat of hell, to which the less worthy will be condemned and which the saved will relish as a sign of their comparative blessedness. See Ron Srigley "The End of the Ancient World: Dostoevsky's Confidence Game" in Richard Avramenko and Lee Trepanier. *Dostoevsky's Political Thought.* (Plymouth, UK: Lexington Books, 2013)

75 See Joseph Frank. *Lectures on Dostoevsky.* (Princeton, NJ: Princeton University Press, 2020) at p. 59

76 See Fyodor Dostoevsky. *The Idiot,* trans. (Hertfordshire, UK: Wordsworth Editions, 1996)

77 Consider that Ivan Karamazov, Stepan Verkhovensky, Nikolai Stavrogin, and even Rashkolnikov all fall into this paradigm of upwardly aspiring but often poor radical intellectuals and insurrectionaries.

78 Albert O. Hirschman. *The Rhetoric of Reaction: Perversity, Futility, Jeopardy.* (Cambridge, MA: The Belknap Press of Harvard University Press, 1991)

79 Again this is one of the respects in which his work is inferior to Dickens or Orwell—not to mention Fanon, Derrick Bell, and a variety of scholars who focus

on racism—who are vastly more sensitive to the way material deprivation and dis-crimination as often warps the inner life of the poor as endows it with grace. Indeed Dostoevsky would have been wise to have considered James Baldwin's rich exami-nation of the impact of racist elitism on both victim and perpetrator.

80 See Fyodor Dostoevsky. *Devils*, trans. Michael R. Katz. (Oxford, UK: Oxford University Press, 2008) at p. 426

81 Julia Kristeva. *Dostoevsky, or the Flood of Language*, trans. Jody Golding. (New York, NY: Columbia University Press, 2022) at p. 17

82 See Joseph Frank. *Lectures on Dostoevsky.* (Princeton, NJ: Princeton University Press, 2020) at pp. 87, 88

83 Jordan Peterson is an exemplary case study here.

84 Albert O. Hirschman. *The Rhetoric of Reaction: Perversity, Futility, Jeopardy.* (Cam-bridge, MA: The Belknap Press of Harvard University Press, 1991)

85 See Fyodor Dostoevsky. "Notes from Underground" in *Great Short Works of Dosto-evsky*, trans. (New York, NY: Perennial Library, 2004)

86 Something echoed a century and more later in Philip K Dick's *A Scanner Darkly* when Bob Arctor (Fred) ruminates on how inhuman and amoral scanners and cam-eras watch and adjudicate everything he does.

87 See Fyodor Dostoevsky. *Crime and Punishment*, trans. Constance Garnett, 2006. Available at https://www.gutenberg.org/cache/epub/2554/pg2554-images.html

88 The thriller and even the detective genre were already gaining traction through writers like Edgar Allan Poe, whose short story "The Purloined Letter" even in-cludes an ingenious detective who reads as a prototype of later sleuths like Sherlock Holmes and Dostoevsky's own Porfiry

89 This will be a key theme to which I will return.

90 I am drawing the terms psychological hedonism and ethical hedonism from Henry Sidgwick. Dostoevsky would of course have not been familiar with them, but they service as the more technical shorthand for the views discussed. See Henry Sidg-wick. *The Methods of Ethics.* (Indianapolis, IN: Hackett Publishing Company, 1981)

91 Fyodor Dostoevsky. *Crime and Punishment*, trans. Constance Garnett, 2006. Avail-able at https://www.gutenberg.org/cache/epub/2554/pg2554-images.html at Part IV, Chapter Four

92 Alasdair MacIntyre. *After Virtue: A Study in Moral Theory: Third Edition* (Notre Dame, IN: University of Notre-Dame Press, 2007)

93 Consider Rashkolnikov's redemption by Sonya in *Crime and Punishment*, the Underground Man's love of Liza in his titular story, Stepan Verhovensky's late con-version by Sofya Matveyevna, and Dmitri's passionate affair with Grushenka.

94 See Leo Tolstoy. *The Kingdom of God Is within You*, trans. Constance Garnett. (Kshetra Books, 2016)

95 See Fyodor Dostoevsky. *The Brothers Karamazov*, trans. Richard Pevear. (New York, NY: Farar, Straus and Giroux, 2002)

96 There are echoes in both Dmitri and Ivan of Kierkegaard's depiction of the aesthetic life in *Either/Or*, in that (contra Plato to Hegel) both the immediacy of crude pleas-ure and even higher intellectual pursuits are characterized in purely and ultimately unfulfilling aesthetic terms. See Soren Kierkegaard. *Either/Or: A Fragment of Life*, trans. Alastair Hannay. (London, UK: Penguin Books, 1992)

97 Julia Kristeva. *Dostoevsky, or the Flood of Language*, trans. Jody Golding. (New York, NY: Columbia University Press, 2022) at p. 62

98 Fyodor Dostoevsky. *The Idiot*, trans. (Hertfordshire, UK: Wordsworth Editions, 1996)

99 Slavoj Zizek. *The Fragile Absolute: Or Why Is the Christian Legacy Worth Fighting For?* (London, UK: Verso Books, 2009)

100 Fyodor Dostoevsky. *The Brothers Karamazov*, trans. Richard Pevear. (New York, NY: Farar, Straus and Giroux, 2002)

101 I've often thought this was a small error on Dostoevsky's part, since by locating the thematic heart of the book so early he does strip it of some tension. This isn't a mistake one sees in *Crime and Punishment*, where Rashkolnikov's climatic dialogues with Sonya and Porfiry on the nature of his wrongdoing take place near the end and coincide more closely with the climax of the plot and add to its power.

102 One recalls here Kierkegaard's observation about how little modern philosophy has advanced beyond Socrates, or at least beyond the satirized Hegelian tautologies mocked in *Concluding Unscientific Postscript to the Philosophical Fragments*.

103 See Goethe. *Faust: Part One*, trans. David Luke. (Oxford, UK: Oxford University Press, 1998) at p. 15

104 See Ellis Sandoz. "Philosophical Anthropology and Dostoevsky's 'Legend of the Grand Inquisitor'" in *Dostoevsky's Political Thought*, ed. Richard Avramenko and Lee Trepanier. (Plymouth, UK: Lexington Books, 2013)

105 Fyodor Dostoevsky. *The Brothers Karamazov*, trans. Richard Pevear. (New York: Farar, Straus and Giroux, 2002) Book V, Chapter Five

106 See Joseph Frank. *Lectures on Dostoevsky*. (Princeton: Princeton University Press, 2020) at p. 178

107 See Joseph Frank. *Lectures on Dostoevsky*. (Princeton: Princeton University Press, 2020) at p. 179

108 See Ron Srigley. "The End of the Ancient World" in *Dostoevsky's Political Thought*, ed. Richard Avramenko and Lee Trepanier. (Plymouth, UK: Lexington Books, 2013) at pp. 217, 218

109 One can see now how Dostoevsky appeals to conservatives like Jordan Peterson, who stress self-improvement in isolation from or even by contrast to political and social activism. See Jordan Peterson. *Twelve Rules to Life: An Antidote to Chaos*. (Toronto, ON: Random House Canada, 2018)

110 See Soren Kierkegaard. *Either/Or: A Fragment of Life*, trans. Alastair Hannay. (London, UK: Penguin Books, 1992)

111 See Obery Hendricks. *The Politics of Jesus: Rediscovering the True Revolutionary Nature of Jesus' Teachings and How They Have Been Corrupted*. (New York, NY: Three Leaves Publishing, 2006) and Paul Tillich. *The Socialist Decision*. (Eugene, OR: WIPF and Stock Publishers, 1977)

112 Soren Kierkegaard. *Attack on Christendom,* trans. Walter Lowrie. (Princeton, NJ: Princeton University Press, 1968)

113 See Joseph Frank. *Lectures on Dostoevsky*. (Princeton, NJ: Princeton University Press, 2020) at p. 181

PART II
Entering the Wasteland

3

BETWEEN GOD AND BAAL I—CULTURE WARS IN THE EARLY 20TH CENTURY

Conservatism in the 20th Century

There were several distinct forms of the political right that gained ascendency in the early 20th century. The first were the various moderate conservative movements and parties which became regular players in the political tos and fros of liberal and social democracies, alongside their various intellectual supporters. These could undoubtedly have a softly authoritarian streak, and leaders like Richard Nixon and Margaret Thatcher weren't above enthusiastically aiding a foppish array of anti-communist conservative dictators who stretched from Santiago to Manila.[1] Many moderate conservatives were not exactly keen on seeing an expansion of democratic, and certainly economic, rights to any more groups than had already made it into the club.[2] In part as a result of conservative antipathy and challenges many modern representative states are best understood—for better or worse—as polyarchal and limited rather than fully demotic. Even states with democratic features have shown themselves quite willing to extend rights to political equality to a narrow range of beneficiaries, rather than everyone (or most everyone) who falls under the jurisdiction of law. Sadly for those of us who believe in democratic political equality there is nothing conceptually immanent or historically inexorable about its extension. As Robert Dahl puts it:

> As we say, the male citizens of Athens did not believe that the Strong Principle [of political equality] applied to majority of adults in Athens— women, metics, and slaves. In Venice, so much admired by republican theorists from Guicciardini to Rousseau, the nobles extended the principle only to themselves, a tiny minority of the Venetian population. In fact, because the Strong Principle does not specify its own scope, its implications are as powerful for aristocrats as for commoners. The principle could

DOI: 10.4324/9781003307952-6

equally well apply to a democracy with universal suffrage and to aristo-cratic institutions like the House of Lords or the College of Cardinals[3]

This applied through the 20th century as conservative and not a few liberal groups would express conciliation toward certain forms of exclusionary democratic par-ticipation,[4] often successfully halting the spread of democratic forms of organiza-tion within different states and social spheres.[5] Nowhere was this more transparent than at the economic level. Connecting two twinned conservative anxieties about the spread of democracy and challenges to property, the hardest lines in the sand have typically been those drawn around the democratization of the economy and property relations.[6] A shared hostility to economic democracy is one of the rea-sons conservatism aligned successfully with various forms of classical liberalism and then neoliberalism in the mid- and late-20th centuries, even those which were broadly committed to the modernist principles of securing a narrow conception of equality and freedom for all.[7] Whether this alliance should or will continue or break apart in the face of more muscular forms of anti-liberal conservatism is be-yond the scope of this book, though the tea leaves don't augur well.[8]

Nevertheless, there is a real sense in which these forms of moderate conserva-tism followed right-Hegelianism's lead and acclimated themselves to a democratic, liberal, and even modestly social democratic era. There are a few reasons for this. First, as Fawcett puts it, the rout of fascist and other far-right movements during World War II had an ideological impact. In the medium term the military and moral abyss into which Nazism sank had the medium-term effect of discrediting the most illiberal and anti-democratic forms of the political right. Second, the ex-istence of the Soviet bloc—for all its tyranny—posed genuine ideological problems for conservatives and liberals who could be pulled to the left due to hegemonic competition with communist soft power.[9] While this was especially true in conti-nental Europe and the developing world, even the proudly capitalist United States wasn't immune to the pull. Coupled with this was the prestige of the Civil Rights, anti-Apartheid, and anti-colonial movements which could compel even hardened opponents like William F. Buckley to budge on race issues.[10]

And finally, there was a genuinely impressive mutation in moderate conserv-ative thought, which rethought many of its primary fetishes through a well-known ability to conserve through adaptation. Sometimes this would take the form of simply conceding or retreating in the face of liberalism, democracy, and equality. At others it would take the form of developing symbiotic contrasts to the most aggressively radical kinds of left-wing rhetoric and concepts. But others developed genuinely novel ways of thinking through what it means to be on the political right.

T.S. Eliot and the Wasteland of the Modern World

T.S. Eliot was indisputably the greatest poet writing in English in the twentieth century...His social and political vision is contained in all his writings, and has been absorbed and reabsorbed by generations of English and American readers-upon whom it exerts and almost mystical fascination, even when they are moved, as many are, to reject it. Without Eliot, the philosophy of Toryism would have lost all substance during the last century. And, while not explicitly intended it, he set his philosophy on a higher plane, intellectually, spiritually and stylistically, than has ever been achieved by the socialist idea.[11]

T.S. Eliot is a figure who, like Dostoevsky, was a man of genius. He clearly belongs within the conservative tradition even as he sits there more uncomfortably than Roger Scruton might admit. This is because, to a far greater extent than Dostoevsky, Eliot consistently enacts a withdrawal from politics, even as he is inexorably drawn back to it by the vulgarities unleashed by modernity. One can see this continuously in his non-fiction writings, which will often claim to diagnose a profound problem in the culture of a de-Christianizing society and locate its source in a combination of the market, democratic mass society, and the desacralization enacted by technology and science. A more stridently political person would take this as a call to action against liberalism, but Eliot unceasingly pulls back whenever the possibility of program or partisanship threatens to emerge from his criticisms. The following passage from *The Idea of Christian Society* is representative.

> You cannot, in any scheme for the reformation of society, aim directly at a condition in which the arts will flourish: these activities are by-products for which we cannot deliberately arrange the conditions. On the other hand, their decay may always be taken as a symptom of some social ailment to be investigated. The future of art and thought in a democratic society does not appear any brighter than any other, unless democracy is to mean something very different from anything actual. It is not that I would defend a moral censorship: I have always expressed strong objections to the suppression of books possessing, or even laying claim to literary merit. But what is more insidious than any censorship, is the steady influence which operates silently in any mass society organized for profit, for the depression of standards of art and culture.[12]

This is a rich paragraph whose productive ambivalences are largely tapered over by a unified vision sufficiently strong to ride if not master them. However we begin with a sentiment, known to Burke but mostly likely Augustinian in inspiration, that the improvement of society is far less likely than its rot. This is of course a pessimistic and even cynical viewpoint, at odds with even the Millenarian and agapeic forms of Christianity common in less doubt ridden individuals and epochs. Eliot then moves on to a discussion of decay and links it squarely to the roots of democratic society, which he will link to a number of other social institutions and cultural transformations with which he draws an elective affinity to democracy. But Eliot's tone throughout can't even be called resignation, since it is shockingly closer to uncertainty. Anxious about a potentially serious problem he diagnoses within liberal democracies, Eliot reverts to a legalistic liberalism to emphatically decry the censorship of artistic works, even those of questionable merit. This is then followed by rationalizing that the problem is bigger than any law could fix, reverting us to the mode of reasoning at the beginning of the discussion but striking an even more defeatist note. Eliot holds that society's supplication to the market, which in effect engenders mass society and transforms the masses' demands into a ruling behemoth, has reduced high culture to the venal. And there is no clear solution to that—or at least one which doesn't bring with it larger risks that Eliot is unwilling to contemplate.

There are complex reasons for Eliot's taciturnity in politics and culture. One is the special status Eliot ascribes to the transcendent calling of poetry, which is supposed to rise above crude polemics and organic intellectualism. At points Eliot stresses that this isn't to dismiss the value of topical writing or journalism, which has its place and charms.[13] But there is little doubt he doesn't think these kinds of writing are estimable as high art. Of course to alchemically mold the clay of immediacy into the gold of eternity is a goal of many a high artist. One could even adapt such Platonic and Christian aesthetics into a more subjectivist Kantian parlance and say the great artist aspires to universalize the particular. In such cases Eliot likely thought that commonplace polemics or programs that periodize themselves through hyper-specific content would immediately date and debase the work.[14]

A more critical reading of Eliot would be that he falls into the expansive cadre of powdery conservative authors for whom partisan political commentary is already precipitously close to a kind of demotic writing. After all political and cultural commentary must inevitably take into account the needs and feelings of the mediocre mass if it is to be practical and convincing.[15] Faced with devolution to such Samaritan considerations as how people will keep a roof over their heads or how to feed the hungry 5,000, it can be very comforting to retreat into abstract aesthetic and meta-political questions about values where dirt won't crust on your fingers.

But a more important reason for Eliot's taciturnity is he was simply unsure about how to transcend the vulgarities of modernity. In this Eliot undoubtedly spoke for many conservatives not on the far right in the early 20th century. In the opening of his book *The Conservative Mind*—which includes a hagiographic discussion of Eliot—Russell Kirk observes that conservatives had lost nearly every major battled they'd fought between 1789 and the 1950s.[16] While he would never put it in such a brazenly partisan and irreligious vernacular, Eliot would likely agree that all efforts to turn back the tide of egalitarian mass modernity had failed. His unforgettable depiction of the Hollow Men as "paralyzed force, gesture without motion" applies as equally to critics as it does to the straw-headed and sugar-hearted boobs who were now masters of the universe.

One of Eliot's key problems is the same as Prufrock's. Eliot's early training in the British idealist tradition of F.H. Bradley made him aware of the extent to which modernity's guiding philosophy of the subject held that consciousness is enclosed within itself but always desires contact with an "other" outside its own representations.[17] Politically this has the democratic quality of wanting to create a shared world together which simultaneously instantiates both our own subjectivity and that of the others we cooperate with. But such cooperation becomes impossible without a shared language and, more importantly, a sense of the sacred, without which everything devolves into pagan polytheism. Consequently Eliot wanted to restore Christian and English tradition and culture. As Wilson puts it, "Eliot...rearticulated what Burke and Coleridge had initiated: the idea of culture was the quintessentially conservative phenomenon."[18] But this led to the paradox that any "restoration" of a cultural tradition entails a process of conscious invention by the poet or thinker. As Scruton puts it, "Eliot argues that true originality is possibly only within a tradition, and that every tradition must be re-made by the original artist, in the very act of creating something new."[19]

What is never mentioned here by Scruton, but was better understood by Eliot, is precisely how Romantic and modern this sounds. By taking a measure of self-conscious distance toward the tradition, the poet of tradition invariably desublimates and even has to deconstruct it rather than living within it. The poet can hope that this will enrich and rejuvenate the tradition, but there is always the risk of revealing its contingency and delegitimating the foundations. Tradition itself becomes plastic. This is very different from the rather unself-conscious idylls put forward by someone like Burke or De Maistre and testifies to the vast loss that occurred in the conservative confrontation with egalitarian modernity.

Now, rather like how a Marxist might insist that contradiction can only be overcome through praxis, a traditionalist might respond to the paradox by adopting the fully revolutionary claim that to save old traditions something radically new must be introduced. And sometimes Eliot seems attracted to this prospect, despite its perils. As he put it in "Little Gidding": "What we call the beginning is often the end/And to make an end is to make a beginning/The end is where we start from." In more dramatic moments in Eliot's poetry one finds the rather proto-Heideggerian insight that a restoration can only be achieved by beginning again, which would necessarily be destructive rather than reparative act. Such a conservative radicalism of course attracted Ezra Pound to fascism, which Eliot wisely rejected as too plebian and too pagan in its inspiration for the man of taste. In the end Eliot settled for a more modest politics of elitist artistic community committed to the aesthetics of Christian society and criticizing the ugliness of the modern world and its democracy. As he put it in *The Use of Poetry and the Use of Criticism*:

> When the poet finds himself in an age in which there is no intellectual aristocracy, when power is in the hands of a class so democratized that

while still a class it represents itself to the whole nation; when the only alternatives seem to be to talk to a coterie or soliloquize, the difficulties of the poet and the necessity of criticism become greater.[20]

Except is it so ugly, and is Eliot in fact particularly Christian? Certainly the seriousness with which Eliot took the idea of a Christian society might suggest that he is. But it is a Christianity and a Christian society which appeal to him for philosophical and aesthetic reasons rather than human and material ones. And a faith whose central figure is a God who becomes human suffers and dies for his flock while even momentarily coming to doubt his own legitimacy on the Cross is not well understood on these lines.[21] Indeed I'd venture to say the kind of aesthetic Christianity advanced by Eliot is a misunderstanding of the faith. It isn't Christ's mercy, humanity, or justice that attracts Eliot to religion—that things should be just on earth as they are in heaven. It is Christ's transcendence, glory, and kingdom—the Dantean universe where paradiso and inferno equally are the creation of an eternal love which orders, ranks, and condemns as much or more than it forgives and saves. It certainly isn't the Christ who came to level kingdoms, castigated the rich, and proclaimed that the "the wretched of the earth [will] learn that God is on their side."

In other words it is really Aristotelian-inflected scholasticism which is to Eliot's taste. Eliot is so committed to the Scholastic vision of a hierarchically complementary and orderly universe that he will even correctly castigate other conservatives for wanting to keep elements of Christian moralism while abandoning its metaphysical grandeur for scientific materialism.

> To justify Christianity because it provides the foundation of morality, instead of showing the necessity of Christian morality from the truth of Christianity, is a very dangerous inversion; and we may reflect, that a good deal of the attention of totalitarian states has been devoted, but a steadiness of purpose not always found in democracies, to providing their national life with a foundation of morality-the wrong kind perhaps, but a good deal more of it. It is not enthusiasm, but dogma, that differentiates a Christian from a pagan society.[22]

Ironically this is a devastating argument against many later conservatives who will try to defend on Christian dogma on the basis that a non-egalitarian Christian morality is attractive, particularly post-liberals and self-help gurus like Jordan Peterson. But even Eliot's conception of morality as a kind of ascription of divine meaning guts it of tangibility and practicality. Eliot can hang with the noble poets of England if he wishes, but Christ walked among the prostitutes, lepers, beggars, and tax collectors of Galilei. Eliot's continuous disdain for "the cheap and rapid-breeding cinema" which will lead the "lower classes…to drop into the same state of protoplasm as the bourgeoise," his concern for the decadence that comes from sufficient material prosperity to ward off disaster, and his preference for exceptional over common people suggest he would have little sympathy for Christ's own social tastes.[23] Predictably the side of Christian morality stressed by him is integration into the greater cosmology of Thomism, where human activity assumes sublime aesthetic qualities through participation in God's plan. It is rarely anything as concrete as the cruelty of those institutions that make up society, or what we justly owe to one another as moral equals in God's eyes. Sometimes this leads Eliot to the crudest forms of elitism married to Hirschman's perversity rhetoric:

> By destroying traditional social habits of the people, by dissolving their natural collective consciousness into individual constituents, by licensing the opinions of the most foolish, by substituting instruction for education, by encouraging cleverness rather than wisdom the upstart rather than the qualified, by fostering a notion of getting on to which the alternative is hopeless apathy, Liberalism can prepare the way for that which is its own negation: the artificial, mechanised or brutalised control which is a desperate remedy for its chaos.[24]

In moments like this we realize Eliot forgets that a Christian society would be one where the least among us is my neighbor to the utmost.[25]

Michael Oakeshott's Critique of Rationalism

> To be conservative, then, is to prefer the familiar to the unknown, to prefer the tried to the untried, fact to mystery, the actual to the possible, the limited to the unbounded, the near to the distant, the sufficient to the superabundant, the convenient to the perfect, present laughter to utopian bliss. Familiar relationships and loyalties will be preferred to the allure of more profitable attachments; to acquire and to enlarge will be less important than to keep, to cultivate and to enjoy; the grief of loss will be more acute than the excitement of novelty or promise. It is to be equal to one's own fortune, to live at the level of one's own means, to be content with the want of greater perfection which belongs alike to oneself and one's circumstances. With some people this is itself a choice; in others it is a disposition which appears, frequently or less frequently, in their preferences and aversions, and is onto itself chosen or specifically cultivated. Now, all this is represented in a certain attitude towards change and innovation; change denoting alterations we have to suffer and innovation those we design and execute.
>
> (Michael Oakeshott, "On Being Conservative")

Perry Anderson said the four greatest right-wing philosophers of the 20th century were Leo Strauss, Carl Schmitt, F.A. Hayek, and Michael Oakeshott. Of these Anderson stressed that Oakeshott was undoubtedly the least known, and commented on how his passing in 1990 generated barely a ripple even in the conservative press. This was in spite of his being the "most original thinker of post-War conservatism" and even the "wayward voice of an archetypical English conservatism…"[26] No doubt Oakeshott himself would have been little surprised at this reception, even if his reputation has only grown exponentially over the years.[27]

Oakeshott was an unusual personality and figure. His father was a socialist and part of a Fabian group which played an important formative role in the Labor Party. While Oakeshott apparently shared some of these predispositions early on, the technocratic and scientist mode into which British socialism sank wore at his early Romantic enthusiasm.[28] As a young man Oakeshott rejected the virtually ubiquitous analytical turn in contemporary philosophy spearheaded by Bertrand Russell and came under the spell of Hegelian-influenced British idealism. Despite his work assuming more recognizably Tory forms by the mid-20th century, this early influence never goes away and one can detect the shadow of Hegel falling over Oakeshott's important analyses of Hobbes. After chalking up a solid fighting record in World War II, Oakeshott seems to have been allergic to pursuing a career in the more prestigious Oxbridge institutions. Instead he opted to teach at the London School of Economics, where he continued to lecture until the 1980s. Not exactly a precursor to the MeToo movement Oakeshott had many affairs and several marriages, including a dalliance with Iris Murdoch and his son's girlfriend. His lifestyle was an unusual mixture of bohemianism and luddism, with Oakeshott hosting legendary drinking parties that would last well into the morning while on the surface living a contemplative life in the country. A man after my own heart really.

These biographical ambivalences are by no means separable from Oakeshott's intellectual legacy, which often seems to tug in different directions and has been interpreted as variably liberal and conservative. Even an effort to explain these away by associating Oakeshott with the legendary pragmatism of British Toryism runs askew, since at various points he rejected partisan involvement and even refused honors from Margaret Thatcher.

Oakeshott was above all else a man of affect, and one can conceive of his work as contending with the desacralization of existence characteristic of modernity. Like Carlyle and Eliot, this eventually assumes anti-progressive and anti-democratic forms. But unlike them Oakeshott makes few appeals to religiosity or mythologization, aside from those of his own construction. One might be tempted to construe Oakeshott as a strict Burkean, particularly given his famous condemnations of rationalism and his traditionalism. And undoubtedly there are parallels. But Oakeshott's philosophy is considerably more individualistic than Burke's. A part of this is a difference in epoch. Burke wrote when the egalitarian forces of modernity had just erupted and posed a potentially lethal threat to the Ancien regimes of Europe. In such historical times, a single resolute statesman might still hope to make a substantial difference. Oakeshott came of age during the era of totalitarianism abroad and technocratic managerialism at home, and though his writing resists and lays blame for these trends he rarely seems optimistic that things might be turned around.

But unlike Eliot, Oakeshott also doesn't let this bring him down. He continuously emphasizes the open textured nature of existence, wherein new choices might bring about small-scale reconfigurations. At the very least it was still possible that the pursuit of what Oakeshott called "adventurous" lifestyles as an end in themselves might inadvertently bring about a reordering of political existence.[29] But of course most people wouldn't aspire to this, and much of Oakeshott's resentment is directed against the fact that uninteresting masses have gained so much political power. This inevitably leads to the emergence of a technocratic bureaucracy working in blandly efficient way to secure their modest pleasures.

At the epicenter of Oakeshott's work is a critique of rationalism. Like many such critiques it contains a paradoxical tension.[30] Despite his romantic investment in the choice of leading an adventurous life and even becoming a kind of singular individual Oakeshott is deeply critical of the rationalist idea that we are purely self-creating individuals. Or that by extension political associations are nothing more than the plastic creations of hyper-theoretical self-conscious actors. Part of this is because, conceived in this way, rationalism becomes horizontally limitless in its aspiration to understand and reorder the world. While at the same time it collapses any vertical hierarchy where the experience of certain facets of reality enjoys a higher aesthetic status. This includes dismissing the traditionalist practices and ways of experiencing and "understanding" reality, which often ascribed to existence an extra-empirical meaning bound up in the ordinary conditions of life which gave it a thickness of meaning lacking in the rationalist approach. To the rationalist all modes of experience operate at the same flat level. Consequently the only kind of understanding modern rationalism acknowledges is technical and scientific knowledge, which claims to exhaust what we can "know" about the world with certainty even as they gut it of the various forms of meaning-making which take place within it. More worryingly rationalism also litigates against forms of knowledge which don't conform to its leveling schema.

Ironically this rationalist quest for certainty leads to a profound ignorance of the actual significance of the traditionalist activities which order real human beings, which make no sense within the framework. So the quest for rational knowledge about the world requires denying huge swathes of inconvenient facts about the social world. The result is that rationalists in fact understand very little about humanity. So they set about, at best clumsily and at worst tyrannically, trying to bring order to something they do not understand by forcing it to conform to what little they do happen to understand. It becomes a kind of fundamentalist project insistent on perfectibility, made all the uglier through a continuous negation of its own dependence on faith.[31]

Rationalism marries very easily to the crudest kind of utilitarian calculus, which replicates the rationalist's epistemic leveling at the aesthetic and normative levels. Individual choices about which desires are worth pursuing are regarded as purely a matter of subjective taste. For classical liberals in the vein of Locke it was left to individuals to pursue their desires, since the classical liberal tradition demarcated sharply between the political role of the state in protecting personal autonomy and individual's natural right to pursue happiness and property exclusively within the market. And of course utilitarian push for extending state power to advance happiness in the 19th and 20th provoked widespread backlash as a betrayal of the liberal ethos.[32] But for Oakeshott this was both scientifically and historically naïve. Even Locke had already gone too far beyond Hobbes in his endorsement of a representative government accountable to the aggregated interests of the masses, limited by the thin fig leaf of respect for natural rights.[33] Once belief in natural rights faded away, as it inevitably would in a secular age, nothing stood in the way of demanding technocratic management by state power to manage and satisfy desires as efficiently as possible. This aligns with the democratic spirit of the era, since naturally the simplest way for state actors to adduce the most beneficent utilitarian outcome is to ask what most people want. But the end result of this is that the state and its administration gradually inflate and assume more and more control over life to complete this task, eventually leveling out forms of life and behavior seen as hostile or even unnecessary in the pursuit of its instrumental ends. As Elizabeth Campbell Corey puts it:

> Such is the politics of faith. Human life is understood to be a condition in which people strive for a mundane perfection not merely individually, but as a society. In this striving they are oriented and organized by a government that steps in to enforce a plan. Dissent is discouraged, for who could doubt the goodness of transforming the human condition from one of manifest ills to one of perfection? The great virtue of this style of politics — and indeed, its great vice, from Oakeshott's perspective — is that it pursues perfection in one direction. It posits a "single road" and is "content with the certainty that perfection lies wherever it leads." The politics of faith presumes not only that "human power is sufficient... to procure salvation," but that perfection denotes a "single, comprehensive condition of human circumstances.[34]

There is certainly something to Oakeshott's epistemic critique of the early Enlightenment's quest for certainty. In terms of its moral implications much of the force of "Rationalism in Politics" comes less from the specificity of its arguments and more from its appeal to an extraordinary form of the Hirschman's "perversity thesis." Rationalism sets out for certainty and perfectibility, but ends in ignorance and tyranny, or, what may be even worse, pure boredom.[35] By horizontally flattening the experience of life through reason, the rationalist robs it of dimension and excitement. By contrast Oakeshott's reification of the traditional modes of understanding embodied in practices seems beatified next to the icy epistemic disintegration enacted by rationalistic imperialism. Moreover, unlike rationalistic leveling, traditional and practical forms of understanding are chauvinistic and exclusive. They may well only be accepted by those who participate in a given practice and regard it as moral, while appearing obscure or even incomprehensible to everyone else. This not only gives traditional modes of knowledge a kind of beauty, in the Burkean sense of being localized and small products of human creation, but also connects them with higher and more sublime qualities through being an often unconscious and continuous creation carried on as a particularized inheritance from our past.

Oakeshottian Idealism and Human Conduct

Oakeshott's critique of rationalism is undoubtedly his most famous contribution to political thought. But it can only be fully appreciated in the context of the systematic philosophy presented in *On Human Conduct*. Undoubtedly Oakeshott's greatest, but most mercurial work, it draws heavily on Aristotle, Hobbes, and above all Hegel and can be compared fairly to the *Phenomenology of Spirit* in terms of its structure if not the book's ambitions. The *Phenomenology* tells a revolutionary story of spirit's passage to ever higher forms of historical freedom. The chief lesson of *On Human Conduct* is the opposite; while human beings are irrevocably defined by their historical situatedness there is no teleological end point to which human life aspires and to which the present can be compared. The practices and very norms of humanity therefore obtain a kind of radical contingency, stripped of any dialectical necessity and so from the power of negation. In the end the effect of reading *On Human Conduct* might be compared to the lesson Wittgenstein drew from the study of language; once one has learned its lessons, the philosophically attuned decides to leave the world exactly as it is but engage with it somewhat wiser and more contented.

The critical thrust of the early parts of *On Human Conduct* is directed against the danger posed by the philosopher critical of practical activity. The philosopher becomes theoretically aware of the idealized structures which generate contingent practices and forms of know-how to a degree the immediate participants do not. He occupies what we might call a (c) meta-conscious level above even the (b) self-conscious reflection of participants engaged in a practice who are assessing its efficacy according to normative standards immanent within it and well above (a) the kinds of immediate application of practical knowledge which requires no reflection at all and may even be slowed by it. This grants the philosopher an elite status relative to the ordinary citizens since he apprehends the structure of practical knowledge in general, while they apprehend it only in its particular reified forms.[36] This might make Oakeshott sound like a Marxist. But unlike a critical theorist Oakeshott does not want the masses to become politicized through adopting a hyper-theoretical sense of remove from traditionalism. This is in part because that constitutes a form of alienation which might be corrosive, but also because such alienation is a precondition for wanting to use critical reason to remake the world in rationalistic ways. It is this possibility that Oakeshott wants to preclude at all costs, even if that means sacrificing the most hallowed tropes of the Western philosophical tradition. Oakeshott even chastises for rarefied modes of Platonic analysis when they seek not just to highlight the contingency of the shadows of the cave but condemn them. This apologia for the cave demonstrates to what extent Oakeshott is willing to go to combat the hyper-rationalistic theoretical tendency.

> And if, in taking part in legal proceedings (as Plato said he might), he were to brush on one side the cave-understanding conditionality of 'the truth, the whole truth, and nothing but the truth' and were to insist that matters be delayed while the question What is truth? Was explored, or if he were to lecture judge and jury about the postulates of justice, those concerned might be expected to become a trifle restless. Before long the more perceptive of the case dwellers would begin to suspect that, after all, he was not an interesting theorist but a fuddled and pretentious 'theoretician' who should be sent on his travels again, or accommodated in a quiet home. And the less patient would be disposed to run him out of town as an impudent mountebank. In short, what the cavedwellers resent is not the theorist, the philosopher (him they are inclined to admire even if they have not much use for his concern with postulates), but the 'theoretician,' the *philosophe,* the 'intellectual'; and they resent him, not because they are corrupt or ignorant but because they know just enough to recognize an imposter when they meet them.[37]

In other words, it is not the analysis of a practice as contingent and applicable only to its particular context which is the issue. That's just the reality of the world revealed by meta-conscious modes of ideal theorizing. It is the *philosophe's* weaponization of this contingency by perversely aligning it with doxa, heteronomy, ideology, or discourse which is where the problem lies. This becomes even worse when the untruth of doxastic understanding and the forms of civil condition which emerge from it come to be contrasted with the rationalistic ideal of a higher truth and justice compared to which real practices will always fall short. This leads inexorably toward utopian thinking and the aspiration to perfect the world.

Oakeshott's account of the civil condition that follows is radically historicist to a degree unimaginable to Hegel, but likely very familiar to someone like Strauss.[38] Human association is conceived not as a matter of "affection, of a choice to be related in the pursuit of a common substantive purpose, or of the conscription in such an enterprise, and not that of self-moved bargainers negotiating with one another for the satisfaction of their chosen egoistic or altruistic wants" but solely as a matter of a "practice or language of intercourse" which is participated in by intelligent individuals for no higher end than those intrinsic to the practice itself.[39] These practices and their intrinsic ends may vary widely in space and time, and consequently so may the system of morals which bind people together vary widely.

That there should be many [moral] languages in the world, some perhaps with familial likeness in terms of which there may be a profitable
exchange of expressions, is intrinsic to their character. This plurality cannot be resolved by being understood as so many contingent and regret-
table divergencies from a fancied perfect and universal moral intercourse
(a law of God, a utilitarian critical morality, or a so called 'rational morality.') But it is hardly surprising that such a resolution should have been
attempted: human being are apt to be disconcerted unless they feel themselves to be upheld by something more substantial than the emanations of
their own contingent imaginations. This unresolved plurality teases the
monistic yearnings of the muddled theorist, it vexes a moralist with ecu-
menical leanings, and it may disconcert an unfortunate who, having 'lost'
his morality (as others have been known to 'lose' their faith), must set about
constructing for himself and is looking for uncontaminated 'rational' principles out of which to make it. But it will reassure the modest mortal with
a self to disclose and a soul to make who needs a familiar and resourceful
moral language…to do it in and who is disinclined to be unnerved because
there are other such languages to which he cannot readily relate his own.[40]

Looking past the genteel langue, this is a stunning paragraph. It holds to a
meta-ethical position so radically relativist and anti-foundationalist that almost
no other conservative, and indeed not even a leftist historicist like Foucault (with
his ethics of the self), let alone Marx (the Aristotelian-Hegelian advocate for
cooperative human flourishing), would endorse it. It adopts the more prescrip-
tive language of liberal pluralism about moral views on the good life, historicizes
it into a broader meta-ethical description of the utter incommensurability of
moral views, and then offers no resolution to the problems raised other than a
kind of pragmatic acceptance. Anyone who becomes discontented with this is
chided for a dispositional lack of conservative modesty.

Taken seriously this kind of radical moral pluralism could very well open
the gate to endless forms of anti-social and nihilistic behavior. The only barrier would be dispositional temperament. And of course Oakeshott suggests we
be modest in accepting the radically foundation-less contingency of our moral
views without succumbing to nihilism while at the same time not seeking to
disrupt others living their own truth by an excess of zealous universalism and
reformism.[41] But any such dispositional barriers would be extremely thin. Oakeshott chides the rationalist for her leveling morality, but at least she is committed
to an ideal universal belief system against which actual human behavior can be
continually checked. This imposes an intrinsic moral constraint on action and is
ironically far sterner stuff than the conservative modesty Oakeshott puts forward,
which could be tossed aside merely in the event that one doesn't adopt such a
disposition toward the moral language one is educated in. From a purely philosophical standpoint all Oakeshott can do is pathologize a refusal to adapt to one's

moral language and practices or attempt to zealously impose one's own moral language and practices on others as a kind of arrogance.

Yet both realistically and theoretically this is thin beer. It is unrealistic since such a pathologization depends on implausible views of human nature. If in fact the moral language I inherited is contingent and foundationless, why shouldn't I feel licensed to ignore or remake them if they don't accord with my wishes? What makes the moral language I am brought up to understand more authoritative than the one I might create if both are equally contingent, but the latter is more to my taste and I want to see others adopt it? It is theoretically implausible since Oakeshott's metaethical insistence that morality is simply the internal acceptance of a moral language and practices which cannot be compared to external standards doesn't need to lead to such a radical acceptance of pluralism. It would always be open to an Oakeshottian individual to simply redefine any aspiration to impose their own moral language and practices on others as an internal aspiration of the practice itself rather than in terms of universal rationalism. One could easily accept the claim that my practices are radically contingent meta-ethically while still holding that an imperative of our-oh so contingent mores is that everyone should adopt them, and moreover that the use of compulsion is permissible in such an "adventure."[42] "Throughout history my people have deigned to impose our particular way of life on others" is by no means an impossible statement in the Oakeshottian universe.

Oakeshott's answer to these irresolvable theoretical problems is to revert to the Hobbesian appeal to state power, which operates over and above the disparate and relativized conceptions of the good operative within its boundaries to maintain order. But it is not a Hobbesian state which is imaginatively conceived as the creation of its members, let alone one which is justified along utilitarian lines as an instrument for protecting their most foundational desire to live a long and pleasure-filled life. Indeed Oakeshott largely disregards the very notion of citizenship and social freedom in terms of rights and active political participation. Political freedom lies in internal participation with the practices set by the conditions of civil association and

> cannot be increased by the enjoyment of a right to participate in the care and custody of respublica; it is not decreased by the absence of such a right; and those who have the authority to make or to amend the provisions of a respublica are neither more nor less 'free' than those who do not.[43]

It is again the thoroughly historicized state which also happened to emerge through contingent processes, but whose power and longevity is sufficient to warrant a belief in its authority for all effective purposes. Indeed Oakeshott chastises those "modern" states which seek to justify their authority through an appeal to their legitimacy. He mocks the "most implausible and gimcrack beliefs which few can find convincing for more than five minutes together and which bear little or no relation to the governments concerned: the 'sovereignty of the people' or of 'the nation,' 'democracy,' 'majority rule,' 'participation' etc."[44] This gets the matter backward, since it again implies that legitimacy is some transhistorical and rational foundation to which the authority of the state is beholden and its operations can be meaningfully compared. But in fact it is the exercise of power which establishes authority and so legitimates itself in the opinions of those it rules. Power is its own argument.

> This conspicuous failure of most modern European states (and all the imitation states elsewhere in the world) to acquire governments with firmly recognized authority has provoked the belief that authority is of no account. Governments have become inclined to commend themselves to their subjects merely in terms of their power and their incidental achievements, and their subjects have become inclined to look only for this recommendation. Indeed, it is long since *this rejection of the idea of authority began to infect of thought about the constitution of government.*[45]

This puts Oakeshott in an unusual position. Since power is what establishes authority and legitimates itself, is any such system might be acceptable or are there conditions where one might rebel against it? As a radical relativist but also a conservative, Oakeshott is ambivalent on these points. His own dispositional preference is once again for a kind of modest acquiescence to the way things are at the state level to avoid nihilistic anarchy, backed by Hobbesian power, but coupled with an abiding distaste for any totalizing exercise of state power which seeks to annihilate the pluralism of moral practices and beliefs in the world as a whole or even domestically. And Oakeshott admits that in such (and other) circumstances there may be those who challenge the authority of the state and even want to overthrow it, and that he has some sympathy for them. But the question remains in the name of what are they trying to overthrow such a totalizing state? It cannot be because it is illegitimate, because even a moral language which commits itself to the extermination of all other moral languages and their participants cannot be criticized from a more foundational standpoint. Oakeshott can only chastise the totalizing application of state power for a lack of modesty. The irony is that a moral universalist committed, say, to endorsing pluralism for foundationalist reasons can offer a far sterner defense against state power than Oakeshott himself can.

In the end Oakeshott's thinking embodies a kind of conservatism which winds up endorsing philosophical perspectives more radical than those of any liberalism or even progressivism to date. His deracinated Hegelianism is so stripped of universal normative content that it winds up describing the world through a dialectic that acknowledges and accepts without ever being able to affirm. Though Oakeshott would dread the word, he winds up producing something very much like the positivism Marx detected in Hegel's philosophy of right: one that immanently nods to power without fully endorsing or criticizing since either endorsement or criticism would entail appealing to some more external ideal which doesn't exist. To the extent there is a Hegelian moral in Oakeshott, it is a suspicion of negation in favor of a modest affection for the familiarity of practices we understand and accept while recognizing their contingency. Though even there it is one that acknowledges the finite power of such affection before negation's ultimately infinite power.[46] Given this it is no wonder Oakeshott's work became so abidingly popular in a time period where conservatism was so much on the defense, since it is so resolutely defensive.

Patrick Devlin on the Enforcement of Morals[47]

Lord Patrick Devlin is chiefly remembered for his infamous debate with the legal positivist H.L.A. Hart on the subject of decriminalizing homosexuality, and his arguments for the enforcement of "morals" through law. This has become tragically ironic in the face of credible accusations from Devlin's daughter which allege that he sexually abused her many times when she was young. This was atop disturbing forms of emotional manipulation and authoritarian control within the family.[48] It will be useful to remember this backdrop when considering Devlin's arguments, since it helps foreground the considerations of power and privilege which are yawningly absent in his writings about the importance of preserving traditional sexual hierarchies. In this respect Devlin is an important figure for understanding how very often the populist kind of conservatism that Devlin advanced, for all its rustic appeals to the common man, is the ideology of maintaining power without accountability or even demonstrable utility.[49]

One of the distinctive features of Devlin's arguments is the extent to which they enact a synthesis of two seemingly incompatible positions. However Devlin's arguments about homosexuality and morality reveal the extent to which he has completely internalized—at least in an official capacity—the most radical forms of socio-historical relativism to emerge in modern era. Except for rare flourishes here and there, his (Devlin's) writings don't build substantive case as to why homosexuality should be considered repugnant.[50] Even more remarkably, given the broader debate around homosexuality concerning whether a largely Christian population should enforce an illiberal Christian morality, Devlin even acknowledges that the presence of different religions (not to mention differences within Christian denominations) complicates the question of the faith's truth. He grants that other states may hold different opinions on the matter, and within their jurisdiction it is their right to decide which religion and morality to hold and enforce.

In this respect Devlin is vulnerable to Straussian accusations of being under the spell of historicism while lacking even the respectability of Oakeshott's sophisticated Anglo-Hegelianism. In *The Enforcement of Morals*, Devlin's global arguments for a kind of socio-historical relativism often consist of armchair anthropology. Devlin observes that there are different conceptions of religious morality in the world and seems to acknowledge the impossibility, or at least great difficulty, of deciding between them on the basis of any transcendent or even rationalist conception of truth. He observes that

> ...between the great religions of the world, of which Christianity is only one, there are much wider differences. It may or may not be right for the State to adopt one of these religions as the truth, to found itself upon its doctrines and to deny to any of its citizens the liberty to practise any other. If it does, it is logical that should use the secular law wherever it thinks it necessary to enforce the divine. If it does not, it is illogical that it should concern itself with morals as such. But if it leaves matters of religion to private judgement, it should logically leave matters of morals also. A State which refuses to enforce Christian beliefs has lost the right to enforce Christian morals.[51]

Devlin later props these historicist and localist observations with a more functionalist argument about the role social morality plays in serving as what Ian Shapiro aptly called a kind of "glue" which binds society together.[52] Devlin himself prefers architectonic metaphors, referring to a house which cannot stand without the stability provided by shared belief.

> What makes a society of any sort is community of ideas, not only political ideas but also ideas about the way its members should behave and govern their lives; these latter ideas are its morals. Every society has a moral structure as well as a political one: or rather, since that might suggest two independent systems, I should say that the structure of every society is made up both of politics and morals. Take, for example, the institution of marriage. Whether a man should be allowed to take more than one wife is something about which every society has to make up its mind one way or the other. In England we believe in the Christian idea of marriage and therefore adopt monogamy as a moral principle. Consequently the Christian institution of marriage has become the basis of family life and so part of the structure of our society. It is there not because it is Christian. It has got there because it is Christian, but it remains there because it is built into the house in which we live and could not be removed without bringing it down. The great majority of those who live in this country accept it because it is the Christian idea of marriage and for them the only true one.[53]

The "for them the only true one" line is quite telling, constituting a retreat into moral subjectivism and relativism so striking that it is hard to see how Devlin imagines his perspective would possibly be enough to secure a foundation for society. It is also remarkably idealist in its orientation. So what we have in Devlin is a paradoxical mess: ideas hold society together. Not true ideas, since we have no way of ascertaining transcendent or even rational truths. But ideas whose only stability lies in their being widely accepted in spite of their lack of foundations;

indeed it is precisely this foundationless quality which requires an intensification of faith through the employment of state power to consecrate them.

This last point is important since it leads us to one of the few moral absolutes which surface in Devlin's argument: society's right to perpetuate itself.[54] At the core of his whole position is an anxiety that if faith in shared morality falters and/or people no longer believe the state is entitled to enforce a shared morality, society will collapse. That he could have reached such a Hobbesian sounding position shouldn't surprise us, since he starts from a philosophical standpoint toward morality whose relativism absolutely echoes Hobbes' in *Leviathan*.[55] And like Hobbes, Devlin recognizes that for this absolute right to social order to be secure, it will be necessary for the state to uphold a shared public religion—even if it turns out that the rational arguments for any such religion don't hold water. It is, in Schmittian terms, a political theology. But one which, like Hobbes, concedes quite a bit to liberalism.[56]

Devlin operates pretty clearly in the tradition of British "ordered liberty" conservatism, and so continuously tips his hat to the importance of individual liberty and the independence of the private life. This sits uneasily next to his assertions about the need for a functional moral glue to hold society together which can be coercively enforced by the state, even against the private dispositions of some of its members. Philosophically it is very uncomfortable relying on a kind of Hobbesian subjectivist relativism with some historicist flourishes one minute, before arguing the subjective moral values of some are outweighed by the functionalist need to enforce a shared morality the next. Devlin only manages to prevent a fall into transparent contradiction by reinscribing the moral absolute of society's right to preserve itself through the enforcement of architectonic morality into his argument. This is a sufficiently pressing concern that might be capable of doing the heavy lifting Devlin wants it to. But one is immediately struck by the objections of Hart and Dworkin that by conceding so much to modernist relativism Devlin has backed himself into a corner where he must show that a failure to enforce any particular moral norm in fact poses an existential threat to society. Anything else would seem, as Hart observed, to impose restrictions comparable to slavery on the behavior of individuals which causes no direct harm to another but merely provokes in them irrational feelings of disgust or disapproval.[57] Needless to say Devlin did not achieve this in *The Enforcement of Morals*, and indeed offers no evidence that decriminalizing homosexuality posed such a threat. In hindsight we can see how pitifully frightened and inaccurate were his worries that allowing gay and lesbian couples the same freedoms to argue over Netflix as heterosexuals would prove such a moral shock that it would bring the whole rotten edifice down.

Devlin and the Origins of Modern Right-Populism

> How is the law-maker to ascertain the moral judgements of society? It is surely not enough that they should be reached by the opinion of the majority; it would be too much to require the individual assent of every citizen.

English law has evolved and regularly uses a standard which does not depend on the counting of the heads. It is that of the reasonable man. He is not to be confused with the rational man. He is not expected to reason about anything and his judgement may be largely a matter of feeling. It is the viewpoint of the man in the street-or to use an archaism familiar to all lawyers-the man in the Clapham omnibus. He might also be called the right-minded man. For my purpose I should like to call him the man in the jury box, for the moral judgement of society must be something about which any twelve men or women drawn at random might after discussion be expected to be unanimous. This was the standard the judges applied in the days before Parliament was as active as it is now and when they laid down rules of public policy. They did not think of themselves as making law but simply as stating principles which every right-minded person would accept as valid. It is what Pollock called 'practical morality', which is based not on theological or philosophical foundations but 'in the mass of continuous experience half-consciously or unconsciously accumulated and embodied in the morality of common sense.[58]

(Patrick Devlin, *The Enforcement of Morals*)

So far Devlin's arguments have been most interesting for demonstrating how he has internalized and reconfigured very modern forms of socio-historical relativism for fundamentally conservative purposes. While the result is an intellectually unsound project prompted by an issue that would be utterly decided against Devlin mere years later, it does demonstrate an important feature of the political right. Namely, its sometimes extraordinary creativity in appropriating the philosophies and styles of egalitarian modernity and deploying them for inegalitarian ends. In this case discriminating against LGBTQ individuals.

The cleverness of Devlin's social theorizing lies in its ability to concede to a soft relativism about values while weaponizing that to insist on the legal enforcement of morals to ensure social stability. This is a very different position from Burke to whom Devlin is sometimes compared.[59] This is because Burke was, contra Strauss, never a mere historicist.[60] Burke considered the social order to be predicated on a sublime social contract between living and dead backed by the wisdom of providence. Consequently, it was only capable of being undermined by rare forces of corruption. Writing with a century and a half of liberal and socialist victories behind him, for Devlin the distintegrationist movements of modernity were not only ubiquitous but frankly right to regard society and its values as very much historical and contingent creations of finite human intelligence. But this contingent fragility was precisely why conservatives needed to abandon the lofty realms of sublimated theorizations for the more explicit power of law in the enforcement of whatever system of morals society—or at least its conservative elements—happened to believe in.

Yet Devlin was no mere decisionist. Like Schmitt, he recognized the ideological potential of the democratic era while wanting to curb its disturbing alliance with liberal egalitarianism.[61] The ingenious way he achieved this was by linking democratic rhetoric to illiberalism without actually making any concessions to further democratization in practice. By accomplishing this within legal theory, Devlin was able to identify a populist basis for conservative law which didn't require a grant of equal rights to those deemed undesirable and whose behaviors were consequently to be restricted. Nor did it require mass deliberation on the legitimacy of these restrictions. Indeed, it doesn't even require explicit majority support. As Devlin puts it: when it comes to common mores

> it is surely not enough that they should be reached by the opinion of the majority; it would be too much to require the individual assent of every citizen. English law has evolved and regularly uses a standard which does not depend on the counting of the heads.[62]

Devlin goes on to stress how his populist standard of the reasonable person is the one "judges applied in the days before Parliament was as active as it is now and when they laid down rules of public policy" and is the one he is applying in this case. The reasonable person, or "man on the Clapham omnibus," will become an enormously impactful conservative fiction going forward. While he is rarely encountered in sterling form out in the wild, the man in the Clapham omnibus occupies a space in the conservative imaginary as the embodiment of the ideal man of prejudice. He is Scruton's man who is

> tolerant of the burdens that life lays on him, and unwilling to lodge blame where they seek no remedy, seek fulfillment in the world as it is—to accept and endorse through their actions the institutions and practices into which they are born.[63]

This tolerant attitude toward the inequities he faces results in part because, while the reasonable man may not enjoy great wealth or tremendous political power, this in turn helps insulate him from recognizing—but certainly not from enjoying—the very real (if often slight) privileges he enjoys in knowing that his minimal status and prejudices will be upheld by the law. He is a person whom conservative elites like Devlin give a taste of status, and consequently claim to speak on behalf of in their more demotic moments. And quite often those who recognize the reasonable person in themselves will rise to the occasion, supporting even elitist conservative political movements, including those that entrench their comparative marginalization, in return for the protection and enforcement of those minimal privileges and prejudices threatened by the left.

To the extent he conforms to this archetype the reasonable person has often been an object of praise by conservative populists, from the "beef, bullets and Bibles" folk of Bolsonaro's tropical Brazil to the Timmies and tax breaks of real Canadians in Stephen Harper's true north. And it has proven extremely effective as an ideological fiction with which millions will identify for the sake of protecting their material and social interests. But it is important to notice how minimal these concessions by populists like Devlin really are. While he is happy to appeal to the common sense of the reasonable person while upholding restrictions on homosexuality, Lord Devlin never has any doubt that he is the one entitled to decide what the common sense of the reasonable person is. Or that conservative judges are to be the proper arbiters of this common sense in the future.

Devlin enacted an extraordinary synthesis between conservative juristocratic rule and populism which would seem extremely unlikely, but would in fact prove quite tenable in the Anglosphere. It would echo Scruton and Jordan Peterson's fawning admiration for the wisdom of judge-made common law one minute while decrying the aloofness of liberal elites and their hallowed institutions the next. In an American context one would see an even more successful series of ideological links made between originalist conservative judges overturning dec-ades-old precedents and popular pieces of legislation, but managing to do so in the name of the "people."[64] Originalists claim that the people themselves are the only ones who should decide for whether the constitution is to be changed. Consequently, by giving originalist interpretations of the dead letter of the law imposed by racist slaveholders for centuries, conservative jurists are in fact being more respectful of democracy than their liberal peers. This is true when mak-ing transformative decisions which further entrench the power of the wealthy to influence politics,[65] roll back popular abortion rights,[66] or make it harder to challenge racially discriminatory restrictions on the right to vote.[67]

But more importantly, Devlin teaches us something more general about the features that would come to stamp many—though by no means all—forms of right-wing populism through the 20th century. First, it is parasitically intellectual and rhetorically dependent on many of the same modern epistemologies whose consequences conservatives decry elsewhere where they lead to more egalitarian or liberal solutions. Second, it is willing to break from the conservative tradition in demotically expressing admiration for certain kinds of ordinary people and their values. Typically these belong to the petit bourgeois rung of society, and can be mobilized to support more elite forms of privilege and status in return for the protection of their own if sufficiently galvanized by disgust or fear. In Devlin's case, of homosexuality. Third, and most importantly, conservative pop-ulism will ape the tropes of democracy while withdrawing from its substance where they think that will lead to political defeat. Often through claiming that the decisions of non-elected and elitist institutions and personalities are more authentic and dependable expressions of the will of conservative fictions like the "reasonable man" than their counterparts. This can even assume a paradoxical form as when it becomes vital to undermine genuinely majoritarian outcomes to ensure the populists' "real" people get the outcome they are entitled to.

Leo Strauss and the Resurrection of Classical Political Philosophy

With the passage from Devlin to Strauss we move to more rarefied intellectual territory, though also more ambiguous. This is in part because many of Strauss' exoteric writings are characterized by a level of scholarly removal and erudition which is rare even in the most academic forms of political philosophy. This is coupled with a generous mind uncommon even in intellectual circles. While Strauss was never afraid to rank thinkers, and many liberals and progressives came up short, there is rarely any of the partisanship and chauvinism one finds in the intellectual genealogies of comparable figures like Scruton.[68] Locke, Kant, and even Marx are revered as great thinkers, and Strauss went out of his way to single out the accomplishments of important contemporary progressives like his frenemy Alexandre Kojev.[69] These talents mean even someone dedicated to applying an anti-reactionary hermeneutics of suspicion would be stupid to deny the insights of wisdom and genius that pervade Strauss' writings. Strauss is also a difficult author to analyze because so much of his work is presented in the form of scholarly, even pedantically meticulous,[70] analyses of texts. That Strauss is first and foremost a teacher is undeniable, but whether he is teaching his own doctrine or even that of another is not. Nonetheless there are recognizable themes which are central to his major works and repeated throughout. Many of these have had an important influence on the political right, especially in the United States, from the mid-century onward. Though whether that means Strauss himself is properly labeled a man of the right was a point about which even he was legendarily taciturn and is a question his admirers debate sharply.[71]

At the epicenter of Strauss' thinking is a concern to restore the dignity of classical political philosophy, which had been undermined by successive waves of modernity and the creeping threat of nihilism.[72] This project was profoundly inspired by Strauss' complex relationships to the great modernist reactionaries Nietzsche and Heidegger. This may seem unusual given that his explicit commentary on either is fairly minimal compared to the voluminous words dedicated to Plato and Machiavelli. But the immense importance of both on Strauss is widely[73] acknowledged, and it is very easy to recognize their shadow across many of his writings.[74] Like Nietzsche and Heidegger, Strauss is profoundly impressed by the philosophical and socio-political discourse of antiquity and often foregrounds its nobility against the decay of the moderns. All three thinkers associate the entry to modernity with the spread of nihilism, though how that is textured varies between them. But as we will see later both Nietzsche and Heidegger remained convinced that the critiques of modernity had so devastated classical philosophy that there could be no returning to it in good faith. What was needed was a reboot or new beginning of the philosophical tradition along their preferred lines. Or as some on the far right put it, a new inceptual moment in the history of Being.[75] One whose political consequences will of course entail a radical rejection of the egalitarianism of modernity for something like aristocratic radicalism or the most banal forms of nationalist chauvinism.

Strauss' own response to the nihilistic egalitarianism of modernity is more recognizably conservative than Nietzsche or Heidegger's, emphasizing a return to core values rather than a break. And of course many on the political right have interpreted Straussian lessons in precisely this way, even mobilizing them on behalf of the American culture war.[76] But a closer look shows that in fact there are radical dimensions to Strauss writings which resist this reductionism.

An obvious example flows from his rejection of historicism, which Strauss identifies as a or *the* governing philosophy of our decadent and relativistic age. A less courageous conservative approach would be to diagnose the ubiquity of historicist relativism as flowing from the pen of a preferred progressive bogey-man; Marx, or more recently post-modern neo-Marxism, immediately leap to mind. The author would then carefully insulate everyone in the conservative tradition from the sharp edges of her own critique. Much like how conservative authors inspired by Nietzsche's anti-egalitarianism, but still interested in defending Judeo-Christian values, will largely ignore his far more dangerous arguments that socialism, democracy, etc. constitute secularized Christian doctrines.[77] Strauss will have none of that.

This can be seen in Strauss' emphatic rejection of conservative icons like Edmund Burke, who is subjected to extraordinarily effective critique in *Natural Right and History*. Here Strauss makes the rather shocking claim that Burke is the founder of the historicist political tradition whose later partisans include Hegel and Karl Marx. On this interpretation Burke and Burkean conservatism's conviction that the value systems and political institutions of a society emerge through an evolutionary process which make them appropriate to that setting, and only that setting, is inherently relativistic and so nihilistic.[78] Burke obviously gives this a conservative interpretation. But Strauss rightly points out that it is a very short step from Burkeanism to the (vulgar) Marxist judgment that, if it is the case that values and institutions are merely the contingent products of history, there is nothing intrinsically truthful or natural to them. Consequently they can be subjected to revolutionary criticism and replacement if it is in the material interest of the working classes. After all, to most of us, Burke's auspicious aristocratic tradition looks a lot like mere class hegemony, and there is no way of arbitrating between these two judgments without appeal to transhistorical principles ala the universal "rights of man," which a consistent Burkean historicism must deny exist. As Strauss puts it in *Natural Right and History*:

> Whereas Burke's 'conservatism' is in full agreement with classical thought, his interpretation of his 'conservatism' prepared an approach to human affairs which is even more foreign to classical thought that was the very 'radicalism' of the French Revolution. Political philosophy or political theory had been from its inception the question for civil society as it ought to be. Burke's political theory is, or tends to become, identical with a theory of the British constitution, i.e., an attempt to discover the 'latent wisdom which prevails' in the later...Transcendent standards can be dispensed with if the standard is inherent in the process; 'the actual and the present is the rational.' What could appear as a primeval equation of the good with the ancestral is, in fact, a preparation for Hegel.[79]

Strauss' root-and-branch critique of perennially popular historicist flavors of conservatism has never been comprehensively answered, even if its case against Burke himself can be overstated.[80] We've seen how it echoes in the work of figures like Oakeshott and Devlin. One limitation is that there is no doubt that the genealogical account of natural rights given by Strauss in his most famous book is decidedly modernist—even historicist—in its approach.[81] But more importantly Strauss work seems vulnerable to the philosophical objection that it never rebuts historicism on its own ontological and epistemological grounds. It largely focuses on demonstrating the negative consequences that flow from historicism. Consequently Strauss' compelling moral objection to modernity and historicism never demonstrates more than that their consequences might be undesirable, not that they are untrue. In a Nietzschean vein, Strauss very clearly converges on his beliefs about truth and the good by following the pathology of his moral inclinations. Strauss himself seems deeply aware of this limitation as when he claims that the

> seriousness of the need for natural right does not prove that the need can be satisfied. A wish is not a fact. Even by proving that a certain view is indispensable for living well, one proves merely that the view in question is a salutary myth: one does not prove it to be true. Utility and truth are two entirely different things.[82]

It is to his deep credit that Strauss was willing to acknowledge this problem and confront it honestly. This reflects Strauss' commitment to the task of political philosophy as he saw it, which is another point where painting him as a conservative seems to fall apart. Strauss understood the goal of the political philosopher to be frequently antithetical to the ambition of achieving a settled social order. Indeed Strauss recognizes that the unhindered quest for truth and ideal justice characteristic of real philosophy may well be such a permanent threat to conservative social orders. Consequently the philosopher must learn to present her teachings in a responsible or even concealed manner.[83] But that only moderates and can never eliminate the danger posed by philosophy.

Strauss' template for the classical political philosopher is Socrates, whose life was lived challenging the doxastic traditions of the time and who died being accused of undermining patriotism and faith in the gods of the city. In this respect Socrates is undoubtedly one of the first "critical theorists," if by this one simply means a figure who uses dialectic to undermine the hegemonic forces of her day. But Strauss would respond that he is absolutely not a modern critical theorist, in the sense of being committed to emancipation and equality for their own sake. These ambitions have a deep affinity with the relativism of modernity, whereas for Socrates the task of a critical dialectic was to transform erotic love for the world as it is into love for what is eternally true and beautiful. This will invariably prove a threat to all historically constituted systems of power and thought, ranging from the demotic to the nationalistic and idolatrous.

The Natural Law of Inequality

Distinctively Strauss manages to combine this radical interpretation of philosophy as a fundamentally critical enterprise that is a threat to the status quo with an elitist sensibility which is more naturally amenable to the political right. His writings are replete with references to the distinction between the genuine philosopher or statesman and the masses who are on balance genuinely unconcerned with the pursuit of excellence and eminently capable of being manipulated by any number of demagogues and Fuhrers. The genuine philosopher for Strauss is a Platonic figure: someone who inquires into the nature of the good and the true without infection by opinion or self-interest. Since these qualities, along with the intelligence required to make use of them, are in short supply, societies will almost invariably slip into doxastic complacency at best and tyranny at worst.

What fascinates Strauss to no end is the way that modern philosophy framed itself as a project of radical intellectual and political emancipation from these antiquarian positions and the elitism they entail, while eventually descending into apologias for the most monstrous regimes that ever polluted the earth. Modern philosophy paved the way for this through jettisoning classical notions of natural right and excellence and locating the basis of political legitimacy squarely in securing the conditions and rights needed for everyone to pursue his or her private desires. This was found most notably in the writings of Machiavelli, Hobbes, and Locke who form the early modern trifecta that effectively carried out this profound revaluation of all values. One of Strauss' key anxieties is the fragility of this basis for political order, since locating legitimacy in the protection of an individual's right to pursue their own desire without any consideration of a higher goods or ends moves us very close to nihilism and relativism. For Strauss this remains true no matter how ostentatiously modern political philosophers will dress up their thinking in the decaying language of classical natural law and right. As he put it with reference to Locke:

> Locke's teaching on property, and therewith his whole political philosophy, are revolutionary not only with regard to biblical tradition but with regard to the philosophical tradition as well. Through the shift of emphasis from natural duties or obligation to natural rights, the individual, the ego, has become the center and origins of the moral world, since man-as distinguished from man's end-had become the center or origin...Man is effectively emancipated from the bonds of nature, and therewith the individual is emancipated from those social bonds with antedate all consent or compact, but the emancipation of his productive acquisitiveness, which is necessarily, if accidentally, beneficent and hence susceptible of becoming the strongest social bond; restraint of the appetites is replaced by a mechanism whose effect is humane.[84]

Desire becomes the basis of the good and the endless striving for its gratification is a joyless quest for joy. From there it is a short step to historicism and positivism, two seemingly disparate philosophies which converge on the belief that what is "good" is simply a matter of the predominant views of any given time. Consequently the goal of political thought is not to ask questions about whether what is considered good is actually so, as though from a transhistorical perspective. Instead it is simply to describe society impartially as it exists now and ascertain how these existent desires and interests can be better organized and regulated to maximize people's happiness. Political action becomes focused on instrumental techniques rather than the attainment of justice. This creates the conditions where there are no inherent moral barriers to power doing whatever it must to achieve greater utility, including sweeping aside even the minimal barriers of liberal and legal rights. Like the proverbial self-swallowing serpent, the morality of permissiveness that was to be guaranteed by freedom and rights will be devoured by an impetus to maximize pleasure at all costs. The door becomes open for any number of horrific regimes, each professing to reflect the general will and to be more ruthless in pursuing its interests, up to and including the genocide of all those who stand in the way of achieving earthly utopia.

Whatever one thinks of this analysis, it is no doubt powerful and morally serious. We can also locate Strauss' attraction to conservatives in this deep wariness of modernity and the appeal of returning to antiquity for insight against vulgarity and tyranny. Ironically it is precisely this level of historical awareness that enables him to imaginatively reconstruct the perspective of ancient philosophers as they might have understood themselves so effectively in order to evaluate modernity from their standpoint. This is a talent lacking in a cruder take on the same era, like Popper's *The Open Society and Its Enemies*, a book which reads Plato as some kind of failed communist.[85] But more importantly Strauss' is merciless in his dialectical willingness to link the different instantiations of modern thought together, showing how they feed off and depend on one another and so cannot be crudely demarcated in the way unreflective liberals and socialists want. To give one example, the popular literature would portray something like Nazism as a fall from the progressive and liberal democratic Weimar ideal. But a Straussian would explain how National Socialism was in fact a parasitic mutation of mass politics and nationalist relativism only possible in the modern era, thereby implicating the political institutions and principles of Weimar in their own fall. In other words it is a totalizing critique of modernity which can tempt one to a wholesale rejection of the modern world; though how to do that without becoming just another failed revolutionary or reactionary outburst is an open question throughout Strauss' work.

But more importantly, to accomplish a wholesale rejection (or redemption) of modernity at more than just the political or moral level would require a world-historical thinker on the level of Plato or Kant. When Strauss was living the only one he thought came close was Heidegger, who himself became tempted by a false start. This is because to genuinely replace modern thinking one would ultimately need to not just overcome its politics, but the metaphysical foundation on which it rested. Namely modern science, which even Strauss recognized had proven as spectacularly successful in describing the natural world as it could be a disaster when its techniques were applied to improving the human one. This is a point even many Straussians ignore as they launch impotent political critique after political critique on the basis of antiquarian metaphysics that appears help-lessly quaint in the face of modern sciences' endless secular miracles.[86] Strauss was capable of recognizing that in the face of this metaphysical dominance there was no going back to Plato and Aristotle, no matter how much one may wish to.

Strauss' own response to modernity was consequently far more modest, and mostly focused on the need to provide a first-class education to American and European elites who would go on to assume positions of power. The ambition was to create statesmen of wisdom and character who possessed an insight into the philosophical dimensions of the political problems they faced. But what the content of this Straussian education should be is extremely ambiguous. It isn't clear that it should uncritically teach Platonism in light of its metaphysical fail-ings by modern standards. It isn't clear that it should uncritically teach rationalis-tic liberalism in the face of its clear moral failing by antiquarian standards, even if it does align better with the science of the era. One of the reasons for the split in West and East Coast Straussianism is of course a debate over whether one should try to Platonize liberalism or give up on it wholesale. Though both tend to em-phasize pedagogical issues related to the need to better educate leaders and the public on (carefully selected) works of Western philosophy, and usually couple it with a rather charmless mania toward anything that smacks of wokeness, political correctness, or excess activism.[87]

In the end one of the deflating truths about Straussianism is that, for all its grandiosity, the practical lesson of his teaching often seems to boil down to: read the great works of the canon carefully and that will make you a more virtuous person and political actor. And that consequently it is a major task to educate the aristocratic scions of the era before they came into their own so they can in turn elevate or manage the dangerously despotic masses. Strauss doesn't appear to have thought his thinking incompatible with a cautious support for liberal republicanism, though this would be much in the Churchillian vein of accepting it as the worst system except for all the others. The goal would be to align mod-ern liberalism more with its classical antecedents, leaning heavily on figures in the liberal tradition that stressed the need to cultivate statesman-like virtues and intellect. In an American context Strauss' more liberal and patriotic interpreters, like Harry Jaffa, would try to find this in the lives and works of the Founding Fathers through figures like Abraham Lincoln.[88] Though of course stressing that the "freedoms" and "equality" they guaranteed were not applicable to "the exhi-bitionism of lesbians, sodomites, abortionists, drug addicts, and pornographers." Freedom was only to be freedom "within the moral law," which as it turns out means unfreedom for many millions who might wish to harmlessly live in ways other than those Jaffa respected. This would be coupled with an attitudinal wariness of extensive democracy and an acceptance of inequitable distributions of power and influence where that roughly matched the abilities and virtues an individual had cultivated. This point is clearly articulated by McAllister in his useful book on Strauss and Voegelin:

> A conservative principle related to this affirmation of the social character of the individual is the belief that a proper social and political order requires a hierarchy that is roughly commensurate with abilities and effort. Here conservatives swim upstream against a rather vigorous current of equalitarianism. Conservatives recognize two forms of equality: equality before God and equality before the law. (They do not even embrace equality of opportunity because they cannot separate that formally from equality of condition. Otherwise, they see an enormous variety of talents that deserve distinct place. Here they stand upon the Platonic definition of justice in which each person receives his or her due. Hierarchy extends well beyond a simple concern for social justice, and it must do so, I think, because conservatives who are given to a justification of class distinction based upon natural talent fail to explain how this just distribution of privileges might work, except to say that no human system can achieve justice fully. Perhaps more important to the conservative defense of hierarchy is an abhorrence for its opposite: mass society.[89]

In case the paragraph didn't make it clear, it is quite obvious that Strauss and his disciples weren't worrying themselves to sleep over whether material affluence might have enabled some of their prized students the leisure to become the educated elite destined for political greatness; a luxury millions of potentially talented and virtuous individuals are denied through mere accidents of birth. Throughout their writings there is an extensive concern with virtue, intellectual excellence, and annoying university relativists but very little with housing, plumbing, or the presence of lead in the homes of African Americans brought about by de jure and de facto racist segregation. In other words they don't care much about most of the socio-political issues which matter to living citizens everyday, which are often unexciting and solvable only through the kind of midbrow technocratic deliberations Strauss himself found so tediously nihilistic. This gives Straussianism a well-mocked reputation for aloofness that gestures to a more foundational philosophical problem: the relentless idealism Strauss seems to have picked up from Heidegger.

Strauss is extremely suspicious of the modern distinction between facts and norms, even if he acknowledges the difficulty of overcoming it without appealing to a discredited metaphysics. This is in part because the distinction between facts and norms contributed to the emergence of modern positivism and technocratic management, which intellectually and morally constitute a steep drop from the glories of Plato's dialogues and Thucydides' sweeping histories. Historicism, and consequently historical materialism, doesn't fare much better. One of the oddities of this attitude is that many of Strauss' best works, from *Natural Right and History* and the essay "What is Political Philosophy?" are eminently historical and even genealogical. They trace the development of a complex sequence of ideas, examining their mutual impact on one another, and then extrapolate very general conclusions about the society and culture. Consequently it is hard not to read Strauss as more beholden to historicist methods than he admits.[90] His own big story essentially inverts the teleological orientation of cheesier progressive historiographies by describing Western history in terms of a steep fall rather than improvement and the expansion of freedom and democracy. The close of his chapter on "modern natural right" with the "joyless quest for joy"[91] quote and the concluding ruminations on the "crisis" of modernity rhetorically emphasize the point.[92]

But the more important question is whether Strauss successfully avoids the charms of crypto-idealism which have proved so irresistible to the German right[93] (and for that matter those influenced by them). Strauss' undeniably grand narrative on the decline and fall of natural rights ascribes overwhelming influence on the history of ideas, and those of political and metaphysical philosophy in particular. This is perhaps an inevitable chauvinism from a proud philosopher, but it is no less reductive for it. Even Strauss' treatment of Thucydidean history, which arguably took a rather pessimistic view of the influence of ideas over power and action, tends to foreground the ideological and even archetypal bifurcations replete in *The Peloponnesian War* over its nitty-gritty and military details.[94]

This is a foundational problem since it means that Strauss' account of the movement toward modernity misses a great deal that is fundamental about it beyond its philosophical and high political transitions. There is little or nothing about political economy and the way it transformed relations between men and the natural world as profoundly as any institutional transitions. Strauss' treatment of technology and science is inevitably framed in the grammar of political philosophy, rarely addressing them as independently interesting forces of transformation and inquiry. In this respect Strauss doesn't even rise to Heidegger's level of analysis, even if they share a predictable Luddism.[95] Perhaps most frustratingly there is little interest in the concreteness or lived conditions in which most people live, shit, sweat, eat, reproduce their social life, and then die.

Finally, Strauss' crypto idealist take on modernity is problematic for its failure to go far enough, as he carefully exonerates the ancients from the force of his own accusations even while stressing their influence. A more ambitious and complete critique of the fall into modernity couldn't take such pains to exonerate Plato and the Ancients for their own culpability in the descent. It might need to be daring enough to go all the way with Nietzsche and Heidegger in locating the source of the rot in the originary moment of Western philosophy and tracing its mutation through antiquity and Christianity into modernity. If Nietzsche and Heidegger have any virtues compared to Strauss, it is that their hermeneutics of suspicion is coldly impartial toward even cherished peaks. By contrast there is something deflating about Strauss careful and scholarly insulation of the Ancients from criticism. An attitude of "this far, but no further."

In making accusations of crypto-idealism I am not trying to fault Strauss for a lack of moral seriousness. That's (one of) Heidegger's failings. But it does show the degree to which his account of modernity is wildly overdetermined by its emphasis on the impact of ideas, and indeed the most highbrow and removed ideas. In his hands, the trickle-down effect of ideas possesses enough explanatory power to account for a great deal that can in fact only be explained through multi-variate analysis. This descriptive overdetermination also means that Strauss is insufficiently balanced in his normative appraisals of modernity. This is an understandable fault given his close experience of totalitarianism, and the deep awareness of the potential for modern authoritarian regimes to commit themselves to industrialized murder. But an account of modernity which doesn't ascribe significant weight to the tangible benefits (and costs) of technological improvement, the construction of public goods and infrastructure, the invention and distribution of new medicines like penicillin, and so many more operates at too immaterial a level to be considered accurate or even compelling.

On the other front his critique of contemporary liberal democracy and technocratic positivism as prone[96] to advancing nothing but the hedonistic and relativistic pursuit of self-interest misses the extent to which liberal philosophers from the beginning were deeply committed to conceiving alternative conceptions of the good life. For instance, even the Millsian philosophical liberalism with which Strauss was familiar wasn't committed to liberty purely for its own sake or even for the purposes of utility maximization. Mill's conception of the good life was one where the just state withdrew from regulating the moral lives of individuals beyond the parameters set by the harm principle so that they could more easily engage in various experiments in living. This would allow both the individual and society to assess different conceptions of the good life through the application of the fallibilist method, and Mill was under no doubt they would gradually move closer and closer to the best prospects. This is much closer to the Socratic disposition of moderate skepticism coupled with meta-ethical optimism than Strauss or many Straussians acknowledged.

But going further, Mill had no doubts that to create happy and good citizens, liberal states would need to do more than just ease up on moral regulation. In this respect Mill was far less prone to ideation and more sensitive to materialism than Strauss. Mill argued that one would need to radically transform political institutions and the economy to allow more democratic and solidaristic forms of life to emerge, where those governed by laws had a say in them and the surplus created by industrial production was spread more fairly.[97] This would in turn elevate human beings through fostering a greater sense of mutual respect and recognition.[98] To the extent that Mill is a far more complete liberal than Locke, Hobbes, or any of Strauss' usually early modern targets. This severely blunts the impact of the critical analysis of the broader tradition. Now whatever one thinks about this kind of liberalism it is far more robustly committed to a distinct conception of the good life than Strauss implies. For that matter the same is true of Mill's socialism. It may not be the Platonic good which Strauss himself is attracted to, but then Strauss himself has never been able to fully believe in Platonism.

In the end what Strauss presents us with is a philosopher who is fundamentally uncertain, isolated between past and present through not loving the liberal society he lived in while rejecting a nostalgic return to a Republic that never was and perhaps never could be. Like fellow Jewish emigres Adorno and Horkheimer, one senses Strauss was riven by despairing contempt toward the vulgar liberal capitalist regime which provided him with refuge while having to endure the complex reality that a more spiritually attuned country like Germany would give itself over to Nazism with vigor. Perhaps given the immensity of the problems he faced, it was inevitable that Strauss would seek and find answers in idealist philosophy, even if those answers never resulted in concrete solutions.

Conclusion

The early and mid-20th century was a period when more moderate conservatives felt the world slipping away. By which I mean "felt the cultural consensus was slipping away from them." The air of melancholic resignation and even futility that pervades authors of this period is partly explainable in terms of the catastrophes of the time. But it is also reflective of an epoch when liberalism and communism seemed to be advancing everywhere, mutually radicalizing one another, and for conservatives both threatening to reduce culture to a series of Tim Allen Christmas specials. That the far right had been utterly discredited for having already sunk the world into the moral oblivion of genocide and hatred is a theme often backgrounded in their writings. This leads authors like Oakeshott and Strauss to make peace with more moderate strands of liberalism while Eliot and Devlin looked to either a Christian elite or the populist masses to turn things around. And eventually, they would turn as we begin to look at the period of conservatism's unabashed triumph. We should be quite familiar with this time period since we've endured it for four decades.

Notes

1　Another important form was indeed conservative dictatorship and various residual feudal forms of socio-political organization. These dominated much of Latin America, Africa, the Middle East, and East Asia through the latter half of the 20th century, along with European states like Francoist Spain and Greece under the Colonels.

2　See Albert O. Hirschman. *The Rhetoric of Reaction: Perversity, Futility, Jeopardy.* (Cambridge, MA: The Belknap Press of Harvard University Press, 1991)

3　See Robert Dahl. *Democracy and Its Critics.* (New Haven, CT: Yale University Press, 1989) at p. 32

4　A helpful and timely example is the use of populist rhetoric around race and economic issues to mobilize mass support and activist movements in the United States. Political leaders from George Wallace to Donald Trump would often employ consciously democratic language about bringing power back to the people to mobilize support. But the "people" very invariably conceived along highly exclusionary lines which excluded any moral obligation to accept the unworthy—often determined by race—as members of the community entitled to political agency. Ironically these could even allow American conservatives to frame the impositions of racialized constraints on voting and political participation as necessary to securing real democracy for those entitled to it. This appropriation of democratic language stripped of an expansive egalitarian ethos and intended to retrench forms of exclusionary power would have a long history on the political right in America and elsewhere. I will discuss this at some length later. For now see Joseph E. Lowndes. *From the New Deal to the New Right: Race and the Southern Origins of Modern Conservatism.* (New Haven, CT: Yale University Press, 2008)

5 Eric Hobsbawm. *The Age of Extremes: A History of the World 1914–1991.* (New York, NY: Vintage Books, 1996)

6 See Robert A. Dahl. *On Democracy.* (New Haven, CT: Yale University Press, 2000) at 90 and Robert A. Dahl. *A Preface to Economic Democracy.* (Oakland: University of California Press, 1986)

7 Jessica Whyte. *The Morals of the Market: Human Rights and the Rise of Neoliberalism.* (London, UK: Verso Books, 2019)

8 See Matthew McManus. *The Rise of Post-Modern Conservatism: Neoliberalism, Post-Modern Culture, and Reactionary Politics.* (Gewerbestrasse, Switzerland: Palgrave MacMillan, 2019)

9 See Eric Hobsbawm. *The Age of Extremes: A History of the World 1914–1991.* (New York, NY: Vintage Books, 1996)

10 Edmund Fawcett. *Conservatism: The Fight for a Tradition.* (Princeton, NJ: Princeton University Press, 2020)

11 Roger Scruton. *A Political Philosophy: Arguments for Conservatism.* (London, UK: Bloomsbury, 2006) at p. 191

12 See T.S. Eliot. *Selected Prose,* ed. John Hayward. (London, UK: Penguin Books, 1953) at p. 241

13 See T.S. Eliot. *Selected Prose,* ed. John Hayward. (London, UK: Penguin Books, 1953) at pp. 44–47

14 Immanuel Kant. *Critique of Judgement,* trans. Nicholas Walker. (Oxford, UK: Oxford University Press, 2009)

15 Heidegger as we will discover is an exemplar.

16 See Russell Kirk. *The Conservative Mind: From Burke to Eliot.* (Washington, DC: Gateway Editions, 2016)

17 See Langdon Hammer. "T.S. Eliot." Yale University Courses, December 6th, 2012. https://www.youtube.com/watch?v=eUO-ICj6PHQ

18 James Matthew Wilson. *The Vision of the Soul: Truth, Goodness and Beauty in the Western Tradition.* (Washington, DC: The Catholic University of America Press, 2017) at p. 11

19 Roger Scruton. *A Political Philosophy: Arguments for Conservatism.* (London, UK: Bloomsbury, 2006) at p. 193

20 Cited in Roger Scruton. *A Political Philosophy: Arguments for Conservatism.* (London, UK: Bloomsbury, 2006) at p. 201

21 Obery Hendricks. *The Politics of Jesus: Rediscovering the True Revolutionary Nature of Jesus' Teachings and How They Have Been Corrupted.* (New York, NY: Three Leaves Publishing, 2006). On the point about Christ coming to doubt God on the Cross see Slavoj Zizek. *The Fragile Absolute: Or Why Is the Christian Legacy Worth Fighting For?* (London, UK: Verso Books, 2009)

22 T.S. Eliot. *Selected Prose,* ed. John Hayward. (London, UK: Penguin Books, 1953) at p. 212

23 T.S. Eliot. *Selected Prose,* ed. John Hayward. (London, UK: Penguin Books, 1953) at p. 239

24 See T.S. Eliot. *Christianity and Culture: The Idea of a Christian Society and Notes Towards the Definition of Culture.* (New York, NY: Harvest Books, 1949) at p. 12

25 Again, a point which Tolstoy did not forget. See Leo Tolstoy. *The Kingdom of God Is within You*, trans. Constance Garnett. (Kshetra Books, 2016)

26 Perry Anderson. "The Intransigent Right at the Turn of the Century." *London Review of Books*, September 24th, 1992

27 There is a Michael Oakeshott Association, a consistent stream of monographs and essays on his work, and young conservatives seem especially taken with him. See Nate Hochman. "Michael
Oakeshott, 30 Years Later." *National Review*, December 18th, 2020

28 See Terry Nardin. "Michael Oakeshott." *Stanford Encyclopedia of Philosophy*, February 14th, 2020

29 See Michael Oakeshott. *On Human Conduct.* (Oxford, UK: Oxford University Press, 1975)

30 Michael Oakeshott. *Rationalism in Politics and Other Essays: New and Expanded Edition.* (Indianapolis, IN: Liberty Press, 1991)

31 Michael Oakeshott. *The Politics of Faith and the Politics of Skepticism.* (New Haven, CT: Yale University Press, 1996)

32 Ludwig von Mises. *Liberalism.* (Auburn, AL: Mises Institute, 1985)

33 See Michael Oakeshott. *On Human Conduct.* (Oxford, UK: Oxford University Press, 1975) at p. 245

34 See Elizabeth Campbell Corey. "The Politics of Faith and the Politics of Skepticism." *Voeglin View*, January 21st, 2010

35 Michael Oakeshott. *Rationalism in Politics and Other Essays: New and Expanded Edition.* (Indianapolis, IN: Liberty Press, 1991)

36 Oakeshott would not care for this word of course, but I do.

37 See Michael Oakeshott. *On Human Conduct.* (Oxford, UK: Oxford University Press, 1975) at pp. 30, 31

38 Leo Strauss. *Natural Right and History.* (Chicago, IL: University of Chicago Press, 1953)

39 Michael Oakeshott. *On Human Conduct.* (Oxford, UK: Oxford University Press, 1975) at p. 182

40 Michael Oakeshott. *On Human Conduct.* (Oxford, UK: Oxford University Press, 1975) at pp. 80, 81

41 See Michael Oakeshott. "On Being Conservative" in *Rationalism in Politics and Other Essays: New and Expanded Edition.* (Indianapolis, IN: Liberty Press, 1991)

42 I draw some inspiration in this critique from the work of Jeremy Waldron and Brian Barry.

43 Michael Oakeshott. *On Human Conduct.* (Oxford, UK: Oxford University Press, 1975) at p. 314

44 Michael Oakeshott. *On Human Conduct.* (Oxford, UK: Oxford University Press, 1975) at p. 191

45 Michael Oakeshott. *On Human Conduct.* (Oxford, UK: Oxford University Press, 1975) at p. 192

46 Karl Marx. *Early Writings*, trans. Rodney Livingstone. (London, UK: Penguin Classics, 1992)

47 Given the gravity of the accusations against him, and their credibility, I deliberated upon writing this section. It is not my intention to uphold the merits of Devlin's contributions in spite of what he has been accused of, but even including references to him in an academic work may be taken as such. After some reflection I decided it was important to criticize his work, not just because on its own merits it falls flat, but precisely because it defends the kinds of entrenched privileges which allows powerful men to uphold their prejudices and predatory behavior through the force of law. And

indeed the populist streak that appears in Devlin's work will be actively deployed by other sexual predators like Donald Trump in the future.

48 See Beatrix Campbell. "Our Silence Permits Perpetrators to Continue: One Women's Fight to Expose a Father's Abuse." *The Guardian*, July 25th, 2021. https://www.theguardian.com/uk-news/2021/jul/25/our-silence-permits-perpetrators-to-continue-one-womans-fight-to-expose-a-fathers-abuse

49 It also makes Devlin's reference to prohibitions on incest early in his condemnation of homosexuality staggeringly hypocritical.

50 In this respect Devlin differs profoundly from a legal theorist like John Finnis, who remains convinced that homophobia can be made to look like right. See John Finnis. "Law, Morality, and Sexual Orientation" in John Corvino. *Same Sex: Debating the Ethics, Science, and Culture of Homosexuality*. (Lanham, NY: Rowman and Littlefield 1997) and John Finnis *Natural Law and Natural Rights: Second Edition*. (Oxford, UK: Oxford University Press, 2011)

51 See Patrick Devlin. *The Enforcement of Morals: Maccabean Lectures in Jurisprudence*. Online pp. 132, 133

52 See Ian Shapiro. "The Burkean Outlook." Yale Courses, *The Moral Foundations of Politics*. April 8th, 2011. https://www.youtube.com/watch?v=hkDqadw-fJE&t=3s

53 See Patrick Devlin. *The Enforcement of Morals: Maccabean Lectures in Jurisprudence*. Online pp. 136, 137

54 Dworkin rightly highlights this dimension of Devlin's argument, and chastises those who don't recognize it. See Ronald Dworkin. "Lord Devlin and the Enforcement of Morals" *The Yale Law Journal*, Vol 75, No 6, 1966 at p. 989

55 Thomas Hobbes. *Leviathan*. (London, UK: Penguin Books, 2017). For the relativist reading see Richard Tuck. *Hobbes: A Very Short Introduction*. (Oxford, UK: Oxford University Press, 2002)

56 This alleged weakness in Hobbes' position was stressed by Schmitt, who we will discuss later. See Carl Schmitt. *The Leviathan in the State Theory of Thomas Hobbes*. (Chicago, IL: The University of Chicago Press, 2008)

57 See H.L.A. Hart. *Law, Liberty, and Morality*. (Stanford, CA: Stanford University Press, 1963)

58 See Patrick Devlin. *The Enforcement of Morals: Maccabean Lectures in Jurisprudence*. Online at pp. 141, 142

59 Ian Shapiro. "The Burkean Outlook." Yale Courses, *The Moral Foundations of Politics*. April 8th, 2011. https://www.youtube.com/watch?v=hkDqadw-fJE&t=3s

60 Leo Strauss. *Natural Right and History*. (Chicago: University of Chicago Press, 1953)

61 See Carl Schmitt. *Constitutional Theory*, trans. Jeffrey Seitzer. (Durham, NC. Duke University Press, 2008)

62 See Patrick Devlin. *The Enforcement of Morals: Maccabean Lectures in Jurisprudence*. Online at p. 141

63 See Roger Scruton. *The Meaning of Conservatism: Third Edition*. (South Bend, IN: St Augustine's Press, 2002) at p. 111

64 See Steven G. Calabresi. *Originalism: A Quarter-Century of Debate*. (Washington, DC: Regnery Publishing Inc., 2007) and Antonin Scalia. *A Matter of Interpretation: Federal Courts and the Law*. (Princeton, NJ: Princeton University Press, 1997)

65 See *Citizens United v. Federal Election Commission*, 558 U.S. 310 (2010)

66 See *Dobbs v. Jackson Women's Health Organization*, No. 19–1392, 597 U.S (2022)

67 See *Brnovich v. Democratic National Committee*, 594 U.S (2021)

68 Compare Leo Strauss. *Natural Right and History*. (Chicago, IL: University of Chicago Press, 1953) and Roger Scruton. *Conservatism: An Invitation to the Great Tradition*. (New York, NY: All Points Books, 2017) and Roger Scruton. *Fools, Frauds, and Firebrands: Thinkers of the New Left*. (London, UK: Bloomsbury Continuum, 2015)

69 See his extensive discussion of Kojev's views in "Restatement on Xenophon's Hiero." Included in Leo Strauss. *What Is Political Philosophy? And Other Studies*. (Chicago, IL: University of Chicago Press, 1988)

70 Even fans will sometimes roll their eyes at Strauss' tendency to engage in numerological analysis of a text, carefully counting out this or that reference as is deciphering cryptograms. See Ted V. McAllister. *Revolt against Modernity: Leo Strauss, Eric Voegelin, and the Search for a Postliberal Order.* (Lawrence: University of Kansas Press, 1995)

71 Carson Holloway's description of Strauss as "not a conservative, not so much because he was *opposed* to being a conservative as because he was—in a sense—*above* being a conservative" seems accurate to me. See Carson Holloway. "Leo Strauss and American Conservatism." *Public Discourse*, December 16th, 2014

72 Strauss is not shy about stressing the superiority of the ancients over the moderns, even claiming that "compared with classical political philosophy, all later political thought, whatever its merits may be, and in particular modern political thought, has a derivative character." See Leo Strauss. *What Is Political Philosophy? And Other Studies.* (Chicago, IL: University of Chicago Press, 1988) at p. 28

73 The Jewish Strauss even attended lectures by the Heidegger and was emphatic in labeling him a "great" thinker even if Strauss was horrified by his decision to support the Nazi party. Somewhat uncharitably Strauss even compares his own supervisor, Cassirer, unfavorably to Heidegger. He points out how in terms of his influence on modern German thinker "Heidegger surpasses all his contemporaries by far." By contrast "Cassirer represented the established academic position. He was a distinguished professor of philosophy but he was no philosopher. He was erudite but he had no passion. He was a clear writer but his clarity and placidity were not equaled by sensitivity to the problems." Personally I find it much easier to admire a thinker who stridently opposed Nazism, even if he wasn't a philosopher of the first rank, and far harder to admire a man whose great imagination led him to ruminate on the varied possibilities offered by racist nationalism. See Leo Strauss. *What Is Political Philosophy? And Other Studies.* (Chicago, IL: University of Chicago Press, 1988) at p. 246.

74 The importance of both thinkers to Strauss is stressed by Tucker Landy. See Tucker Landy. *After Leo Strauss: New Directions in Platonic Political Philosophy.* (Albany, NY: SUNY Press, 2014)

75 Michael Millerman. *Beginning with Heidegger: Strauss, Rorty, Derrida, Dugin and the Philosophical Constitution of the Political.* (London, UK: Arktos Media, 2021)

76 See Allan Bloom. *The Closing of the American Mind: How Higher Education has Failed Democracy and Impoverished the Souls of Today's Students.* (New York, NY: Simon and Schuster, 2012)

77 See Jordan Peterson. *Maps of Meaning: The Architecture of Belief.* (New York, NY: Routledge Press, 1999)

78 These objections could be stated somewhat differently in terms of that Straussian distinction between political thought, embedded very much in the opinions and needs of the time, and the timeless inquiries of political philosophy. Strauss points out that Burke "did not write a single work on the principles of politics. All his utterances on natural right occur in statements ad hominem and are meant to serve immediately a specific practical purpose." See Leo Strauss. *Natural Right and History.* (Chicago, IL: University of Chicago Press, 1953) at p. 295

79 Leo Strauss. *Natural Right and History.* (Chicago, IL: University of Chicago Press, 1953) at p. 319

80 This point is emphasized by James Matthew Wilson, who responds to Strauss by highlighting the emphasis on providence and aesthetics in Burke and reading them in a Platonic manner. See James Matthew Wilson. *The Vision of the Soul: Truth, Goodness and Beauty in the Western Tradition.* (Washington, DC: The Catholic University of America Press, 2017)

81 This is a limitation that is more ubiquitous than one might expect. It also haunts the similarly modern work of someone like Alasdair MacIntyre.

82 See Leo Strauss. *Natural Right and History.* (Chicago, IL: University of Chicago Press, 1953) at p. 6

83 Much of Strauss concern with esoteric and exoteric writing centers on this.

84 See Leo Strauss. *Natural Right and History.* (Chicago, IL: University of Chicago Press, 1953) at p. 248

85 See Karl Popper. *The Open Society and Its Enemies.* (Princeton, NJ: Princeton University Press, 2013)

86 One Straussian who does understand this is Landy, who at least tries to respond to modern metaphysics at a genuinely metaphysical level. See Tucker Landy. *After Leo Strauss: New Directions in Platonic Political Philosophy.* (Albany, NY: SUNY Press, 2014)

87 Many Straussians also adopt a fairly arbitrary cut-off point for what is considered an acceptable part of the canon, with anything to the left of classical liberalism usually connoted as beyond the pale no matter its intellectual merits or influence. In this they're typically more dogmatic than the master himself, who, if nothing else, can't be faulted for something as base as partisan prejudice. This is rather depressing, because as other conservative-leaning authors have noted, figures like Adorno developed sweeping critiques of modernity which overlap with Strauss' on a surprising number of points. See Jeffrey L. Nicholas. *Reason, Tradition, and the Good: Macintyre's Tradition Constituted Reason and Frankfurt School Critical Theory.* (Notre Dame, IN: University of Notre Dame Press, 2012)

88 See Harry Jaffa. "The American Founding as the Best Regime." *Claremont Review of Books,* July 4th, 2007

89 Ted V. McAllister. *Revolt against Modernity: Leo Strauss, Eric Voegelin, and the Search for a Postliberal Order.* (Lawrence: University of Kansas Press, 1995) at p. 268

90 A similar charge can and has been leveled against MacIntyre, who formulated an equally rich account of modernity's fall that remains rather beholden to its historicist impulses. See Alasdair MacIntyre. *After Virtue: A Study in Moral Theory: Third Edition* (Notre Dame, IN: University of Notre-Dame Press, 2007)

91 Leo Strauss. *Natural Right and History.* (Chicago, IL: University of Chicago Press, 1953) at p. 251

92 This is perhaps why, of all the modern thinkers associated with the left, Strauss often seems to have the most sympathy for Rousseau. For all his revolutionary credentials, the basic Rousseauean story is one of decline for an initially benighted state.

93 I will discuss this shortly.

94 See Leo Strauss. *The City and Man.* (Chicago, IL: The University of Chicago Press, 1978)

95 See Martin Heidegger. *The Question Concerning Technology and Other Essays.* (New York, NY: Harper Perennial, 2013)

96 I saw prone because, as mentioned, Strauss admitted that liberalism needn't fall into this paradigm.

97 See Helen McCabe. *John Stuart Mill: Socialism.* (Montreal, QC: Queens-McGill University Press, 2021)

98 These themes come through most prominently in John Stuart Mill. *On the Subjection of Women*, reprinted. In Richard Vandeweetering and Lesley Jacobs. *John Stuart Mill's The Subjection of Women: His Contemporary and Modern Critics.* (Delmar, NY: Caravan Books, 1999)

4

BETWEEN GOD AND BAAL II—
CULTURE WARS IN THE LATE
20TH CENTURY

Bring on the Culture War

> We Americans have chosen, in our foolishness, to disunite the country
> through stupid immigration, economic, and foreign policies. The level of
> unity America enjoyed before the bipartisan junta took over can never be
> restored. But we can probably do better than we are doing now. First, stop
> digging. No more importing poverty, crime, and alien cultures. We have
> made institutions, by leftist design, not merely abysmal at assimilation but
> abhorrent of the concept. We should try to fix that, but given the Left's
> iron grip on every school and cultural center, that's like trying to bring
> democracy to Russia. A worthy goal, perhaps, but temper your hopes—
> and don't invest time and resources unrealistically.
>
> (Michael Anton, "United 93 Election")

Seen in purely quantitative terms the "culture war" that ignited in the 1950s has
likely seen more conservative energies dedicated to it than any other issue in history. That its seminal minds would choose to devote so much of their attention
to policing the activism and reading habits of first-year undergrads tells you a lot
about the quality of right-wing media's obsessions. And there is undoubtedly a
lot about it that from the beginning was amusingly trite, from William Buckley
making the curriculum content of elite Ivy schools a matter of national concern
to Allan Bloom educating us all about the evils that flow from Mick Jagger's
shaking pelvis. But the culture war tells us much that is important about the
political right in its moment of political ascendency and triumph. Not least of
which is that all the political power in the world can't compensate for the enduring feeling that a democratizing culture is inexorably slipping away from them.

DOI: 10.4324/9781003307952-7

The political right would respond to these enduring anxieties with remarkable energies and innovation that did much to shape our current moment.

One of the most important things to note about conservatism and the right in the late 20th century is that, like everything, it becomes spectacularly Americanized. This was first and foremost due to the sheer hegemony of American influence, which could not be completely resisted even if one wanted to. It was sufficiently ubiquitous that by the 2000s even resolutely nationalist French politicians like Marine le Pen were parroting American talking points about the dangers of "wokisme."

Second, and less appreciated, is that the influence of American conservatism flowed from its status as the leading anti-Communist country from 1948 onward. It's a dark truth that in the earlier part of the century many European conservatives would have preferred a right-wing or even fascist dictatorship to even democratically mandated socialist reforms.[1] One of the features of the Nazi invasion of the Soviet Union which is sometimes underplayed is the extent to which it was conceived and presented as a pan-rightest assault against a mortal enemy which rallied significant support from anti-Communists and collaborators across Europe.[2] But with its discrediting in the gas chambers of Auschwitz many had to settle for the undeniably more liberal and democratic republic as the lesser of two evils, even if American conservatives themselves often seemed to have little good to say about their country in the years between Roosevelt and Reagan.[3]

Third, from the Cold War through the illegal Iraq War, American liberals and conservatives often (very so reluctantly I'm sure) accepted the imperialist imperatives imposed upon them by geopolitical superpower status. This meant they were infamously not above propping up conservative regimes in Latin America, Europe, and Asia where necessary to halt the spread of communism. Or even engaging in that sanitized term "regime change" where the people of a country happen to choose the wrong political ideology. This of course meant many of these client states either imported, or had imposed upon them, certain features of American anti-Communism and natal neoliberalization at minimum.[4]

Finally—and here is something of a paradox—American conservatism was in many ways far better suited to succeed and even flourish than many of its counterparts. This is because the technological and communicative transformations wrought by the mid-20th century had so profoundly restructured the political landscape that the kleptocratic elitism of conservative dictatorship—while by no means disappearing—largely proved unstable if left to their own accord.[5] Autarkic Francoism and Salazarian corporatism crumbled within years of their namesake's passing. Kemalism was too secular and enamored with modernization. Pinochet was not even being able to keep a lid on Chilean democracy for a solid 20 years before confronting a dangerously egalitarian precedent by potentially becoming the first former head of state prosecuted under international law. And military dictatorships like Brazil's weren't even able to relish prestige when times were good let alone when they frantically tried to maintain their rule over a crumbling economy.

By contrast, from the 19th century onward, American conservatives had had to compete in a very high stakes and high-profile contest for mass support. This included being able to win elections of course, but also recognizing how and when to manipulate electoral infrastructure to hemorrhage influence and capacity to those they felt deserved it. Whether by exploiting or simply relying on the more minoritarian features of American constitutionalism.[6] By the time Goldwater ran in 1964 they had already developed much of the ideological infrastructure and media savvy needed to remain electorally competitive well into the 21st century, even when domestic majorities soured on them.[7] In other countries it would take the right some time to learn from these techniques. But learn they would.

The emphasis on culture wars is also interesting for the dialectical tensions within contemporary politics it reveals. American political culture is inexorably stamped with the legacy of Enlightenment and modernity for better and worse. This includes a certain ineradicable commitment to the revolutionary principles of equality and freedom ensconced in documents like the *Declaration of Independence*, which occupies such a hallowed place in the social imaginary that all but the most ambitious American conservatives pay homage to them. The way conservatives would adapt to the culture war is consequently sensitive to these modern and egalitarian impetuses, sometimes displaying ingenuity in reinventing them for reactionary purposes and sometimes resting content with transparent inconsistency where consistency would compromise preferred outcomes.[8]

For those willing to align the right with the Enlightenment, it was easy enough to castigate progressive cultural demands as a regression from the more overtly elitist forms libera Enlightenment ideology can take. This includes a kind of possessive individualism, a belief in the universality of American exceptionalism, a commitment to meritocratic defenses of the market, and a wariness of extensive democracy. For those more hostile to Enlightenment, drawing on a long history of Southern conservatism especially, progressive cultural demands were the ultimate radicalization of the Enlightenment project which real Americans had always been wary of.[9] American conservatives have also had a complex relationship to the language of democracy, statism, and free thought. They are typically willing to appeal to the demotic spirit of Enlightenment where that insulates them from social and state interference. While at the same time turning on Enlightenment where its principles lead to unacceptable conclusions on the environment, crime, and much else. Someone like Thomas Sowell may even appeal to both modes without recognizing or at least acknowledging the tension, castigating the "anointed" liberal elites for their removal from everyday life one minute and justifying restrictions on democratic participation the next.[10] While in intellectual tension with one another both positions flow organically from the constant in right-wing America's approach to the culture wars: the conviction that liberal and leftist organizers are dangerously ignorant of the ugly realities of life, and will bring about tyranny in the quest for equality if left unchecked. Overeducated academics and activists will give too much political power to those who don't know how to exercise it responsibly, and who'll consequently bring society to ruin.[11] Seen from this perspective the intellectual contradictions of the American right are resolved by a kind of faux realism suckled on paranoia.

This brings us to the most startling tension within the American culture wars, which is the remarkable ability of American conservatives to mobilize populist anger against elite intellectualism to advance ultimately revanchist and anti-democratic policies. As we've seen conservatives have been doing this since Burke complained about the "licentious and giddy coffee houses" and De Maistre the "fundamentally destructive" influence of the *philosophes*. But American conservatives have successfully refined this into a *modus operandi* vaster and more refined than any other. In part because it aligns so advantageously with the more demotic features of Enlightenment and above all with the social Darwinian ethos and even the value relativism and forms of reification exacerbated by modern capitalism. American conservatives will combine a popular antipathy to withdrawn intellectualism and apply that to progressivism wholesale, painting it as an elitist effort to organize society along the lines of their preferred pattern rather than allowing natural or divinely ordained "differences"—including racial differences—to express themselves in hierarchical form. Oftentimes this is given a rationalist defense by figures like von Mises or Ayn Rand, but American conservatives haven't been above appealing to the language of value pluralism to condemn those progressives who think they're smart and good enough to impose their vision of justice on everyone over convictions of the authentic "people." Robert Bork's expressions of rage against the "New Class" of American progressives who have no respect for "particularity-respect for difference, circumstance, history, and the irreducible complexity of human beings and human societies."[12] Of course by "respect for difference" what Bork means is the difference between the meritorious and the vulgar or the deserving and undeserving. Not between queer and heteronormative or anything so unvirtuous as that...

What is undeniable is the power of the culture way to mobilize and give pathological expression to many of the deepest anxieties of American and global conservatives about a cultural moment which is becoming irrevocably corrupted. This is true even though Marxists are correct that the cultural logic of late capitalism leads liberals and conservatives to instinctively—or even consciously—fixate political energies on culture war clashes as a distraction from material and class disputes.[13]

Fusionism, or Getting God and Capital into Bed Together

Capitalism and Christianity should have very little to do with one another. This is true whether one is a left- or right-wing Christian. From Old Testament stipulations on forgiving debts to Christ's declaration in Matthew 19:24 that it is easier for a camel to pass through the eye of the needle than for a rich man to enter the kingdom of heaven, scripture and history weigh heavily against such a marriage between Jesus and Mammon.[14] Nietzsche is close to the mark when he describes the genealogical origin of Christianity as slave morality which is the root of most every radically egalitarian movement down to socialism and democracy. Even if one wants a more conservative take, for much of its history more right-wing forms of Christianity were aligned with the teleological conception of nature and the social philosophy of naturalized hierarchical complementarity. For many conservatives this vision of nature has been an enduring ideological fetish from which they have never entirely weaned themselves. And yet the dynamics of capitalism, as Marx and Carlyle both recognized on opposing sides of the political spectrum, didn't just disrupt this society and its social philosophy. It mercilessly trampled it underfoot.

And yet a right-wing version of Christianity and a gloves-off form of capitalism have not only found a way to coexist but to flourish together in the United States, even if there is evidence the marriage is fracturing due to irreconcilable differences.[15] Part of this can be explained by extrapolating from Weber's brilliant theory of the protestant work ethic.[16] Weber accounts for how the development of more individualist and liberal forms of Christianity brought about by the Reformation became aligned with the Protestant notion of the "calling." This held that God conceived of us not in the medieval sense of being passive recipients of his grace and Aristotelian contributors to maintaining a static whole. Instead we were to be active (if not necessarily free in the metaphysical sense) participants in the improvement of creation, even quasi-divine and creative beings in the spirit of Mirandola's "Oration on Human Dignity."[17] Ann Coulter embodied the culmination of this trend when she said "God gave us the earth. We have dominion over the plants, the animals, the trees. God said, 'Earth is yours. Take it. Rape it. It's yours.'"[18]

This coincided with the elevation of labor to a sacrosanct status it was largely denied in antiquity and the Medieval era, and was complemented by an index of vices framed around hostility to sloth and indolence. Weber's archetype for this figure is the prototypically waspy Benjamin Franklin, who was thrifty, diligent, and refrained from relaxation, alcohol, and other hedonistic behaviors.[19] Over time the ontotheological basis of this ethic became increasingly unnecessary— but never entirely abandoned—as the ethic became hegemonic enough to withstand secularization through alignment with the political economy of the new era. What emerges is a spirit of capitalism that justifies inequalities by appeal to individual merits and hard work. But now, at best, for no higher purpose than the rational progress and utility maximization brought about by the advance of the market system. Or at worst as yet another kind of secularized competitive mechanism to allow the hard working and intelligent to rise while the inferiors remain at the bottom. To Weber's observations we can add a qualification and an additional argument.

The qualification is that Weber sometimes goes too far in pushing his own anxieties about secularization and desacralization, not recognizing how older forms of ideological justification could assume new skins or persist even under the pressures of rationalization. This is especially important when grasping reactionary movement's response to modernity. First, we can readily see now that even if the work ethic can sustain itself without Christianity, that by no means requires the latter's abandonment. American conservatives have found the allure of mapping Christianity and capitalism together irresistible, and they have been aided in part by the more abstract dimensions of political economy. Twentieth-century neoliberals like Hayek tended to conceive the market as a kind of "sublime" object which was the providential product of a long evolutionary history and could be known to work in a largely beneficent way even if its actual processes could never be fully understood let alone controlled.[20] It isn't hard to see how this could—in a remarkable inversion of Weberian expectations—be theologized rather than secularized. The "invisible hand of the market" could be seen as a manifestation of the visible hand[21] of God rewarding and punishing those who deserve it, while withdrawing into impenetrability whenever one tries to grasp his rather mysterious ways. American fusionism was especially talented at forming an ideological linkage of this sort, framing individual choice as the basis for Christian virtue and, consequently, of material reward for those who make smart economic choices and refrain from sinfulness. The emergence of prosperity gospels and the most profane kind of free marketing anti-welfarism by Christian churches embodies this trend.[22]

The argument is that Weber sometimes undervalues how the conception of time operative within Christianity from the beginning could very easily align itself to the more optimistic forms of modern capitalism. The two possess an elective affinity. One tension that persisted within the efforts to harmonize Christian thought with Aristotelian cyclical metaphysics was Christianity's linear and even millenarian vision of history. While there could be some overlap between the rhetoric of cosmological cyclicity and the rust inevitably brought about by original sin, from Paul through Augustine onward Christianity remained committed to the idea that the arc of history would inevitably tilt toward justice. How could it not when Jesus himself entered the world within history to save it, demarcating a clear moment of transformation after which salvation became an option?

This conception of time would prove immensely influential to a huge number of movements who would adapt the language of historical teleology for their own purposes. Now Hirschman is right to point out that this has always been a rhetorical trope more organically aligned with liberalism and the left.[23] But it has never been monopolized by the left, and to the extent Corey Robin is right that the "future" becomes the preferred dimension of time for right-wing intellectuals eager to transform society the progress entailed by moving toward unadulterated domination by capital has always been appealing.[24] This included many of the early capitalists, who, it must be remembered, often saw themselves with some credibility as the creative vanguard of a new and better future for all.[25] In this sense the ongoing conservative depiction of capitalism and its competitive hierarchies as a necessary precondition for social improvement can be said to draw ideological sustenance from a vulgarized Christian view of time as progress. One that perverts Christianity's egalitarian connotations through a strategy of endless withdrawal from moral concern with material conditions and fairness. The market may save us all in the end. But the end is a long ways off, and man's unwillingness to work for $7.50 an hour and no bathroom breaks means the lower orders shouldn't expect too much before then.

These ruminations provide a theoretical basis for why and how a socially conservative and hierarchical Christianity could be fused successfully with the almighty dollar. The fusion found fertile soil in American context where the influence of especially puritanical and evangelizing forms of Protestantism had been linked from the inception with peculiarly American exceptionalism. In the more immediate American context it is impossible to understand the emergence of fusionism without understanding three broad developments which had occurred. The first is the anti-Communism of the Cold War, which galvanized American conservatives and could take on the unmistakable aura of a modern crusade through much of the 1950s.[26] Difficult as it might be to appreciate with the hindsight of 70 years at the time Soviet style communism by no means appeared ideologically toothless. Many conservatives saw both the erosion of the great European empires by radical anti-colonial and anti-imperialist groups and the victory of Mao's Communist Party in China as signs that global capitalism was rapidly losing ground to the Red tide. Coupled with this was a brief period of rapid economic growth on the part of the Soviet Union, along with the horrifying prospect of them having nuclear weapons post-1953. Consequently for many the very real prospects of the future were annihilation or communism, and Stanley Kubrick cynically visualized how for many on the extreme right the former might actually be the winning option.[27] This geopolitical climate created fertile soil in which to enact an alliance between militant defenders of capitalism and socially conservative Christians and traditionalists. This was partially successfully as a mere alliance of strategic necessity, but it was also predicated on more than few shared convictions which flowed organically out of anti-Communism. As Lowndes put it:

> Buckley and other NR [*National Review*] editors linked economic anti-statism and social traditionalism…in a combination that came to be called fusionism. This sometimes uneasy alliance brought together free market ideology with a philosophical commitment to transcendent moral horizons binding individuals in community and tradition. Both libertarians and traditionalists sought an organic basis for social order and were thus hostile to centralized state planning. They also shared a dislike of egalitarian impulses. In the context of the Cold War, anticommunism was a very tangible connection between the two.[28]

The second catalyst for the emergence of fusionism was the changing economic and political climate within developed states. In hindsight many of the extreme right's fears about Communist takeovers from within the United States were overblown, though it was by no means a remote possibility in countries like France or Italy where large Communist parties could win and share power through sheer electoral popularity. But even within states without powerful communist or socialist parties the post-Depression and post-War culture had shifted decidedly toward a social liberalism which was eminently compatible with egalitarian economic policies and high levels of unionization. To a degree that would have been shocking to early generations. One of the reasons an author like Ayn Rand could rise to the top of the 1940s sales charts on the back of a gigantic novel centered around rapey protagonists is that her credo of creeping government collectivism and egalitarian mediocrity resonated with millions during the era of FDR and Eisenhower.[29] Alongside this shift toward social liberalism in the economy was a new cultural egalitarianism in the culture and intellectual sphere embodied in feminist and counter-cultural movements. Most infamously emanating from the universities William Buckley took such issue with.[30] Fusionists of all stripes tended to be comfortable criticizing the egalitarianism, though the more libertarian among sometimes accepted or even welcomed the counter-cultural movements. This would later become the source of considerable tensions within the American conservative movement, but through the heady days of social liberalism's triumph it didn't matter as much since there were shared enemies aplenty to confront.

Last and most uncomfortably the American fusionist movement was undeniably shaped by its response to desegregation and the demand for civil rights and an end to racism. Fusionists had mixed feelings about the Civil Rights movements, though none were zealous proponents and many were suspicious or even critical.[31] Almost all fusionists saw the Civil Rights movements as an opportunity to mobilize the resentments of Southerners for the purposes of a new conservative coalition; one ideologically linking contempt for the federal government's activism on race with its growing ambition to achieve economic equality. Sometimes this could even be cast in a clever enough way to dodge accusations of racism, as with the 1956 piece "The South Girds Its Loins," where the author figured people could be convinced that the "Southern position rests not at all on the question whether Negro and White children should, in fact, study geography side by side; but on whether a central or local authority should make that decision."[32] Undoubtedly Buckley's stance of aristocratic parochialism, articulated in his essay "Why the South Must Prevail," spoke for many:

> The central question that emerges—and it is not a parliamentary question or a question that is answered by merely consulting a catalogue of the rights of American citizens, born Equal—is whether the White community in the South is entitled to take such measures as are necessary to prevail, politically and culturally, in areas in which it does not predominate numerically? The sobering answer is Yes—the White community is so entitled because, for the time being, it is the advanced race.[33]

Over time the antipathy toward civil rights evolved into an ongoing struggle against the more general "Rights Revolution" which broke out in the 1960s, especially as it veered into demands for affirmative action, challenged patriarchal norms in the workplace, and embraced more overtly anti-militaristic and even unpatriotic forms. How to challenge these movements successfully was a hard ideological puzzle for a conservative movement that often attached itself so consciously to the rhetoric of libertarianism. This provided fusionism with far wider mass appeal that it would have had as a purely socially conservative movement and lead to some truly epochal clashes.

Kirk vs. Meyer on Whether Conservatives Can Make Peace with Liberalism

> ...Conservatives pay attention to the principle of variety. They feel affection for the proliferating intricacy of long-established social institutions and modes of life, as distinguished from the narrowing uniformity and deadening egalitarianism of radical systems. For the preservation of a healthy diversity in any civilization, there must survive orders and classes, differences in material condition, and many sorts of inequality. The only true forms of equality are equality at the Last Judgment and equality before a just court of law; all other attempts at levelling must lead, at best, to social stagnation. Society requires honest and able leadership; and if natural and institutional differences are destroyed, presently some tyrant or host of squalid oligarchs will create new forms of inequality.
>
> (Russell Kirk, "10 Conservative Principles")

The Kirk-Meyer debate remains a frequent touchstone for American conservative intellectuals, especially since Trumpism broke apart the fragile consensus in favor of right-wing liberalism and reintroduced many to the Dionysian pleasures of integralist authoritarianism.[34] The debate is emblematic of the stark tensions inherent within a conservative tradition which from the beginning had to conciliate with a muscular form of liberalism. In other ways it is a weird enterprise from start to finish. And that is because our two disputants are rather eccentric figures within the political right, even if they embody recognizable strands of it.

That Kirk should enjoy prestige as the intellectual re-founder of the American conservative tradition is hard to dispute. What's also hard to dispute is the fact that he sits uncomfortably within it. His *The Conservative Mind* was consciously intended as a rebuttal to the arrogant liberal presumption that the right was intrinsically Mill's "stupid party," successful not for the quality of its ideas but because the sheer mass of stupidity within society could often carry it to victory. This offended Kirk deeply, as one might expect for a man who once compared academics to "dull dogs" and referred to his alma mater as "Cow University." And Kirk's work has a kind of noblesse quality to it that undoubtedly gave mid-century conservatism a gloss of sophistication and grandeur. Nevertheless Kirk's fandom for Burkean historicism was hard to reconcile with an attraction to natural law common to both the possessive individualist and right-Christian flanks of American conservatism. Kirk's soft spot for gloomy European snobs like Joseph de Maistre, Arthur Balfour, and the transplant T.S. Eliot, coupled with his luddism, was also hard to square with the American exceptionalism and the optimistic technophilia which infected all but the most immunized. And his rather homey incorporation of proud southern racists like John C. Calhoun into the great conservative tradition left Kirk and, by consequence, everything he touched open to accusations of indifference to racial inequality at best.[35]

Frank Meyer was undoubtedly the lesser intellect between the two. Starting out as a strident Communist, he read Hayek and became an equally zealous proponent of the free market. Much like a mutilated form of Marx's dialectics of class struggle could prove irresistible to those who wanted a Rosetta stone through which all history could be understood, Meyer found in Hayek and Voegelin the heroic story of a single principle-freedom-working its way into pre-eminence. Despite his undoubted limitations as both a scholar and a theorist next to Kirk, Meyer had a gift for economy and monologism too plebian and rationalistic for the former. Above all Meyer had a nose for the diplomatic side of intellectual politics, and could smell a tasteful synthesis when it was simmering. His impressive effort to combine a commitment to personal virtue with a defense of libertine political arrangements had the benefit of looking conceptually plausible enough to work with while being the strategically right idea for the American right. Consequently Meyer's version of fusionism would dominate smoothly and surely for many decades, until the 21st century resurrected a host of Kirkean ghosts to plague him once more.

What is interesting is that Kirk and Meyer both start from a similar affective standpoint: anxiety that the modern liberal or progressive state has become sufficiently powerful to swallow everyone and everything whole. Their difference lies in what the state is trying to destroy. Kirk claims that his position, and consequently conservatism as a whole, defies easy summation. This is because it is not a collection of rationalistic dogma which intends to reform society according to an abstract design, but instead a "way of looking at the civil social order."[36] This is much in the Burkean vein of characterizing politics as more of an outlook or disposition than a political theory. At times this proud lack of a program almost seems to be a way of glamorizing conservatism by characterizing it as either more worldly than its abstract opponents, more profound in its access to a mysterious but transcendent order, or, when feeling particularly greedy, both at the same time. And indeed Kirk will sometimes shift between both rhetorical styles in his writing when trying to condemn liberal and progressive "abstraction." But rather like Burke, Kirk's inability to define his principles exactly has little to do with anything all that mysterious. Anyone at all familiar with the history of conservatism expertly charted in Kirk's *The Conservative Mind* would recognize what is going on plenty quick. The "way" Kirk looks at civil social order repeatedly discovers the same sorts of egalitarian problems and recommends the same anti-egalitarian solutions as have been done by so very many other conservatives before and since. "Absolute equality is the death of all real vigor and freedom in existence," "equality should not extend to equality of condition: that is, society is a great partnership, in which all have equal rights—but not to equal things," "property and freedom are inseparably connected; economic leveling is not economic progress," and plenty more original gems are par for the course.[37]

Because much of Kirk's work is genealogical and commentary there is a degree of reconstruction that has to be carried out to express Kirk's main points successfully. His critique of the left modulates along the same lines as Burke's, Eliot's, and Oakeshott's and situates him comfortably within Anglo tradition. On the one hand he resents the left for its leveling impulse and vulgarity of imagination, and on the other he sees progressivism's emphasis on the small man as inspiring a perverse logic that ironically instantiates itself as a giant and overwhelming despotism which employs tyrannical measures to eradicate meaningful differences in status and merit within society. But since he is not a liberal Kirk doesn't mean by this toleration for individual differences and experiments in living—let alone multicultural toleration. Kirk anticipates someone like Bork caring very tenderly for the "natural" inequalities which make men different, or their differentiated ranks within society, and for a few others.[38] Kirk, following Burke, will sometimes defend this through a more demotic rhetorical mode praising the little platoons and brigades which rank society into so many colorful hierarchies of servitude and despotism.[39] But he was even more emphatic than Burke in comfortably shifting to an elitist rhetoric of the sublime and immense where that suited him. Indeed, in contrast to Burke—who was at least consistent enough in his principles to be wary of the expansiveness of the British Empire[40]—Kirk is enamored of America's "imperial duties" and even wishes for "imperial intellects" which will rise to meet them.[41]

In his "10 Conservative principles," Kirk stresses three times the association between inequality and resistance to leviathan when discussing the "Six Canons of Conservative Thought." Half of Kirk's canons focus to some extent or another on the need to maintain inequality within society. The second canon includes an injunction against the "narrowing uniformity, egalitarianism and utilitarianism of most radical systems." The fourth holds that "freedom and property are closely linked" and that "economic leveling" opens the door to the state becoming "master of all." But it is the third which is the most telling. It concerns the...

> Conviction that civilized society requires orders and classes, as against the notion of a 'classless society.' With reason conservatives have been called 'the party of order.' If natural distinctions are effaced among men, oligarchs fill the vacuum. Ultimate equality in the judgement of God, and equality before courts of law, are recognized by conservatives; but equality of condition, they think, means equality in servitude and boredom.[42]

One might playfully respond to Kirk by reformulating his disposition in the following terms: it isn't the state's job to dominate everyone because the traditional higher orders in society were plenty capable and entitled to do that of their own accord. These inegalitarian arguments are rather unoriginally given a rather surface gloss through Kirk's first canon, which stresses submission to some flavor of transcendent morality. The nature and true existence of which Kirk often doesn't bother to define. One suspects his very inability to define and argue for the sublime order, which invests social stratification with energy and aesthetic legitimacy, is meant to be conceived as a virtue, a testament to the depth that comes from postulating transcendence without arguing for it. Against this lusciously colorful model of hierarchical complementarity and domination, Kirk contrasts the drably rationalized world "sophisters, calculators, and economists" who have the gall to point out how abstract and unreal his mysticism happens to be.[43]

Now in some respects Kirk is simply pouring old wine into new bottles, albeit with literary style and impressive erudition—even if he shares a predilection for Anglo prejudices that better conservative philosophers like Roger Scruton didn't.[44] As a result of his argumentation, Kirk is vulnerable to a huge number of objections. The most obvious is that for all Kirk tries to aestheticize a perverse dialectic of leftist leveling resulting in the expansion of leviathan, his argument falls completely flat. By almost every metric the rights revolution which raged through the mid-20th century, which Kirk opposed even in the moderate forms embodied by the *Brown* decision, eroded despotic systems entrenched by state governments.[45] The "imperial duties" Kirk wanted to see the United States assume as heir apparent to the British Empire contributed to the disruption of any number of orderly societies across the globe through military coercion and, by the 21st century, had left much of the Middle East a ruin.

The ultimate appeal of Kirkeanism was never its historical acumen or even moral argumentation. It was Kirk's aesthetics of meaning. For someone like Kirk the traditional roles which one played in society, along with the mores and dispositions associated with them, provided a sense of significance within the broader social order. That not all roles were equally esteemed, or even close to equally esteemed, was beside the point. This is also where the integral connection between smallness and bigness in his work comes in, since by obediently participating in grander forms of hierarchical order—whether those set by imperial intellects or the very transcendent moral order to which they had access—the lives of little people could be affirmed and ordered into their proper place. As Kirk put it in *The Roots of American Order*, his defense of ordered liberty conservatism, the social order in which one participated would map itself onto the soul as a kind of disciplinary subjectivity which situated all where they belonged.

> The "inner order" of the soul and the "outer order" of society being intimately linked, we discuss in this book both aspects of order. Without a high degree of private moral order among the American people, the reign of law could not have prevailed in this country. Without an orderly pattern of politics, American private character would have sunk into a ruinous egoism. Order is the first need of the soul. It is not possible to love what

one ought to love, unless we recognize some principles of order by which to govern ourselves. Order is the first need of the commonwealth. It is not possible for us to live in peace with one another, unless we recognize some principle of order by which to do justice. The good society is marked by a high degree of order, justice, and freedom. Among these, order has primacy: for justice cannot be enforced until a tolerable civil social order is attained, nor can freedom be anything better than violence until order gives us laws.[46]

What's remarkable about this in a book that is nominally a defense of a moderate form of conservatism is just how extreme this position is. Even if one repudiates the liberal view that enhancing freedom through respect for some kind of natural or deontological rights is the first ambition of society, going back to Plato many would contend that justice is at least the first virtue of social institutions. For Kirk order has primacy over everything, with the mere fig leaf that it be "tolerable" the only thing in place to qualify it. Consequently whether one regards that order as free or loveable is not an overriding concern. Even whether it is in fact just and free from some higher philosophical perspective[47] is a secondary concern. It is hard not to regard this, however much Kirk directs himself against the leviathan, as a defense of authoritarian tendencies so long as they happen to be to his liking and refrain from leveling enterprises. But more importantly they seem especially vulnerable to Meyer's correct observations that a Kirkean society would preclude the very realization of the virtue it is intended to achieve, since a license to compel certain forms of behavior would pollute the capacity of individuals to develop a virtuous character by the very fact that their doing good is coerced.

For these reasons it is obvious why Frank Meyer was long considered the more palatable figure. What becomes tricky is figuring out what is in fact distinctly conservative about Meyer's viewpoint. It is undoubtedly true that he shared with traditionalist figures like Kirk and Oakeshott a fear that the modern egalitarian impetus would lead to an overwhelming statism. But unlike them the moral center of his work is the single individual, and his freedom and property, being threatened by state coercion. While his abiding anxiety was communist takeover, Meyer was also worried by various species of "collectivist liberalism"—a point which sits unhappily next to his robust defense of the socialist liberalism of J.S. Mill.[48] Meyer's emphasis on property of course overlaps nicely with many conservative concerns about egalitarianism, but isn't distinctly different from the classical liberal viewpoints of Locke, Hayek, or Milton Friedman. There is a deep tension in Meyer's writing, as for all those who take the classical liberal imaginary too seriously without testing it against real history, that of course a powerful state is required to establish a system of law and order which will insulate the free individual from interference and create a legal entitlement to property. This is rarely acknowledged by Meyer to the extent that even someone like Hayek not only recognized but defended the need for law and order along propertarian and liberal lines. Instead Meyer's work often gets relatively simplistic narratives echoing Lockean mythologizations about the existence of property rights anterior to the law which it is the state's job to protect.

> The state therefore has two natural functions, functions essential to the existence of any peaceful, ordered society: to protect the rights of citizens against violent or fraudulent assault and to judge in conflicts of right with right. It has a further third function, which is another aspect of the first, that is, to protect its citizens from assault by foreign powers. These three functions are expressed by three powers: the police power, which protects the citizen against domestic violence; the military power, which protects the citizen against violence from abroad; and the courts of law, which judge between rights and rights, as well as sharing with the police power the protection of the citizen against domestic violence.[49]

While I admire his liberalism there is undoubtedly something dissatisfying about much of this. A century and a half after Bentham's *Anarchial Fallacies* and a few decades after Weber's *Economy and Society*, even someone with a convert's zeal should recognize that naturalizing property entitlements circa a throwback appeal to natural rights opens the door to every kind of objection one can imagine. This should have been especially obvious to someone with a background in historical materialism.[50] But to his credit Meyer does organize a popular intellectual defense of natural rights by making possessive individualist forms of liberty the basis of living a virtuous life. While he confronted serious intellectual opponents—from Kirk to Brent Bozell—they never managed to organize their views to make them appealing to the mass of American conservatives for whom "liberty" was as cherished a word as it was to liberals. As Matthew Continentti put it:

> Bozell teased out a knot in Meyer's thinking, but in a way that could neither satisfy the libertarians inside the conservative coalition nor appeal to the majority of Americans who were not traditionalist Catholics. That was one reason the final victory in the dispute went to Meyer. Bozell's politics could not sustain a wide-ranging American Right, much less one that was viable at the polls. 'Fusionism'-the term was Bozell's, based on Meyer's original reference to 'fusion'-also won out through default. By the mid-1960s the writers who might have sustained the argument were either uninterested or unavailable....Finally, fusionism appealed to movement conservatives because it offered the most plausible theoretical explanation for their belief that the continuance of the American republic depended on a complex mixture of both freedom and virtue.[51]

It is here that Meyer's qualified originality lies, at least for the American tradition.

Now of course liberal thinkers like Kant had already formulated a far more sophisticated rebuttal of heteronymous social conservatism by emphasizing how only the good will doing its duty could be truly moral, opening up an expansive concern with motivation still of live interest to analytical philosophers.[52] Even devoutly Christian philosophers have been aware of this problem. At the foundation of Kierkegaard's *Attack on Christendom* is a concern about whether organized forms of religious faith which operate through coercive state systems and even various forms of social pressure generate modes of religious inauthenticity which actually preclude free individuals from the struggles entailed by real faith in God. If they do then socially conservative forms of religiosity are not only problematic but the very barrier to achieving what they claim to want.[53] And to the extent conservatives claim to care about character, virtue, and faith I think these are largely unanswerable objections to any illiberal system committed to authoritarian social order even at the expensive of the freedom and authenticity of the individuals who make it up. Meyer's caustic remark directed against Kirk, that in these situations "persons as such are anathema to the New Conservative doctrine, unless they are mere symbols for orders and ranks and hierarchies, stiffly disposed as in a Byzantine mosaic, signifying the abstract virtue of diversity..." is very on the mark.[54]

Meyer's own discussion of the association between virtue and freedom is considerably more mundane than either Kant's or Kierkegaard's, but warrants commendation for putting similar arguments in the language of American possessive individualism. Now part of his defense of freedom as the locus of virtue flows from a kind of synthesis of Aristotelian and Millsean anthropologies. Meyer stresses the importance of human relations in the formation of both character and meaning, while highlighting how it is often individuals themselves who know best which kind of relations are suited to their abilities and character. But the more important argument is a kind of watered-down Kantian sentiment that the deployment of coercion to produce virtue precludes its very development. Only through being capable of vice can one be good, as it is only when we have the potential to sin that holiness is obtainable. As Meyer puts it programmatically:

A social order is a good social order to the degree that men live as free persons under conditions in which virtue can be freely realized, advanced, and perpetuated. Freedom has its risks because it may not be virtue but vice that men advance, but all existence has its risks. Unless men are free to be vicious, they cannot be virtuous.[55]

In the end Meyer's talents as an expositor allowed him to popularize these important ideas, even if his limitations as a political theorist ensured they would remain vulnerable to more stubborn forms of conservative traditionalism in the future. But in the aftermath of the Cold War, where the kind of right-wing liberalism Meyer endorsed everywhere seemed triumphant, this must have seemed of little consequence.

Neoconservatism, or, Invigorating a Tired Civilization

> In other words, until another great power challenger emerges, the United States can enjoy a respite from the demands of international leadership. Like a boxer between championship bouts, America can afford to relax and live the good life, certain that there would be enough time to shape up for the next big challenge. Thus the United States could afford to reduce its military forces, close bases overseas, halt major weapons programs and reap the financial benefits of the "peace dividend." But as we have seen over the past decade, there has been no shortage of powers around the world who have taken the collapse of the Soviet empire as an opportunity to expand their own influence and challenge the American-led security order.
>
> (*The Project for a New American Century, 2000*)

Neoconservatism, a self-contradicting label for an odd doctrine, rose to prominence during the late 20th century. It enjoyed a brief moment of hegemony in the early 21st century but that was enough for it to be responsible for much of the century's pain so far. That this hasn't much bothered the conscience of its remarkably unrepentant spokesman (and not a few women) testifies to the moral rot that was there from the very beginning. Neoconservatism emerged in the 1960s, largely among disaffected liberals and reformed Marxists who were appalled at the lack of patriotism, 1960s radicalism, and detentism with Communism they saw on the American left. It enjoyed considerable prestige during the Reagan administration, where its combination of exceptionalist patriotism and militant anti-Communism was very much in fashion.

The aftermath of the Cold War presented neoconservatives with both an opportunity and a potential crisis, and it is the dialectical relation between the two prospects that stamped much of neoconservatism between the 1990s and its apex with the Bush Jr. administration. Neocons were critical of both Bush Sr. and Clinton for their lack of ambition and even "imagination"[56] with regard to the possibilities neoconservatives saw as being inherent in American power within a unipolar world. Ironically their own political imagination was rather scanty. Like the proverbial man with a hammer for whom everything becomes a nail, neoconservatives started trying to conceptualize the geopolitical cosmos as an arena of potential targets whose eradication would be both beneficent and exciting. The price paid for this lack of vision was the discrediting of neoconservatism by its disastrous foreign ventures in Iraq and Afghanistan. Their fall would be so steep that as of writing this chapter the neoconservative brand remains toxic even on the American and British right where it was once a dominant intellectual movement.

The defining tension of neoconservatism lay in seeing the fall of communism as both an opportunity and a potential crisis. On the one hand it was an opportunity for the United States and its allies to reinvent the world without any of the geostrategic constraints that would be imposed by the existence of another global power. On the other hand this raised the very real question of what, if anything, can or should be done with unipower. Neoconservatives were deeply concerned that, with the threat of war with a sufficiently powerful rival now gone, the martial edge which had allowed the United States and its allies to succeed would be dulled by continuous budget cuts and rollbacks. But for the more theoretically inclined neoconservatives, an equal and more subtle danger was the prospect of cultural laxity and its attendant nihilism and lack of opportunity for great projects. The young Francis Fukuyama captured this worry expertly in his early essay the "End of History" which described the post-Cold War period as

> a very sad time. The struggle for recognition, the willingness to risk one's life for a purely abstract goal, the worldwide ideological struggle that called forth daring, courage, imagination, and idealism, will be replaced by economic calculation, the endless solving of technical problems, environmental concerns, and the satisfaction of sophisticated consumer demands. In the post-historical period there will be neither art nor philosophy, just the perpetual caretaking of the museum of human history. I can feel in myself, and see in others around me, a powerful nostalgia for the time when history existed.[57]

Fukuyama drew, consciously or not, on the reservations of an already older neoconservative tradition. In one of his better essays "Capitalism, Socialism, and Nihilism" Irving Kristol, the Godfather of the movement, criticized socialism while offering a surprisingly lukewarm endorsement of capitalism. Kristol was deeply concerned that capitalism lacked the moral and spiritual capacity to ward off nihilism, which in the long run might become a more enduring threat to the bourgeois order. This can infect even its most sacrosanct economic principles, contributing to the banalized drive into egalitarian mediocrity.

> Even the very principles of individual opportunity and social mobility, which originally made the bourgeois—liberal idea so attractive, end up— once the spirit of religion is weakened-by creating an enormous problem for bourgeois society. This is the problem of publicly establishing an acceptable set of rules of distributive justice. The problem does not arise so long as the bourgeois ethos is closely linked to what we call the Puritan or Protestant ethos…But from the very beginning of modern capitalism there has been a different and equally influential definition of distributive justice. It says that, under capitalism, whatever is, is just—that all the inequalities of liberal—bourgeois society must be necessary, or else the free market would not have created them, and therefore they must be justified…Will this positive idea of distributive justice commend itself to the people? Will they accept it? Will they revere it? Will they defend it against its enemies? The answer, I submit, is as obvious as it is negative…Ordinary people will see it merely as a self-serving ideology; they insist on a more 'metaphysical'

justification of social and economic inequalities. In the absence of such a justification, they will see more sense in simpleminded egalitarianism than in the discourses of Mandeville or Hume. And so it has been: As the connection between the Protestant ethic and liberal-bourgeois society has withered away, the egalitarian temper has grown ever more powerful.[58]

These anxieties about the rising egalitarian temper required that the American mass had the ideals of their society sublimated elsewhere. If not in domestic struggles, where they were all too quickly coopted by New Left forms of expressive individualism and amoralism, then in the international sphere.

All this should highlight the danger of conflating neoconservatism with some kind of foreign policy realism ala Thucydides. In its best moments realism's disposition was one of wary prudentialism in the face of the world's enormity. Neoconservatism often regarded America as facing enormous problems, but many of them had little time or patience for technocratic prudentialism, let alone economism. Its view of the world was colorful and easily bored. This point was articulated expertly by Corey Robin in *The Reactionary Mind*.

> For conservatives who yearned for and then celebrated socialism's demise, Clinton's promotion of easygoing prosperity was a horror. Affluence produced a society without difficulty and adversity. Material satisfaction induced a loss of social depth and political meaning, a lessening or resolve and heroic verve...For influential neocons, Clinton's foreign policy was even more anathema. Not because the neocons were unilateralists arguing against Clinton's multilateralism, or isolationists or realists critical of his internationalism and humanitarianism. Clinton's foreign policy, they argued, was too driven by the imperatives of free market globalization. It was proof of the oozing decadence taking over the United States after the defeat of the Soviet Union, a sign of weakened moral fiber and lost martial spirit.[59]

The rhetoric neoconservatives would launch against this potential decadence would assume many cadences, testifying to the diverse intellectual heritage and journey of its members. Often neoconservative rhetoric assumed the recognizably reactionary stance of a campaign against materialist decadence. Other times it could present as a kind of neo-realism, even aping Schmittian style injunctions that the United States adopt an agonistic politics toward its rivals. Irving Kristol's argument that "statesmen should, above all, have the ability to distinguish friends from enemies...." is representative.[60] And, much like Schmitt himself, this kind of "realism" could itself speak many languages, from a cynical and even wonkish obsession with the geometries of military intervention and the technology of warfare to a rather Straussian insistence that sometimes only force employed by the virtuous against the wicked could make the world a better place. Most remarkably, it could even (rather unconsciously) ape liberalism's dark history of imperialist justificatory logics to make a case for military intervention as a way of spreading human rights and democracy. Michael Ignatieff managed to combine almost all of these rhetorical styles into a singular whole. As he put it in his influential primer *Empire Lite:*

> To the extent that human rights justify the humanitarian use of military force, the new empire can claim that is serves the cause of moral universalism. Yet is service to the cause is equivocal. If America were consistent about defending human rights everywhere, it would have to dispatch marines to every failed or failing state where populations are threatened with massacre or genocide. Doing so would be both vain and unwise. Empires that are successful learn to ration their service to moral principle to a few strategic zones where the defence of principle is simultaneously the defense of a vital interest, and where the risks do not outweigh the benefits. This is why modern imperial ethics can only be hypocritical.[61]
>
> (Indeed)

Of course, whatever one thinks of it, in the end the neoconservative project for "empire" wasn't "successful." As has since been discredited, and many of the former neocons have been unable to reconcile themselves with the plebian style and overt illiberalism of the right-wing populists who succeeded them. Often this has taken the form of simply accusing Trump and his allies as lacking virtue and tact, along with even more predictable accusations that left-wing radicals were in fact the ones responsible for galvanizing Trumpist extremism with their own extremism.[62] However, while many neoconservatives remain keen to distance themselves from figures like Trump, the reality is that the political rhetoric they deployed—at once patriotic and declinist, grandiose, agonistic, and cynical—along with the practical consequences of distrust, paranoia, and expanding executive power produced by the endless War on Terror, all fed into the banal brutalities of the Trumpist era. In this respect the effort of neoconservatives to insulate themselves from responsibility for Trumpism comes across as insincere or at best naïvely self-flattering. Without neoconservatism there would be no Trumpism.

Assessed as a whole, neoconservatism can be understood as one of the cultural logics which emerged in reaction to the neoliberal era. Unlike earlier forms of conservatism like Kirk and Buckley's that still had a world to win, neoconservatism gained much of its emotive force from anxiety about a world where the right had achieved so many of its domestic and international ambitions it was left wondering what there was left to accomplish. In this neoconservatism was fundamentally stamped by the features of consumerist neoliberalism which they found decadent but were unwilling to structurally critique; indeed neoconservatives typically went out of their way to not only laud the market but insist on a more brutal extension of it across the globe—including by military force if necessary. Like many forms of conservatism the neocons resented the materialism, permissiveness, and legalistic constraints imposed by the purer forms of neoliberal doctrine.[63] Indeed the very affluence neoconservatives saw being generated by the market system they promoted was responsible for the decadence they decried.

Rather than rejecting neoliberalism, their vision was one of complementarity. Unlike conservatives such as Buckley or Kirk, who directed their anxieties on the culture inward, neoconservatives looked abroad for solutions. In many respects this was an inevitable dialectical movement, since it enabled mainstream American and British conservatives to allow market transformations and permissiveness to continue apace at home, while projecting any criticisms to external opponents who could be safely targeted without the need or systematic change. Decadent materialism and domestic softness could be indefinitely excised through an exciting Thucydidean foreign policy abroad, with American imperial power conceived as an endlessly adaptable tool which could be used by great men to remake the world. With its startlingly un-Burkean view of human societies as effectively plastic which could be indefinitely rearranged by the sufficiently strong willed neoconservatism, it testifies to the residue of liberal nominalism which it was never able to shake off even as its major intellectuals moved right, but which made it well adapted to the height of market society. Neoconservatism was the perfect reactionary flavor for the broader post-modern culture which emerged.[64] Karl Rove's (it's most likely him at least) denunciation of the "reality-based community" which didn't appreciate how the scions of "empire" create their "own reality" which nebbish intellectuals will only be left to interpret is an emblematic statement to that effect.[65] But as always it turns out reality is a stubborn thing, and the neoconservatives would have been wiser if they remembered the *Book of Proverbs* sage wisdom about what comes before a great fall.

The Religious Roots of Post-Liberalism

> Liberalism thus culminates in two ontological points: the liberated individual and the controlling state. Hobbes's *Leviathan* perfectly portrayed those two realities: The state consists solely of autonomous (and non-grouped) individuals, and the individuals are "contained" by the state. No other grouping is granted ontological reality. In this world, gratitude to the past and obligations to the future are replaced by a near-universal pursuit of immediate gratification: Culture, rather than imparting the wisdom and experience of the past toward the end of cultivating virtues of self-restraint and civility, instead becomes synonymous with hedonic titillation, visceral crudeness, and distraction, all oriented toward promoting a culture of consumption, appetite, and detachment. As a result, seemingly self-maximizing but socially destructive behaviors begin to predominate in society.
>
> (Patrick Deneen, "Unsustainable Liberalism")

Post-liberalism, as both its enemies and proponents have taken to calling it,[66] is the most sophisticated[67] branch of right-wing theory to have emerged since the "end of history" period. It is also a misnomer, since there is very little "post" about post-liberalism. At least in the dialectical sense of wanting to transcend the limitations of liberal democracy to establish a new kind of society which will nonetheless remain stamped by features of the old. Post-liberalism—as articulated by Adrian Vermeule, Patrick Deneen, R.R. Reno, and the rest of the team—is more driven by nostalgia for the preliberal era than most conventional forms of right-wing thought. In this respect post-liberalism (sometimes consciously) harkens back to the more strident anti-liberalism of De Maistre, Dostoevsky, and Schmitt. Down to echoing the bellicose tone of those with enough free time on their hands to long for a return to the boys from men separating full Latin mass.

While their work varies considerably in its quality and orientation, the basis of the post-liberal's critique is quite uniform. They locate most, if not all, of the contemporary problems in the Western world with the spread of liberalism, seeing in its permissive emphasis on freedom and democratic equality the seeds of almost every form of discontent.[68] This gives post-liberalism a decidedly monological quality which can get a bit tedious. When the villain in your story is not only always the same, but always presented in the same way, it's hard to escape feelings of contrivance. Nevertheless the post-liberals monomaniacal assault on liberal permissiveness and—in a more complicated way—democratic equality has been effective in establishing a school of thought defined by a particular disposition and attitude. This can make the attacks of the more sophisticated post-liberals effective and even powerful within the limits of their analytical frameworks.

As predominantly Roman Catholics, many of the post-liberals echo the long-standing objection that liberalism and other progressive politics are fundamentally nihilistic. Unable to provide meaning to human life by connecting individual activity to the plans of a transcendent deity, life comes to lack a sublime or higher quality and becomes an empty pursuit of pleasure after pleasure, power after power. What gives the better post-liberal condemnations force beyond the kind of moralistic and elitist objections we've seen from Maistre through T.S. Eliot is their ability to develop an immanent critique of liberalism which purports to explain its failures in terms of its very successes. In worse hands this is nothing more than the "perversity" rhetoric dolled up with conventional reactionary appropriations of populist liberal and left rhetoric. A good example of this can be seen in R.R. Reno's claim that the "class war, a war on the weak, is epitomized by the campaign for gay marriage....Marriage has become another plastic, open-ended option for the upper class."[69] Here the only response is to express amusement that one could even think that the biggest problem facing the "poor" is the prospect of a man marrying another man and not...being "poor."[70] Not to mention expressing bewilderment that Reno thinks that gay men and women are not in fact the "weak" despite it being legal in the United States to openly criminalize their lifestyle until *Lawrence v Texas* in 2003 (and will be again if Clarence

Thomas has his way). But in the hands of Patrick Deneen the immanent critique of liberalism as a system which promises freedom and inequality and ends in state intrusion and material inequality is worth analyzing.

On Democratic Faith

The first iteration of Deneen's critique of liberal democratic modernity is presented in his book *Democratic Faith*. Interestingly the account in this book is considerably more nuanced than what appears in the later, more popular, *Why Liberalism Failed*, and can be profitably mined even by those not attuned to Deneen's political convictions. The intention of *Democratic Faith* is to criticize an excess of "democratic faith," which can be seen in a throughline of activists running from Locke through Jefferson and culminating in Dewey and Rorty. These authors all assumed that by liberating human beings from the shackles of, mainly religious, cosmological certainty, they would free human reason up for spectacular projects of human perfectibility. Deneen highlights how, despite often adopting the language of hyper-rationalization, democratic confidence paradoxically rested on a kind of secular faith which was in many respects more blindly optimistic than its religious counterparts. From at least Augustine there was a recognition of the fallen character of human life, and a consequent acceptance that no earthly utopia was possible (at least before the return of Christ). Much of Deneen's book is taken up with a deep analysis of figures like Rousseau, Whitman, and Dewey to demonstrate how much heavy lifting this faith was required to do.

Deneen concludes *Democratic Faith* by drawing on an array of "friendly critics" of democracy such as Plato and Tocqueville who maintain a "profound" sympathy with democratic aspirations but nonetheless sought to "chasten their idealistic democratic counterparts while defending democracy not in the name of human potential for 'perfectibility' but rather on the opposite grounds, namely, based on fundamental and inescapable human imperfection, insufficiency, and frailty. Their endorsement of human equality underlying their devotion to democracy rests upon our shared condition of imperfection and not on a projected future condition of fulfilled human promise.

This sets "friendly critics" of democracy, including Deneen himself, apart from more stridently anti-egalitarian thinkers who remain "largely vilified for their fundamental inegalitarianism and, more, their lack of democratic faith."[71]

At this point there is little that any defender of egalitarianism or democracy should object to. For Catholics like Deneen, an emphasis on equality arising from human frailties and sin can of course be more deeply connected to acknowledging each person as the equal child of God's agapeic love. By constructing a defense of democracy that echoes these theological convictions, even cast in secularized language, Deneen has provided a very helpful bridge for the wary Catholic to embrace modernity without abandoning her deep convictions. Given the long history of Catholic reaction, this is a welcome accomplishment. But even for the secular commentator Deneen is undeniably right that an excess of faith in democracy some of us are given to can lead to an ignorance of the more ugly and evil human qualities which will always be with us. More importantly, Deneen and authors like the late Peter Lawler have rightly drawn attention to how these more perfectionist strains of democratic faith very readily attach themselves to surprisingly inegalitarian outlooks. The hyper-meritocratic libertarianism which always creeps up, in the United States particularly, can very quickly operationalize democratic language about equal opportunity into an apologia for staggering levels of wealth and a minimal sense of communitarian obligation to our fellow citizens.[72] After all, if democratic perfectibility entails the best rising on their own merits, this can easily lead to a sense of narcissistic self-idolization, where the successful feel they alone were responsible for their success and consequently owe nothing to anyone else.[73] Drake's "Started from the Bottom" insists he's "gonna worry bout me, give a fuck about you" for a reason. By contrast an emphasis on our all-too-human frailties undeniably has a potent egalitarian dimension to it. It compels us to look at failure and suffering and recognize that there but for the grace of God go I.

However, as Deneen well knows, democracy and liberalism are by no means synonymous. And as early as *Democratic Faith* one can see him working through the ideas that would form the basis for his post-liberal views. This is because contemporary liberalism married to democracy constitutes the most aggressive and successful form of idealistic faith in human perfectibility. Deneen acknowledges that some earlier liberals once held a more pessimistic view about the "rational capacities of ordinary citizens" but regards these as having been "largely overcome" by the time we get to Mill and Dewey. These liberals believed in endless "moral progress through education, open deliberation, and the scientific control of nature…"[74] This led to its modern commitment into the

> most idealistic, even 'religious' transformative impulse [which] jettisons the accompanying tradition's religious belief in ineradicable human sinfulness, self-interest, and self-deception. It regards the prosect of universal reason and democratic deliberation as eminently realizable; it is not viewed as 'utopian' but as a practicable goal. The failure to realize a fully deliberative polity lies not in the nature and limitations of human character but rather is attributable to an insufficiently realized democratic populace…To the extent that people fail to demonstrate their receptiveness to liberalism's 'transformative' character, liberalism exhibits is foundational hostility toward nontransformed, average people.[75]

This final set of populist remarks are very difficult to square with the rather dark approximation of human nature at the beginning, and are irreconcilable with

Deneen's attraction to aristocratically minded "friendly critics" of democracy who also expressed consistent resignation at the failures of ordinary citizens to approximate higher ideals. In a populist vein Deneen chastises liberals for having too much faith in humankind and being disappointed when they don't live up to this ideal. But the basis of this populism is an even more highly elitist view that this faith is misguided because it asks more of the common man than he could possibly achieve of his own effort. Indeed, for Deneen, far more likely than perfectibility is a kind of tyrannical social leveling. Paradoxically each person is individuated by being thrown back on their own power to pursue hollow pleasures. While at the same time coming to looking like everyone else because of the widespread resentment directed against any cultural pressure to commit to sublime projects where those aligned with an acknowledgment of variable human excellence. Given this, it is unsurprising that Deneen remains fascinated with Tocqueville's lengthy rumination on the functionalist need for religion to permeate the liberal democratic order to instill a sense of transcendence in citizen's profane enterprises.

Has Liberalism Failed?

Deneen's *Why Liberalism Failed* is the most comprehensive and clear indictment yet produced by the post-liberal tradition, and also the most demonstrative of its technique of immanent critique. In the opening sections Deneen stresses how, at the turn of the 20th century, it seemed that liberalism was everywhere triumphant. It had overcome its most sustained rivals on the right (fascism) and left (communism) and become the official ideology of the "end of history." And yet by the silver jubilee of the peak 1989–1991 years there was no doubt liberalism was everywhere in crisis. Though notably, Deneen is silent about the role his allies played in bringing it there, which is rather like pouring gasoline on a burning house and then condemning it for shoddy fireproofing. Populist "illiberal" politicians like Victor Orban, Donald Trump, and Jair Bolsonaro seemed to be everywhere ascendant, leading to dime a dozen analyses from panicked classical liberals and ordered liberty conservatives about how the root of the problem was an insufficient commitment to liberalism. Donald Trump and Orban had exposed our failures in defending Enlightenment reason,[76] or how we'd strayed too much from the enduring wisdom of the American Founders,[77] or how easily people can be taken in by grifters of low moral character.[78] Deneen took a more immanent perspective and held that in fact liberalism hadn't failed because of an excess of commitment to its principles. It had failed because it had succeeded too well, like a nihilistic abyss that swallowed all the "preliberal" little platoons and cultures that sustained it to end by imploding.

> Liberalism's own successes makes it difficult to sustain reflection on the likelihood that the greatest current threat to liberalism lies not outside and beyond liberalism but within it. The potency of this threat arises from the

fundamental nature of liberalism, from what they are thought to be its very strengths-especially its faith in its ability of self-correction and its belief in progress and continual improvement-which make it largely impervious to discerning its deepest weaknesses and even self-inflicted decline. No matter our contemporary malady, there is no challenge that can't be fixed by a more perfect application of liberal solutions.[79]

Deneen goes on to call Francis Bacon the real founder of liberal metaphysics. By denying a teleological quality to nature Bacon undercut the basis of right in natural law. Instead Bacon adopted what Peter Lawler describes as a "nominalist" ontology, holding that all matter could be put up on the rack and manipulated for human purposes and through intellectual power.[80] Nature was seen as an infinitely plastic entity to be manipulated by liberated human beings for the purposes of gratifying our self-interest. Nature was also seen as the primary source of barriers to human flourishing which could be overcome through the exercise of reason, rather than fulfilling any teleological function higher than what humans ascribed to mere matter in motion.

Deneen goes on to extend his outlook to liberal politics, highlighting how Hobbes and Locke took a dim view of human community and culture by putting the infamous atomized individual at the core of their thought. This atomized individual also looked upon all human communities as artificial and consequently regarded any obligation imposed upon her which was not entirely voluntaristic as fundamentally illegitimate. Initially this took the form of a rebellion against feudal and medieval aristocratic statism and its remnants such as slavery, a point which Deneen begrudgingly grants liberalism some qualified credit for.[81] But Deneen then turns the screw by pointing out how, since liberalism's most rigid commitment is to liberate the individual from all unchosen commitments— including cultural and even natural ones—it was inevitable that liberal subjects would demand an expansion of the state. After all "individualism and statism advance together, always mutually supportive, and always at the expense of lived and vital relations that stand in contrast to both the starkness of the autonomous individual and the abstraction of our membership in the state."[82] The state was the only power sufficiently great to completely liquidate unchosen forms of attachment, including traditional and religious ones.

Liberals went on to tear down traditional forms of citizenship, allied to market forces which generated immense inequality, empowering a "new aristocracy" to engage in endless Millsian "experiments in living. Custom has been routed: much of what today passes for culture—with or without the adjective 'popular'— consists of mocking sarcasm and irony..."[83] which snidely dismisses any return to tradition as a loss of free individuality even as its proponents look and sound the same. Both classical and progressive liberalisms contribute to this: the former by allowing the market to generate intense selfishness and inequality and the latter by using state power to destroy any traditionalist barriers to experimentalism. Meanwhile the working class, unable to insulate itself from the corrosion wrought by these transformative projects, is increasingly destitute, devoid of local community institutions, and haughtily mocked by the "liberalocracy."

One of the most disappointing features of *Why Liberalism Failed* is, oddly, how unambitious it actually is. Deneen could hardly be more disparaging of the Promethean liberal metaphysics associated with Bacon, who he describes as wanting "master nature" to liberate humans from its limits with the end result being an "assault on cultural norms and practices developed alongside nature."[84] For all this fire and brimstone one would think the essence of Deneen's critique would therefore be a complete dissection of Baconian materialism and its offshoots. Something along the line of a *Summa* or at least a *Theology and Social Theory*.[85] But instead we get almost no ontological or epistemological arguments whatsoever, and by conservative standards not even particularly good putdowns.[86] This is quite shocking. Any liberal who paused for a minute might retort that, even if everything Deneen said about the moral and political implications of liberal metaphysics were right (and it isn't), that does nothing to actually discredit liberal metaphysics. Something can be undesirable and still true. To quote Strauss one more time

> …a wish is not a fact. Even by proving that a certain view is indispensable for living well, one proves merely that the view in question is a salutary myth: one does not prove it to be true. Utility and truth are two entirely different things.[87]

Rebutting Francis Bacon, Kant, Russell, and so on by appealing to Charles Murray is a bit like trying to refute optics by pointing to Michael Bay movies; rhetorically persuasive to a select few, but besides the point. It is quite telling that for all the sturm und drang directed against the rationalistic liberal metaphysics tied to the scientific revolution, the best post-liberals have been to marshal against has been….aesthetic theory and poetics.[88]

But even at the political level Deneen's sweeping indictment of liberalism is highly intellectualized, conflating the conceptual idealizations of liberalism and the disintegrationist material practices of capitalist markets. An important limitation to *Why Liberalism Failed* is how its abstract reliance on liberal philosophy as the basis for criticism is largely devoid of any serious analysis of political economy and the concrete power relations which spring from it. Indeed, for all Deneen's undeniably sincere concerns about inequality and the working class, almost all his objections follow in the R.R. Reno vein of cultural condemnation. Deneen even refuses to give progressive individualism, let alone democratic socialism, any credit for welfarism or any reforms which actually increased the political agency of the lower orders. He dismissively conflates progressive individualism and classical liberalism's possessive individualism by suggesting the "embrace of economic equality was not intended to secure an opposite outcome to classical liberalism: rather, it sought to extend the weakening of social forms and cultural traditions already advanced by classical liberalism, with an end to increasing political consolidation."[89] His main villain in the chapter from which this quote comes is J.S. Mill. But Mill was a self-described socialist who condemned classical liberalism's exacerbation of inequality and the spread of anomie resulting from capitalist exploitation. His solution was the spread of workplace democracy, more material flourishing, and increasingly political suffrage for those it had long been denied. Mill was also very concerned with adding a solidaristic dimension to liberalism and was convinced that this could never be achieved simply through cultural or political transformations. Instead workplace democracy was useful in generating local ties of affection through direct participation in reproducing social life and disseminating its rewards more fraternistically.[90] Compared to Mill and other progressive liberals anyone should find Deneen's efforts to graft class agitation to a crusade against gay marriage...insincere and not enough.[91] In fact not much at all.

And while Deneen, Ahmari, and others are correct in describing certain rights-based constraints on the political freedoms of conservatives to uphold traditionalist norms as a constraint on freedom, their view is deeply unbalanced.[92] Adrian Vermeule may lose some freedom when he is not allowed to implement anti-sodomy laws. But these freedoms are vastly less substantial than those of LGBTQ persons who would essentially become criminalized because of such restrictions.[93] In this respect it is hard to see how the post-liberal program of socially conservative illiberalism could be implemented without resorting to more strident authoritarianism than the one they critique. This concern turns to irritation when one remembers the scorn with which Deneen describes the voluntaristic basis of liberal thinking, and becomes anger when discovering the post-liberal fanboyism toward tin-pot illiberal autocracies like Hungary and Poland.[94] And finally a sense of disappointment given the depth of Deneen's early analysis of democracy, which suggests a different path forward than the one they decided to take.

National Conservatism

Along with post-liberalism another recent development has been the rise of national conservatism. It has enjoyed unusually high levels of institutional support, which has allowed it to host a yearly conference of luminaries agitating for anti-liberal politics and flirting around the edge of acceptable defenses of soft authoritarianism.[95] While there is considerable overlap with the agonistic and even substantial aims of post-liberalism, national conservatism takes a more stridently nationalistic and organicist approach than its counterpart. The chief theorist of national conservatism is Yoram Hazony. In his readable books *The Virtue of Nationalism* and *Conservatism: A Rediscovery* Hazony lays out a systematic case for national conservatism as a response to the vulgarities of our liberal and egalitarian moment. Strikingly Hazony takes a more transparently anti-egalitarian tone than the post-liberals, even going so far as to reject liberal modernity's defense of universal human freedom and especially equality.

The human individual is not born free and equal. On the contrary, he is born weak, dependent, and ignorant—in the lowest position within a family hierarchy in which everyone he meets is stronger, wiser, and more capable than he is. However, there is a natural progression in every human hierarchy, whereby the young begin at the bottom, in positions having the least importance. In these lower positions, they give honor to their superiors and elders, treating their words and actions as having great weight. It is this, and only this, which permits the young to learn and attain competence and wisdom in any kind of endeavor. With time, these youths gain in knowledge, experience, and skill, and they rise in status until they take the place of their elders, who have died or stepped aside. What "equality" exists in this progress of human society results from the fact that the young may advance in knowledge and status, until one day they will acquire the importance and weightiness that now belongs to their elders and superiors. Then they will be parents and teachers, rulers and commanders, proprietors and accomplished scholars. And when this day comes, they themselves will be honored by the young, who will in this way repay them for having honored their own parents and teachers.[96]

This position is considerably more critical and candid than Deneen's or even Vermeule's, whose Catholicism one suspects makes them reticent to abandon at least a nominal commitment to human equality. Hazony's argument, building on the positions of Burke, Selden, and others, is that the liberal belief in universal freedom and equality flows from its basis in rationalism. Developed by Descartes as a "worthless" rival to the eventually triumphant empirical sciences, rationalism's scientific failures haven't prevented it from being political influential. A long line of

> political theorists embraced it and it remains the dominant view. Descartes's method was adopted by Thomas Hobbes and John Locke in England, and later imported back into France by Jean-Jacques Rousseau's *The Social Contract* and into Germany in the form of Kant's political essays such as *Perpetual Peace*.[97]

These rationalistic philosophies hold that all individuals are equal and free, and so disregard authority and hierarchies which have proven themselves over time. For Hazony, the way to determine whether authoritative hierarchies have proven themselves over time is through applying a method of "historical empiricism" which holds that the

> authority of government derives from constitutional traditions known, through the long historical experience of a given nation, to offer stability, well-being, and freedom. These are refined through trial and error over many centuries, with repairs and improvements being introduced where

necessary, while seeking to maintain the integrity of the inherited national edifice as a whole. Such historical empiricism entails a skeptical standpoint with regard to the divine right of the rulers, the universal rights of man, and all other abstract, universal systems.[98]

This of course immediately leads to a conundrum: on what basis to criticize liberal principles insofar as they are reframed as part of the national heritage—as, for instance, they have been in many Western states? If the only basis for measuring an ideology and its form of government is their endurability then hasn't liberalism proven itself historically and empirically? Hazony is often cagey on this point. Sometimes he holds out olive branches to at least "anti-Marxist" liberals, while in other he condemns the whole of liberalism without qualifications. Hazony stresses how the egalitarian and emancipatory core shared by liberalism and Marxism leads to a "dance" where liberals are inexorably coaxed toward leftist extremism by the immanent logic of their own rationalism.[99] For this reason his usual tone is one of rejection even for moderate liberalism.

Hazony holds that those hierarchies associated with national identities are those that have proven themselves to be the most durable and conducive to human well-being over time. He even quietly smuggles in some distinctly Millsian sounding language to describe nationalism as not just conducive to the well-being of a nation's members, but to humanity as a whole because it allows us to run a variety of "experiments" to test which forms of life are best. As he puts it in *Conservatism: A Rediscovery* where

> we are unable to obtain certainty by examining nature and revelation, the best way to proceed is by experiment, with each nation maintaining its own customs and practices until a repair is obviously required. Such a procedure will not please the revolutionaries, who insist that all questions have certain and universally valid answers. But it will uphold laws and a way of life that is suited to the history and character of a particular people.[100]

Hazony argues that a world of nation-states, emulating the Westphalian state system which emerged post-1648, would be less prone to violence and imperialist wars than an international system oriented by cosmopolitan universalism.[101] It would also be one where various conservative democracies would flourish without imperialist interference from liberal internationalism. These nationalist conservative democracies would be more militant in upholding a public religion, mandate a kind of religious education, and adopt an ethno-chauvinistic approach to migration policies. Hazony is generally cagey about what all of this would mean for religious, sexual, and ethnic minorities already living within candidate states for conservative democratization. At points Hazony suggests that, where these groups pose no large-scale challenge to the predominant conservative order, they may be entitled to a "carve out" of freedom from ethno-religious norms.[102] Less explicitly stated is that these "carve outs" could not be framed in liberal terms as "rights" against the national or religious majority, but instead exceptions to the general rule to be grant by those in power. To the extent Schmittian anxieties about the failure of efforts at political-theological inclusion haunt liberalism, they positively influence it in these circumstances.

There are many problems with Hazony's analysis.

First, as Hazony occasionally grudgingly admits, many liberals—including some of the most progressive—are clearly empiricists who don't fit into the rationalist box where Hazony wants to fit them. Even Kant was a transcendental idealist who, in addition to making important astronomical contributions, certainly didn't think it was possible to deduce scientific facts about the phenomenal world through pure reason. And both rationalist and empiricist liberals tended to be far more willing to stress the limitations of human reason than Hazony gives them credit for. Indeed, given the lengthy defense of theological transcendence embodied by variable traditions in *Conservatism: A Rediscovery*, it is quite clear that Kant, Mill, Popper, Rawls, and the rest of the gang are far more willing to accept skeptical limitations to human knowledge than Hazony.[103] Indeed Hazony's "historical empiricism" turns on a great many real abstractions which are certainly not empirically existent. After all the reified "nation" is not an empirical object but an abstract "imagined community" which exists only in the convictions and practices of its members. Hazony might respond in a Burkean vein that at least his preferred abstractions have proven themselves over time, but that brings us to the next problem.

Second, for a "historical empiricist," it is ironic that the weakest dimension of Hazony's work is its historical details. The Westphalian era of nationalist competition which Hazony nostalgically lionizes was noteworthy for three things. European states jealously guarding their sovereignty, ethnic groups within them causing mass disruption in the name of national self-determination, and the most expansive imperialism the world has ever seen. Britain, France, the United States, and almost all the other countries Hazony points to as models for his nation-statism were intensely imperialist powers. And much of their imperialism was transparently motivated by various combinations of liberal-national, ethno-nationalist, religious-nationalist, white-supremacist, and every other flavor of chauvinism. In its more benign forms nationalism undoubtedly served as a liberatory and even anti-colonial force. But conservative and not a few progressive nationalists were more prone to reifying the nation and appealing to its greatness as a justification for hyper-expansionist policies.[104] Even more baffling are Hazony's efforts to evade the reality of fascist ultra-nationalism through redefining Nazi expansionism as imperialism and consequently not motivated by a genuine nationalism.[105]

Third, and most importantly, as mentioned, Hazony occasionally refers to Enlightenment rationalism as an unskeptical quest for truth. I highlighted that in many respects figures like Kant were far more willing to accept the consequences of enduring epistemic limitations than Hazony. This has political consequences since, in fact, historical empiricism very quickly turns into a kind of idealism whose dependency on real abstractions is very apparent. There is a deeply De Maistrean sense in which Hazony clearly objects to the modernist tradition for submitting the reified real abstractions of nation, tradition, and faith to an endless and equal questioning of all rather than regarding them as sublime transcendent objects to be adorned and submitted to. As he puts it:

> Enlightenment rationalism supposes that individuals, if they reason freely about political and moral subjects without reference to tradition, will quickly discover the truth concerning these matters and move toward a consensus. But experience suggests just the opposite: When people reason freely about political and moral questions, they produce a profusion of varying and contradictory opinions, reaching no consensus at all. Indeed, the only thing that reasoning without reference to some traditional framework can do with great competence is identify an unlimited number of flaws and failings, both imagined and real, in whatever institutions and norms have been inherited from the past. Where individuals are encouraged to engage in this activity, the process of finding flaws in inherited institutions proceeds with ever greater speed and enthusiasm, until in the end whatever has been inherited becomes a thing of lightness and folly in their eyes. In this way, they come to reject all the old ideas and behaviors, uprooting and discarding everything that was once a matter of consensus. This means that Enlightenment rationalism, to the extent that its program is taken seriously, is an engine of perpetual revolution, which brings about the progressive destruction of every inherited institution, yet without ever being able to consolidate a stable consensus around any new ones.[106]

This maps onto Hazony's hierarchical vision of society and his rejection of human equality. But more importantly, for a man of faith, it denies the importance of authenticity and individuation in one's relation with God so stressed by figures like Kierkegaard, Derrida. Faith depends on making the way to God harder by stressing the distance between God and the world, and so intensifying the relationship. Authentic faith will always include precisely the kind of relentless and scrupulous questioning Hazony wants to banish. By reducing religion to a kind of nationalist glue holding a people together, Hazony risks turning the divine into a kind of idol. In this respect it is hard to think of a greater enemy to true faith than the nationalist conservative movements which claim to be defending it.

Conclusion

If Devlin, Oakeshott, and the rest speak with the voice of a conservatism which is convinced it has lost the modern world, then Kirk, Deneen, and Hazony represent it on the offensive. By contrast neoconservatism is the existential loss of meaning which accompanies any triumph so thoroughly that it liquidates the will to live through the absence of resistance and struggle. To the extent that conservatism is compelled to greater intellectual and aesthetic heights in its struggle with liberalism and progressivism, a paradox is that in this success we see some of its most underwhelming figures. Kirk was undoubtedly an important and prolific author, but he cannot be meaningfully compared with a generous scholar like Strauss or a giant like Eliot or Dostoevsky. Meyer's blending of liberalism with virtue ethics was a canny philosophy for the moment, but it pales next to the efforts of those who'd done it before and better. And neoconservatism's post-modern Thucydideanism was so unconvincing even under the ideal conditions of an endless War on Terror, where one would expect it to flourish, its moment in the sun didn't even last out a few decades. But regarded from the standpoint of someone critical of conservatism, the least that can be said for these positions is they are comparatively tempered. Indeed part of their appeal is a consistent supplication before a good many liberal and democratic norms, even if they're repurposed for right-wing projects. The same cannot be said for the far right, which will produce some of the greatest and worst—and most evil—thinkers on the political right.

Notes

1 Robert O. Paxton. *The Anatomy of Fascism*. (New York, NY: Vintage Books, 2005)
2 See Richard Evans. *The Third Reich at War*. (London, UK: Penguin Books, 2010) and Robert O. Paxton. *The Anatomy of Fascism*. (New York, NY: Vintage Books, 2005)
3 See Rick Perlstein. *Before the Storm: Barry Goldwater and the Unmaking of the American Consensus*. (New York, NY: Nation Books, 2001)
4 Chile is just the most notorious and brazen example. See Jessica Whyte. *The Morals of the Market: Human Rights and the Rise of Neoliberalism*. (London, UK: Verso Books, 2019) and David Harvey. *A Brief History of Neoliberalism*. (Oxford, UK: Oxford University Press, 2007)
5 Singapore and the remaining Middle Eastern monarchies are partial exceptions to this rule.
6 See Robert Dahl. *How Democratic Is the American Constitution?* (New Haven, NC: Yale University Press, 2003)
7 See Rick Perlstein. *Before the Storm: Barry Goldwater and the Unmaking of the American Consensus*. (New York, NY: Nation Books, 2001) and Joseph E Lowndes. *From the New Deal to the New Right: Race and the Southern Origins of Modern Conservatism*. (New Haven, CT: Yale University Press, 2008)
8 Contemporaneously, reconciling the rhetoric of populism with a reliance on the most overtly anti-majoritarian and elitist features of the American constitution is a good example.
9 See Peter Augustine Lawler. *Postmodernism Rightly Understood: The Return to Realism in American Thought*. (Lanham, MA: Rowman and Littlefield, 1992)
10 See Thomas Sowell. *Intellectuals and Society*. (New York, NY: Basic Books, 2009) at p. 56 and Thomas Sowell. "Misinformed Electorate Shouldn't Vote." *Fox Business*, September 18th, 2015 https://www.youtube.com/watch?v=ENBKr2DZ0dI
11 See especially Curtis Yarvin. *A Gentle Introduction to Unqualified Reservations*. Unqualified Reservations, January 8th, 2009
12 Robert Bork. *Coercing Virtue: The Worldwide Rule of Judges*. (Toronto, ON: Vintage Canada, 2002) at p. 5
13 See Fredric Jameson. *Postmodernism, or, the Cultural Logic of Late Capitalism*. (Durham, NC: Duke University Press, 1991)

14 See Obery Hendricks. *The Politics of Jesus: Rediscovering the True Revolutionary Nature of Jesus' Teachings and How They Have Been Corrupted.* (New York, NY: Three Leaves Publishing, 2006)

15 Adrian Vermeule. *Common Good Constitutionalism: Recovering the Classical Legal Tradition.* (Cambridge, UK: Polity Press, 2022)

16 See Max Weber. *The Protestant Work Ethic and the Spirit of Capitalism,* trans. Talcott Parsons. (Mineola, NY: Dover Publications, 1958)

17 This is true regardless of whether one adopts a more humanistic view of individuals as freely laboring to improve the world or the Calvinistic position that earthly prosperity was ordained by God for those who he'd already decided were worthy of salvation.

18 See Ann Coulter. *If Democrats Had Any Brains They'd Be Republicans.* (New York, NY: Three Rivers Press, 2007) at p. 104

19 See Max Weber. *The Protestant Ethic and the Spirit of Capitalism,* trans. Talcott Parsons. (Mineola, NY: Dover Publications, 1958) at pp. 48–50.

20 Quinn Slobodian. *Globalists: The End of Empire and the Birth of Neoliberalism.* (Cambridge, MA: Harvard University Press, 2018)

21 Hayek was deeply opposed to these meritocratic, let alone religious, ways of reasoning about the market. Though he saw a role for religion in providing for social order. See F.A. Hayek. *The Constitution of Liberty: The Definitive Edition.* (Chicago, IL: University of Chicago Press, 2011)

22 See Obery Hendricks. *Christians against Christianity: How Right Wing Evangelicals Are Destroying Our Nation and Our Faith.* (Boston, MA: Beacon Press, 2021)

23 See Albert O. Hirschman about the left's tendency to lean into rhetoric about being on the right side of history. See Albert O. Hirschman. *The Rhetoric of Reaction: Perversity, Futility, Jeopardy.* (Cambridge, MA: The Belknap Press of Harvard University Press, 1991)

24 Corey Robin. *The Reactionary Mind Second Edition: Conservatism from Edmund Burke to Donald Trump.* (Oxford, UK: Oxford University Press, 2018) at p. 51

25 See Robert Heilbroner. *The Worldly Philosophers: The Lives, Times, and Ideas of the Great Economic Thinkers-Seventh Edition.* (New York, NY: Simon and Schuster, 1995)

26 Rick Perlstein. *Before the Storm: Barry Goldwater and the Unmaking of the American Consensus.* (New York, NY: Nation Books, 2001)

27 See Eric Hobsbawm. *The Age of Extremes: A History of the World 1914–1991.* (New York, NY: Vintage Books, 1996)

28 Joseph E. Lowndes. *From the New Deal to the New Right: Race and the Southern Origins of Modern Conservatism.* (New Haven, CT: Yale University Press, 2008) at p. 49

29 See Ayn Rand. *The Fountainhead: Student Edition.* (New York, NY: Signet Books, 1993) and Jennifer Burns. *Goddess of the Market: Ayn Rand and the American Right* (Oxford, UK: Oxford University Press, 2009)

30 See William Buckley. *God and Man at Yale: The Superstitions of Academic Freedom.* (Wilmington, DE: ISI Conservative Classics, 2001)

31 Kirk's veneration of Southern conservatism while barely mentioning slavery or segregation is indicatory.

32 See National Review. "The South Girds Its Loins." *National Review,* February 29th, 1956

33 See William Buckley. "Why the South Must Prevail." *National Review,* 1957 https://adamgomez.files.wordpress.com/2012/03/whythesouthmustprevail-1957.pdf

34 See Ben Sixmith. "The Fusionism That Failed" *First Things,* June 2019 and R.R. Reno. "A New Fusionism" *First Things,* April 2020

35 See Miles Smith. "Russell Kirk and the South." *The Imaginative Conservative,* September 15th, 2014

36 See Russell Kirk. "Ten Conservative Principles." *The Russell Kirk Center,* https://kirkcenter.org/conservatism/ten-conservative-principles/

37 See Russell Kirk. "The Essence of Conservatism." *The Russell Kirk Center,* March 19th, 2007

38 Robert Bork. *Coercing Virtue: The Worldwide Rule of Judges*. (Toronto, ON: Vintage Canada, 2002)

39 Kirk's veneration of Burke was a consistent theme of his work, even after his conversion to Catholicism. See Russell Kirk. "The Living Edmund Burke." *Modern Age*, Summer/Fall 1982

40 See Uday Singh Mehta. *Liberalism and Empire: A Study in Nineteenth-Century British Liberal Thought*. (Chicago, IL: The University of Chicago Press, 1999)

41 See Russell Kirk. "The Living Edmund Burke." *Modern Age*, Summer/Fall 1982

42 Russell Kirk. *The Conservative Mind: From Burke to Eliot*. (Washington, DC: Gateway Editions, 2016) at pp. 8, 9

43 Hayek and Kirk infamously had rather testy exchanges, and it is quite possible that the former had Kirk in mind when he accused conservatism of a willful and even proud "obscurantism." See F.A. Hayek. "Why I Am Not a Conservative." *Foundation for Economic Education,* 2016 and Matthew Continetti. "The Forgotten Father of American Conservatism." *The Atlantic,* October 19th, 2018

44 Kirk's unwillingness to learn from Hegel due to his influence on Marx is representative.

45 See Russell Kirk, "Now Perhaps Schools Can Get Down to Education," To the Point, General Features Division, August 11th, 1974

46 See Russell Kirk. *The Roots of American Order*. (Wilmington, DE: Intercollegiate Studies Institute, 2003) at Chapter One

47 At points Kirk is very vulnerable, as all Burkeans are, to a Straussian style immanent critique of his historicism.

48 Frank Meyer. *In Defense of Freedom and Related Essays*. (Indianapolis, IN: Liberty Fund, 1996) at pp. 164–169

49 Frank Meyer. *In Defense of Freedom and Related Essays*. (Indianapolis, IN: Liberty Fund, 1996) at pp. 99, 100

50 Meyer even theorizes that Burke might have come round to natural rights discourse, not excepting his criticisms of its rhetorical misemployment by the French Revolutionaries. See Frank Meyer. *In Defense of Freedom and Related Essays*. (Indianapolis, IN: Liberty Fund, 1996) at p. 62

51 Matthew Continetti. *The Right: The Hundred Year War for American Conservatism*. (New York, NY: Basic Books, 2022) at pp. 148, 149

52 There are extensive debates about this in the various forms of Kantian constructivism seen today, particularly on the question of the extent to which Rawlsian-style hypostatized empirical interests can play a role in moral motivation without corrupting the integrity of the deontological project. See Allen Wood. *Kant's Ethical Thought*. (Cambridge, UK: Cambridge University Press, 1999)

53 Soren Kierkegaard. *Attack on Christendom*, trans. Walter Lowrie. (Princeton, NJ: Princeton University Press, 1968)

54 Frank Meyer. *In Defense of Freedom and Related Essays*. (Indianapolis, IN: Liberty Fund, 1996) at p. 130

55 Frank Meyer. *In Defense of Freedom and Related Essays*. (Indianapolis, IN: Liberty Fund, 1996) at p. 148

56 See Christopher DeMuth and William Kristol. *The Neoconservative Imagination: Essays in Honor of Irving Kristol*. (Washington, DC: American Enterprise Institute, 1995)

57 See Francis Fukuyama. "The End of History?" *The National Interest*, 1989 at p. 18

58 See Irving Kristol. *Neo-Conservatism: The Autobiography of an Idea*. (New York, NY: Free Press, 1995) at pp. 100, 101

59 See Corey Robin. *The Reactionary Mind: Conservatism from Edmund Burke to Donald Trump*. (Oxford, UK: Oxford University Press, 2011) at pp. 210, 211

60 See Irving Kristol. "The Neoconservative Persuasion." *The Weekly Standard*, August 25th, 2003

61 See Michael Ignatieff. *Empire Lite*. (Toronto, ON: Penguin Canada, 2003) at p. 94

62 A typical screed in this mode is Jonah Goldberg. *Suicide of the West: How the Rebirth of Tribalism, Nationalism and Socialism Is Destroying American Democracy.* (New York, NY: Crown Forum, 2020)

63 Many forms of neoliberalism were distinctively legalistic in their outlook, perhaps inevitably given their desire to constrain state power and consequently put a cap on how it could be used even by "great" men in the pursuit of vainglory. Interestingly many neoliberals were concerned that even domestic law would be insufficient and called for the creation of more robust international legal systems which neoconservatives came to despise. See F.A. Hayek. *Law, Legislation, and Liberty.* (Chicago, IL: University of Chicago Press, 1978) and Jessica Whyte. *The Morals of the Market: Human Rights and the Rise of Neoliberalism.* (London, UK: Verso Books, 2019)

64 Fredric Jameson. *Postmodernism, or, the Cultural Logic of Late Capitalism.* (Durham, NC: Duke University Press, 1991)

65 See Ron Suskind. "Faith, Certainty, and the Presidency of George W. Bush." *New York Times,* October 17th, 2004

66 See Patrick Deneen's forthcoming "Regime Change: Toward a Postliberal Future" with Sentinel Press for an example.

67 Also significant are the various forms of "national conservatism" which have emerged since at least the victory of Trump and which will be discussed shortly. The critiques of the national conservatives overlap with post-liberals in distinct ways, but their solutions tend to be more Burkean and historicist in orientation—with all the inevitable Straussian problems this entails. This has led to an occasionally fierce battle between the two. For the most sophisticated defense of national conservatism see Yoram Hazony. *Conservatism: A Rediscovery.* (Washington, DC: Regnery Press, 2022)

68 Discussed with great nuance by Deneen in Patrick Deneen. *Democratic Faith.* (Princeton, NJ: Princeton University Press, 2005)

69 R.R. Reno. *Resurrecting the Idea of Christian Society.* (Washington, DC: Regnery Faith, 2016) at p. 62

70 It is striking how far this tradition has descended from its great thinkers. Compare these rather rote bits of social conservatism to the careful and rich analysis of someone like MacIntyre in his dialogue with the Marxist tradition. See Alasdair MacIntyre. *Marxism and Christianity.* (Notre Dame, IN: University of Notre Dame Press, 2003)

71 Patrick Deneen. *Democratic Faith.* (Princeton, NJ: Princeton University Press, 2005) at p. 191

72 Peter Augustine Lawler. *American Heresies and Higher Education.* (South Bend, IN: St Augustine Press, 2016)

73 The deepest analysis of the basis of these views remains MacPherson's classic analysis of possessive individualism. See C.B. MacPherson. *The Political Theory of Possessive Individualism: Hobbes to Locke.* (Don Mills, ON: Oxford University Press, 1962)

74 Patrick Deneen. *Democratic Faith.* (Princeton, NJ: Princeton University Press, 2005) at p. 25

75 Patrick Deneen. *Democratic Faith.* (Princeton, NJ: Princeton University Press, 2005) at p. 26

76 See Steven Pinker. *Enlightenment Now: The Case for Reason, Science, Humanism, and Progress.* (London, UK: Penguin Books, 2019)

77 See George F. Will. *The Conservative Sensibility.* (New York, NY: Hachette Books, 2020)

78 See Jonah Goldberg. *Suicide of the West: How the Rebirth of Tribalism, Nationalism and Socialism Is Destroying American Democracy.* (New York, NY: Crown Forum, 2020)

79 See Patrick Deneen. *Why Liberalism Failed.* (New Haven, CN: Yale University Press, 2018) at pp. 28, 29

80 Peter Augustine Lawler. *Postmodernism Rightly Understood: The Return to Realism in American Thought.* (Lanham, MA: Rowman and Littlefield, 1992)

81 Patrick Deneen. *Why Liberalism Failed.* (New Haven, CT: Yale University Press, 2018) at pp. 52, 53

82 Patrick Deneen. *Why Liberalism Failed.* (New Haven, CT: Yale University Press, 2018) at p. 46

83 Patrick Deneen. *Why Liberalism Failed.* (New Haven, CT: Yale University Press, 2018) at p. 146

84 Patrick Deneen. *Why Liberalism Failed.* (New Haven, CT: Yale University Press, 2018) at p. 71

85 John Milbank and Catherine Pickstock and Graham Ward. *Radical Orthodoxy.* (London, UK: Routledge, 1999) and John Milbank. *Theology and Social Theory: Beyond Secular Reason-Second Edition.* (Oxford, UK: Blackwell Publishing, 2006)

86 One partial exception is an interesting essay on time in Patrick Deneen. *Conserving America: Essays on Present Discontents.* (South Bend, IN: St Augustine Press, 2016)

87 See Leo Strauss. *Natural Right and History.* (Chicago, IL: University of Chicago Press, 1953) at p. 6

88 See James Matthew Wilson. *The Vision of the Soul: Truth, Goodness and Beauty in the Western Tradition.* (Washington, DC: The Catholic University of America Press, 2017)

89 Patrick Deneen. *Why Liberalism Failed.* (New Haven, CN: Yale University Press, 2018)

90 Helen McCabe. *John Stuart Mill: Socialist.* (Montreal, QC: Queens-McGill University Press, 2021)

91 See Patrick Deneen. "How Will Future Historians Treat Same-Sex Marriage." *The Public Discourse,* July 10th, 2013

92 See Sohrab Ahmari. *The Unbroken Thread: Discovering the Wisdom of Tradition in an Age of Chaos.* (New York, NY: Convergent Books, 2021)

93 See Adrian Vermeule. *Common Good Constitutionalism: Recovering the Classical Legal Tradition.* (Cambridge, UK: Polity Press, 2022)

94 See Jozef Andrew Kosc. "Poland and the Future of Europe." *First Things,* June 14th, 2018

95 See Rod Dreher. "What Conservatives Must Learn from Hungary." *National Conservatism,* November 2nd, 2021 https://www.youtube.com/watch?v=BEB7FdogGS4

96 Yoram Hazony. *Conservatism: A Rediscovery.* (Washington, DC: Regnery Press, 2022) at pp. 132, 133

97 Yoram Hazony. *Conservatism: A Rediscovery.* (Washington, DC: Regnery Press, 2022) at p. 106

98 See Yoram Hazony. "Conservative Democracy: Liberal Principles Have Brought Us a Dead End." *First Things,* January 2019

99 Yoram Hazony. "The Challenge of Marxism." *Quillette,* August 16th, 2020

100 Yoram Hazony. *Conservatism: A Rediscovery.* (Washington, DC: Regnery Press, 2022) at p. 10

101 See Yoram Hazony. *The Virtue of Nationalism.* (New York, NY: Basic Books, 2018)

102 See Yoram Hazony. "Why National Conservatism?" *National Conservatism,* July 15th, 2019 https://www.youtube.com/watch?v=4cpyd1OqHJU&t=1725s

103 See Yoram Hazony. *Conservatism: A Rediscovery.* (Washington, DC: Regnery Press, 2022) at pp. 189–207

104 Eric Hobsbawm. *The Age of Revolution 1789–1848.* (New York, NY: Vintage Books, 1996)

105 See Yoram Hazony. *The Virtue of Nationalism.* (New York, NY: Basic Books, 2018) at pp. 207, 208

106 See Yoram Hazony. *Conservatism: A Rediscovery.* (Washington, DC: Regnery Press, 2022) at pp. 146, 147

5

THE FAR RIGHT, WAR, AND GENOCIDE

What Makes Someone "Far Right?"

The right has long had an -—often self-ascribed- —reputation for preferring moderation over radicality, improvement over revolution, and restraint over bellicosity. In the United States, where liberalism is so engrained into the cultural fabric that conservatives can even claim to be "conserving" the principles of classical liberalism, [1] these sentiments often express themselves in the language of a minimal or "small state" which can give the political right an anti-authoritarian gloss which sits uncomfortably with many of its policy preferences.[2] Indeed even some popular conservative authors have even so internalized this conviction that they can parrot a faux progressive sounding language; Dave Rubin no doubt speaks for millions of partisans when he claims the Right is

> "exponentially more tolerant, way more respectful toward individuals, way more supportive of individual thought, way more interested in diversity, way more progressive, way more inclusive, and honestly, just a way more fun side. The Right is a toga party with a bunch of people drinking and smoking and sharing different and often competing ideas."[3]

These kinds of tropes can make the mere existence of the far right seem like a paradox to the faithful, and more conventional conservatives like Jonah Goldberg or Thomas Sowell have consequently tried to explain the far right-—particularly fascism- —away by reading it as essentially just another form of progressive radicalism in a (very good) disguise:

> "The usual image of the political spectrum among the intelligent-sia extends from the Communists on the extreme left to less extreme

DOI: 10.4324/9781003307952-8

left-wing radicals, more moderate liberals, centrists, conservatives, hard right-wingers, and ultimately Fascists. But, like so much that is believed by the intelligentsia, it is a conclusion without an argument, unless endless repetition can be regarded as an argument. When we turn from such images to specifics, there is remarkably little difference between Communists and Fascists, except for rhetoric, and there is far more in common between Fascists and even the moderate left than between either of them and traditional conservatives in the American sense."[4]

All this distorts a very real history of right-wing radicalism in theory and practice. From the beginning the political right has never been afraid of taking dramatic action where such has been required to halt the advance of democratic and egalitarian movements. Historically these have ranged from conducting vast counter-revolutionary wars to instituting Holy Alliances around which the entire globe is to orbit.[5] Many right-wing intellectuals gravitate towards dramatic and even consciously frightening rhetoric and ideas, designed to shock and galvanize. From the beginning the snide but measured tones of Burkeanism were complemented by De Maistre's insistence that all power and greatness rest with the executioner, who emulates God inby being the author of punishment.[6] But the mere fact that figures on the political right are willing to act and think in extreme ways means we have to ask: extreme compared to what?

Moderate forms of conservatism, especially in the 20th century, are characterized by their accepting and even defending important facets of modernist political projects committed to moral equality, liberal freedoms, and political participation. This is achieved by leaning heavily into the facets of classical liberalism which emphasize respect for property rights and the importance of maintaining the rule of law: both of which intersect vitally with conservative concerns for order and hierarchy. But the political right can be more conciliatory still. For someone like Oakeshott or Scruton, even a minimal welfare state might be reconcilable with ordered liberty conservatism-—whether as a means of maintaining order, preventing radicalization, or out of a sense of noblesse oblige.[7] These conciliations with egalitarian modernity can be cast in tragic and pragmatic terms, or, with George Will, even defined as intrinsic to patriotic conservatism in what are by now longstanding liberal democratic states.[8]

Firstly, the far right is far more emphatic in its rejection of the egalitarian aspirations of modernity. The far right typically rejects even this most slender of concessions to equality. In its darkest forms this can be given racist expression through an insistence on the biological inferiority of "lower" peoples, as in the writings of a Calhoun or a Gobineau. But far-right thinking by no means needs to have a racist bent, and thinkers like Nietzsche and Heidegger can even dismiss biological (though not "'spiritual'") racism as vulgar and excessively beholden to modern materialism and scientism. Far-right authors may even follow Alexander Dugin in regarding expressions of biological racism as a potential barrier to coalition building against liberalism. What is important is the insistence that human beings and peoples are not equal, cannot be made equal, and that any artificial aspiration to make them equal has brought about decadence and decline.

Secondly, the far right has historically been far less prone to describing its efforts in terms of conservation. If things have fallen so far, what is there left to conservative? As Glenn Elmers put it in his subtly titled essay "Conservatism is No Longer Enough."

> "The conservative movement" still matters because if the defenders of America continue to squabble among themselves, the victory of progressive tyranny will be assured. See you in the gulag. On the off chance we can avoid that fate, it will only be if the shrinking number of Americans unite and work together. But we can't simply mandate that conservatives "set aside" their differences, no matter how urgent it is that they do so. So my goal here is to show why we must all unite around the one, authentic America, the only one which transcends all the factional navel-gazing and pointless conservababble. Practically speaking, there is almost nothing left to conserve. What is actually required now is a recovery, or even a refounding, of America as it was long and originally understood but which now exists only in the hearts and minds of a minority of citizens."[9]

So calling the far right a species of conservatism would be incorrect. The far right insists that only radical transformations can successfully overcome the decay which has overtaken so much of society. Often they will follow conservatives in expressing nostalgia for a more gilded past; fascism's palingenetic project of restoration is predicated on a sense of national right having been denied through a fall from greatness. But even here this needn't always be the case, and the far right has often prided itself on a kind of futuristic innovation by insisting that its idealized state has never or rarely been fully realized or even conceived. In this respect far- right authors can sound something like radical progressives, and some might even follow Dugin in having a soft spot for the revolutionary scope of a doctrine like Marxism. But the kind of radical change they wish is violently opposed to the egalitarian ambitions of liberals and progressives. Sometimes both a nostalgic and futurist rhetoric can even be synthesized, as in Alexander Stephens' "Cornerstone" speech defending the American Confederacy. This remarkable document reaches to the far past by invoking the Magna Carta and respect for inherited rights, even aping elements of American liberalism through its defense of state and property rights. But the "Cornerstone Speech" is more emphatic in its ambitious vision for the future. Stephens applauds the Confederacy above all else for its novelty in being the first society in the world to entrench racial inequality as its cornerstone.

> "Our new government is founded upon exactly the opposite idea; its foundations are laid, its corner-stone rests, upon the great truth that the negro is not equal to the white man; that slavery subordination to the superior race

is his natural and normal condition. This, our new government, is the first, in the history of the world, based upon this great physical, philosophical, and moral truth."[10]

One consequence of this radicalism is that far- right figures may express wariness or even hostility towards more moderate forms of conservatism, which can come to symbolize excessive acquiescence or even collaboration with the intolerable. Part of the appeal of the far right is its ability to assume a countercultural veneer through the radicalness of its convictions and an unwillingness to compromise, which can even take the form of condemning moderate conservatives for upholding the status quo while lacking energy and imagination. This becomes especially dangerous in moments where liberal centrism and its institutions appear weak, which presents both an opportunity and a threat to the far right. The opportunity is obvious. The threat lies in the fact that more sweeping forms of leftism might be the ones to profit from the center being unable to hold. In these contexts the demands of the far right can become especially urgent, and moderate conservatives may be overwhelmed or compromise by bringing in more extremist elements to the mainstream to benefit from their zeal. This happened in both Italy and Germany, where conservative groups like the monarchy, big business, and the German National People's Party tried to tame fascism by allying with it.[11]

Thirdly, far- right authors experience a greater sense of alienation from the world as it is than moderate conservatives. As we've seen many conservatives who felt discontented with vulgar modernity adopted a stance of tragic resignation towards it. This is where much of the far right's contempt for moderate conservatism can be found, since resignation is not what it wants. A consequence of this is that the far right is paradoxically more willing to be experimental and daring in its efforts to conceive comprehensive alternatives to a status quo which is increasingly conceived as unacceptable. As part of these efforts far- right intelectuals may appropriate staggeringly eclectic sets of ideas-—even from strange ends of the political spectrum-—which would be utterly toxic to conventional conservatives. Carl Schmitt found surprising support for a popular fascist dictatorship in Rousseau by claiming the Fuhrer embodied the general will. Alexander Dugin is willing to appropriate insights from an array of leftist post-modern theorists to argue that Eurasian authoritarianism reflects a unique civilizational culture which Western imperialist universalism is in no position to criticize. The far right will also be more willing to reject basic planks of moderate right-wing movements. Nietzsche and Evola outdid the most contemptuous Marxists in their hatred for Christianity, seeing it as a debased manure out of which modern emancipatory movements grew. Fascist ultranationalists may come to see capitalism and even private property as forces of decadent materialist individualism and seek to subordinate the economy to the cause of the ultranation.

One disturbing result of this is that far- right thinking is often more ambitious than its moderate conservative counterparts. While the overwhelming number of the right's crackpots and cranks crawl out from the extreme ends of the spectrum, it is undeniably true that some of the most sparkling right-wing intellects defend the most extreme and evil aspirations. There is no comparing the work of Devlin or Meyer to that of Heidegger or Schmitt. Moderation is an easy route to intellectual mediocrity, since by leaning on conventional wisdom one avoids both absurdity and innovation.

Nietzsche, the Aristocratic Rebel

> "The great majority of men have no right to life, and serve only to disconcert the elect among our race; I do not yet grant the unfit that right. There are even unfit peoples."
>
> (Friedrich Nietzsche, *The Will to Power*)

Nietzsche is the greatest right-wing thinker in history. His genius and originality are so acknowledged that even the most self-conscious radical leftists find themselves inexorably attracted to his work.[12] Partly as a result of this there will be plenty of progressives who resent Nietzsche's even being in a book like this. For many years the line ran that the most one could say is that Nietzsche "influenced" a number of right-wing movements and thinkers, while attaching a million caveats about how profoundly they misrepresented Nietzsche's work.[13] His grip on the radical imagination is so firm because Nietzsche is a radical in the most stringent sense of the word: getting at the roots and pulling them.

This is one of the reasons why Nietzsche's philosophy has proven excessively strong stuff for more moderate conservatives who are vested in maintaining the world as it is. For the more superficial analysts on the right, Nietzsche is either another symptom of the godless atheism and bohemianism which has swept the world or a neat critic of egalitarianism whose ideas can be selectively deployed where useful while the more troubling claims associated with these criticisms are simply ignored. Ben Shapiro's description of Nietzsche in *The Right Side of History* as an atheist immoralist and proto post-modernist represents one side of that coin.[14] Douglas Murray's (who apparently thinks appealing to the anti-Christ is a good way of propping up Judeo-Christian values) cheap use of Nietzsche's theory of "ressentiment" and Dinesh D'Souza's lazy condemnation of Nordic social democracy as a society of "last men" represent the other.[15] At either pole these takes do Nietzsche the tremendous disservice of not taking him seriously by simply using his talking points as a sounding board for rearticulating more narrowly partisan views.

More sophisticated conservative thinkers like George Grant or Jordan Peterson are better. They tend to follow Nietzsche in conceiving grand genealogies of modern history, but take Nietzschean thought as potentially dangerous. Grant's description of Nietzsche as a thinker who abandoned the transcendent notion of eternity for a conception of time as history which culminates in his own elevation of the will to power as the highest ideal, backed by the might of modern technology, is an intriguing one.[16] Peterson's take on Nietzsche as a thinker who both celebrated and mourned the death of God, anticipating that the fall of religiosity would see both tyrannical new secular creeds and sweeping nihilism, has become increasingly popular.[17]

> "It does not require a particularly careful reader to note that Nietzsche described God, in *The Gay Science*, as 'the holiest and mightiest of all that the world has yet owned' and modern human beings as 'the murderers of all murderers.' These are not the sorts of descriptions you might expect from a triumphant rationalist celebrating the demise of superstition. It was instead a statement of absolute despair. In other works, particularly in *The Will to Power*, Nietzsche describes what would occur in the next century and beyond because of this murderous act. He prophesied (and that is the correct word for it) that two major consequences would arise...As the purpose of human life became uncertain outside the purposeful structure of monotheistic thought and the meaningful world it proposed, we would experience an existentially devastating rise in nihilism, Nietzsche believed. Alternatively, he suggested, people would turn to identification with rigid, totalitarian ideology: the substitute of human ideas for the transcendent Father of All Creation."[18]

The problem with these readings is that they are far too timid in handling someone like Nietzsche. Both Grant and Peterson, as moderate conservatives deeply influenced (though in the latter's case probably without knowing it) by Canadian idealism, want to rewrite Nietzsche's story of secularization to conserve a giant space for traditional religious views by reconceiving secularism as a tragedy which still might be overcome. In Grant's case Nietzschean thinking itself becomes symptomatic of the very nihilism Nietzsche sought to overcome;, a view shared by Alasdair MacIntyre amongst others.[19] Whereas in the hands of someone as easily frightened as Peterson, Nietzsche can become a neutered intellectual prop to uphold the Judeo-Christian civilization he despised above all else.

The shocking reality is that it is on the far right alone that you see any internalization of Nietzsche's view that only a total critique of the history of Western thought, accompanied by a comprehensive transformation of the existing world, is sufficient to combat the decadent spread of nihilistic egalitarianism-—the slave morality. This will require the creation of a genuinely new kind of "aristocratic radicalism" which is entirely unprecedented. Indeed, while he occasionally expresses some nostalgia for the master moralities of antiquity, even on these points Nietzsche is resolute that they failed for good reasons. And just as surprisingly, he adamantly rejects all the new secular idols put forward by 19th- century conservative thinkers for being either unworthy or polluted by the very morality they try to resist. The ultra-nation, the blood of a master race, and capitalist hierarchies of merit all appear completely unworthy to Nietzsche. Given this it is perhaps unsurprising that so few on the right have been willing or even capable of going as far as Nietzsche.

Nietzsche's Critique of Resentiment and Slave Morality I

Nietzsche's thinking can be understood as a response to the problem of nihilism, which he regards as the creeping cultural condition of the modern world. Its critical dimension is directed towards diagnosing the roots of this nihilism and pulling them out. In doing so Nietzsche is gleefully irreverent. Beginning with a complex response to Schopenhauerian pessimism and Wagnerian nationalism, Nietzscheanism eventually evolves into an attempt to overturn the entire downward trajectory of Western thought. The positive side of Nietzsche's programme is oriented around the creation of "life affirming values" which embody an aesthetics of health and greatness. This will include new forms of great politics which have never been seen before.[20] Nietzsche is giddy about the horror this will bring about since violence will be a sign that the peoples of the earth are not yet entirely exhausted.

> "I know my destiny. There will come a day when my name will recall the memory of something formidable—a crisis the like of which has never been known on earth, the memory of the most profound clash of consciences, and the passing of a sentence upon all that which theretofore had been believed, exacted, and hallowed. I am not a man, I am dynamite. And with it all there is nought of the founder of a religion in me. Religions are matters for the mob; after coming in contact with a religious man, I always feel that I must wash my hands.... ..... I require no "believers, " it is my opinion that I am too full of malice to believe even in myself; I never address myself to masses....I am the harbinger of joy, the like of which has never existed before; I have discovered tasks of such lofty greatness that, until my time, no one had any idea of such things. Mankind can begin to have fresh hopes, only now that I have lived. Thus, I am necessarily a man of Fate. For when Truth enters the lists against the falsehood of ages, shocks are bound to ensue, and a spell of earthquakes, followed by the transposition of hills and valleys, such as the world has never yet imagined even in its dreams. The concept "politics" then becomes elevated entirely to the sphere of spiritual warfare. All the mighty realms of the ancient order of society are blown into space—for they are all based on falsehood: there will be wars, the like of which have never been seen on earth before. Only from my time and after me will politics on a large scale exist on earth."[21]

Because he accepts the secular conclusion that "good" and "evil" have become outdated terms in a context where they cannot be transhistorically grounded in a foundation like God, Nietzsche struggles to invent an entirely new terminology

to express the concept of higher aristocratic and lower slavish values. He understands that this will entail going beyond morality without simply smuggling it
back in as so many others did. In some moments Nietzsche will even contend
that his constructive project will mean overcoming the very binary between
truth and falsehood, since this merely repeats the Platonic "appearance and
reality" distinction in vulgarized Christian form and is at the root of so much
modern nihilism. His yearning to have a value system without morality, and a
philosophy of existence without truth, was in many respects an impossible task.
But it is one to which Nietzsche remained committed to until his last sane day,
in part because the will to overcome such distinctions was itself a sign of strength
and health even if its object can never be fulfilled.

From *The Birth of Tragedy* onwards Nietzsche detects something fundamentally wrong with modern culture, which he will frame in a number of different
ways throughout his intellectual career. His first book is one of the only occasions
where Nietzsche's thinking operates according to a relatively simply bifurcation
between Apollonian and Dionysian principles. The young Nietzsche comes to
the rather vulgar Hegelian conclusion that some synthesis of the two principles is
required for a culture to be at its best.[22] In terms of its political reception, if *The
Birth of Tragedy* was all that Nietzsche ended up writing, he would have fallen
into the category of being a more conventional and moderate reactionary critic.
The book launches an even-by-then familiar critique of rationalism coded as
Apollonian logocentrism, written in an upbeat nostalgic register. But *The Birth
of Tragedy* is already distinctive in calling for a cultural rejuvenation through
returning to a Dionysian spirit which predates Christianity and even the Greek
philosophers who so influenced Christian philosophy. While the book is not as
fierce on this point as Nietzsche's later work, a creative reader might draw the
conclusion that what is required is a more wholesale rejection of Apollonian
reason as embodied in the Greek philosophers. This would implicate much of
the Aristotelian-Christian worldview, which more generic reactionaries to this
day find so addictive, in the spread of nihilism. And Nietzsche does suggest the
problem goes all the way back to Socrates:

> "The most acute word, however, about this new and unprecedented value
> set on knowledge and insight was spoken by Socrates when he found that
> he was the only one who acknowledged to himself that he knew nothing,
> whereas in his critical peregrinations through Athens he had called on the
> greatest statesmen, orators, poets, and artists and had everywhere discov-
> ered the conceit of knowledge. To his astonishment he perceived that all
> these celebrities were without a proper and sure insight, even with regard
> to their own professions, and that they practiced them only by instinct...
> This is what strikes us as so tremendously problematic whenever we con-
> sider Socrates, and again and again we are tempted to fathom the meaning
> and purpose of this most questionable phenomenon of antiquity. Who is
> it that may dare single-handed to negate the Greek genius that, as Homer,

Pindar, and Aeschylus, as Phidias, as Pericles, as Pythia and Dionysus, as the deepest abyss and the highest heights, is sure of our astonished veneration? What demonic power is this that dares to spill this magic potion into dust?"[23]

Here one can find in natal form many of the objections which Nietzsche will later systematize more brilliantly. At a pathological level Socrates conceals an arrogant sense of his own superiority under the veneer of skeptical purity. He alone knows that he knows nothing, but unlike the aristocratic men he condemns, Socrates is unwilling to rest with a mere "instinct" which feels it has immediate access to reality and even a right to command it and others. In this way the will to truth is transformed into a moral project that develops into a relentless critique of existing power on behalf of an idealized justice Socrates isn't even able to define. This is because Socrates' ultimate motivation is in fact a kind of hatred well camouflaged as righteousness. Even Socrates' death is not so much noble as a kind of concealed revenge. Socrates must have known that he would become the "new ideal, never seen before, of noble Greek youths" who would consequently internalize this as feelings of guilt over their aristocratic status.[24] Socrates is Nietzsche's first creature of resentment: unable to live in the world, but constantly needing to project a transcendent dimension which validates his pathological disdain and which can be appealed to in order to render the instinctively mighty impotent.

Already with Socrates we see the advent of Western nihilism: acidic and corrosive under the mask of righteous and inquiring. But things became far worse with Plato, against whom Nietzsche directs himself more fully than any other major philosopher. Heidegger's reading of Nietzsche as a kind of anti-Platonism does a disservice to his novelty, but does capture a sense of the stakes at play.[25] Because Plato is the most significant founder of Western thought, and Western thought ended in Christian nihilism, nihilism's deepest roots lie in Plato's thought through its systematic elevation of Socratic ressentiment into philosophy. One of the most important clues lies in Plato's mania for systematicity; his need to unify a theory of the good, the beautiful, and the true into either a singular ideal form or a multiplicity of forms if he is to be content with the world. Nietzsche is endlessly mocking of this, since Plato was amongst the first clever enough to convince himself that the just and beautiful world in his head is somehow also truer and more real than the actual one he inhabits. In this Plato compares almost pitifully to other Grecian authors like Thucydides, who still embodied some of the pre-Socratic virtues.

"In respect to Plato I am a thorough sceptic and have always been unable to join in the admiration of Plato the artist which is traditional among all scholars. After all, I have here the most refined judges of taste of antiquity themselves on my side…Ultimately my mistrust of Plato extends to the very bottom of him: I find him deviated so far from all the fundamental instincts of the Hellenes, so morally infected, so much an antecedent Christian-he already has the concept of 'good' as the supreme concept-that I should prefer to describe the entire phenomenon 'Plato' by the harsh term 'higher swindle' or, if you prefer, 'idealism,' than by any other...Courage in the face of reality ultimately distinguishes such natures as Thucydides and Plato: Plato is a coward in the face of reality-consequently he flees into the ideal; Thucydides has himself under control-consequently he retains control over things..."[26]

This includes creating a uniform notion of human beings, whose material differences and distinct capabilities are to be scrubbed away through the invention of a human soul that exists within everyone's body while being higher than the body. Plato does give this an elitist quality through insisting on the philosopher's superior access to the true and beautiful world, and consequently the quality of her soul. But the effacement of human differences paves the way for the kind of egalitarianism anticipated in the *Meno* where Socrates proves the slave is in fact not so different from the master because his soul can equally yearn for the truth. The forced unity of existence in Platonic ideals means the real world and real people will never be able to live up to it, which leads Plato to call for immense political efforts to realize a utopia where the gap between the ugly world of "appearance" and the truer world of "reality" will be bridged through political changes.

Here it is important to note the form Nietzsche's objection takes. As authors like Bull note, Nietzsche will rarely argue directly against the long and meticulous arguments Plato makes for his philosophical distinctions in *The Republic* and many other works.[27] Instead Nietzsche pathologizes Plato's philosophical arguments into expressions of his moral and psychological yearnings-—and ultimately Plato's degeneracy in the face of reality. In *The Genealogy of Morals* Nietzsche applies his hermeneutics of suspicion to declare that these "moral (or immoral) intentions in every philosophy constituted the real germ from which the whole plant had grown" and Plato's is no different.[28] These moral and immoral intentions find intellectual expression in the work of major philosophers, but Nietzsche regards them as both symbolic of, and generative of, the broader culture.

Now one might respond to Nietzsche in several ways.

Firstly one might shift the discursive terrain back to rationalistic thinking, and criticize Nietzsche for (quite remarkably) not taking Plato's technical arguments seriously. Indeed, not really responding to them at all. After all the theory of the "forms" may have a moral connotation, but it is also an epistemic claim about the importance general categories have as applied to particulars and an ontological argument about the status of non-empirical entities like numbers and justice. Is Plato ultimately motivated by a "moral or immortal" intention when he claims that number cannot be a particular thing or an appearance? Maybe, but the argument would still independently stand.[29]

Secondly, one might take Nietzsche's pathologization on their own terms and contend that he doesn't really understand Plato--a man who even from a Nietzschean standpoint can only be described as a figure of tremendous energy, will, and imagination. If one were feeling petty and greedy, one could even point out that if Nietzsche is right and the "health" of a philosopher determines the worth of their outlook then noble Plato the broad- shouldered is more worthy of emulation than the ever-sickly Nietzsche. Plato's own philosophy exploits the disjunction between the ideal of justice and the "reality" of the world as a continuous prompt for action on the part of the philosopher, whose responsibility to the city persists even when she becomes attracted to the transcendent beauty of the forms. In this respect the unreality of the world of doxastic appearance becomes a continuous call for overcoming on the part of the philosopher and eventually the polis. This can readily transform into a philosophy of praxis, as when Marx predicts that with the final arrival of socialism the reified social world will disappear and humankind will confront its own productions in their true form for the first time.

But these somewhat technical arguments miss the main point of Nietzsche's analysis, which is both historical and political. When Nietzsche refers to great figures of the past critically, it is important to recognize he is not simply or even primarily being critical of their work or actions in themselves. This is even true of his ultimate opponent Christ, who is treated with shocking respect in *The Anti-Christ*. Pointing out that Nietzsche is unfair to Plato misses what is important and dramatic in his message. It is not so much the originators of doctrines but their disciples and second -handers who are the problem, since it is in their hands that values calcify into the nihilistic thoughtlessness of morality and dogmatics. Nietzsche is by no means as crude as Heidegger in assuming that a philosopher like Plato is singularly constitutive of the metaphysical basis of an era. Nietzsche often sounds quite materialist in his relentless emphasis on the phenomenology of the body and, more importantly, the instantiation of power in culture.[30] But he does describe philosophers as emblematic of trends towards decadence or vitality in a culture. Nietzsche consequently uses the good name of Plato as a whipping boy to condemn the long slow rot of nihilism that his thinking facilitated. This will become even more transparent with the transition to Christianity, which strips away the residual Grecian aristocratism and anti-democratic sentiments of Plato and becomes firmly a philosophy for the resentful "masses."

Nietzsche's Critique of Resentiment and Slave Morality II

"And let us not underestimate the fatality that has crept out of Christianity even into politics! No one any longer possesses today the courage to claim special privileges of the right to rule, the courage to feel a sense of reverence towards himself and towards his equals-the courage for a pathos of distance....Our politics is morbid from this lack of courage-The aristocratic outlook has been undermined most deeply by the lie of equality of souls;

and if the belief in the 'prerogative of the majority' makes revolutions and will continue to make them-it is Christianity, let there be no doubt about it, Christian value judgement which translates every revolution into mere blood and crime! Christianity is a revolt of everything that crawls along the ground directed against that which is elevated: the Gospel of the lowly makes low..."[31]

Nietzsche's critique Christianity is the most sweeping ever initiated. Much like his critique of Plato, little of it consists of responding to the dense ontotheological defense of Christianity stretching from Augustine to Thomism which provides the scholastic backdrop of many religious movements to this day. —including those on the political right. Nietzsche largely takes for granted both the secularizing implications of discoveries in the 19th- century empirical sciences and the epistemological limitations to human reason delineated by German idealism moving from Kant to Schopenhauer. Also of formative importance, as it was to Karl Marx and many others, was the burgeoning secular or even atheistic treatment of religion and Jesus pioneered by Strauss, Feuerbach, and others. To many educated Germans some combination of these factors weighed heavily against the idea of God, or at least seemed to make him superfluous. Where this generated problems, starting with Kant, bourgeois Germans found a way to either to adapt faith to reason or at minimum to save core moral convictions of Christianity in secularized form. Indeed, in many important ways, the fact that the eschatological project of Christian morality could no longer be consummated in transcendence made it all the more urgent to achieve the kingdom of God on earth.[32] Nietzsche thus found himself in the unusual position of being both far more critical of Christianity than many of his counterparts, while, at the same time, taking the consequences of secularization far more seriously. This stems from his conscious decision to not try and save the Christian legacy but to treat it antagonistically.

On the one hand Nietzsche is contemptuous of the secular convictions that Christian morality can be detached and saved from the decline of its metaphysics. While this is philosophically achievable, Nietzsche conceives it as a sign of weakness and decadence. It constitutes an addiction to foundationless Christian morality; a kind of yearning to a rise above nihilism by standing atop nothing. This is one reason his condemnation of Christianity is so relentlessly psychological, since Nietzsche understood, as Marx did, that the basis of religion's appeal was never the truth of the doctrine. It was the way Christianity made the suffering of the world intelligible and purposive. But while the young Marx thought the humanist impulses of Christianity could be preserved and rationalized through a secular transition to socialism Nietzsche regards both Christian morality and its socialist descendants as nihilistic sublimations of the herd's ressentiment.[33]

It is this remarkable genealogical link of Christianity with progressive movements that distinguishes Nietzsche from those on the political right who share his convictions about the demonstrable superiority of the few over the many along with his anxieties about modern nihilism. For less courageous thinkers, the kind of throne and altar Christianity agitated for by De Maistre served as a stabilizing force for earthly tradition and authority through sublimating elevated particular individuals with divine authority. While he is close to figures like De Maistre in criticizing Enlightenment universalism and humanism through an emphasis on particularity, Nietzsche takes a completely different view than De Maistre on the uses of Christianity. As Losurdo points out:

> "Diehard opponents of revolutionary France denounced its ideologues and leaders sometimes as nihilists (and atheists), sometimes as suffering, more or less, from religious fanaticism......Nietzsche went far further back, and saw nihilism as arising not from a heresy that distorted and perverted 'authentic" Christianity but precisely from Christianity, or rather the Jewish-Christian tradition, as such."[34]

From a Nietzschean perspective almost everything about the conservative appropriation of Christianity is lopsided and self-serving because it lacks the courage of its convictions. It takes a doctrine of universal love and equality before the throne of God, whose founder demanded that the poor be elevated on earth as they would be in heaven and promised the wretched of the earth that God is on their side, and tries to reconceive it as historical force maintaining authority structures and hierarchical complementarity. Nothing could be so ridiculous as ignoring the ideological Christian origins of revolutionary egalitarianism, or so vulgar as the conservatives' failure to wean themselves off of Christianity when they clearly wish to banish its levelling impulses. For Nietzsche, there is a direct genealogical link between Christianity and its secularized offspring, which he variably describes as liberalism, democracy, and socialism (the "residue of Christianity and Rousseau" as he put it in *The Will to Power*). Even so partial an achievement as equal rights for all is repudiated by Nietzsche for its noxious association with Christian thinking and values:

> "The poison of the doctrine 'equal rights for all'-—this has been more thoroughly sowed by Christianity than by anything else, from the most secret recesses of base instincts, Christianity has waged a war to the death against every feeling of reverence and distance between man and man, against, that is, the precondition of every elevation, every increase in culture-—it has forged out of the ressentiment of the masses its chief weapon against us...."[35]

Or again and even more emphatically.

"Whom do I hate most heartily among the rabbles of today? The rabble of Socialists, the apostles to the Chandala, who undermine the workingman's instincts, his pleasure, his feeling of contentment with his petty existence—who make him envious and teach him revenge.... .... Wrong never lies in unequal rights; it lies in the assertion of "equal" rights.... ....

What is bad? But I have already answered: all that proceeds from weakness, from envy, from revenge. — The anarchist and the Christian have the same ancestry."[36]

This willingness to undertake a totalizing critique of egalitarianism and assault even those idols which the stock thinkers of the political right revere distinguishes Nietzsche. It will have an immense impact on a new generation of anti-Christian thinkers on the political right: from Heidegger through super-fascists like Evola.

Nietzsche also breaks from conservative narratives of secularization as a kind of cultural development external to Christian thinking. Instead the move to a secular society is given a suitably Grecian cast by Nietzsche.[37] For the De Maistres , Newmans, and Deneens of the world the fall into decadent materialism and egalitarian libertinism can be understood by hermetically drawing a cordon around the metaphysically sanitized core of Christian doctrine and regarding secularism as an external force arising from scientific rationality. Or at worst the immanentization of various heresies into modernity; Protestantism and Gnosticism being a familiar culprits.

For Nietzsche this misunderstands two truths about Christianity. The first is the extent to which egalitarian libertinism of the liberal democratic and socialist type is the end point of the herd's levelling slave morality, which ultimately tears down even the kind of rarefied Christianity cherished by the stubborn but still weak. But second and more importantly, it rejects the kind of exalted inquiries carried out by Christianity's defenders which were themselves doomed to self-secularization by attaching the faith to Platonism and Aristotelianism. The Christian's (especially Pauline's) unwillingness to the accept the metaphysical lack of foundations for faith and root itself in purely in the will and ressentiment of the slave meant synthetsizing it with the prestige of Greek philosophy in an effort to reconcile faith and reason. Even these more intellectually high- falutin efforts have a proto-democratic quality to them since they aspired to give Christianity a kind of universal validity that any and every person would accept as natural law. This yearning for affirmation and validity through universal reason displays a slavish attitude that rarefied personalities don't require and even pride themselves on rejecting. And it was doomed to failure, since the Christian reason which constantly searched for affirmation of the truth and beauty of God leads inexorably to the awful moment of self-overcoming:

"All great things bring about their own destruction through an act of self-overcoming: thus the law of life will have it, the law of the necessity of 'self-overcoming' in the nature of life-the lawgiver himself eventually receives the call....In this way Christianity as a dogma was destroyed by its own morality, in the same way Christianity as morality must now perish too: we stand on the threshold of this event. After Christian truthfulness has drawn one inference after another, it must end by drawing its most striking inference, its inference against itself; this will happen, however, when it poses the question 'what is the meaning of all will to truth?'" [38]

So what we have in Nietzsche is a right-wing critic of Christianity who regards it as both the basis of the progressive movements he despised and self-immolating due to the immanent tendencies of its own value system. This alone would have won for Nietzsche a unique place in the history of reactionary thought. But his most enduring and popular contribution came from theorizing on the ressentiment that underpinned the Christian value system. This gutted Christianity's claims to moral superiority, and the critique was extensive enough to ultimately tarnish the successor doctrines of secularized Christian egalitarianism which Nietzsche condemned with venom.

The theory of ressentiment hasn't been particularly well understood even by conservative popularizers like Douglas Murray or Dinesh D'Souza who are eager to appropriate it for polemical purposes. In their hands ressentiment becomes just a version of super- actuated envy. But from a Nietzschean standpoint envy may well be a healthy disposition if it stirs a person to vital enterprises; after all, a desire for what others have and I don't is one of the great inspirations in life. Resentiment is what appears precisely when an individual or "race" is neither strong nor willful enough to aspire to the satisfactions available to superior people. This leads them to internalize a sense of personal inferiority which is then externalized as hatred of the superior person. —but at least initially in an impotent way. What makes ressentiment so toxic and unhealthy to Nietzsche is the fact that it constitutes a yearning for revenge against the superior individual who makes one feel inferior. But precisely because the inferior person lacks the strength to overcome the object of their hatred, it is a yearning for revenge that remains unsatisfied and so cyclically turns back on itself.

Now in a healthy society Nietzsche thinks this would be the last word on the subject. But what is remarkable about the "Jewish" people and Christians is that this cycle of ressentiment had the effect of deepening their psychology. It engendered the creation of new kinds of emotion like guilt and Kierkegaardian despair;, the most profound kinds of sadness which emerge when the self is distressed not because it cannot fulfill its desire, but simply because it is this very self and can never become anything better.[39] This had the effect of layering profundity onto the human soul which was lacking in the one-dimensional aristocratic protagonists of "master morality" like Achilles or Aeneus. But more importantly, this creative form of ressentiment almost paradoxically became active through the construction of a new "slave morality" which inverted the value system of master morality. Courage became wrath, love of life became attachment to the things of this world, and of course love of one's self became the ultimate sin of pride. And remarkably, Nietzsche acknowledges that the slave morality triumphed when its morality was internalized by the masters, who became sickened and weakened by experiencing the new feelings of guilt and uncertainty it engendered.[40]

In this manner the world came undone, and we moved irrevocably towards the culture of nihilism rooted in ressentiment that constitutes the modern, revolutionary era of democratic nothingness. The unworthy rabble miraculously conquered the truly superior people in society without needing to lift a finger, since they surrendered power of their own accord. As Ronald Beiner puts it:

> "For Nietzsche, the advent of modernity means, above all, the displacement of genuine cultures (which are all premodern) by mere pseudo-culture, or at least the appreciation of past cultures as a replacement for the capacity to produce or generate authentic culture. Christianity as the ultimate boundary between antiquity and modernity is crucial to Nietzsche's narrative. This is in Nietzsche's view the true crime of Christianity and why he hates it so much....Christian morality presented itself as a higher morality than 'antique virtue' and on that basis delegitimized and debunked ancient cultures as representing the peak of human possibilities. Once antiquity was associated with an inferior morality, culture as the ancients experienced it became utterly irrecoverable, and the ultimate result of that debunking iof pagan culture by Christianity is what comes to be known as 'modernity.'"[41]

Nietzsche's Defense of Aristocratic Values and Superior Men

> "A tremendous hope finds expression in this work. After all, I have absolutely no reason to renounce the hope for a Dionysian future of music. Let us look a century ahead, and let us suppose that my attempt to destroy two millenniums of hostility to Nature and of the violation of humanity be crowned with success. That new party of life-advocates, which will undertake the greatest of all tasks, the elevation and perfection of mankind, as well as the relentless destruction of all degenerate and parasitical elements, will make that *superabundance of life* on earth once more possible, out of which the Dionysian state will perforce arise again. I promise the advent of a tragic age: the highest art in the saying of yea to life, "tragedy," " will be born again when mankind has the knowledge of the hardest, but most necessary of wars, behind it, without, however, suffering from that knowledge......"

(Nietzsche, *Ecce Homo*)

The end point of Christian humanism and egalitarianism is the formation of a nihilistic society. Not simply because the death of God through Christianity's immanent self-secularization guts the metaethical foundation of its morality and the offshoots. But because Christianity's roots in the ressentiment of the slave meant that the successor cultures are invariably crass, materialistic, and decadent. In other words, a world where ordinary human beings are in fact happy and content because they are treated well by others. In his less optimistic moments

Nietzsche even posits the potential arrival of the "last men"-—a culture where "things will continue to go down, down, to become thinner, more good-natured, more prudent, more comfortable, more mediocre, more indifferent, more Chinese, more Christian."[42] As Bull points out, this pleasant last man is a "mutually incompatible" challenge to the possibility of the Superman arriving.[43] It is the path humankind will take without the defeat of slave morality through new forms of "great politics."[44]

Nietzsche's political solutions to the problems of nihilism are invariably aristocratic and don't preclude the use of slaves, as put bluntly in *Beyond Good and Evil*:

> "Every elevation of the type "man," has hitherto been the work of an aristocratic society-and so it will always be: a society which believes in a long scale of orders of rank and differences of worth between man and man and needs slavery in some sense or other. Without the pathos of distance such as develops from the incarnate differences of classes, from the ruling caste's constant looking out and looking down on subjects and instruments and from its equally constant exercise of obedience and command, its holding down and holding at a distance, that other, more mysterious pathos could not have developed either...in short precisely the elevation of the type 'man', the continual 'self-overcoming of man,' to take a moral formula in a supra-moral sense."[45]

Nietzsche discusses the pathological basis of his Superman in detail, though the content of the Superman's value system is never discussed at great length. While this project may have been carried out had his planned masterpiece, *The Will to Power* (not to be confused with the book of fragments compiled by his sister), been carried out, in some ways Nietzsche's own amoralism and aesthetic fixation precludes a high degree of specificity. For the Superman to be the Superman he'd have to will his own values into being, which will necessarily not be Nietzsche's values; Zarathustra is after all the prophet of a new era and not its consummation.[46] From a psychological standpoint what is surprising is how this new era will bring about a dialectically familiar kind of consciousness. Nietzsche is unwilling to abandon the pathos of depth established by Christianity for a strict return to the pathos of distance that defined antiquity. Nietzsche's passing reference to the Superman as a "the Roman Caesar with Christ's soul" in *The Will to Power* is in many respects his highest impossible yearning. The Superman would be a combination of the strong and healthy antiquarian hero who would nevertheless possess the kind of absolute self-consciousness emblematic of modernity without any of the sickening doubt or need to sublimate his values into universalistic morality.

Indeed the Superman would immediately recognize the demotic temptation inherent in universalism as the inability to simultaneously will into creation his own values without making them into something other than his own through the fiction that they would also be affirmed and welcomed by others. From the standpoint of the demos, the aristocratic Superman well be conceived and portrayed as evil in their moral system. In one of Nietzsche's more striking parables, he points out how the lambs invariably regard the eagle as menacing and even fixated upon them, when in fact the bird of prey admires the lambs as a means to satiate his hunger. It is worth noting here how little the philosophical emphasis on anti-universalism and difference endorsed by post-structuralist thinkers inspired by Nietzsche necessarily requires a progressive or inclusive politics.[47] Much as Burke discovered when theorizing about the "little platoons" in society, an emphasis on difference can mean each playing their role in a system of hierarchical complementarity. But Nietzsche is far more exacting than Burke in decoupling his argument for aristocratic difference from any obligation or even care to those who will belong to the lower orders, beyond tentative gestures implying they will benefit from participating in the life-affirming projects set by the Superman.[48]

Beyond just psychological descriptions aplenty, Nietzsche also analyzed various kinds of "aristocratic" societies throughout his writings as potential templates for producing his modern superman who will bring life-affirming values back into the world. It is in these instances that we can see more clearly the kind of horrifying political orderings Nietzsche might have endorsed; though this never becomes systematized to the extent of providing a clear blueprint for a state ordered by aristocratic radicalism. It is also where we can see Nietzsche's surprising attentiveness to hierarchical particularism in his stress on the fundamental unequalness of societies relative to one another and the unequalness of their internal members.[49]

It is in these moments that Nietzsche's work can approximate a more vulgar reactionary genre in its nostalgia and fables of decline and fall brought about by the mass age. Nietzsche will often refer to Grecian and occasionally Medieval aristocracies with approval for their stratified hierarchies, militarism, and lack of mass politics. He is contemptuous of the modern liberal and workers' movements which have enabled the inferior types to put constraints on the enterprises of superior people. In his darkest writings Nietzsche isn't above echoing the rhetoric of a Southern slaveholder and appealing to the self-interestedness of the actually existing and inadequate aristocracy; chiding them for the foolish decision to educate the masses to be participants rather than slaves.

> "The stupidity, fundamentally the instinct degeneration which is the cause of every stupidity today, lies in the existence of a labor question at all.... There is absolutely no hope left that a modest and self-sufficient kind of human being, a type of Chinaman, should here form itself into a class: and this would have been sensible, this was actually a necessity. What has one ever done? Everything designed to nip in the bud even the prerequisites for it-through the most irresponsible thoughtlessness one has totally destroyed the instincts by virtues of which the worker becomes possible as a class,

possible for himself. The worker has been made liable for military service, he has been allowed to form unions and to vote: no wonder the worker already feels his existence to be a state of distress (expressed in moral terms as a state of injustice). But what does one want?-—to ask it again. If one wills an end, one must also will the means to it: if one wants slaves, one is a fool if one educates them to be masters-—"[50]

Nietzsche also makes it clear that his preferred societies will not be pacific. While he sometimes ruminates about the possibility of a well-armed people choosing to consciously disarm themselves after years of war and conquest, the more typical Nietzsche delights in the edifying prospect of violence. As in *The Gay Science* when Nietzsche says:

> "we 'conserve' nothing, neither do we want to return to any past periods, we are not by any means 'liberal'; we do not work for 'progress'; we do not need to plug up our ears against the sirens who in the market place sing of the future: their songe about 'equal rights,' 'a free society,' 'no more masters and no more servants' has no allure for us. We simply do not consider it desirable that a realm of justice and concord should be established on earth... we are delighted with all who love, as we do, danger, war, and adventure, who refuse to compromise, to be captured, reconciled, and castrated; we count ourselves among conquerors; we think about the necessity for new orders, also for a new slavery-—for every strengthening and enhancement of the human type also involves a new kind of enslavement."[51]

In these kinds of passages it is very easy to see why, while Nietzsche disliked crude biological racism and nationalism, he would prove fascinating to many fascist writers and movements.[52] The political interpretation of Nietzsche as a far-right anti-egalitarian vital to fascist intellectualism has been argued for with such force that it is increasingly hard to deny.[53] As Bull put it, "equality has had no fiercer critic than Nietzsche, whose 'fundamental insight with respect to the genealogy of morals is that social inequality is the source of our values concepts, and the necessary condition of value itself."[54] For those committed to egalitarianism in any flavor -—liberal, democratic, socialist-—this may be enough to reject Nietzscheanism wholesale. This would strike me as going too far in the direction of abandoning the sparkling insights and genius of the work. But any future progressive appropriation of Nietzschean ideas should be more self-conscious about the violence being done to his fundamental convictions.

A complete critique and reappropriation of Nietzsche would need to (1) comprehensively defend egalitarian modernity against his charge that it is ultimately a decadently nihilistic culture whose highest values are in fact founded on nothing more than the ressentiment of the herd and (2) demonstrate why the aristocratic radicalism he proposes in its place is deficient, either by resuscitating morality to combat Nietzschean aesthetics, or by showing that Nietzsche's aesthetic reverence for the superman is in fact ugly on its own terms and that equality is more life- affirmingly and beatific.

The most important start to such a project has been initiated by Wendy Brown in her book *In the Ruins of Neoliberalism.*[55] She acknowledges the reality of ressentiment as the basis of many progressive movements, including in the wounded attachments of the marginalized for whom their very identity as victims becomes an object of pathological fixation from which they are unable to detach themselves.[56] However Brown follows other recent commentators by arguing that Nietzsche is profoundly misguided in asserting that feelings of ressentiment only appear amongst the slaves and wretched of society.[57] Brown draws attention to how the ressentiment of privilege and status can be just as nihilistic and pathological a source of political motivation as the ressentiment of the slave. And this often leads to far more destructive consequences.

While the ressentiment of the victim may take the form "if I can't have it, no one will" the ressentiment of elites, or the aspiring, assumes the more vindictive "no one else should enjoy what I have." Pathological attachment to positions of power and status for their own sake can be generative of profound feelings of ressentiment when these are threatened by egalitarian movements, which may even engage in self-destructive behavior to avoid sharing them. Ironically even Nietzschean-inspired art has given expression to this. In *The Fountainhead* Ayn Rand—herself very influenced by Nietzsche[58]—has the "heroic" architect Howard Roark demolish a public housing project rather than see his aesthetic vision compromised.[59] At its most extreme even sharing status at no significant material cost to elites may be resented. Consider George Wallace's threat to eliminate public education in Alabama rather than see black children attend school with white children. Or when Hitler commanded the destruction of Germany itself rather than seeing its resources and people fall into the despised hands of wretched Jews and Communists.[60]

There is a deep sense in which the incompleteness of Nietzsche's analysis of ressentiment is implicated in the more nefarious projects of nationalism and racism to which he provided unwitting ideological support. His failure to analyze the ressentiment around which elites would mobilize, imagining themselves licensed by virtue of being intrinsically superior men, meant that Nietzsche didn't predict how radically inegalitarian philosophies might lead not to great politics. Instead they would lead to the crudest and cruelest vulgarity thinly masked by the veneer of bombast—the parodic imitation of a great politics whose practical power became inextricably coupled to an ability to mobilize the very masses it simultaneously despised. In this respect the worse judgement against the faux-aristocratic politics Nietzsche inspired is just how tacky and tasteless it was in between bouts of uncreative destruction.

But the more basic problem with Nietzsche is that his hermeneutics of suspicion, which sees every philosophy as animated by its morality and every morality not predicated on his crude understanding of strength as flowing on ressentiment, finds in everything what it is looking for but not what is really there. There is a genuine and deeper strength that comes from love of one's neighbour as one's self, and it is expressed in the ability to self-consciously bear the suffering, not just of my life but of everyone's life, without bending or breaking. And then to reciprocally transcend the dehumanization of suffering by transvaluating it into a demand for justice for ourselves, for others, and for all; —a demand which has the power to teleologically suspend the ethical and aesthetic dogmas of the world. Nietzsche could never understand how the egalitarian Christian ethic became not just intellectually creative, but strong enough to overcome master morality. Here Nikos Kazantzakis seems to have the right answer:

> "He felt terrible pains in his hands, feet and heart. His sight cleared; he saw the crown of thorns, the blood, the cross. Two golden ear-rings and two rows of sharp, brilliantly-white teeth flashed in the darkened sun. He heard a cool mocking laugh, and rings and teeth vanished. Jesus remained hanging in the air alone. His head quivered. Suddenly he remembered where he was, who he was and why he felt pain. A wild indomitable joy took possession of him. No, no, he was not a coward, a deserter, a traitor. No, he was nailed to the cross. He had stood his ground honourably to the very end; he had kept his word. The moment he cried ELI ELI and fainted, Temptation had captured him for a split-second and led him astray. The joys, marriages and children were lies, the decrepit degraded old men who shouted coward, deserter, traitor at him were lies. All-all were illusions sent by the Devil. His disciples were alive and thriving. They had gone over sea and land and were proclaiming the Good News. Everything had turned out as it should, glory be to God! He uttered a triumphant cry: IT IS ACCOMPLISHED! And it was as though he had said: Everything has begun."[61]

Heidegger on the Nihilism of the Modern Subject

Heidegger occupies a curious position as a far-right thinker. Like Nietzsche he is undeniably a brilliant philosopher. Heidegger's work has had a truly astonishing influence on the broader intellectual culture, including across the political spectrum. Authors as diverse as Jacques Derrida, Jordan Peterson, Richard Rorty, and Alexander Dugin have all described him as a formative influence. On the other hand however, unlike Nietzsche, Heidegger directly leant his name and prestige to the most sinister political party of all time. Not only that-—contrary to the official line at the time-—Heidegger's involvement with Nazism was neither casual nor purely opportunistic. It flowed from deep convictions formed during the 1920s, often in dialogue with or influenced by the other figures of the "German Revolution," who were animated by hostility to the Weimar rRepublic. These reactionary dispositions evolved into providing both intellectual credibility to the Nazi party when it came to power in 1933 and lending it institutional support during Heidegger's brief tenure as Rector of Freiburg.[62]

All this would seem to make Heidegger a recognizably political author, even someone like Burke or De Maistre who served a dual function as both an intellectual and an activist. And yet compared to almost everyone else in this book Heidegger's philosophical writings can superficially appear resolutely apolitical. Excepting the odd throwaway line about Russia and America being "metaphysically the same" or the singularness of the German nation one would be hard pressed to find much transparently political or moral material in his work. Conventional apologists for Heidegger's work will sometimes point to this lack of overtly political language as a sign that the profound core of his philosophy needn't be touched by the personal errors of his Nazism.[63] Heidegger never apologized for his involvement with Nazism but certainly did downplay it whenever possible. In a 1976 *Der Spiegel* interview, one of the few moments where he allowed the issue to be directly discussed, Heidegger largely sidestepped the years between 1933– and 1936. He then insisted that anyone who listened to his 1936 lectures on Nietzsche would recognize them as a *very* coded "confrontation" with National Socialism.[64] Even this unconvincing rhetoric of exoneration retrenches the narrative of Heidegger as an apolitical thinker, since a "confrontation" with National Socialism which consists of a long scholarly analysis of Nietzsche suggests a level of remove from social life distinct even by the alpine standards of German academia.

While the surface of Heidegger's writing can seem, beyond just its well-known density, amoral and apolitical, this is not because Heidegger is either. In fact Heidegger is convinced of the fallen nature of nihilistic modernity. As a result the conventional language of politics and morality, inherited from the history of Western metaphysics, is inadequate and potentially complicit in the problem.[65] An entirely new vocabulary may be required, and this will of necessity reject the occlusive everydayness of norms surrounding good and evil, freedom, and equality. In this respect Heidegger follows Nietzsche in the totality of his critique of Western modernity, though his dialectic is almost always ontological rather than psychological and aesthetic. To this day Heidegger's myriad neo-fascist progeny are so impressed by this critique they portray it as the catalyst to search for another beginning which will evade the limitations of Western metaphysics and its immanent collapse into the nihilism of Being's withdrawal.[66]

The history of big B Being's withdrawal over the long course of Western metaphysics is the major political story of Heidegger's work and vital to understanding his rejection of liberalism, socialism, and democracy. Complicating this is the reality that Heidegger's thinking has been very profitably mined for philosophical projects which have little to do with politics, [67] and even for political projects radically contrary to Heidegger's own.[68] As Duff stresses, Heidegger's thinking is not "coextensive" with Nazism, and he has had a major influence on at least three political traditions very different than neo-fascism, including "Iranian revolutionaries...environmentalists and Greens [and] Cold War dissidents."[69] A further complication is that Heidegger's most famous work and chef d'ouevre is *Being and Time*: a remarkable work of existential phenomenology which appears to have little to say about politics until the concluding sections on authenticity and the dangers of the mass "they."

Heidegger regards modern thought as pivoting around the philosophy of the subject which from Descartes through Kant assumes universalistic characteristics. Framing the subject in such a universalistic way has a distinctly egalitarian flavor by undermining claims about the intrinsic superiority of the few over the many.[70] Reacting to this humanist and democratic dimension is one of the reasons Heidegger is critical of the philosophy of the subject. Nevertheless, even those committed to humanism would be foolish to reject the often remarkable insights of Heidegger's thinking purely on that basis, provided they are handled with sufficient delicacy. The kind of possessive individualist variations of the philosophy of the subject put forward, especially by early modern thinkers, were both anthropologically and politically damaging. They deserve the widespread condemnation they've received. *Being and Time* does a great deal to blur the crudities of the Cartesian subject/object divide, and both Heidegger's major book and *Kant and the Problem of Metaphysics* follows Husserl in successfully critiquing transcendental idealism's demotion of the ontical world of the subject's experience to mere phenomena constituted by reason.[71]

At the basis of *Being and Time* is Heidegger's concern for the forgetting of Being, though why this is politically significant isn't clear until near the end. His critique of the philosophy of the subject takes the form of rejecting the Cartesian-Kantian insistence that at the basis of human life is reason and its apprehension of the objects of thought and experience. Instead Heidegger claims that the structural primordiality of Dasein-—that entity which "in its being this being is concerned about its very being."[72]- —is not reason but care:

> "As a possibility of being of Dasein, together with the Dasein disclosed in it, anxiety provides the phenomenal basis for explicitly grasping the primordial totality of being Dasein. Its being reveals itself as care. The ontological development of this fundamental existential phenomenon demands that he differentiate it from phenomena which at first might seem to be identified with care. Such phenomena are will, wish, predilection, and urge. Care cannot be derived from them because they themselves are founded upon it."[73]

This position obviously draws a great deal from the existential tradition which preceded Heidegger, most importantly from Soren Kierkegaard who launched a similar critique of vulgar-Hegelian hyper-rationalism in favor of a view of life where "truth was subjectivity." This isn't to say that truth is subjective, but that truth only has meaning for a subject whose life is committed to living the truth and so whose own selfhood can become a problem for it where this commitment anxiously wavers.[74] Heidegger is to be commended for systematizing the insights of earlier existential thinkers and massively broadening their scope to weigh on other areas of the philosophy of the subject, ranging from epistemology to praxis.

One example is how Heidegger rethinks Dasein's phenomenological apprehension of its "world" not in terms of the initially passive rationalistic subject who impartially evaluates sense data, but in terms of the projects it sets itself within time. Moreover Heidegger stresses how this results in a pluralistic onto-epistemology, since each Dasein may apprehend its world differently depending on both the nature of their projects and the historical contexts which circumscribe them. To a traditionalist German peasant in the Black Forest a river may appear as a part of the natural ecology of the environment vital for the watering of crops, while to a rationalistic technocrat it appears as a moving collection of hydro-carbon molecules which can be technically manipulated to generate electrical power.[75] While both enframings of the river have a degree of validity, neither are fully ontological and Heidegger makes it very clear which he prefers even at the ontical level.

Finally, Heidegger adds another original contribution through theorizing an ecstatic phenomenology of time. He demonstrates how the rationalistic idea that Dasein's experience of time is purely presentist cannot explain how its moods and projects are very much determined by an ecstatic relationship with past and future. Think about a hockey player taking a shot, reaching into the past to rely on skills honed over the years and a sense of guilt over having not lived up to her potential, while also projecting herself into the future anxiously concerned to score the winning goal. Any hermeneutics of her activity would be entirely empty if it did not comprehend this ecstatic relationship between past, present, and future and how each folded in on one another as she skates.

Heidegger goes on to argue that conventional philosophers of the subject made a serious error through their inadequate understanding of the phenomenology of time and its relationship to care. Kant comes under special chastisement for his homologation of Newtonian time and human being's transcendental intuition of time, characterizing both as a linear progression to and from fixed points. Kant didn't appreciate how his own postulate of a "transcendental imagination" was more radical than it seemed, playing a role akin to care in *Being and Time* through ecstatically linking past, present, and future together. As Heidegger puts it in *Kant and the Problem of Metaphysics*,

> "it is not because time functions as a 'form of intuition' and was interpreted as such at the point of entry into *Critique of Pure Reason,* but because the understanding of Being must be projected upon time from out of the ground of the finitude of Dasein in man, that time in essential unity with the transcendental power of imagination, attained the central metaphysical function in the *Critique of Pure Reason*. This *Critique of Pure Reason* itself thus rattles the mastery of reason and the understanding. 'Logic is deprived of its pre-eminence in metaphysics, which was built up from ancient times. Its idea has become questionable."[76]

Had things ended here, more or less with the content of *Division I* of *Being and Time*, there would be nothing especially objectionable about the political connotations of Heidegger's project. He would have contributed in important ways to a reconceptualization of the rationalistic subject by correcting for its excesses and drawing attention back to the subject's contextual embeddedness in a richly temporal world of projects. Perhaps the only criticism one could make is that Heidegger doesn't go far enough; one of the lingering hangovers of Husserl's influence is Heidegger's continued fixation on the idealist philosophy of consciousness even as he tries to break out of it. It would take later phenomenologically oriented materialists like Merleau Ponty and Simone de Beauvoir to firmly escape through foregrounding the philosophical importance of body in a way that had been marginalized in Western philosophy since Plato.

Heidegger's Deconstruction of Western Metaphysics

This leads us to the more critical points. Both the technical sharpness of Heidegger's critique and the apocalyptic-—and frankly often bombastically self-aggrandizing- —rhetoric later surrounding it can't disguise the fact that he remains firmly situated within the modern philosophy of the subject. This is true even if Heidegger dramatically reworks its basic obsessions and overcomes its rationalistic limitations (with an awful lot of help from Nietzsche and Kierkegaard which often goes less acknowledged than it should be).[77] Without a doubt this must have caused Heidegger considerable frustration. As Habermas puts it with admirable clarity:

> "So little does Heidegger free himself from the pregiven problematics of transcendental consciousness that he can burst the conceptual cage of the philosophy of consciousness in no other way than by abstract negation. Even in the 'Letter on Humanism' which sums up the results of the Nietzsche interpretations of the previous decade, Heidegger cannot characterize his own procedure otherwise than through implicit reference to Husserl: He wants, as he puts it there, to 'retain the essential help of the phenomenological way of seeing and to dispense with the inappropriate concern with science and research."[78]

Not only does Heidegger not free himself from the philosophy of the subject in any remarkable way in the first *Division* of *Being and Time*, the latter half of the book and almost all his subsequent work doubles down on its idealist connotations in particularly vulgar ways. Heidegger's attempt to overcome the rationalistic subject through an analysis of Dasein's finitude and the critique of inauthenticity, coupled with the long deconstruction of the history of Western metaphysics and a rejection of "'science and research,'" leads him to a highly idealized and politically purple philosophy of history which compares very poorly with those of Hegel and Marx.[79] As Habermas observes,

> "The history of philosophy had already become a key to philosophy of
> history for Hegel. The history of metaphysics holds a comparable rank
> for Heidegger; through it the philosopher masters the sources from which
> each epoch fatefully receives its own light. This idealistic perspective has
> consequences for Heidegger's critique of modernity."[80]

And it is here that the problems arise, and overwhelmingly where Heidegger will
find his most enthusiastic support on the contemporary far right.

The broad stroke of Heidegger's political philosophy is that the history of
Western metaphysics is one of continuous decline from the "beginning" of
Parmenides and the pre-Socratics. In a charitable mood Plato and Aristotle may
round off the epochal period of the West's golden age, but in a more critical
disposition Heidegger will already portray Plato as a step down through his con-
flation of Being with discrete ideas, leading to the philosophy of Being as the
Being of beings apprehended by the rational subject's mind.[81] With the transition
to Cartesian modernity even the Platonic characterization of ideas as real was
abandoned, with a subject-object binary becoming central to Western thinking.
All significant ontological questioning about the "meaning of Being" faded as
even an awareness of Being withdrew from human life. While Heidegger casts
this in secular language, many have understandably detected a strong echo of
Christian onto-theology in this story of the fall, and unsurprisingly his work has
been attractive to religious thinkers in part for this reason.[82] The modern subject
enframed the world in increasingly technical and instrumental terms as nothing
more than "standing reserve" to be manipulated for the purposes of satisfying
human needs.

> "Enframing blocks the shining-forth and holding-sway of truth. The des-
> tining that sends into ordering is consequently the extreme danger. What
> is dangerous is not technology. There is no demonry of technology, but
> rather there is the mystery of its essence. The essence of technology, as a
> destining of revealing, is the danger...The threat to man does not come
> in the first instance from the potentially lethal machines and apparatuses
> of technology. The actual threat has already affected man in his essence.
> The rule of Enframing threatens man with the possibility that it could be
> denied to him to enter into a more original revealing and haence to experi-
> ence the call of a more primal truth. Thus, where Enframing reigns, there
> is danger in the highest sense."[83]

The reduction of the world to a subject who sees objects and consequently regards Being as nothing but the "Being of beings" to be manipulated for her
purposes perverts the "essence" of humankind. It reduces us to a present-minded
and inauthentic "they" committed to the trivial satisfaction of everyday needs,
something which was always a temptation in every epoch, but which is distinctively characteristic of the modern world. While symptoms of this were

diagnosed by Hegel and Nietzsche, Heidegger's two vacillating candidates for exemplifying the "end" of Western metaphysics, he holds that neither was able to escape it. There is no saving the tradition by looking to the intellectual resources available within it—unless they happen to be Heidegger's. This necessitates the overcoming of all Western metaphysics, along with its last Gods, and initiating a new beginning that will capture the glory of the pre-Socratic time without replicating its immanent failures. In this only the "great and unrevealed individuals" will play a major role.[84]

Much has been made of the affinity between Heidegger's critique of the history of Western metaphysics—and indeed Western history as a whole—and the Nietzschean precedent which so inspired him. Not least by Heidegger himself.[85] This cannot disguise the fact that Heidegger's history constitutes a considerable regression from the far more sophisticated takes of Nietzsche, Marx, Adorno, and even Hegel. In each of these figures the philosophy of history is very much conceived in terms of a process whose moments can only be understood in dialectical relation to one another, and whose complexity increases as more distant periods still contain within them the originary problems but in more developed form. This increasing complexity is in part because of the dynamic relation between the ideational forms through which history is conceived by human subjects, including in more sophisticated forms by self-reflective forms of consciousness,[86] and the material practices which both determines and instantiates these forms. By contrast the centrality of philosophy—and not even all philosophy, but only the history of Western metaphysics as the story of Being's withdrawal—in Heidegger's story is simultaneously self-aggrandizing, bordering on self-parodying. It also means that the inceptual moment where metaphysics comes into the world is given far grander status than the millennia long developments that followed. The historical development of metaphysics becomes wildly over-determined as the Rosetta stone through which all historical moments are to be interpreted and compared as a movement of decline.[87] This metaphysical centrality naturally makes a philosopher like Heidegger not only an impressive figure within his own discipline, but something approximating a secular prophet who has a deep insight into the nature of all that has occurred since the inception of Western metaphysics and is entitled to pass a kind of cosmic judgement upon them on Being's behalf.

Now of course Heidegger isn't the first or the last philosopher to fall victim to this kind of megalomania. But as the thinker without a sense of humor par excellence Heidegger is undoubtedly the funniest. Nietzsche and Marx would have smiled at the conceit that idiosyncratic developments in philosophy are what makes the world go round. His megalomania might even have a kind of charm to it if it didn't result in Heidegger making appalling metaphysical conflations, such as his infamous comparison of the Nazi gas chambers to industrial agriculture: "farming is now a motorized food industry, in essence the same as the fabrication of corpses in gas chambers and extermination camps, the same as the blockade and starving of the peasantry, the same as the fabrication of the hydrogen bomb."[88] The justification for such a pathetically stupid homology is that all of these are instantiations of the nihilistic technical metaphysics which has risen to historical primacy. It only makes sense where one ascribes such paramount analytical importance to idealist metaphysics that the materiality of producing food to preserve life and murder on an industrial scale becomes undifferentiated. Mere ontical phenomena of secondary importance compared to a new translation of Aristotle.[89] This has implications in exonerating Heidegger himself from his own concrete political commitments, relegating them to mere analytical errors. As Ronald Beiner puts it with venomous accuracy:

> "On Heidegger's view one needs to think in centuries. He assumed that people would be reading him for centuries (just as one continues to read Aristotle or Hegel). The twentieth century was a lost cause...But eventually people would forget Mussolini and Hitler and remember Heidegger. Three hundred years from now, people would see that philosophically, Heidegger was right, even if he made some tactical mistakes in the 30s. (Over the span of centuries, who would care what happened in the 1930s?) Gadamer once said (in the context of defending Heidegger!) that Heidegger, 'true visionary' that he was, was so preoccupied by modernity's forgetfulness of Being that even the Nazi genocide 'appeared to him as something minimal compared to the future that awaits us.' That seems correct. For Heidegger, the extermination of European Jewry was 'small change' compared with what modernity is doing to the experience of Being."[90]

What Beiner could have added is that it is precisely this idealist flattening of all real events to historicized metaphysical instantiations, and the anti-egalitarian dimensions that obtain, which makes the Heideggerian critique of the West so palatable to the far right. It enables a solipsistic form of self-congratulation for the philosopher and the disciples who understand him, while licensing the dehumanization and even the transformation into thinghood of real human beings who become nothing more than the "masses" whose lives gain meaning through the projects to which they are set by their authentic betters. Alexander Dugin's neo-fascistic denunciation of the "senseless masses, both ancient and modern" whom a "true thinker" need pay no attention to in *Heidegger: The Philosophy of a New Beginning* is representative.[91] This brings us to the crux of Heidegger's politics: his conviction that fascist leadership will be required to lead the masses out of the nihiism embodied in technicist liberalism and socialism.

The Jargon of Authenticity in Defending Nazism

In his *Introduction to Metaphysics* Heidegger makes the geopolitical convictions of his philosophical views spectacularly clear. Presented during the peak of the Nazi (counter) revolution in 1935 as a summer course, one imagines what Heidegger's students must have thought. It isn't exactly summertime fun. The lectures find Heidegger lamenting that philosophy can "never directly supply the forces and create the mechanisms and opportunities that bring about a historical state of affairs, if only because philosophy is always the direct concern of the few."[92] However he is under no illusions that a dramatic transformation in historical affairs is necessary, and Heidegger is delighted one seems to be occurring.[93] The planet is currently riven between two seemingly great opponents, who are in fact united in embodying the crassness of the modern mass age.

> "...Europe, it its unholy blindness always on the point of cutting its own throat, lies today in the pincers between Russia on one side and America on the other. Russia and America, seen metaphysically are both the same: the same hopeless frenzy of unchained technology and the rootless organization of the average man. When the farthest corner of the globe has been conquered technologically and can be exploited economically...when a boxer counts as a great man of a people; when the tallies of millions at mass meetings are a triumph; then, yes then, there still looms like a spectore over all this uproar the question: what for?-—where to?-—and what then? The spiritual decline of the earth has progressed so far that peoples are in danger of losing their last spiritual strength, the strength that makes it possible even to see the decline..."[94]

Heidegger goes on to link these dark trends directly to the levelling effect of egalitarian America and Russia, whose metaphysics "aggressively destroys all rank and all that is world-spiritual, and portrays these as a lie."[95] The "darkening of the world is happening. The essential happenings in this darkening are: the flight of the gods, the destruction of the earth, the reduction of human beings to a mass, the pre-eminence of the mediocre."[96] Against this stands the German people or *volk*, which is spiritually and geographically equipped for "subduing the danger of the darkening of the world, and thus taking over the historical mission of our people, the people of the center of the West."[97]

Here we undoubtedly see Heidegger presenting a more nationalistic interpretation of authentic Dasein than was given in *Being and Time;*, following on from the infamous "Rectoral Address" where he successfully called on German students to submit to the leadership of Adolph Hitler.[98] Some might characterize this as a shift in focus from what seemed initially like the more individualistic philosophy of *Being and Time*. Here authenticity is often taken to be an individual rejection of the mass in favor of an "anticipation of death" which lifts us out of the vulgar presentism of common-sense notions of time. It also drives away the ontical "endless multiplicity of closest possibilities offering themselves-those of comfort, shirking, and taking things easy" through a commitment to ontologically minded projects.[99] But in fact Heidegger explicitly rejects just such an individualistic account, which would invariably constitute a kind of vulgar romantic or existential humanism. Instead Heidegger stresses that choosing an authentic "destiny" is always something that is done with "others:":

> "With this term [destiny], we designate the occurrence of the community of a people. Destiny is not composed of individual fates, nor can being-with-one another be conceived of as the mutual occurrence of several subjects. These fates are already guided beforehand in being-with-one-another in the same world and in the resoluteness for definite possibilities. In communication and in the struggle the power of destiny first becomes free."[100]

But what is the content of this destiny to which an authentic community of people must commit itself. And more importantly who gets to decide on this destiny? The ontological language Heidegger so often uses obscures these political questions by implying a destiny is something "fated" by the history of Being. Moreover sublimating the choice at the level of ontology means it necessarily exists "beyond" considerations of good and evil. It is to be evaluated by the uniquely Heideggerian existential aesthetics in so far as it reinscribes an existential awareness of the loss of Being into a people's behavior.

All this gives a sublime gloss to the far more banal reality that those who decide the "destiny" of an authentic people are the rarefied few who can be recognized by the especially sensitive philosopher. While he never gives anything approximating the criteria for recognizing these leaders, Heidegger evidently saw something he liked in Hitler, Goering, and the others something he liked. When the Nazis turned out to be disappointments, Heidegger didn't apologize. He instead claimed to have misread the tea leaves by failing to recognize that Nazism was just another symptom of the Western drive to nihilistic domination of the world through technology. [101] Whoops. In this respect we once more see the impoverished quality of Heidegger's philosophy of history, as the specificity the Holocaust fades into the sweeping ideations of the larger story. From *Letter on a Humanism* onwards Heidegger drops some of this Nietzschean flavored rhetorical excess and retreats into the familiar language of reactionary pastoralism. Dasein becomes ontologically attuned less through a people's grand destiny and more through being the "shepherd" of Being who allows entities to unconceal the truth of what they are.[102] All while awaiting a more sincere new beginning where the history of metaphysics can finally be overcome.

In *The Jargon of Authenticity* and *Negative Dialectics*, Theodor Adorno rightly diagnoses the failure of Heidegger's project as a residual attachment to the aesthetic purity of ontological essentialism, from which his crypto-idealism never allowed him to escape.[103] While the notion of ecstatic time seemed to break Dasein out of the contingencies of the present, Heidegger carefully tames the emancipatory potential of such a call by insisting that an authentic project is one where an individual's, and indeed the community's, whole being becomes totally committed to their authentic "destiny" as the philosopher understands it. Authenticity so conceived in the idealist terms of *Being and Time* onwards is abstracted from the real-life conditions and actions required to achieve it. And so also from all considerations of power and authority which might seem central to invigorating real struggles against the tyranny. There is almost no consideration of power at all in Heidegger, who is far more frightened of the influence of everyday people and their mediocrity than the might allocated to deserved "rank."

In this way a philosophical enterprise which initially set itself against the triteness of the bourgeois everyday came to lend ideological support to the most brutal kind of inauthenticity. This came from Heidegger's unawareness of the totalizing effects of material power on the soul and body of real human beings. In one of the greater ironies to ever befall the intellectual far right, a thinker who prided himself on seeing further than anyone was completely blind to the fact that the politics he supported would lead to the very ends he most feared. Heidegger imagined that the people could be elevated from mere "masses" by unaccountable leaders committed to something bigger than themselves. It would have occurred to anyone with any sense that by calling for the even the minimal bourgeois freedoms guaranteed by democracy to be stripped away, Heidegger was facilitating what Hitler would ultimately do. Flatten the people out before manipulating them into becoming banal killing machines.

Carl Schmitt on Liberalism, the God That Failed

> "The political is the most intense and extreme antagonism, and every concrete antagonism becomes that much more political the closer it approaches the most extreme point, that of the friend-enemy grouping. In its entirety the state as an organized political entity decides for itself the friend-enemy distinction."
>
> (Carl Schmitt, *The Concept of the Political*)

Despite engaging in some polite exchanges during the peak of the Nazi era Heidegger allegedly castigated Schmitt for still thinking too much like a liberal."[104] Beyond just showing the depths of Heidegger's own political radicalization, it surely would have stung Schmitt. Nevertheless there is some truth to the accusation. Schmitt was one of the rare far-right thinkers who remained fascinated rather than repelled by liberalism, awed both by its mythological power and the very way it neutered accusations of mythologization.[105] This makes Schmitt the most conventionally reactionary of the figures we've looked at. For some this might make Schmitt a less original thinker than Nietzsche or Heidegger. While true, this also gives his critique of liberalism and egalitarian modernity the disturbing force which comes from familiarity and proximity. Nietzsche and Heidegger wanted to reject liberalism and socialism wholesale, which means liberals and socialists can just reject them in turn.[106] Schmitt's critique of liberalism is an immanent one that takes aim at many of the tradition's most cherished idols. That means no thoughtful liberal can responsibly ignore it.

The sharpness of his critique means Schmitt has been of enduring interest to plenty of conservative and far-right critics down to the present day.[107] The acknowledged power of his objections means he has also been of longstanding fascination to liberals,[108] democrats,[109] and even left-wing radicals[110] who are variably committed to defending liberalism, reforming it, or overcoming its inegalitarian and anti-democratic limitations. The attraction for the latter is somewhat understandable given how Schmitt's is undoubtedly a radical critique of liberalism. But it should very much not be one that appeals to progressives, for reasons Heiner Bielefeldt made clear:

> ….Schmitt systematically undermines the liberal principle of the rule of law. He wants it to be replaced by an authoritarian version of democracy, a democracy based upon the 'substantial homogeneity' of the collective unity of the people rather than one resting upon the principles of participatory republicanism. Although Schmitt until 1933 opposed the Nazi party, his ardent anti-liberalism entails from the outset the potential for fascism. It is thus more than a pure coincidence that he finally proved able to espouse the political ideology of the Third Reich and to take up for some time the role of a legal adviser to the Nazi regime, without substantially changing his previously developed political concepts.[111]

I even toyed around with Schmitt during my undergraduate, when all the cool kids at Carleton University experimented with the tools of *Political Theology* to explain the illiberal horrors unleashed by the neoconservative Bush administration (ah to be young again).[112] Since then I have grown wary of these kinds of progressive Schmittian experiments. If they are going to be conducted it needs to be done with tremendous care to ensure that the critique of liberalism is genuinely emancipatory and not reactionary.[113] Seen in such a light this section can be read as a more personal effort to wean people off the temptations offered by Schmittianism.

Schmitt was born into a conservative petit bourgeois Catholic family in 1888. The Kaiser's German Empire was at the height of its domestic and international prestige and influence. While he was later excommunicated the stamp of revanchist Catholicism is implanted deep into Schmitt's writing through all its twists and turns. Like De Maistre (a longstanding influence on him), Kirk, and others, Schmitt's Christianity had a distinctly pessimistic tone stressing the fallenness of man and the inexorability of sin. Like Burke, De Maistre, and Heidegger and unlike Carlyle, Oakeshott, or Eliot, Schmitt, his writing is not at its most original and engaging in moments of reflective triumph or even tragic defeat. It draws vampire-like sustenance from ongoing and agonistic confrontation with a worthy foe.

So not coincidentally Schmitt's creative peak was a long stretch between 1920 and 1938 during which almost all the books which made his name were prepared and published. This includes *Political Theology, The Crisis of Parliamentary Democracy, The Concept of the Political,* his opus *Constitutional Theory,* and Schmitt's highly original and viciously anti-Semitic take on Hobbes' *The Leviathan in the State Theory of Thomas Hobbes.* These works provide a running commentary on the decline and fall of the Weimar Republic Schmitt (mostly) despised but whose fall he was initially uncertain about. Weimar, in its heyday one of the most progressive and democratic republics in the world and initially dominated by the powerful German Social Democratic Party,[114] very much became a petri dish from which Schmitt extrapolated larger political lessons about liberalism and democracy. Its ultimate failure seems to have affirmed his gloomiest predictions about both the theological instability of liberal politics and the need to replace it with a popular form of authoritarian "democracy" oriented by a leader embodying the general will. Schmitt got his chance to help create such a society between 1933 and 1936 when he served as the crown jurist of the Third Reich.

After this cure proved far worse than the disease and Schmitt's career was in shambles due to his rapprochement with Nazism, he spent the rest of his life as a cult figure for the European far right even if he was a persona non grata among West German academics.[115] Living until near the end of the Cold War, Schmitt was somewhat less prolific and considerably less original. His *The Nomos of the Earth* mainly operationalizes the ideas directed against domestic liberal legal systems and extends them into an equally pointed, but more predictable[116] criticism of emerging international law.[117]

Schmitt's regard for liberalism ranges from puzzlement to outright hostility, reflecting in his attitudes the vacillations liberal politics itself engages in. For Schmitt, all significant modern political concepts are secularized theological concepts.[118] They concern the ultimate ends to which life is directed, or if one prefers the terminology of Protestant theology, what is of highest or ultimate "concern" in life.[119] This attraction to political theology is very much in keeping with the long history of reactionary thought which seeks to transvalue the profanity of human existence by attaching it to a transcendent sublime. We have seen this before in the writings of figures like De Maistre and T.S. Eliot. But where Schmitt is far more modern than these authors is in combining his attraction to politics raised to theological intensity with a remarkable indifference and even skepticism about grounding his theic preferences in any kind of philosophical or scholastic foundation. Schmitt's is a political theology without the theology, which even at his most irrationalist one could not accuse De Maistre of. For Schmitt there is no evading a political theology, but its content is almost entirely determined by human decision.

In this Schmitt's acknowledged debt to the commitment-driven existential Christianity of Soren Kierkegaard is abundantly clear. For Kierkegaard, an authentic commitment to the life of faith had tremendous power—it could even teleologically suspend the ethical world of norms for the single individual who came to believe God's will required something higher from him. Where Schmitt differs from the melancholy Dane is his belief that these questions can be dissolved for the individual through the exercise of exceptional sovereign power. Political sovereignty can answer the riddles of existence for, and even in defiance of, the single individual. This has the virtue of overcoming the anxious vacillations and uncertainty which were so emblematic of the early 20th century and post-Nietzschean Weimar Germany in particular. From Schmitt's standpoint the irresolution Kierkegaard diagnosed so effectively can never be solved individually, but only through power. Liberalism's wish to avoid this exemplifies why so many liberal subjects end up as Kierkegaardian losers whose lives never come into genuine theological focus. As Loschenkohl puts it:

> From a Schmittian perspective, however, the question arises whether the young man's decision not to decide is in the end any different from mere indecisiveness – whether he does not 'suspend the decision at the crucial point by denying that there was at all something to be decided' and instead indulges in what Schmitt criticizes as the 'everlasting conversation' of parliamentary democracies characterises such romanticist attitude as the 'essence of liberalism'; paraphrasing Donoso Corte's, he writes that liberalism reverts to 'negotiation, a cautious half measure', all 'in the hope that the definitive dispute, the decisive bloody battle, can be transformed into a parliamentary debate and permit the decision to be suspended forever.[120]

These existential themes run throughout Schmitt's work and bring us to the first horn of his critique of liberalism. On the one hand liberal materialism attempts to do away with the transcendent dimensions of life by endlessly delaying the moment of theological decision and existential commitment. Liberals do this to achieve a prudentialist pacification of the intense political conflict they associate with religiosity, itself almost certainly a residue of liberalism's birth pains during the age of Reformation and large-scale religious conflict. This also has an egalitarian dimension to it.[121] By attempting to avoid theological decisions political liberals can try to claim for themselves a special tolerance of diverse "conceptions of the good life" which will be treated equally under the law.[122] Consequently liberals are never required to face any genuine political "enemies"; at least insofar as illiberal doctrines miraculously decide to relegate themselves to minority positions within liberal states and stop trying to impose their own homogenizing political theology.

This reflects liberalisms' privileged self-understanding as a neutral guarantor of freedom and equality compared to authoritarian regimes. But in practice liberalism relied on majoritarian acceptance of its basic convictions to evade decision and confrontation. The theoretical and practical poverty of this view comes into focus when one looks at the everyday politics of governing a mass of people, whose deep dissatisfactions with liberal democracy liberals shockingly take pride in since they reflect pluralistic variety. All of this was exposed by the failures of the Weimar Republic, as Schmitt never tires of reminding us:

> The method of will formation through simply majority vote is sensible and acceptable when an essential similarity among the entire people can be assumed. For in this case, there is no voting down the minority…One must assume that, but virtue of being part of the same people, all those similarly situated would in essence will the same thing. If the assumption of an indivisible, national commonality is no longer tenable, then the abstract, empty functionalism of pure mathematical majority determinations is the opposite of neutrality and objectivity. It is only the quantitatively larger or smaller, forced subordination of the defeated, and, therefore, suppressed minority.[123]

This brings us to the second horn of Schmitt's critique.

Dictatorship and Democracy

The first horn of Schmitt's critique of liberalism holds that it denies its own theological base and asserts the neutrality of liberal law with respect to competing visions of the good life. Liberalism does this in the name of social equality and freedom at the level of principle, and a concern to avoid genuine political struggle against enemies at the level of prudence. Schmitt's most Nietzschean moments occur when he snidely observes these efforts by liberals to avoid moments of decision. He takes them to be reflective of an abiding lack of resolution. Much of Schmitt's acidic commentary on the efforts of liberal positivists to locate the political legitimacy of liberalism in mere legalism, while simultaneously denying any explicit moral content to the law, reflects this disdain.[124] Schmitt's bemusement at the endless delaying characteristic of parliamentarian talk is another.

> A constitution that would not dare to reach a decision on this question; one that forgoes a substantive order, but chooses instead to give warring factions, intellectual circles, and political programs the illusion of gaining satisfaction legally, of achieving their party goals and eliminating their enemies, both by legal means; such a constitution is no longer even possible today as a dilatory formal compromise; and as a practical matter, it would end by destroying its own legality and legitimacy. It will necessarily fail at the critical moment when a constitution must prove itself.[125]

But this leads us to Schmitt's potentially more damaging horn. Liberalism's flailing efforts to convince the gullible that its very egalitarian sounding neutrality is the basis of its moral superiority amuse Schmitt. But Schmitt was also convinced that even a liberal politics cannot endlessly postpone moments of decision. He was aware that in many instances liberals could choose to be bolder and simply assert the theological superiority of liberalism through the use of state power when they were required to do so. After all, it was the quintessentially bourgeois thinker Hobbes who had banished political theology and mythology from civil society through inventing the greatest mythological embodiment of state power in history.[126] As mentioned one way liberalism tries to circumvent the gridlock of political divisions is by assimilating democratic elements into liberalism and making legislation turn on the principle of majority rule. This was transparent in all the great bourgeois revolutions—from America to France to Germany— that appealed to some notion of "we the people" as the ultimate sovereign who legitimates liberal constitutionalism. But this democratic fix was a sham since, at most, it meant that representatives elected by a majority of the population were entitled to impose their preferences on the minority without restriction—meaning that in fact the liberal "people" were only a segment of the voting population. Or, perhaps worse, the majority was halted in these ambitions by the structures imposed by constitutional liberal rights. In which case the mere majority of the population weren't even able to express their will through the law.

Consequently who or what ultimately assumes the role of sovereign within the liberal state for Schmitt and Schmittian is an ambiguous—and to some extent contextually sensitive—matter. It may be a parliamentary party that enjoys explicitly majority support, but nevertheless claims the implicit or virtual support of the opposition. It may be a liberal dictatorship of the sort Hayek once supported as an alternative to socialist democracy. For both critical legal theorists and even some on the right it may be Supreme Court. A liberal Supreme Court grants itself the "neutral" role of interpreting the plain meaning of a constitution said to represent the will of liberal polis, while in fact exploiting the penumbra between semantic indeterminacy and moral ambiguity to advance its own untethered political preferences the whole way down.[127]

Remarkably Schmitt openly theorizes that, given these failings, a sovereign dictatorship which constitutes a people out of theological "friends," comes to enjoy their total support, and eliminates internal enemies, may in fact be more democratic than liberalism. Drawing heavily on Rousseau, Schmitt identifies a consecution between the general will embodying the authentic wishes of a national people and a singular figure who instantiates and can direct the general will. Schmitt even gives this an egalitarian connotation. In *Constitutional Theory* he defends the nation as the "essential substantive elements of democratic equality." But it is inherently a chauvinistic and reified equality which denies moral status and equality to those outside of it and even posits the need for further and potentially edifying conflict at the international level.[128] As he puts it,

> democratic equality is essentially similarity, in particular similarity among the people. The central concept of democracy is people and not humanity. If democracy is to be a political form at all, there is only a people's democracy and not that of humanity.[129]

This is very coincident with the fascist ultranation.[130]

Consequently the equality of all those outside the national people is denied, while the equality of the national people is affirmed but only through political idealizations. It is denied in reality since the people's will is determined and known by the dictator and needn't be expressed through active participation or a devolution of power. This latter point is the most important. As critics of Nazism like Erich Fromm have stressed, there is an intrinsic connection between more substantive commitments to equality, the development of personal and collective identity, and respect for individual freedom.[131] A recognition of the moral equality of all individuals entails respecting an entitlement to free development of their personal identity without the intent to impose some supposedly superior national identity on them. Moreover it is only by allowing equal individuals the freedom to develop their personalities that they can form unalienated relationships with others that are predicated on love and civic friendship rather than force.

Now there are many respects in which liberal democracy falls short on this front. Not least because of the enduring inequities produced by capitalist domination. But Schmitt's cure of denying such individual differences through the ambition of creating a shared national identity is far worse than the disease. In the name of achieving a kind of faux nationalistic "democratic equality" through an authoritarian state which is to impose sameness, Schmitt must deny the more substantive equality of individuals to live their lives as they, and not someone else, think best. As with so many far-right thinkers, the social problem is to be resolved through sublimation of the real abstraction of the ultranation into a seamless idol. The practical consequence is not social elevation but mass submission to dictatorial power transformed into totalizing authority. Even more remarkable is how Schmitt condemns the tedious doldrums of liberal mediocrity relative to the sublimity of a genuinely theological politics. And yet Schmitt made the fool's error of not realizing that the Nazi solution he endorsed would produce a far more massified society than the troubled bohemian republic he despised. The Nazi ultranational state's banality would make the kind of inauthenticity Kierkegaard detected in bourgeois Christendom look paltry by comparison.

In the end it's hard not to see Schmitt as a remarkably clever man fleeing the complexities of the world into a fortress of power. What's remarkable is how, starting from a highly modern decisionist standpoint which posits the irrevocably pluralistic and existential division between competing theologies, Schmitt ends with such a demand for absolute national sameness. A sameness which is to be imposed from above by power in the name of a totalizing "democracy" in which the people do not even need to actively participate so long as they subordinate their will to the general will as determined by, and embodied in, the leader. This demonstrates the extent to which Schmitt leans heavily and so undialectically into his famous bifurcations. We can have political enemies or national unity. The political universe will either be divided into the warring Gods of political theology, or the Fuhrer wills fetishized idols into being and commands "Bow!" To which all of us should say: no.

Fascism's 21st-Century Rebranding

Curiously, it seems the Washington demonstrators' success at breaching the Capitol gives them less support in American society today than the unsuccessful French demonstrators of February 1934 acquired in their country. In France, elections in June 1936 had a highly contested outcome: the installation of a Jew and a Socialist, Leon Blum, as the French Prime Minister. French fascists remained active opponents of Blum until opportunity came for them again in June 1940 with Hitler's defeat of the French Army, and the replacement of the French parliamentary republic with the authoritarian Vichy regime. In the United States, after the ignominious failure of a shocking fascist attempt to undo Biden's election, the new American President can begin his work of healing on January 20. Despite encouraging early signs and the relative robustness of American institutions, it's too soon for a responsible historian to say whether he'll be more successful in sustaining our Republic than European leaders were in defending theirs.

Robert Paxton, "I've Hesitated to Call Trump a Fascist. Until Now."

It was the destiny of 20th-century fascism to cause tremendous suffering before deliquescing into the sewage of history. In a better world that would have been the end of it. But we live in this world, and it wasn't. Nietzsche, Heidegger, and Schmitt provided the intellectual voice for a new kind of political agitation on the right.[132] By unshackling the right from the shackles of traditionalism and the more egalitarian strands of Christian humanism, these far-right authors projected a new kind of utopian ideal. One defined by radically aristocratic inequality, with a rarefied few defined by will, authentic resolve, or embodying the national identity, entitled to rule over the decadent masses. Of course none of these thinkers would have been or were impressed by the actual results. But analogous to Corey Robin's observation that the right has frequently been disappointed when its attraction to violence as an edifying activity collides with the vulgar banality of war, we might say that the lived reality of one's aggrandizing fantasies is usually the quickest route to desublimating them.[133] The quackery of fascism isn't the opposite of "great" politics. It is, as Benjamin pointed out, the material reality of trying to self-consciously will a "great" politics into being before discovering it means nothing but entertaining vulgarity during the rallies and death, defeat, and shame when it enters the battlefield.[134]

I don't want to digress extensively into the long and complex debate about the intersection of theory into fascist reality.[135] Nor do I want to give an intellectual gloss to fascist movements by implying that they were primarily motivated by high intellectual ideals. It is telling that most court fascist intellectuals, from Evola to Alfred Rosenberg, were far less impressive figures than Heidegger or Schmitt.[136] The latter were treated with suspicion by fascist regimes for their heterodoxy on issues like the centrality of biological racism. As an authoritarian movement with totalitarian aspirations (never truly successful)[137] fascism was invariably suspicious of the very kind of radical thinking that led figures like Heidegger or Schmitt to be attracted to it in the first place.

In practice fascists operated very much like other political parties and movements, in that they would syncretically draw on theoretical precedents and practical opportunities to advance their cause with less than a theorist's reverence for consistency. This could include borrowing liberally from liberalism, and even socialism and communism where that seemed politically efficacious. A practice which continues to this day when one thinks of slogans like "white lives matter" or the constant fascist plagiarising of demands for viewpoint diversity and free speech.[138] Fascist movements were also far more willing to draw comprehensively and deeply on the epistemic and scientific revolutions associated with modernity, while rabidly denying the egalitarian connotations liberal and socialists would give them. Indeed the quackish pastiche of pseudo-science, mythology, and nationalism which many associate with fascist irrationalism in fact contributed to its appeal across a broad spectrum of the polis. This is one of the features that gave fascists a kind of revolutionary modernism which contrasts with conventional conservatism. As Gregor stresses with reference to the Nazi eugenics programs:

> the vision of a racially re-engineered society that Hitler espoused may have been described using language familiar to many on the mainstream right, including, sometimes, the language of an angry Protestant nationalism (this was undoubtedly a key element of the appeal). But the vision itself was far from familiar, and bore no relation to anything recognizable in what earlier nationalist or racist movements had sought to achieve.[139]

This syncretic disposition produced something new which owed much to the fertile inegalitarian manure laid by intellects greater than the fascists themselves.[140] What fascism did was take the belief that, in the words of the "left-wing" Nazi Gregor Strasser, "people are unequal, they are unequal from birth, become more unequal in life and are therefore to be valued unequally in their positions in society and in the state..." and radicalize it.[141] It saw in liberal democracy and especially Marxism an existentially deadly rejection of the

> aristocratic principle of Nature and replaces the eternal privilege of power and strength by the mass of numbers and their dead weight. Thus it denies the value of personality in man, contests the significance of nationality and race, and thereby withdraws from humanity the premise of its existence and its culture. As a foundation of the universe, this doctrine would bring about the end of any order intellectually conceivable to man.[142]

Or as Mussolini put it,

> after socialism, Fascism trains its guns on the whole block of democratic ideologies, and rejects both their premises and their practical applications

and implements. Fascism denies that numbers, as such, can be the determining factor in human society; it denies the right of numbers to govern
by means of periodical consultations; it asserts the irremediable and fertile and beneficent inequality of men who cannot be leveled by any such
mechanical and extrinsic device as universal suffrage. Democratic regimes
may be described as those under which the people are, from time to time,
deluded into the belief that they exercise sovereignty, while all the time
real sovereignty resides in and is exercised by other and sometimes irre-
sponsible and secret forces. Democracy is a kingless regime infested by
many kings who are sometimes more exclusive, tyrannical, and destructive
than one, even if he be a tyrant.[143]

And fascism affirmed inequality, not just through negation and reaction. Griffin
observes how classical commentators on fascism tended to define it solely in
terms of what it was opposed to—invariably the kinds of egalitarian politics
associated with liberal parliamentarianism or more transformational forms of
socialism and communism.[144] This has the effect of normalizing convictions
about human equality and conceiving fascism as some visceral reaction against
them. While true, this ignores how an ideological commitment to inequality
can be just as comprehensive as its counterpart. One thing Nietzsche was right
about is that contemporary Western cultures have by now sufficiently internalized the political semiotics of equality so that dramatic deviations from it have
to be defended. What is novel about fascism is how decisively it broke from this,
and, in doing so, licensed a pathological enjoyment of feelings of superiority
without any of attendant guilt or qualification hanging around from Christian
humanism.[145] Fascism was an endorsement not just of inequality but of radical
and aristocratic inequality—historically but by no means exclusively conceived
along ultra-nationalistic and racist lines. This is what made it distinctive.

Fascism coupled a pathos of "noble" distance with a ressentiment and sense
of victimization which is distinctive to far-right movements: a resentment of
the undeserving who claim the status and power which belong to the rarefied
and deserving. It was the hatred emerging from these extraordinarily divalent
but connected poles—a belief in one's radical superiority coupled with resentment at one's perceived radical disinvestment—that fascism drew its emotional
power from. It garnered considerable political support because it was able to reify
this pathos into a hyper-sublime politics of palingenetic ultranationalist recov-
ery which could include millions of Germans and Italians, transforming them
into the racial aristocrats of the world. The dialectical pathos of superiority and
ressentiment could then be directed against the weak and parasitic enemies of
the fascist noble class or master race. This served fascism by elevating the pitch
of edifying conflict and providing a source of ideological stabilization through
projecting blame for the inevitable desublimation and failures of its ambitions on
the weak, unpatriotic, and of course Jews.[146]

In the end the only novel consequence of generic fascism was finding a way of coupling a distinctively horrific kind of human suffering with an equally distinct banality. Beginning with a call for authentic sacrifice and edifying violence, generic fascism ended in a bunker with a madman raving that his people had failed him. The dynamic tension between fascism's claims to superiority and victimization was a source of its power. The impotent struggle of utterly small narcissists to achieve bigness through purifying competition, violence, and death is the enduring source of fascism's disgrace. It wasn't too much to hope that this would be the end of it. But it wasn't.

Dugin's Cosmic War

> I share the vision of René Guénon and Julius Evola, who considered modernity and the ideologies derived from it—individualism, liberal democracy, capitalism, and so on—to be the causes of the coming catastrophe of humanity, and the global domination of Western attitudes as the final degradation of the Earth. The West is approaching its end, and we should not let it pull all the rest of us into the abyss along with.
>
> (Alexander Dugin, *Introduction to Eurasianism*)

> There, other mountain peaks are clear visible, whereas the insignificant swarms in dark valleys below are indiscernable in the present much like long ago. A true thinker knows as little about the details of society in which he lives as he does about those of the times long gone. Yet the voice of Being is audible to him, as it emnates from the ancients clearer and louder than the itching on the part of the senseless masses, both ancient and modern.
>
> (Alexander Dugin, *Heidegger and the Philosophy of a New Beginning*)

In our time we've seen a resurgence of hard and far-right movments, many with a distinctly post-modern quality. How to define and undestand this development has become an important academic enterprise to which this book may make a marginal contribution. But a great deal of the discourse has focused on whether any of these hard and far-right movements warrant being called fascistic, in the full pejorative sense of the term. Here we should be cautious since there are many forms of hard right movements which, however unpalatable on their own terms, lack specifically fascist qualities. But let there be no doubt. There are plenty of modern fascists, with one of the most significant being the far right's pet philosopher Alexander Dugin. I'll begin by explaining why he belongs in the fascist canon, before addressing whether Dugin has made any distinctive "innovations" to the fascist tradition.

Dugin has denied that he is a fascist. He insists that his "Fourth political theory" constitues a new direction forward. Though even here, echoes of fascist talk about a "third way" undercut the authenticty of his claims.[147] Dugin's Western apologists acknowledge his illiberalism, but also deny that he is a fascist. Instead they characterize Dugin as defending a kind of right-wing populism, or even advocating for the rule of Duginite philosopher kings. Some hold Dugin even defends a "Eurasianist concept of democracy" where the people get to participate in their "destiny."[148] Though, of course, the nature of this destiny is determined by the "single ones (the philosophers, historians, and leaders who lead the people to its destiny) who carry out [the] project. A people only truly has a destiny when it chooses to live authentically."[149] Beyond that the people are entitled to few rights to actually determine what they think is politically best.

In fact Dugin's position is largely coextensive with generic fascism, which was also distinctive in appropriating some of the modernist language of mass political participation and rearticulating it in authoritarian terms. Fascism was a different kind of right- politics from the nostalgic defense of aristocratic Ancien regimes characteristic of the 19th century, or even the conservative dictatorships popular in Europe during the early 20th century. Both of these largely divested the population from any meaningful role in political participation. Fascism went in a different but, in the end, no less authoritarian direction. Fascist states made a constant effort to energize the population and engaged in mass propagandistic efforts to convince the people that their collective will was reflected in the directions given by the party or the person of the leader. Indeed in a Schmittian vein some defenders of fascism claimed that authoritarianism was more democratic precisely because the leader had no checks on his power and so was better able to instantiate the national will.[150] The fact that Dugin expresses the same politics of a people participating in its destiny without actual political rights in a rather ugly, but original, jargon changes nothing.[151]

Second Duginite apologists will also argue that Dugin's rejection of crude biological racism shows he is not a fascist. And it is true that, in one of his post-modern modes, Dugin rejects generic fascism's

> racism, xenophobia and chauvinism. These are not only moral failures but also theoretically and anthropologically inconsistent attitudes. Differences between ethnos don't equate to superiority or inferiority. The differences should be accepted and affirmed without any racist sentiments or consideration. There is no common or universal measure to judge different ethnic groups. When one society tries to judge another it applies its own criteria and so commits intellectual violence.[152]

But Dugin never holds to this position consistently. He has been forthright about calling for a global war to destroy the decadent and decaying Western culture which he feels plenty entitled to judge and condemn. He has also made abundant anti-Semitic comments, including railing against "cosmopolitan financial elites and Ukrainian 'Jewish Oligarchs.'"[153] More importantly Dugin is not nearly as allergic to racism and racists as the apologias suggest. Dugin has had positive things to say about the "spiritual racism" of Evola.[154] He has cited the need for Eurasianists and followers of the fourth political theory to align with ethno-chauvinist identitarians like Alain de Benoist ("simply the best" Dugin gushed) and white nationalists where doing so is strategically expedient in the struggle against liberal internationalism.

> I consider the 'White nationalists' allies when they refuse modernity, the global oligarchy and liberal-capitalism, in other words everything that is killing all ethnic cultures and traditions. The modern political order is essentially globalist and based entirely on the primacy of individual identity in opposition to community. It is the worst order that has ever existed and it should be totally destroyed. When "White nationalists" reaffirm Tradition and the ancient culture of the European peoples, they are right.[155]

In either case it would be inaccurate to describe either generic mid-century or later fascism as pivoting around an exclusively biologically racist and hyper-essentialist conception of ultranationalist identity. While the two leading fascist states of the 20th century came to justify themselves in viciously racist terms, there was nothing intrinsically necessary about this. Until the prestige of Nazism eclipsed Mussolini's regime, Italian fascism[156] was inclusive of Jews and stressed the national unity and cultural superiority of the people regardless of skin color.[157] This was both a matter of political necessity for a fascist regime ruling a country highly stratified between north and south and indicated an initial wariness of emulating the kind of crude materialism which seemed to underlie "scientific racism." As Kevin Passmore puts it,

> ...before the 1930s race and still less antisemitism did not inform [Italian] domestic or foreign policy as pervasively as it would in Germany, and Fascists were more interested in raising the birthrate than in eliminating the unfit. Indeed, in his bid for influence in movements outside Italy, Mussolini promoted Fascist universalism as an alternative to Nazi racism. In 1930, he ridiculed biological racism. He regarded race as a 'feeling,' which, by implication anyone could acquire.[158]

Heidegger, Dugin's primary theoretical influence, also defended Nazism while expressing wariness about biological racism in such terms, even if he held many culturally anti-Semitic views. Dugin's post-modern and strategic reformulation of the fascist ultra-nation in terms of a relatively more inclusive Eurasianist "civilization" is an evolution of this approach but not a major break from it.[159]

Lastly, some of Dugin's apologists will stress that because he rejects nationalism in favor of a more expansive Eurasianist vision of the "narod" or "people" he cannot be a fascist.[160] This is the least convincing of all their arguments, since from the very beginning the fascist ultra-nation pushed against the boundaries of conventional nationalism. This was eminently predictable since limiting itself to an ambition for, say, national self-determination would have constrained the imperialist ambitions so dear to Hitler, Mussolini, and Dugin's hearts. As Griffin puts it with his usual clarity:

> In the 1930s, individual ideologues such as Drieu La Rochelle, Jose Streel, and Ezra Pound were already presenting fascism as a pan-European force of rebirth, and doomed attempts were made by some of Mussolini's followers, convinced of their movement's 'universal' civilizational significance, to create a Fascist International. With the war apparently going Hitler's way, an entire bureaucracy was set up by the Third Reich to plan the postwar European New Order....The idea of interwar fascism as an exclusively national phenomenon has long been superseded.[161]

In this respect Dugin's Eurasianist vision of a "Novorossiya" or "Large Russia," whose boundaries have been artificially and unfairly constrained, necessitating a war to recover Ukraine and allied with a pan-illiberal global coalition, is fascist vanilla.[162] Generic fascism also appealed to its dynamic of superiority and victimization as a basis for imperialist politics, where the wronged people would assume their rightful place as lords of the earth.[163] One sees the ressentiment of a person convinced he is superior and unable to understand how the decadent are continuously able to thwart him. Much the same is true in Duginism, which vacillates between utopian imaginaries and fantasies of revenge. *Foundations of Geopolitics* captures this Hitlerite virulence nicely:

> [The] new global ideology will be that of Final Restoration, putting a final end to the geopolitical history of civilizations – but this will not be the end which the globalist spokesmen of the End of History have theorized. The materialistic, atheistic, anti-sacred, technocratic, Atlanticist version of the End will give way to a different epilogue – the final Victory of the sacred Avatar, the coming of the Great Judgement, which will grant those who chose voluntary poverty the kingdom of spiritual abundance, while those who preferred wealth founded on the assassination of the Spirit will be condemned to eternal damnation and torment in hell.[164]

Dugin is a fascist intellectual. In practical terms, as Alexander Reid Ross puts it, he "considers Eurasia a palingenetic territorial imperative, through which the Russian spirit might soar with the advancement of the purity of its soul. Eurasianism must confront 'Atlanticism' in a metaphysical combat between the alchemical elements of water and fire."[165] Or as Toal puts it, "Dugin cast[s] this as spiritual clash between tellurocracy (earth) and thalassocracy (water)."[166] The question then becomes: what, if anything, has he contributed to the far-right intellectual tradition beyond redefining its basic geopolitical obsessions for the 21st century?

Dugin's Post-Modern Fascism

Dugin's main theoretical "contribution" has been improving the right's facility with the language of post-modern philosophy to advance its chauvinistic forms of militant identitarianism. What makes Dugin different from more conventional post-modern conservatives tamped by the cultural conditions of the epoch is the extent to which he is highly self-conscious about this.[167] Indeed what is consistently surprising is the extent to which Dugin expresses a considerable admiration for iconoclastically left authors like Derrida, Foucault, and Deleuze. This comes through most clearly in *The Fourth Political Theory*.

> In the Postmodern critique of historical optimism, universalism and historicism has acquired a systematic character and created the doctrinal prerequisites for a total revision of the conceptual apparatus of Western philosophy. The revision itself is not fully implemented, but what is done (Levi-Strauss, Barthes, Ricoeur, Foucault, Deleuze, Derrida, etc.) are already sufficient to ensure that the inability to use the Dictionary of the Modern without its thorough and meticulous deconstruction.[168]

There is something grimly funny about this. Many conservative critics have condemned post-modern theory for dissolving the epistemic and moral bases for Western universalism and optimism. Dugin agrees that post-modern theorists have accomplished this and praises them for it, but in the service of a geopolitical project vastly more reactionary than any Jordan Peterson would be comfortable with. That he should be attracted to post-modern critiques of Western foundationalism for undermining its universalism isn't entirely unexpected. Far and away Dugin's most significant influence is Martin Heidegger, who was a profound influence on the post-structuralist philosophies which emerged in late 20th-century France and which have long enamored many on the left.

For Dugin, Heidegger is the philosopher of "another beginning." Indeed some on the far-right stress how Dugin offers the most complete understanding of Heidegger's profound message, which entails a rejection of liberal democracy. Indeed, a rejection of millennia of Western history to the extent it led to the emergence of nihilistic modernity.[169] Dugin's reading of Heidegger is very much in a political vein. Heidegger teaches how the nihilistic "postmodern" culture emerging in the 21st-century West is not, as the more superficial reactionaries suppose, a consequence of abandoning Enlightenment reason. It isn't even as Nietzsche predicted a consequence of Christian egalitarianism running its course.[170] Instead it is the withdrawal and then forgetfulness of Being, initiated with the Platonic reduction of Being to beings, which is the culprit. From there, Grecian thought decayed into Christian scholasticism, upon which few innovations were made for almost 1,000 years. With Cartesianism we saw an undeniably energetic but lethal turn toward apprehending the world in terms of subject–object dualism. Being was now simply the thinghood of standing reserve to be manipulated by the inauthentic "swarming masses" for their contentment.[171] The political theories which emerge from this inauthenticity are liberalism and communism, which both work against the possibility of a new and more authentic beginning.

> Americanism (liberalism, 'planetary idiocy') and Communism (Soviet Bolshevism) are the opponents of fundamental ontological transition to another beginning, both being the extreme expressions of Western European metaphysics...Therefore, only the return of the End's phenomena to their end i.e., the final destruction of Liberalism and Communism, will be the manifestation of mankind authentically taking the leap into another Beginning and the dawn of Being's return.[172]

Of course Heidegger saw Germany, the nation of the center, as having a crucial role to play in confronting America and Russia. Dugin now regards Russia or Eurasia, apparently the quintessential power of the land,[173] as the only force which could possibly confront the Atlantic coalition which he so despises. This is telling. Dugin talks a great deal about authenticity and the people willing its destiny. Yet to an even greater extent than Heidegger—who at least had philosophical originality to excuse him—Duginism runs directly into the contradictions that befall any authoritarian system which apes the language of authenticity and integrity. Which is that any political theory which in practice demands not only obedience in action but subordination of the soul to the "destiny" willed for it by fascist intellectuals can only end in the mutilation of the soul by commanding its submission to a horrific lie. And a lie of the worst sort: one so corrosive and widespread it will parasitically eat away at the very society it is intended to homogenize into a "people."

What Plato understood, and what Dugin never will, is that the most important kind of democracy is the democracy of the human soul. We are each of us divided into many parts, which confront and live in one another producing the drama that makes us human. The jargon of fascist authenticity which wishes to smelt the democracy of the soul into a singular will commanded by the philosopher or leader distorts this human quality. The irony is that by demanding authenticity from those who cannot will otherwise the philosopher or leader precludes the very possibility of being authentic, because being authentic means carrying the burden of choosing between one's deepest inclinations to become a singularly unique individual.

In the hands of the Nazis and earlier fascists these perversions led to tragedy on an unimaginable scale. But Dugin's 21st-century fascism began with shrill cries that the "destiny" of the Russian people lay elsewhere. It has concluded with geriatrics firing Soviet weapons at Ukrainian soldiers. Duginism reminds us of Marx's truth: history repeats itself first as tragedy, then as utter farce.

Notes

1 George F. Will. *The Conservative Sensibility*. (New York, NY: Hachette Books, 2020)

2 Particularly on carceral and race issues.

3 See Dave Rubin. *Don't Burn This Country: Surviving and Thriving in our Woke Dystopia*. (New York, NY: Sentinel Books, 2022) at p. 7

4 See Thomas Sowell. *Intellectuals and Society*. (New York, NY: Perseus Books, 2011) at p. 99

5 See Eric Hobsbawm. *The Age of Revolution 1789–1848*. (New York, NY: Vintage Books, 1996)

6 See Joseph De Maistre. *The Generative Principle of Political Constitutions: Studies on Sovereignty, Religion, and Enlightenment*, ed. Jack Lively. (London, UK: Routledge, 1965)

7 See Roger Scruton. *The Meaning of Conservatism: Third Edition*. (South Bend, IN: St Augustine's Press, 2002) at pp. 170–172

8 See George F. Will. *The Conservative Sensibility*. (New York, NY: Hachette Books, 2020)

9 Glenn Ellmers. "Conservatism Is No Longer Enough." *The American Mind*, March 23rd, 2021

10 See Alexander Stephens. "Cornerstone Speech." March 21st, 1861. https://www.battlefields.org/learn/primary-sources/cornerstone-speech

11 Robert O Paxton. *The Anatomy of Fascism*. (New York, NY: Vintage Books, 2005)

12 See especially the work of Gilles Deleuze and Michel Foucault. See Gilles Deleuze. *Nietzsche and Philosophy,* trans. Hugh Tomlinson. (New York, NY: Columbia University Press, 1983) and Michel Foucault. *The Foucault Reader*, ed. Paul Rabinow. (New York, NY: Pantheon Books, 1984)

13 Historians have found it easier than political theorists and philosophers to accept the association between Nietzsche and the far right because that is simply a part of the historical record, and historians can largely shrug their shoulders over whether these figures actually got his thinking correct.

14 See Ben Shapiro. *The Right Side of History: How Reason and Moral Purpose Made the West Great*. (New York, NY: Broadside Books, 2019)

15 See Douglas Murray. *The War on the West*. (New York, NY: Broadside Books, 2022) at pp. 205–206 and Dinesh D'Souza. *United States of Socialism: Who's Behind It. Why It's Evil. How to Stop It*. (New York, NY: All Points Books, 2020) at p. 137

16 George Grant. *Time as History*. (Toronto, ON: University of Toronto Press, 2001)

17 While narrowly correct, this is nonetheless not a particular good interpretation. It allows less ambitious conservative thinkers like Peterson to have their cake and eat it, appropriating bits of Nietzschean lore to criticize secularism and the left while ignoring Nietzsche's belief that Christianity was a self-secularizing faith whose successors are in fact progressive movements.

18 See Jordan Peterson. *Twelve Rules to Life: An Antidote to Chaos*. (Toronto, ON: Random House Canada, 2018) at p. 162

19 See Alasdair MacIntyre. *After Virtue: A Study in Moral Theory: Third Edition* (Notre Dame, IN: University of Notre-Dame Press, 2007)

20 See Hugo Drochon. *Nietzsche's Great Politics*. (Princeton, NJ: Princeton University Press, 2016)

21 Friedrich Nietzsche. "Ecce Homo" in *Basic Writings of Nietzsche*, trans. Walter Kaufmann. (New York, NY: The Modern Library, 2000) at p. 783

22 His own later analysis of the book as "offensively Hegelian" and apolitical in *Ecce Homo* is accurate, if a bit unfair to its many merits.

23 Friedrich Nietzsche. *Basic Writings of Nietzsche*, trans. Walter Kaufmann. (New York, NY: The Modern Library, 2000) at p. 88

24 Friedrich Nietzsche. *Basic Writings of Nietzsche*, trans. Walter Kaufmann. (New York, NY: The Modern Library, 2000) at p. 89

25 Martin Heidegger. *Nietzsche: Volume One and Two*, trans. David Farrell Krell (San Francisco, CA: HarperCollins, 1961)

26 Friedrich Nietzsche. *Twilight of the Idols and the Anti-Christ*. (London, UK: Penguin Books, 2003) at pp. 117, 118

27 Malcolm Bull. *Anti-Nietzsche*. (London, UK: Verso Press, 2014)

28 Friedrich Nietzsche. *Basic Writings of Nietzsche*, trans. Walter Kaufmann. (New York, NY: The Modern Library, 2000) at p. 203

29 And remains viable. Physicists like Roger Penrose will appeal to Platonic ideas in their account of number. See Roger Penrose. *The Road to Reality: A Complete Guide to the Laws of the Universe*. (New York, NY: Random House, 2004)

30 See Eagleton's discussion of Nietzsche in Terry Eagleton. *Materialism*. (New Haven, CT: Yale University Press, 2016)

31 Friedrich Nietzsche. *The Twilight of the Idols and the Antichrist: Or How to Philosophize with a Hammer*. (London, UK: Penguin Classics, 1990) at pp. 168, 169

32 See Alasdair MacIntyre. *Marxism and Christianity*. (Notre Dame, IN: University of Notre Dame Press, 2003)

33 For a deep account of the relationship between Marx and Nietzsche see Nancy S. Love. *Marx, Nietzsche, and Modernity*. (New York, NY: Columbia University Press, 1986)

34 See Domenico Losurdo. *Nietzsche, the Aristocratic Rebel*, trans. Gregor Benton. (Chicago, IL: Haymarket Books, 2021) at p. 515

35 Friedrich Nietzsche. *The Twilight of the Idols and the Antichrist: or How to Philosophize with a Hammer*. (London, UK: Penguin Classics, 1990) at p. 186

36 Friedrich Nietzsche. *The Twilight of the Idols and the Antichrist: Or How to Philosophize with a Hammer*. (London, UK: Penguin Classics, 1990) at p. 191

37 My interpretation on this point is directly inspired by Nancy S. Love. *Marx, Nietzsche, and Modernity*. (New York, NY: Columbia University Press, 1986)

38 See Friedrich Nietzsche. "The Genealogy of Morals" in *Basic Writings of Nietzsche*, trans. Walter Kaufmann. (New York, NY: The Modern Library, 2000) at p. 597

39 See Soren Kierkegaard. *The Sickness unto Death. A Christian Psychological Exposition for Upbuilding and Awakening,* trans. Howard V. Hong. (Princeton, NJ: Princeton University Press, 1983)

40 See Friedrich Nietzsche. "The Genealogy of Morals" in *Basic Writings of Nietzsche*, trans. Walter Kaufmann. (New York, NY: The Modern Library, 2000)

41 See Ronald Beiner. *Dangerous Minds: Nietzsche, Heidegger and the Return of the Far Right*. (Philadelphia: University of Pennsylvania Press, 2018) at p. 39

42 See Friedrich Nietzsche. "On the Geneaology of Morals" in *Basic Writings of Nietzsche*, trans. Walter Kaufmann. (New York, NY: Basic Books) at p. 480

43 See Malcom Bull. *Anti-Nietzsche*. (London, UK: Verso, 2011) at p. 74

44 See Hugo Drochon. *Nietzsche's Great Politics*. (Princeton, NJ: Princeton University Press, 2016)

45 See Friedrich Nietzsche. *Beyond Good and Evil*, trans. Walter Kaufmann. (London, UK: Penguin Books, 1990) at p. 192

46 Friedrich Nietzsche. *Thus Spoke Zarathustra: A Book for Everyone and No One*, trans. Graham Parkes. (Oxford, UK: Oxford University Press, 2009)

47 Eagleton stresses this point in his critique of post-modern progressivism. See Terry Eagleton. *The Illusions of Postmodernism*. (Hoboken, NJ: Wiley-Blackwell, 1996)

48 See Malcolm Bull. *Anti-Nietzsche*. (London, UK: Verso Press, 2014)

49 Here one might take up Brian Barry's point that the meta-ethics of cultural incommensurability, suggesting one cannot compare cultural value systems, is incompatible with a belief that all cultures are equal precisely because that would entail ranking and comparing cultures to one another and deciding they are in fact equal. Interestingly Nietzsche's work embraces both potentially incompatible forks in a different respect, since he often implies different cultural value systems cannot be morally compared while clearly ranking some as higher than others. His recourse to

a purely aesthetic vocabulary to justify this is less than convincing. See Brian Barry. *Culture and Equality: An Egalitarian Critique of Multiculturalism*. (Boston, MA: Belknap Press of Harvard University Press, 2002)

50 Friedrich Nietzsche. *The Twilight of the Idols and the Antichrist: Or How to Philosophize with a Hammer*. (London, UK: Penguin Classics, 1990) at p. 106

51 Friedrich Nietzsche. *The Gay Science: With a Prelude in Rhymes and an Appendix of Songs*, trans. Walter Kaufmann. (New York, NY: Vintage Books, 1974) at p. 338

52 See Richard Evans. *The Coming of the Third Reich*. (London, UK: Penguin Books, 2005) and Ronald Beiner. *Dangerous Minds: Nietzsche, Heidegger, and the Return of the Alt Right*. (Philadelphia: University of Pennsylvania Press, 2018)

53 See Ronald Beiner. *Dangerous Minds: Nietzsche, Heidegger, and the Return of the Alt Right*. (Philadelphia: University of Pennsylvania Press, 2018) and Domenico Losurdo. *Nietzsche, The Aristocratic Rebel*, trans. Gregor Benton. (Chicago, IL: Haymarket, 2020) and Matthew McManus. *Nietzsche and the Politics of Reaction: Essays on Liberalism, Socialism, and Aristocratic Radicalism*. (Gewerbestrasse, Switzerland: Palgrave MacMillan, 2022)

54 See Malcolm Bull. *Anti-Nietzsche*. (London, UK: Verso Press, 2011) at p. 153

55 Wendy Brown. *In the Ruins of Neoliberalism: The Rise of Antidemocratic Politics in the West*. (New York, NY: Columbia University Press, 2019)

56 Wendy Brown. *States of Injury: Power and Freedom in Late Modernity*. (Princeton, NJ: Princeton University Press, 1995)

57 See Paul Elliott Johnson. *I the People: The Rhetoric of Conservative Populism in the United States*. (Tucaloosa: The University of Alabama Press, 2022) and Corey Robin. *The Reactionary Mind Second Edition: Conservatism from Edmund Burke to Donald Trump*. (Oxford, UK: Oxford University Press, 2018)

58 See Jennifer Burns. *Goddess of the Market: Ayn Rand and the American Right* (Oxford, UK: Oxford University Press, 2009) at pp. 41–43

59 See Ayn Rand. *The Fountainhead*. (New York, NY: Signet Books, 1996)

60 See Jonathan Holloway. "From Sit Ins to Civil Rights." *Yale University Courses,* 2010 https://www.youtube.com/watch?v=HsZ8wlviG7Q&t=1s

61 See Nikos Kazantzakis. *The Last Temptation*. (London, UK: Faber and Faber, 1975) at p. 575

62 All this is exhaustively discussed in Emmanuel Faye. *Heidegger: The Introduction of Nazism into Philosophy*, trans. Michael B. Smith. (New Haven, CT: Yale University Press, 2009)

63 This was the interpretation of Rorty for example. See Richard Rorty. "On Heidegger's Nazism" in *Philosophy and Social Hope*. (London, UK: Penguin Books, 2000)

64 See Rudolph Augstein and Georg Wolff. "Martin Heidegger." *Der Spiegel*, May 31st, 1976

65 This point is stressed in Alexander S. Duff. *Heidegger and Politics: The Ontology of Radical Discontent*. (Cambridge, UK: Cambridge University Press, 2015)

66 Neofascists and their apologists have found fertile material in Heidegger's work. See Alexander Dugin. *Heidegger: The Philosophy of Another Beginning*, trans. Nina Kouprianova (Arlington, VA: Radix Press, 2014); Michael Millerman. *Beginning with Heidegger: Strauss, Rorty, Derrida, Dugin and the Philosophical Constitution of the Political*. (London, UK: Arktos Media, 2021); and Michael Millerman. *Inside "Putin's Brain": The Political Philosophy of Alexander Dugin*. (Montreal, QC: Millerman School, 2002)

67 See Hurbert L. Dreyfus. *What Computers Still Can't Do: A Critique of Artificial Reason*. (Boston, MA: The MIT Press, 1992)

68 See Hannah Arendt. *The Human Condition*. (Chicago, IL: University of Chicago Press, 1998)

69 See Alexander S. Duff. *Heidegger and Politics: The Ontology of Radical Discontent*. (Cambridge, UK: Cambridge University Press, 2015) at p. 7

70 Dialectical materialism rejects universalistic sameness while carrying on much the same spirit of egalitarian politics in most of its iterations, though on a different normative basis, stressing the mutuality of satisfying human needs.

71 See Martin Heidegger. *Being and Time*, trans. Joan Stambaugh. (New York, NY: SUNY Press, 2010) and Martin Heidegger. *Introduction to Metaphysics,* trans. Greogry Fried and Richard Polt. (New Haven, CT: Yale University Press, 2000)

72 See Martin Heidegger. *Being and Time*, trans. Joan Stambaugh. (New York, NY: SUNY Press, 2010) at p. 11

73 See Martin Heidegger. *Being and Time*, trans. Joan Stambaugh. (New York, NY: SUNY Press, 2010) at p. 177

74 See Soren Kierkegaard. *The Sickness unto Death. A Christian Psychological Exposition for Upbuilding and Awakening*, trans. Howard V. Hong. (Princeton, NJ: Princeton University Press, 1983)

75 See Martin Heidegger. *The Question Concerning Technology and Other Essays.* (New York, NY: Harper Perennial, 2013)

76 Martin Heidegger. *Kant and the Problem of Metaphysics,* trans. Richard Taft. (Indianapolis: University of Indiana Press, 1997) at pp. 170, 171

77 This point has long been highlighted by the Frankfurt school of critical theory, which has also pointed out how readily Heideggerianism lends itself to the most banal kinds of subjectivist enterprises under the auspices of "living authentically." See Theodor Adorno. *The Jargon of Authenticity*, trans. Knut Tarnowski and Frederic Will. (New York, NY: Routledge, 2003) and Theodor Adorno. *Negative Dialectics,* trans. E.B Ashton. (New York, NY: Continuum, 2007)

78 Jurgen Habermas. *The Philosophical Discourse of Modernity*, trans. Frederick Lawrence. (Boston, MA: The MIT Press, 1987) at p. 138

79 Some might wonder why, after essentially discussing *Division I* of *Being and Time* in the first section (with some supplementary material), this section would leap forward to Heidegger's philosophy of history. The answer is that the full philosophy of history developed later is helpful in understanding the critique of everydayness, mass society, and inauthencity in the latter half of *Being and Time.*

80 Jurgen Habermas. *The Philosophical Discourse of Modernity*, trans. Frederick Lawrence. (Boston, MA: The MIT Press, 1987) at p. 132

81 Martin Heidegger. *What is Called Thinking?*, trans. J. Glenn Gray. (New York, NY: Harper and Row, 1968)

82 See John D. Caputo. *Hermeneutics: Facts and Interpretation in the Age of Information.* (London, UK: Pelican Books, 2018) and Michael Inwood. *Heidegger: A Very Short Introduction.* (Oxford, UK: Oxford University Press, 2019)

83 Martin Heidegger. *The Question Concerning Technology and Other Essays.* (New York, NY: Harper Perennial, 2013) at p. 28

84 Martin Heidegger. *Contributions to Philosophy (From Enowning)*, trans. Parvis Emad and Kenneth Maly. (Bloomington: Indiana University Press, 1999) at p. 291

85 See Martin Heidegger. *Nietzsche: Volume One and Two*, trans. David Farrell Krell (San Francisco, CA: HarperCollins, 1961) and Martin Heidegger. *Nietzsche: Volume Three and Four*, trans. David Farrell Krell. (San Francisco, CA: HarperCollins, 1961). For an erudite analysis of the links see Leo Strauss. "On German Nihilism" *Interpretation,* Vol 29, No 3, 1999

86 These include through aesthetics, religion, philosophy, and critical praxis.

87 Consider how in all his discussions of the enframing of the world by technology, there is barely a single discussion of the role materialist changes in social and economic relations played, even though more interesting commentators from the left (Marx, Adorno) to the right (Schmitt, Max Weber) had already diagnosed their centrality.

88 Quoted in Bruce Heinly, reply by Peter E. Gordon. "Heidegger and the Gas Chambers." *New York Review of Books,* December 4th, 2014

89 Martin Heidegger. *The Question Concerning Technology and Other Essays.* (New York, NY: Harper Perennial, 2013)

90 Ronald Beiner. *Dangerous Minds: Nietzsche, Heidegger, and the Return of the Alt Right.* (Philadelphia: University of Pennsylvania Press, 2018) at p. 107

91 See Alexander Dugin. *Heidegger: The Philosophy of Another Beginning,* trans. Nina Kouprianova (Arlington, VA: Radix Press, 2014)

92 Though as indicated, the fact that the few can't directly supply these forces in the short run doesn't diminish their cosmic importance over time.

93 Martin Heidegger. *What Is Metaphysics?,* trans. Richard Polt. (New Haven, CT: Yale University, 2014) at p. 11

94 Martin Heidegger. *What Is Metaphysics?,* trans. Richard Polt. (New Haven, CT: Yale University, 2014) at p. 40

95 Martin Heidegger. *What Is Metaphysics?,* trans. Richard Polt. (New Haven, CT: Yale University, 2014) at p. 48

96 Martin Heidegger. *What Is Metaphysics?,* trans. Richard Polt. (New Haven, CT: Yale University, 2014) at p. 47

97 Martin Heidegger. *What Is Metaphysics?,* trans. Richard Polt. (New Haven, CT: Yale University, 2014) at p. 52

98 See Martin Heidegger. "The Self Assertion of the German University" *The Review of Metaphysics,* Vol 38, No 3, March 1985

99 Martin Heidegger. *Being and Time,* trans. Joan Stambaugh. (New York, NY: SUNY Press, 2010) at p. 365

100 Martin Heidegger. *Being and Time,* trans. Joan Stambaugh. (New York, NY: SUNY Press, 2010) at p. 366

101 For more on this see Emmanuel Faye. *Heidegger: The Introduction of Nazism into Philosophy,* trans. Michael B. Smith. (New Haven, CT: Yale University Press, 2009)

102 Martin Heidegger. *Basic Writings: Revised and Expanded Edition,* ed. David Farrell Krell. (San Francisco, CA: Harper Collins, 1993)

103 Theodor Adorno. *The Jargon of Authenticity,* trans. Knut Tarnowski and Frederic Will. (New York, NY: Routledge, 2003) Theodor Adorno. *Negative Dialectics,* trans. E.B. Ashton. (New York, NY: Continuum, 2007)

104 Emmanuel Faye. *Heidegger: The Introduction of Nazism into Philosophy,* trans. Michael B. Smith. (New Haven, CT: Yale University Press, 2009) at pp. 151–172

105 His most pronounced book to that effect is Carl Schmitt. *The Leviathan in the State Theory of Thomas Hobbes.* (Chicago, IL: The University of Chicago Press, 2008)

106 Or at least the worst elements of their thinking.

107 Perhaps his most famous contemporary disciple is Adrian Vermeule. See the very Schmittian Adrian Vermeule. "All Human Conflict is Ultimately Theological" *Church Life Journal,* July 26th, 2019

108 See David Dyzenhaus. *Law as Politics: Carl Schmitt's Critique of Liberalism.* (Durham, NC: Duke University Press, 1996)

109 See David Dyzenhaus. "Liberalism After the Fall: Schmitt, Rawls and the Problem of Justification" *Philosophy and Social Criticism,* Vol 22, 1996

110 See Giorgio Agamben. *State of Exception, trans.* Kevin Attell (Chicago, IL: University of Chicago Press, 2002) and Chantal Mouffe. *The Return of the Political.* (London, UK: Verso Press, 2005)

111 See Heiner Bielefeldt. "Carl Schmitt's Critique of Liberalism: Systematic Reconstruction and Countercriticism" in David Dyzenhaus. *Law as Politics: Carl Schmitt's Critique of Liberalism.* (Durham, NC: Duke University Press, 1996) at p. 23

112 Our manual of choice was Amy Bartholomew. *Empire's Law: The American Imperial Project and the 'War to Remake the World.'* (London, UK: Pluto Press, 2006)

113 I am not convinced everyone was so cautious. Many of the criticisms in this vein leaned very heavily on the anti-universalistic strands of Schmittian thinking to condemn the tyranny of liberal rationalism. In its more imperialist forms this is all well and good, but plenty of commentators paid little attention to how simply affirming the particularism of traditional identity can very much have conservative and even hard right implications. Indeed, as this book itself has shown, historically that has

often been the case and it remains so today. See Alexander Dugin. *Eurasian Mission: An Introduction to Eurasianism.* (London, UK: Arktos Media, 2014). For a good critique of these forms of militant particularism see Brian Barry. *Culture and Equality: An Egalitarian Critique of Multiculturalism.* (Boston, MA: Belknap Press of Harvard University Press, 2002)

114 See Richard Evans. *The Coming of the Third Reich.* (London, UK: Penguin Books, 2005)

115 Perhaps because of the more transparently political nature of his work and involvement in the Nazi regime, perhaps because he had fewer important backers like Hannah Arendt and Jean Paul Sartre, Schmitt never enjoyed the kind of post-War Teflon like existence Heidegger had until quite recently.

116 Though it is not without its proponents, especially on international legal scholars influenced by post-structuralist theory. See Martti Koskenniemi. *The Gentle Civilizer of Nations: The Rise and Fall of International Law 1870–1960.* (Cambridge, UK: Cambridge, University Press, 2001)

117 Carl Schmitt. *The Nomos of the Earth in the International Law of Jus Publicum Europeaum.* (Candor, NY: Telos Press, 2006)

118 See Carl Schmitt. *Political Theology.* (Chicago, IL: The University of Chicago Press, 2005)

119 See Paul Tillich. *Dynamics of Faith.* (New York, NY: Harper Collins, 2001) at p. 1

120 See Birte Loschenkohl. "Occasional Decisiveness: Exception, Decision and Resistance in Kierkegaard and Schmitt" *European Journal of Political Theory,* Vol 18, at p. 98

121 Carl Schmitt. *The Concept of the Political: Expanded Edition.* (Chicago, IL: The University of Chicago Press, 2007)

122 For a Schmitt inspired critique of Rawlsian style political liberalism see David Dyzenhaus. "Liberalism After the Fall: Schmitt, Rawls and the Problem of Justification" *Philosophy and Social Criticism,* Vol 22, 1996

123 See Carl Schmitt. *Legality and Legitimacy,* trans. Jeffrey Seitzer (Chicago, IL: University of Chicago Press, 2004) at pp. 27, 28

124 See Carl Schmitt. *Legality and Legitimacy,* trans. Jeffrey Seitzer (Chicago, IL: University of Chicago Press, 2004) at p. 9

125 See Carl Schmitt. *Legality and Legitimacy,* trans. Jeffrey Seitzer (Chicago, IL: University of Chicago Press, 2004) at p. 94

126 Carl Schmitt. *The Leviathan in the State Theory of Thomas Hobbes.* (Chicago, IL: The University of Chicago Press, 2008)

127 See John. P. McCormick. "Three Ways of Thinking 'Critically' About the Law." *American Political Science Review,* Vol 93, 1999 and Adrian Vermeule. *Common Good Constitutionalism: Recovering the Classical Legal Tradition.* (Cambridge, UK: Polity Press, 2022)

128 Carl Schmitt. *The Nomos of the Earth in the International Law of Jus Publicum Europeaum.* (Candor, NY: Telos Press, 2006)

129 Carl Schmitt. *Constitutional Theory, trans.* Jeffrey Seitzer. (Durham, NC: Duke University Press, 2008) at p. 263

130 See Roger Griffin. *Fascism.* (Cambridge, UK: Polity Press, 2018)

131 Erich Fromm. *Escape from Freedom.* (New York, NY: Henry Holt and Company, 1994)

132 The fact that there was something genuinely—and disturbingly—new about fascism which distinguished it from earlier right, and even extreme right, positions was once occluded by the tendency to define them in purely reactionary terms. It was in some respects easier to describe fascists by what they opposed than to define them by what they endorsed. Fortunately more recent scholarship has gone a long way to correcting this problem. See Robert O. Paxton. *The Anatomy of Fascism.* (New York, NY: Vintage Books, 2005) and Roger Griffith. *Fascism.* (Cambridge, UK: Polity Press, 2018)

133 Corey Robin. *The Reactionary Mind Second Edition: Conservatism from Edmund Burke to Donald Trump.* (Oxford, UK: Oxford University Press, 2018) at pp. 87, 88

134 See Walter Benjamin. *The Work of Art in an Age of Mechanical Reproduction.* (London, UK: Penguin Books, 2008)

135 For an important analysis of this topic in the contemporary era see Benjamin R. Teitelbaum. *War for Eternity: Inside Bannon's Far-Right Circle of Global Power Brokers.* (New York, NY: Harper Collins, 2020)

136 Saying that it is important to stress that fascist movements were not simply affairs of the gut, and were capable of articulating their politics in explicitly theorized ways. As Corey Robin notes in his otherwise laudatory review of Paxton's book "though Paxton is an excellent guide to the political maneuverings that send elites rushing into the arms of the fascists, he is less helpful explaining how the fascists deliver the masses to the elites. (Though again we should be careful: most working-class voters, particularly in the labor movement and leftist parties, voted against the fascists.) For Paxton, fascism's appeal is primarily emotional. It is an 'affair of the gut' not 'of the brain,' a swamp of 'mobilizing passions' rather than a set of 'reasoned propositions.' This, unfortunately, is a view all too common among analysts of right-wing politics. Discounting the force of ideas on the right, Paxton is unable to recognize or unwilling to acknowledge that the popular classes may actually assent, rationally, to fascism's basic claims. As a result, he fails to see how fascists adapt traditional notions of deference and hierarchy to a mass audience, how they package and sell feudal ideas of higher and lower orders to a society of presumably democratic sensibilities." See Corey Robin. "Fascism and Counterrevolution" *Dissent Magazine,* Summer 2005

137 Richard Evans highlights how, even at the height of Nazi power, it never achieved anything like the totalizing control over German society which it aspired to. Much like the notion of the terrifyingly efficient Nazi war machine belied the chaotic and often kleptocratic Fuhrerocracy the state evolved into, many Germans remained ambiguous or instrumental in their attitudes toward Nazism. Its peak successes in 1938 and 1940, with the Munich Agreements and fall of France, were interludes rather than typical. See Richard Evans. *The Third Reich in Power.* (London, UK: Penguin Books, 2006). Payne makes a similar point about Italian fascism. See Stanley Payne. *Fascism: Comparison and Definition.* (Madison: University of Wisconsin Press, 1983)

138 See Enzo Traverso. *The New Faces of Fascism: Populism and the Far Right.* (London, UK: Verso Books, 2019)

139 See Neil Gregor. *How to Read Hitler.* (New York, NY: W.W. Morton, 2005) at p. 77

140 This included influencing those lesser court intellectuals. Evola's most important book leans heavily on Nietzsche's condemnation of Christianity, even defending the Medieval period by describing what was best in it—hierarchies, chivalry, submission to the nobility—as fundamentally un-Christian. See Julius Evola. *Revolt against the Modern World.* (Rochester, NY: Inner Traditions, 1995)

141 Quoted in Barbara Miller Lane and Leila J. Rupp. *Nazi Ideology before 1933: A Documentation.* (Austin: University of Texas Press, 1978) at pp. 88–95

142 See Yad Vashem. "Extracts from Mein Kampf by Adolph Hitler." The World Holocaust Remembrance Center. 2022

143 See Benito Mussolini. "The Doctrine of Fascism." San Jose State University, https://sjsu.edu/faculty/wooda/2B-HUM/Readings/The-Doctrine-of-Fascism.pdf

144 Roger Griffin. *Fascism.* (Cambridge, UK: Polity Press, 2018)

145 See Erich Fromm. *Escape from Freedom.* (New York, NY: Henry Holt and Company, 1994)

146 This last point was made by Zizek. See Slavoj Zizek. *The Sublime Object of Ideology.* (London, UK: Verso Press, 2009

147 Alexander Dugin. *The Fourth Political Theory,* trans. Nina Kurpianova, Maria Tokmakova, Olga Schief, Vaan Maas, Valentin Cherednikov, Zhirayr Ananyan, Fedor Smirnov, Cyril Lazareff, Ivan Fedorov (Moscow, RU: Eurasian Movement, 2012)

148 I say at points because Dugin, who is nothing if not prolific, will engage in frequent terminological shifts and reconceptualizations. This means that ideas which may be expressed in a post-modern idiom one day can be rearticulated in geopolitical or Heideggerian terms the next. Beyond just being hermeneutically frustrating this has helped cloak his work with a kind of ambiguity which is itself a source of appeal for many on the right.

149 See Michael Millerman. *Inside "Putin's Brain": The Political Philosophy of Alexander Dugin.* (Montreal, QC: Millerman School, 2022) at pp. 36, 37

150 Carl Schmitt. *Constitutional Theory*, trans. Jeffrey Seitzer. (Durham, NC. Duke University Press, 2008)

151 Theodor Adorno. *The Jargon of Authenticity*, trans. Knut Tarnowski and Frederic Will. (New York, NY: Routledge, 2003)

152 Alexander Dugin. *The Fourth Political Theory*, trans. Nina Kurpianova, Maria Tokmakova, Olga Schief, Vaan Maas, Valentin Cherednikov, Zhirayr Ananyan, Fedor Smirnov, Cyrill Lazareff, Ivan Fedorov (Moscow, Russia: Eurasian Movement, 2012) at pp. 204, 205

153 Quoted in Marlene Laruelle. "Alexander Dugin and Eurasianism" in Mark Sedgwick. *Key Thinkers of the Radical Right.* (Oxford, UK: Oxford University Press, 2019) at p. 162

154 Marlene Laruelle. "Alexander Dugin and Eurasianism" in Mark Sedgwick. *Key Thinkers of the Radical Right.* (Oxford, UK: Oxford University Press, 2019) at p. 162 and Julius Evola. *Revolt against the Modern World.* (Rochester, NY: Inner Traditions, 1995)

155 Alexander Dugin. *Eurasian Mission: An Introduction to Eurasianism.* (London, UK: Arktos Media, 2014) at p. 129

156 Though from the beginning the language of biological racism was more easily applied to Africans.

157 Stanley Payne. *Fascism: Comparison and Definition.* (Madison: University of Wisconsin Press, 1983)

158 Kevin Passmore. *Fascism: A Very Short Introduction.* (Oxford, UK: Oxford University Press, 2014) at p. 117

159 Responding to militant Islamaphobes Dugin claims "Muslims form a part of the Russian population, and are an important minority. Therefore, Islamophobia implicitly calls for the break-up of Russia." See Alexander Dugin. *Eurasian Mission: An Introduction to Eurasianism.* (London, UK: Arktos Media, 2014) at p. 129

160 See Michael Millerman. *Inside "Putin's Brain": The Political Philosophy of Alexander Dugin.* (Montreal, QC: Millerman School, 2022) at pp. 31–33

161 See Roger Griffin. *Fascism.* (Cambridge, UK: Polity Press, 2018) at p. 112

162 See Gerard Toal. *Near Abroad: Putin, The West, and the Contest Over Ukraine and the Caucasus.* (Oxford, UK: Oxford University Press, 2017) at p. 246

163 And as Evans points out the most powerful fascist movements truly thought global. See Richard Evans. *The Third Reich at War.* (London, UK: Penguin Books, 2010)

164 See Alexander Dugin. "From Sacred Geography to Geopolitics," trans. Jafe Arnold and John Stachelski. *Eurasianist Archive,* 2019. https://eurasianist-archive.com/2019/10/29/alexander-dugin-from-sacred-geography-to-geopolitics/

165 See Alexander Reid Ross. *Against the Fascist Creep.* (Chico, CA: AK Press, 2017) at p. 171

166 See Gerard Toal. *Near Abroad: Putin, The West, and the Contest Over Ukraine and the Caucasus.* (Oxford, UK: Oxford University Press, 2017) at p. 77

167 See Matthew McManus. *The Rise of Post-Modern Conservatism: Neoliberalism, Post-Modern Culture, and Reactionary Politics.* (Gewerbestrasse, Switzerland: Palgrave MacMillan, 2019)

168 Alexander Dugin. *The Fourth Political Theory*, trans. Nina Kurpianova, Maria Tokmakova, Olga Schief, Vaan Maas, Valentin Cherednikov, Zhirayr Ananyan,

Fedor Smirnov, Cyrill Lazareff, Ivan Fedorov (Moscow, Russia: Eurasian Movement, 2012) at p. 142

169 Michael Millerman. *Beginning with Heidegger: Strauss, Rorty, Derrida, Dugin and the Philosophical Constitution of the Political.* (London, UK: Arktos Media, 2021)

170 Part of Dugin's Eurasianist opportunism is that he isn't as brazenly willing to target Christianity as either Nietzsche, Heidegger, or Evola. This is unsurprising since Orthodox Christianity plays a significant role in the conservative Russian society Dugin defends and admires.

171 Alexander Dugin. *Heidegger: The Philosophy of Another Beginning,* trans. Nina Kouprianova (Arlington, VA: Radix Press, 2014)

172 Alexander Dugin. *Heidegger: The Philosophy of Another Beginning,* trans. Nina Kouprianova (Arlington, VA: Radix Press, 2014) at p. 168

173 Though recent failures in Ukraine beg to differ.

CONCLUSION

The World Out of Joint

To the extent that diversity is a strength the political right is very strong, as it is one of the most diverse political traditions in the world. This book is by no means comprehensive, and should not be considered anywhere near a full intellectual history of the right. Rather it is meant to reflect the views of some of the most significant, or at least most representative, right-wing thinkers and provide a glimpse into the tradition as a whole. And as we've seen, the political right includes its fair share of cranks and crackpots, as well as men of genius and even profundity. There is no other way to understand the contributions of figures like Elliot, Dostoevsky, and even evil men like Nietzsche. In this I echo Corey Robin in hoping that *The Political Right and Inequality* persuades my fellow progressives that the political right may have many stupid people within it, but it is by no means exclusively Mill's "stupid party."[1]

However this is not entirely a commendation. The political right's intellectual imagination and mercuriality have helped it withstand revolutionary global movements for equality and freedom, sometimes through conciliation and adaptation and at other times through outright rejection and counter-revolution. This has persisted to this day, where from seeming defeat and melancholia in the mid-century the right rose like a phoenix to unprecedented levels of power between the 1980s and the present. Much of this was propelled by the impulse that the world was out of joint, and only a restoration of sublime authority and hierarchy could repair it. By 2018 virtually every major country on the globe—the United States, Russia, Brazil, the United Kingdom, Italy, India—was governed by right-wing governments willing to outwardly imagine an illiberal future. While the hurricane has receded since then, it is by no means clear whether this is the end or just the eye.

The accomplishment of modernity was to redefine the basis of society on voluntarist terms, centered around secularized and inclusive principles of equality

DOI: 10.4324/9781003307952-9

and liberty for all. These principles have never been fully instantiated, and the failure to do so has opened liberal and progressive movements to justifiable accusations of hypocrisy from conservative groups who claim to better understand the needs of the people. It has enabled revanchism and reaction to present themselves as ways forward, rather than an Orphean fast track back into the pits of history. Just as importantly, and not discussed to nearly the extent needed here, is the enduring impact of capitalist domination in the workplace and across the globe. This has not only a human but also an environmental dimension which should provoke existential anxieties in anyone. And the fact that many liberals have either ignored or apologized for, or even approved of, these negatives constitutes a betrayal of principle and imagination.

But I think there is reason to be optimistic, even if that must necessarily be an optimism of the will first and foremost. Since 2016 we've also seen the resurgence of genuinely socialist and democratic movements in Latin America, many places in Europe, and shockingly even in the United States. The passionate rejection of efforts to roll back abortion and LGBTQ rights, along with deepening concerns about inequality, bodes well. Even developments which have helped the modern right express a popular yearning for power can be more naturally filled with progressive projects. Many of the conservative populist movements emerged in a context where citizens felt that democratic institutions were no longer accountable to those governed by them and that they served the interests of the powerful.[2] This has generated a pronounced sense of alienation where paradoxically anti-democratic populism and neo-fascism can present themselves as unconstrained expressions of popular will, but whose anti-majoritarian and anti-participatory policies contradict this very impulse. A movement for genuinely democratic reform, including and perhaps especially in the economic sphere, which demands better from elected official should be the way forward instead.

As the conservative revolutionary thinking of figures like Nietzsche highlights, it is wrong to see the political right as purely reactionary and incapable of putting forward transformative inegalitarian programs of its own. But there is also no doubt that for several centuries it has been movements for liberty, equality, and democracy which have propelled history forward. While there is no teleological necessity to history, it does inspire hope that while the arc of the moral universe may be long it will bend toward justice. Ronald Reagan plagiarized Thomas Paine when he said we have it in our power to make the world anew. That power is progressive's still and we can use it if we have the will to do so.

Notes

1 Corey Robin. *The Reactionary Mind Second Edition: Conservatism from Edmund Burke to Donald Trump.* (Oxford, UK: Oxford University Press, 2018)
2 See Roger Eatwell and Matthew Goodwin. *National Populism and the Revolt against Liberal Democracy.* (London, UK: Penguin Books, 2018)

BIBLIOGRAPHY

Adorno, Theodor. *Negative Dialectics,* trans. E.B Ashton. (New York, NY: Continuum, 2007)

Adorno, Theodor. *The Jargon of Authenticity,* trans. Knut Tarnowski and Frederic Will. (New York, NY: Routledge, 2003)

Agamben, Giorgio. *State of Exception,* trans. Kevin Attell. (Chicago, IL: University of Chicago Press, 2002)

Ahmari, Sohrab. *The Unbroken Thread: Discovering the Wisdom of Tradition in an Age of Chaos.* (New York, NY: Convergent Books, 2021)

Anderson, Perry. "The Intransigent Right at the Turn of the Century." *London Review of Books,* September 24th, 1992

Anton, Michael. "United 93 Election." *Claremont Review of Books,* September 5th, 2016

Aquinas, St. Thomas. *Introduction to St. Thomas Aquinas,* ed. Anton C. Pegis. (Toronto, ON: Random House, 1948)

Arendt, Hannah. *The Human Condition.* (Chicago, IL: University of Chicago Press, 1998)

Arendt, Hannah. *The Origins of Totalitarianism.* (New York, NY: Harcout, 1955)

Aristotle. *The Basic Works of Aristotle.* (New York, NY: The Modern Library, 2001)

Augstein, Rudolph and Wolff, Georg. "Martin Heidegger." *Der Spiegel,* May 31, 1976

Augustine, St. *City of God.* (London, UK: Penguin Books, 2004)

Augustine, St. *Confessions of Saint Augustine.* (London, UK: Duncan Baird Publishers, 2006)

Augustine, St. *On Free Choice of the Will,* trans. Thomas Williams. (Indianapolis, IN: Hackett Publishing, 1993)

Avramenko, Richard and Trepanier, Lee. *Dostoevsky's Political Thought.* (Plymouth, UK: Lexington Books, 2013)

Barry, Brian. *Culture and Equality: An Egalitarian Critique of Multiculturalism.* (Boston, MA: Belknap Press of Harvard University Press, 2002)

Bartholomew, Amy. *Empire's Law: The American Imperial Project and the 'War to Remake the World.'* (London, UK: Pluto Press, 2006)

Beiner, Ronald. *Dangerous Minds: Nietzsche, Heidegger, and the Return of the Alt Right.* (Philadelphia: University of Pennsylvania Press, 2018)

Benjamin, Walter. *The Work of Art in an Age of Mechanical Reproduction*. (London, UK: Penguin Books, 2008)

Berlin, Isaiah. "Joseph de Maistre and the Origins of Fascism." *The New York Review of Books,* September 1990

Bloom, Allan. *The Closing of the American Mind: How Higher Education has Failed Democracy and Impoverished the Souls of Today's Students*. (New York, NY: Simon and Schuster, 2012)

Boucoyannis, Deborah. "Adam Smith Has Been Greatly Misinterpreted." *London School of Economics,* Blog, February 18th, 2014 at https://blogs.lse.ac.uk/politicsandpolicy/adam-smith-and-inequality/

Brandom, Robert. *A Spirit of Trust: A Reading of Hegel's Phenomenology of Spirit*. (Cambridge, MA: Belknap Press of Harvard University Press, 2019)

Brennan, Jason. *Libertarianism: What Everyone Needs to Know*. (Oxford, UK: Oxford University Press, 2012)

Brown, Wendy. *In the Ruins of Neoliberalism: The Rise of Antidemocratic Politics in the West*. (New York, NY: Columbia University Press, 2019)

Brown, Wendy. *States of Injury: Power and Freedom in Late Modernity*. (Princeton, NJ: Princeton University Press, 1995)

Brown, Wendy. *Undoing the Demos: Neoliberalism's Stealth Revolution*. (Brooklyn, NY: Zone Books, 2015)

Brown, Wendy. *Walled States, Waning Sovereignty*. (Brooklyn, NY: Zone Books, 2010)

Buckley, William. *God and Man at Yale: The Superstitions of Academic Freedom*. (Wilmington, DE: ISI Conservative Classics, 2001)

Buckley, William. "Why the South Must Prevail." *National Review*, 1957. https://adamgomez.files.wordpress.com/2012/03/whythesouthmustprevail-1957.pdf

Bull, Malcolm. *Anti-Nietzsche*. (London, UK: Verso Press, 2014)

Burke, Edmund. *A Philosophical Enquiry Into the Origins of the Sublime and Beautiful: And Other Pre-Revolutionary Writings*. (London, UK: Penguin Books, 1999)

Burke, Edmund. *Reflections on the Revolution in France*. (Oxford, UK: Oxford University Press, 2009)

Burke, Edmund. *Selected Letters of Edmund Burke*. (Chicago, IL: University of Chicago Press, 1983)

Burke, Edmund. "Thoughts and Details on Scarcity." *Select Works of Edmund Burke, Vol IV*. Online Library of Liberty, https://oll.libertyfund.org/title/canavan-select-works-of-edmund-burke-vol-4#lf0005-04_head_011

Burns, Jennifer. *Goddess of the Market: Ayn Rand and the American Right*. (Oxford, UK: Oxford University Press, 2009)

Calabresi, Steven G. *Originalism: A Quarter-Century of Debate*. (Washington, DC: Regnery Publishing Inc, 2007)

Campbell, Beatrix. "Our Silence Permits Perpetrators to Continue: One Women's Fight to Expose a Father's Abuse." *The Guardian,* July 25th, 2021. https://www.theguardian.com/uk-news/2021/jul/25/our-silence-permits-perpetrators-to-continue-one-womans-fight-to-expose-a-fathers-abuse

Caputo, John D. *Hermeneutics: Facts and Interpretation in the Age of Information*. (London, UK: Pelican Books, 2018)

Carlyle, Thomas. *Past and Present*. (Bolton, ON: Anodos Books, 2019)

Carlyle, Thomas. *The Essential Thomas Carlyle,* ed. Kasey James Elliott. (Chico, CA: Anarch Books, 2021)

Continetti, Matthew. "The Forgotten Father of American Conservatism." *The Atlantic,* October 19th, 2018

Continetti, Matthew. *The Right: The Hundred Year War for American Conservatism.* (New York, NY: Basic Books, 2022)

Corey, Elizabeth Campbell. "The Politics of Faith and the Politics of Skepticism." *Voeglin View,* January 21st, 2010

Coulter, Ann. *If Democrats Had Any Brains They'd Be Republicans.* (New York, NY: Three Rivers Press, 2007)

Cunningham, Frank. *The Political Thought of C.B Macpherson: Contemporary Applications.* (Cham, Switzerland: Palgrave MacMillan, 2019)

Dahl, Robert. *Democracy and Its Critics.* (New Haven, CT: Yale University Press, 1989)

Dahl, Robert. *How Democratic is the American Constitution?* (New Haven, NC: Yale University Press, 2003)s

Dahl, Robert. *A Preface to Economic Democracy.* (Oakland: University of California Press, 1986)

Dahl, Robert. *On Democracy.* (New Haven, CT: Yale University Press, 2000)

Deleuze, Gilles. *Nietzsche and Philosophy,* trans. Hugh Tomlinson. (New York, NY: Columbia University Press, 1983)

DeMuth, Christopher and Kristol, William. *The Neoconservative Imagination: Essays in Honor of Irving Kristol.* (Washington, DC: American Enterprise Institute, 1995)

Deneen, Patrick. "After Liberalism: Can We Imagine a Humane, Post-Liberal Future?" Religion and Ethics, December 2014. http://www.abc.net.au/religion/articles/2014/12/11/4146762.htm

Deneen, Patrick. *Conserving America: Essays on Present Discontents.* (South Bend, IN: St Augustine Press, 2016)

Deneen, Patrick. *Democratic Faith.* (Princeton, NJ: Princeton University Press, 2005)

Deneen, Patrick. "How Will Future Historians Treat Same-Sex Marriage." *The Public Discourse,* July 10th, 2013

Deneen, Patrick. "Unsustainable Liberalism." *First Things,* August 2012

Deneen, Patrick. *Why Liberalism Failed.* (New Haven, CT: Yale University Press, 2018)

Devlin, Patrick. "The Enforcement of Morals." *The Maccabean Lecture in Jurisprudence,* March 1959

De Tocqueville, Alexis. *Democracy in America and Two Essays on America.* (London, UK: Penguin Classics, 2003)

Dillenberger, John. *Martin Luther: Selections from His Writings.* (New York, NY: Anchor Books, 1962)

Dostoevsky, Fyodor. *Crime and Punishment, trans.* Constance Garnett, 2006. Available at https://www.gutenberg.org/cache/epub/2554/pg2554-images.html

Dostoevsky, Fyodor. *Devils,* trans. Michael R. Katz. (Oxford, UK: Oxford University Press, 2008)

Dostoevsky, Fyodor. "Notes from Underground" in *Great Short Works of Dostoevsky,* trans. (New York, NY: Perennial Library, 2004)

Dostoevsky, Fyodor. *Poor Folk,* trans. Constance Garnett. (Mineola, NY: Dover Publications, 2007)

Dostoevsky, Fyodor. *The Brothers Karamazov,* trans. Richard Pevear. (New York, NY: Farar, Straus and Giroux, 2002)

Dostoevsky, Fyodor. *The Idiot,* trans. (Hertfordshire, UK: Wordsworth Editions, 1996)

Dreher, Rod. "What Conservatives Must Learn from Hungary." *National Conservatism,* November 2nd, 2021. https://www.youtube.com/watch?v=BEB7FdogGS4

Dreyfus, Hubert L. *What Computers Still Can't Do: A Critique of Artificial Reason.* (Boston, MA: The MIT Press, 1992)

Drochon, Hugo. *Nietzsche's Great Politics*. (Princeton, NJ: Princeton University Press, 2016)

D'Souza, Dinesh. *The United States of Socialism: Who's Behind It. Why Its Evil. How to Stop It*. (New York, NY: All Points Books, 2020)

Duff, Alexander S. *Heidegger and Politics: The Ontology of Radical Discontent*. (Cambridge, UK: Cambridge University Press, 2015)

Dugin, Alexander. *Eurasian Mission: An Introduction to Eurasianism*. (London, UK: Arktos Media, 2014)

Dugin, Alexander. "From Sacred Geography to Geopolitics," trans. Jafe Arnold and John Stachelski. *Eurasianist Archive*, 2019. https://eurasianist-archive.com/2019/10/29/alexander-dugin-from-sacred-geography-to-geopolitics/

Dugin Alexander. *Heidegger: The Philosophy of Another Beginning*, trans. Nina Kouprianova (Arlington, VA: Radix Press, 2014)

Dugin, Alexander. *The Fourth Political Theory*, trans. Nina Kurpianova, Maria Tokmakova, Olga Schief, Vaan Maas, Valentin Cherednikov, Zhirayr Ananyan, Fedor Smirnov, Cyrill Lazareff, Ivan Fedorov. (Moscow, Russia: Eurasian Movement, 2012)

Dworkin, Ronald. "Lord Devlin and the Enforcement of Morals" *The Yale Law Journal*, Vol 75, No 6, 1966 at pgs 986–1005

Dyzenhaus, David. *Law as Politics: Carl Schmitt's Critique of Liberalism*. (Durham, NC: Duke University Press, 1996)

Dyzenhaus, David. "Liberalism After the Fall: Schmitt, Rawls and the Problem of Justification" *Philosophy and Social Criticism*, Vol 22, 1996 at pgs 9–37

Eagleton, Terry. *Materialism*. (New Haven, CT: Yale University Press, 2016)

Eagleton, Terry. *The Illusions of Postmodernism*. (Hoboken, NJ: Wiley-Blackwell, 1996)

Eatwell, Roger and Goodwin, Matthew. *National Populism: The Revolt Against Liberal Democracy*. (London, UK: Pelican Books, 2018)

Eliot, T.S. *Christianity and Culture: The Idea of a Christian Society and Notes Towards the Definition of Culture*. (New York, NY: Harvest Books, 1949)

Eliot, T.S. *Selected Prose*, ed. John Hayward. (London, UK: Penguin Books, 1953)

Ellmers, Glenn. "Conservatism Is No Longer Enough." *The American Mind*, March 23rd, 2021

Engels, Friedrich. "A Review of *Past and Present* by Thomas Carlyle." Marxists.Org https://www.marxists.org/archive/marx/works/1844/df-jahrbucher/carlyle.htm

Evans, Richard. *The Coming of the Third Reich*. (London, UK: Penguin Books, 2005)

Evans, Richard. *The Third Reich in Power*. (London, UK: Penguin Books, 2006)

Evans, Richard. *The Third Reich at War*. (London, UK: Penguin Books, 2010)

Evola, Julius. *Revolt Against the Modern World*. (Rochester, NY: Inner Traditions, 1995)

Fawcett, Edmund. *Conservatism: The Fight for a Tradition*. (Princeton, NJ: Princeton University Press, 2020)

Fawcett, Edmund. *Liberalism: The Life of An Idea: Second Edition*. (Princeton, NJ: Princeton University Press, 2018)

Faye, Emmanuel. *Heidegger: The Introduction of Nazism into Philosophy*, trans. Michael B. Smith. (New Haven, CT: Yale University Press, 2009)

Filmer, Robert. *Patriarcha*. (Published by Daniel M. Bring, 2019)

Finnis, John. "Law, Morality, and Sexual Orientation" in *Same Sex: Debating the Ethics, Science, and Culture of Homosexuality*, ed. John Corvino. (Lanham, MD: Rowman and Littlefield 1997)

Finnis, John. *Natural Law and Natural Rights: Second Edition*. (Oxford, UK: Oxford University Press, 2011)

Foucault, Michel. *Discipline and Punish: The Birth of the Prison*. (New York, NY: Vintage Books, 1995)

Foucault, Michel. *The Foucault Reader*, ed. Paul Rabinow. (New York, NY: Pantheon Books, 1984)

Frank, Joseph. *Lectures on Dostoevsky*. (Princeton, NJ: Princeton University Press, 2020)

Friedman, Milton. *Capitalism and Agency: Fortieth Anniversary Edition*. (Chicago, IL: University of Chicago Press, 2002)

Friedman, Milton and Friedman, Rose. *Free to Choose: A Personal Statement*. (Orlando, FL: Harcourt, Inc., 1980)

Fromm, Erich. *Escape from Freedom*. (New York, NY: Henry Holt and Company, 1994)

Fukuyama, Francis. *Identity: The Demand for Dignity and the Politics of Resentment*. (New York, NY: Farar, Straus, and Giroux, 2018)

Fukuyama, Francis. "The End of History?" *The National Interest*, 1989

Goldberg, Jonah. *Suicide of the West: How the Rebirth of Tribalism, Nationalism and Socialism is Destroying American Democracy*. (New York, NY: Crown Forum, 2020)

Goldwater, Barry. *The Conscience of a Conservative*. (Mansfield, CT: Martino Publishing, 2011)

Gottfried, Paul Edward. *The Search for Historical Meaning: Hegel and the Postwar American Right*. (Dekalb: North Illinois University Press, 2010)

Grant, George. *Technology and Justice*. (Toronto, ON: House of Anansi Press, 1991)

Grant, George. *Time as History*. (Toronto, ON: University of Toronto Press, 2001)

Gray, John. *Hayek on Liberty: Third Edition*. (London, UK: Routledge, 2016)

Gregor, Neil. *How to Read Hitler*. (New York, NY: W.W. Norton, 2005)

Griffin, Roger. *Fascism*. (Cambridge, UK: Polity Press, 2018)

Habermas, Jurgen. *The Philosophical Discourse of Modernity*, trans. Frederick Lawrence. (Boston, MA: The MIT Press, 1987)

Hall, Edith. *Aristotle's Way: How Ancient Wisdom Can Change Your Life*. (London, UK: Penguin Press, 2018)

Hamilton, Alexander and Madison, James and Jay, John. *The Federalist Papers*, ed. Charles R. Kesler. (New York, NY: Signet Classics, 2003)

Hammer, Langdon. "T.S Eliot." Yale University Courses, December 6th, 2012. https://www.youtube.com/watch?v=eUO-ICj6PHQ

Harper, Stephen. *Right Here, Right Now: Politics and Leadership in an Age of Disruption*. (Toronto, ON: Signal Books, 2018)

Hart, H.L.A. *Law, Liberty, and Morality*. (Stanford, CA: Stanford University Press, 1963)

Harvey, David. *A Brief History of Neoliberalism*. (Oxford, UK: Oxford University Press, 2007)

Hayek, F.A. *Law, Legislation, and Liberty*. (Chicago, IL: University of Chicago Press, 1978)

Hayek, F.A. *The Constitution of Liberty: The Definitive Edition*. (Chicago, IL: University of Chicago Press, 2011)

Hayek, F.A. "The Use of Knowledge in Society." *The Library of Economics and Liberty*. https://www.econlib.org/library/Essays/hykKnw.html

Hayek, F.A. *The Road to Serfdom: The Definitive Edition*. (Chicago, IL: The University of Chicago Press, 2007)

Hayek, F.A. "Why I Am Not A Conservative." *Foundation for Economic Education*, 2016

Hazony, Yoram. *Conservatism: A Rediscovery*. (Washington, DC: Regnery Press, 2022)

Hazony, Yoram. "Conservative Democracy: Liberal Principles Have Brought Us A Dead End." *First Things*, January 2019

Hazony, Yoram. "The Challenge of Marxism." *Quillette*, August 16th, 2020

Hazony, Yoram. *The Virtue of Nationalism.* (New York, NY: Basic Books, 2018)

Hazony, Yoram. "Why National Conservatism?" *National Conservatism,* July 15th, 2019. https://www.youtube.com/watch?v=4cpyd1OqHJU&t=1725s

Hegel, Georg. W.F. *Lectures on the Philosophy of History,* trans. Robert F. Brown and Peter C Hodgson. (Oxford, UK: Oxford University Press, 2019

Hegel, Georg. W.F. *Lectures on the Philosophy of Religion: Introduction and the Concept of Religion,* trans. Peter C Hodgson. (Oxford, UK: Oxford University Press, 2006)

Hegel, Georg. W.F. *The Phenomenology of Spirit,* trans. J.N. Findlay. (Oxford, UK: Oxford University Press, 1977)

Hegel, Georg W.F. *The Philosophy of Right,* trans. S.W. Dyde. (Mineola, NY: Dover Press, 2005)

Hegel, Georg W.F. *The Science of Logic,* trans. A.V. Miller. (Melbourne, AUK: George Allen and Unwin, 1969)

Heilbroner, Robert. *The Worldly Philosophers: The Lives, Times, and Ideas of the Great Economic Thinkers-Seventh Edition.* (New York, NY: Simon and Schuster, 1995)

Heidegger, Martin. *Basic Writings: Revised and Expanded Edition,* ed. David Farrell Krell. (San Francisco, CA: Harper Collins, 1993)

Heidegger, Martin. *Being and Time,* trans. Joan Stambaugh. (New York, NY: SUNY Press, 2010)

Heidegger, Martin. *Contributions to Philosophy (From Enowning),* trans. Parvis Emad and Kenneth Maly. (Bloomington: Indiana University Press, 1999)

Heidegger, Martin. *Introduction to Metaphysics,* trans. Greogry Fried and Richard Polt. (New Haven, CT: Yale University Press, 2000)

Heidegger, Martin. *Kant and the Problem of Metaphysics,* trans. Richard Taft. (Indianapolis: University of Indiana Press, 1997)

Heidegger, Martin. *Nietzsche: Volume One and Two,* trans. David Farrell Krell. (San Francisco, CA: HarperCollins, 1961)

Heidegger, Martin. *Nietzsche: Volume Three and Four,* trans. David Farrell Krell. (San Francisco, CA: HarperCollins, 1961)

Heidegger, Martin. *The Question Concerning Technology and Other Essays.* (New York, NY: Harper Perennial, 2013)

Heidegger, Martin. "The Self Assertion of the German University" *The Review of Metaphysics,* Vol 38, No 3, March 1985 at pgs 467–502

Heidegger, Martin. *What is Called Thinking?,* trans. J. Glenn Gray. (New York, NY: Harper and Row, 1968)

Heidegger, Martin. *What is Metaphysics?,* trans. Richard Polt. (New Haven, CT: Yale University, 2014)

Heinly, Bruce, reply by Peter E.Gordon. "Heidegger and the Gas Chambers." *New York Review of Books,* December 4th, 2014

Hendricks, Obery. *Christians Against Christianity: How Right Wing Evangelicals Are Destroying Our Nation And Our Faith.* (Boston, MA: Beacon Press, 2021)

Hendricks, Obery. *The Politics of Jesus: Rediscovering the True Revolutionary Nature of Jesus' Teachings and How They Have Been Corrupted.* (New York, NY: Three Leaves Publishing, 2006)

Hicks, Stephen. *Explaining Postmodernism: Skepticism and Socialism from Rousseau to Foucault.* (China: Ockham's Razor, 2004)

Hirschman, Albert O. *The Rhetoric of Reaction: Perversity, Futility, Jeopardy.* (Cambridge, MA: The Belknap Pres of Harvard University Press, 1991)

Hobbes, Thomas. *Leviathan.* (London, UK: Penguin Books, 2017)

Hochman, Nate. "Michael Oakeshott, 30 Years Later." *National Review,* December 18th, 2020

Holloway, Carson. "Leo Strauss and American Conservatism." *Public Discourse,* December 16th, 2014

Holloway, Jonathan. "From Sit Ins to Civil Rights." *Yale University Courses,* 2010. https://www.youtube.com/watch?v=HsZ8wlviG7Q&t=1s

Honderich, Ted. *Conservatism: Burke, Nozick, Bush, Blair?* (London, UK: Pluto Press, 2005)

Hobsbawm, Eric. *The Age of Extremes: A History of the World 1914–1991.* (New York, NY: Vintage Books, 1996)

Hobsbawm, Eric. *The Age of Revolution 1789–1848.* (New York, NY: Vintage Books, 1996)

Hume, David. *An Enquiry Concerning the Principles of Morals.* (Indianapolis, IN: Hackett Publishing, 1983)

Hume, David. "Idea of a Perfect Commonwealth." *Liberty Fund.* https://oll.libertyfund.org/page/oll-reader-70

Hume, David. "Of the First Principles of Government." https://davidhume.org/texts/emp/fp

Hume, David. "Of the Original Contract." https://cpb-us-w2.wpmucdn.com/blogs.cofc.edu/dist/8/406/files/2014/09/David-Hume-Of-the-Original-Contract-1kif9ud.pdf

Hume, David. *A Treatise of Human Nature.* (Mineola, NY: Dover Press, 2003)

Ignatieff, Michael. *Empire Lite.* (Toronto, ON: Penguin Canada, 2003)

Inwood, Michael. *Heidegger: A Very Short Introduction.* (Oxford, UK: Oxford University Press, 2019)

Jackson, Roy. *Nietzsche: A Complete Introduction.* (London, UK: Hodder and Stoughton, 2014)

Jaffa, Harry. "The American Founding as the Best Regime." *Claremont Review of Books,* July 4th, 2007

Jameson, Fredric. *Postmodernism, or, the Cultural Logic of Late Capitalism.* (Durham, NC: Duke University Press, 1991)

Johnson, Paul Elliott. *I the People: The Rhetoric of Conservative Populism in the United States.* (Tucaloosa: The University of Alabama Press, 2022)

Kant, Immanuel. *Critique of Judgement,* trans. Nicholas Walker. (Oxford, UK: Oxford University Press, 2009)

Kant, Immanuel. *Critique of Pure Reason,* trans. Abbott Thomas Kingsmill. (Mineola, NY: Dover Classics, 2004)

Kant, Immanuel. *Critique of Practical Reason,* trans. Werner Pluhar. (Indianapolis, IN: Hackett Publishing, 2002)

Kant, Immanuel. *Groundwork to the Metaphysics of Morals,* trans. H.J. Paton. (New York, NY: Harper Torchbooks, 1964)

Kant, Immanuel. *On History,* trans. Lewis White Beck, Robert E. Anchor, and Emil. L Fackenheim. (United States: The Library of Liberal Arts, 1957)

Kant, Immanuel. *Religion Within the Limits of Reason Alone: Revised Edition,* trans. Robert Merrihew Adams. (Cambridge, UK: Cambridge University Press, 2018)

Kant, Immanuel. *The Metaphysics of Morals,* trans. Mary Gregor. (Cambridge, UK: Cambridge University Press, 1996)

Kant, Immanuel. *Toward Perpetual Peace and Other Essays on Politics, Peace, and History,* trans. David Colclasure. (New Haven, CT: Yale University Press, 2006)

Kaufmann, Walter. *Nietzsche: Philosopher, Psychologist, Anti-Christ.* (Princeton, NJ: Princeton University Press, 2013)

Kierkegaard, Soren. *Attack on Christendom,* trans. Walter Lowrie. (Princeton, NJ: Princeton University Press, 1968)

Kierkegaard, Soren. *Either/Or: A Fragment of Life,* trans. Alastair Hannay. (London, UK: Penguin Books, 1992)

Kierkegaard, Soren. *Fear and Trembling,* trans. Alastair Hannay. (London, UK: Penguin Books, 1986)

Kierkegaard, Soren. *Purity of Heart is To Will One Thing,* trans. Douglas V. Steere. (New York, NY: HarperBooks, 2008)

Kierkegaard, Soren. *The Concept of Anxiety: A Simple Psychologically Oriented Deliberation in View of the Dogmatic Problem of Hereditary Sin* trans. Alastair Hannay. (New York, NY: Liveright Publishing Corporation, 2014)

Kierkegaard, Soren. *The Sickness Unto Death. A Christian Psychological Exposition for Upbuilding and Awakening,* trans. Howard V. Hong. (Princeton, NJ: Princeton University Press, 1983

Kirk, Russell. "The Essence of Conservatism." *The Russell Kirk Center,* March 19th, 2007

Kirk, Russell. "The Living Edmund Burke." *Modern Age,* Summer/Fall 1982

Kirk, Russell. *The Conservative Mind: From Burke to Eliot.* (Washington, DC: Gateway Editions, 2016)

Kirk, Russell. *The Roots of American Order.* (Wilmington, DE: Intercollegiate Studies Institute, 2003)

Kirk, Russell. "Ten Conservative Principles." *The Russell Kirk Center.* https://kirkcenter.org/conservatism/ten-conservative-principles/

Kirk, Russell, "Now Perhaps Schools Can Get Down to Education." *To The Point, General Features Division,* August 11 1974

Kosc, Jozef Andrew. "Poland and the Future of Europe." *First Things,* June 14th, 2018

Koskeniemmi, Martti. *The Gentle Civilizer of Nations: The Rise and Fall of International Law 1870–1960.* (Cambridge, UK: Cambridge, University Press, 2001)

Kristeva, Julia. *Dostoevsky, or the Flood of Language,* trans, Jody Golding. (New York, NY: Columbia University Press, 2022)

Kristol, Irving. *Neo-Conservatism: The Autobiography of an Idea.* (New York, NY: Free Press, 1995)

Kristol, Irving. "The Neoconservative Persuasion." *The Weekly Standard,* August 25th, 2003

Kymlicka, Will. "Multiculturalism's Moral Impulse." *Carnegie Council for Ethics in International Affairs,* November 25th, 2014. https://www.youtube.com/watch?v=2W689QD849Y

Landy, Tucker. *After Leo Strauss: New Directions in Platonic Political Philosophy.* (Albany, NY: SUNY Press, 2014)

Lane, Barbara Miller Lane and Rupp, Leila J. *Nazi Ideology before 1933: A Documentation.* (Austin: University of Texas Press, 1978)

Lawler, Peter Augustine. *American Heresies and Higher Education.* (South Bend, IN: St Augustine Press, 2016)

Lawler, Peter Augustine. "Conservative Postmodernism, Postmodern Conservatism." *Intercollegiate Institute,* October 8th, 2014

Lawler, Peter Augustine. *Postmodernism Rightly Understood: The Return to Realism in American Thought.* (Lanham, MD: Rowman and Littlefield, 1992)

Lendvai, Paul. *Orban: Hungary's Strongman.* (Oxford, UK: Oxford University Press, 2018)

Lewis, C.S. *The Problem of Pain.* (New York, NY: HarperOne, 2015)

Lidz, Joel Warren. "Medicine as Metaphor in Plato" *The Journal of Medicine and Philosophy,* Vol 20, 1995 at pgs 527–541

Little John, Brad. "Richard Hooker: A Forgotten Father of National Conservatism." *The American Conservative,* September 23rd, 2020

Locke, John. "A Letter Concerning Toleration." *Online Library of Liberty,* 2021

Locke, John. *First Treatise of Government.* Johnlocke.net. https://www.johnlocke.net/major-works/two-treatises-of-government-book-i

Locke, John. *Second Treatise on Government.* (Indianapolis, IN: Hackett Publishing, 1980)

Loschenkohl, Birte. "Occasional Decisiveness: Exception, Decision and Resistance in Kierkegaard and Schmitt" *European Journal of Political Theory,* Vol 18 at pgs 89–107

Losurdo, Domenico. *Liberalism: A Counter-History,* trans. Gregory Elliot. (London, UK: Verso Press, 2014)

Losurdo, Domenico. *Nietzsche, The Aristocratic Rebel,* trans. Gregor Benton. (Chicago, IL: Haymarket, 2020)

Love, Nancy S. *Marx, Nietzsche, and Modernity.* (New York, NY: Columbia University Press, 1986)

Lowndes, Joseph E. *From the New Deal to the New Right: Race and the Southern Origins of Modern Conservatism.* (New Haven, CT: Yale University Press, 2008)

Lowry, Rich. "The Only Middle Finger Available." *National Review,* October 26th, 2020

Luther, Martin. *Selections from His Writings,* ed. John Dillenberger. (New York, NY: Random House, 1962)

MacIntyre, Alasdair. *After Virtue-A Study in Moral Theory: Third Edition.* (Notre Dame, IN: University of Notre-Dame Press, 2007)

MacIntyre, Alasdair. *Marcuse.* (Roermond, NL: Fontana, 1970)

MacIntyre, Alasdair. *Marxism and Christianity.* (Notre Dame, IN: University of Notre Dame Press, 2003)

Macintyre, Alasdair "The Virtues, the Unity of a Human Life, and the Concept of a Tradition" in *Liberalism and Its Critics,* ed. Michael Sandel. (New York, NY: New York University Press, 1984)

MacIntyre, Alasdair. *Whose Justice, Which Rationality?* (Notre Dame, IN: University of Notre-Dame Press, 1989)

Macpherson, C.B. *Burke.* (Oxford, UK: Oxford University Press, 1980)

MacPherson, C.B. *The Political Theory of Possessive Individualism: Hobbes to Locke.* (Don Mills, ON: Oxford University Press, 1962)

Maistre, Joseph De. *Considerations on France,* trans. Richard A. Lebrun. (New York, NY: Cambridge University Press, 1994)

Maistre, Joseph De. *Essay on the Generative Principle of Political Constitutions,* trans. (Krakow, Poland: New Direction, 2019)

Maistre, Joseph De. *St. Petersburg Dialogues,* trans. Richard A. Lebrun. (Montreal, QC: McGill-Queens University Press, 1993)

Maistre, Joseph De. *The Generative Principle of Political Constitutions: Studies on Sovereignty, Religion, and Enlightenment,* ed. Jack Lively. (London, UK: Routledge, 1965)

Marino, Gordon. *Basic Writings of Existentialism.* (New York, NY: Random House, 2004)

Martin, Robert Ivan. *The Most Dangerous Branch: How the Supreme Court of Canada has Undermined our Law and our Democracy.* (Montreal, QC: McGill-Queens University Press, 2003)

Marx, Karl. *Capital Volume One: A Critique of Political Economy,* trans. Ernest Mandel. (London, UK: Penguin Books, 1990)

Marx, Karl. *Capital Volume Two: A Critique of Political Economy,* trans. Ernest Mandel. (London, UK: Penguin Books, 1993)

Marx, Karl. *Capital Volume Three: A Critique of Political Economy,* trans. Ernest Mandel. (London, UK: Penguin Books, 1993)

Marx, Karl. "Critique of the Gotha Program." May, 1875. Available at https://www.marxists.org/archive/marx/works/1875/gotha/index.htm

Marx, Karl. *Early Writings,* trans. Rodney Livingstone. (London, UK: Penguin Classics, 1992)

Marx, Karl. *Grundrisse: Introduction to the Critique of Political Economy.* (London, UK: Penguin Books, 1973

Marx, Karl and Engels, Friedrich. *The Communist Manifesto.* (Oxford, UK: Oxford University Press, 2008)

Marx, Karl and Engels, Friedrich. *The German Ideology.* (Amherst, NY: Prometheus Books, 1998)

McAllister, Ted V. *Revolt Against Modernity: Leo Strauss, Eric Voegelin, and the Search for a Postliberal Order.* (Lawrence: University of Kansas Press, 1995)

McCabe, Helen. *John Stuart Mill: Socialist.* (Montreal, QC: Queens–McGill University Press, 2021)

McCormick, John P. "Three Ways of Thinking 'Critically' About the Law" *American Political Science Review,* Vol 93, 1999

McManus, Matthew. *A Critical Legal Examination of Liberalism and Liberal Rights.* (Gewerbestrasse, Switzerland: Palgrave MacMillan, 2020)

McManus, Matthew. "A Critical Legal Conception of Human Dignity" *Journal of Human Rights,* Online, 2019

McManus, Matthew. *Liberalism and Socialism: Mortal Enemies or Embittered Kin?* (Cham, Switzerland: Palgrave MacMillan, 2021)

McManus, Matthew. *Nietzsche and the Politics of Reaction: Essays on Liberalism, Socialism, and Aristocratic Radicalism.* (Gewerbestrasse, Switzerland: Palgrave MacMillan, 2022)

McManus, Matthew. "The Politics of Dialectics." *Historical Materialism.* Online, 2020. *https://www.historicalmaterialism.org/book-review/politics-dialectics*

McManus, Matthew. *The Rise of Post-Modern Conservatism: Neoliberalism, Post-Modern Culture, and Reactionary Politics.* (Gewerbestrasse, Switzerland: Palgrave MacMillan, 2019)

McManus, Matthew. *What is Post-Modern Conservatism: Essays on Our Hugely Tremendous Times.* (Winchester, UK: Zero Books, 2019)

McManus, Matthew and Burgis, Ben and Hamilton, Conrad and Trejo, Marion. *Myth and Mayhem: A Leftist Critique of Jordan Peterson.* (Winchester, UK: Zero Books, 2020)

Mehta, Uday Singh. *Liberalism and Empire: A Study in Nineteenth-Century British Liberal Thought.* (Chicago, IL: The University of Chicago Press, 1999)

Meyer, Frank. *In Defense of Freedom and Related Essays.* (Indianapolis, IN: Liberty Fund, 1996)

Meikle, Scott. "History of Philosophy: The Metaphysics of Substance in Marx" in *The Cambridge Companion to Marx,* ed. Terrell Carver. (Cambridge, UK: Cambridge University Press, 1991)

Milbank, John and Pickstock, Catherine and Ward, Graham. *Radical Orthodoxy.* (London, UK: Routledge, 1999)

Milbank, John. *Theology and Social Theory: Beyond Secular Reason-Second Edition.* (Oxford, UK: Blackwell Publishing, 2006)

Millerman, Michael. *Beginning with Heidegger: Strauss, Rorty, Derrida, Dugin and the Philosophical Constitution of the Political.* (London, UK: Arktos Media, 2021)

Millerman, Michael. *Inside "Putin's Brain": The Political Philosophy of Alexander Dugin.* (Montreal, QC: Millerman School, 2022)

Mill, John Stuart. *On Liberty.* (Kitchener, ON: Batoche Books, 2001)

Mill, John Stuart. *On the Subjection of Women,* reprinted. In Richard Vandewetering and Lesley Jacobs. *John Stuart Mill's The Subjection of Women: His Contemporary and Modern Critics.* (Delmar, NY: Caravan Books, 1999)

Mills, Charles W. *Black Rights/White Wrongs: A Critique of Racial Liberalism.* (Oxford, UK: Oxford University Press, 2017)

Mirandola, Giovanni. "Oration on the Dignity of Man" trans. Available online. http://web.mnstate.edu/gracyk/courses/web%20publishing/pico_oration.htm

Mises, Ludwig von. *Liberalism.* (Auburn, AL: Mises Institute, 1985)

Mouffe, Chantal. *The Return of the Political.* (London, UK: Verso Press, 2005)

Montesquieu, Charles de Secondat. *The Spirit of the Laws,* trans. Thomas Nugent. (New York, NY: Batoche Books, Kitchener, 2001)

Murray, Douglas. *The War on the West.* (New York, NY: Broadside Books, 2022)

Mussolini, Benito. "The Doctrine of Fascism." *San Jose State University.* https://sjsu.edu/faculty/wooda/2B-HUM/Readings/The-Doctrine-of-Fascism.pdf

Nardin, Terry. "Michael Oakeshott." *Stanford Encyclopedia of Philosophy,* February 14th, 2020

National Review. "The South Girds Its Loins." *National Review,* February 29th, 1956

Neill, Edmund. *Conservatism.* (Cambridge, UK: Polity Press, 2021)

Nicholas, Jeff. *Reason, Tradition, and the Good: Macintyre's Tradition Constituted Reason and Frankfurt School Critical Theory.* (Notre-Dame, IN: University of Notre Dame Press, 2012)

Nietzsche, Friedrich. *Basic Writings of Nietzsche,* trans. Walter Kaufmann. (New York, NY: The Modern Library, 2000)

Nietzsche, Friedrich. *On the Advantage and Disadvantage of History for Life*, trans. Peter Preuss. (Indianapolis, IN: Hackett, 1980)

Nietzsche, Friedrich. *The Gay Science: With A Prelude in Rhymes and an Appendix in Songs,* trans. Walter Kaufmann. (New York, NY: Random House, 1974)

Nietzsche, Friedrich. "On Truth and Lying in a Non-Moral Sense," trans. Walter Kaufmann. In *The Portable Nietzsche.* (New York, NY: Penguin Books, 1968)

Nietzsche, Friedrich. *Thus Spoke Zarathustra: A Book for Everyone and No One,* trans. Graham Parkes. (Oxford, UK: Oxford University Press, 2009)

Nietzsche, Friedrich. *The Twilight of the Idols and the Antichrist: or How to Philosophize with a Hammer.* (London, UK: Penguin Classics, 1990)

Norman, Jesse. *Edmund Burke: The Visionary Who Invented Modern Politics.* (London, UK: William Collins, 2013)

Nozick, Robert. *Anarchy, State, and Utopia.* (New York, NY: Basic Books, 2013)

Nussbaum, Martha. *Creating Capabilities: The Human Development Approach.* (Cambridge, MA: Belknap Press of Harvard University Press, 2011)

Nussbaum, Martha. *Political Emotions: Why Love Matters for Justice.* (Cambridge, MA: Belknap Press of Harvard University Press, 2015)

Oakeshott, Michael. *On Human Conduct.* (Oxford, UK: Oxford University Press, 1975)

Oakeshott, Michael. *Rationalism in Politics and Other Essays: New and Expanded Edition.* (Indianapolis, IN: Liberty Press, 1991)

Oakeshott, Michael. *The Politics of Faith and the Politics of Skepticism.* (New Haven, CT: Yale University Press, 1996)

Pascal, Blaise. *Pensees,* trans. A.J. Krailsheimer. (London, UK: Penguin Books, 1995)

Passmore, Kevin. *Fascism: A Very Short Introduction.* (Oxford, UK: Oxford University Press, 2014)

Paxton, Robert O. "I've Hesitated to Call Trump a Fascist. Until Now." *Newsweek,* January 11th, 2021

Paxton, Robert O. *The Anatomy of Fascism.* (New York, NY: Vintage Books, 2005)

Payne, Stanley. *Fascism: Comparison and Definition.* (Madison: University of Wisconsin Press, 1983)

Penrose, Roger. *The Road to Reality: A Complete Guide to the Laws of the Universe.* (New York, NY: Random House, 2004)

Perlstein, Rick. *Before the Storm: Barry Goldwater and the Unmaking of the American Consensus.* (New York, NY: Nation Books, 2001)

Peterson, Jordan. *Beyond Order: Twelve More Rules for Life.* (Toronto, ON: Random House Canada, 2021)

Peterson, Jordan. "Open the Damn Country Back Up, Before Canadians Wreck Something We Can't Fix." *National Post,* January 10th, 2022

Peterson, Jordan. *Maps of Meaning: The Architecture of Belief.* (New York, NY: Routledge Press, 1999)

Peterson, Jordan. *Twelve Rules to Life: An Antidote to Chaos.* (Toronto, ON: Random House Canada, 2018)

Pinker, Steven. *Enlightenment Now: The Case for Reason, Science, Humanism, and Progress.* (London, UK: Penguin Books, 2019)

Plato. *Parmenides,* trans. Mary Louise Gill. (Indianapolis, IN: Hackett Classics, 1996)

Plato. *The Republic,* trans. G.M.A Grube. (Indianapolis, IN: Hackett Publishing, 1992)

Popper, Karl. *The Logic of Scientific Discovery.* (New York, NY: Routledge Classics, 2002)

Popper, Karl. *The Open Society and Its Enemies: One Volume Edition.* (Princeton, NJ: Princeton University Press, 2013)

Rand, Ayn. *The Fountainhead.* (New York, NY: Signet Books, 1996)

Robin, Corey. "Fascism and Counterrevolution." *Dissent Magazine,* Summer 2005

Robin, Corey. *The Enigma of Clarence Thomas.* (New York, NY: Metropolitan Books, 2019)

Robin, Corey. *Fear: The History of a Political Idea.* (Oxford, UK: Oxford University Press, 2004)

Robin, Corey. *The Reactionary Mind Second Edition: Conservatism from Edmund Burke to Donald Trump.* (Oxford, UK: Oxford University Press, 2018)

Rorty, Richard. *Philosophy and Social Hope.* (London, UK: Penguin Books, 2000)

Ross, Alexander Reid. *Against the Fascist Creep.* (Chico, CA: AK Press, 2017)

R.R. Reno. *Resurrecting the Idea of Christian Society.* (Washington, DC: Regnery Faith, 2016)

R.R. Reno. *Return of the Strong Gods: Nationalism, Populism, and the Future of the West.* (Washington, DC: Regnery Faith, 2019)

Ryan, Alan. *On Aristotle: Saving Politics from Philosophy.* (New York, NY: Liveright, 2014)

Ryan, Alan. *On Augustine: The Two Cities.* (New York, NY: Liveright, 2016)

Saad, Gad. *The Parasitic Mind: How Infections Ideas are Killing Common Sense.* (Washington, DC: Regnery Publishing, 2020)

Scalia, Antonin. *A Matter of Interpretation: Federal Courts and the Law.* (Princeton, NJ: Princeton University Press, 1997)

Schmitt, Carl. *Constitutional Theory,* trans. Jeffrey Seitzer. (Durham, NC. Duke University Press, 2008)

Schmitt, Carl. *Legality and Legitimacy,* trans. Jeffrey Seitzer. (Chicago, IL: University of Chicago Press, 2004)

Schmitt, Carl. *Political Theology.* (Chicago. The University of Chicago Press, 2005)

Schmitt, Carl. *The Concept of the Political.* (Chicago: University of Chicago Press, 1996)

Schmitt, Carl. *The Concept of the Political: Expanded Edition.* (Chicago: The University of Chicago Press, 2007)

Schmitt, Carl. *The Leviathan in the State Theory of Thomas Hobbes.* (Chicago, IL: The University of Chicago Press, 2008)

Schmitt, Carl. *The Nomos of the Earth in the International Law of Jus Publicum Europeaum.* (Candor, NY: Telos Press, 2006)

Schneewind, J.B. *The Invention of Autonomy: A History of Modern Moral Philosophy.* (Cambridge, UK: Cambridge University Press, 1998)

Schumpeter, Joseph A. *Capitalism, Socialism, and Democracy: Third Edition.* (New York, NY: Harper Collins, 2008)

Scruton, Roger. *Conservatism: An Invitation to the Great Tradition.* (New York, NY: All Points Books, 2017)

Scruton, Roger. *Fools, Frauds, and Firebrands: Thinkers of the New Left.* (London, UK: Bloomsbury Continuum, 2015)

Scruton, Roger. *How to Be a Conservative.* (London, UK: Bloomsbury Continuum, 2014)

Scruton, Roger. *On Human Nature.* (Princeton, NJ: Princeton University Press, 2017)

Scruton, Roger. *The Meaning of Conservatism: Third Edition.* (South Bend, IN: St Augustine's Press, 2002)

Scruton, Roger. *A Political Philosophy: Arguments for Conservatism.* (London, UK: Bloomsbury, 2006)

Scruton, Roger. *The Soul of the World.* (Princeton, NJ: Princeton University Pres, 2014)

Scruton, Roger. "Why I Became a Conservative." *The New Criterion,* September 2003

Sedgwick, Mark. *Key Thinkers of the Radical Right: Behind the New Threat to Liberal Democracy.* (Oxford, UK: Oxford University Press, 2019)

Shapiro, Ben. *The Right Side of History: How Reason and Moral Purpose Made the West Great.* (New York, NY: Broadside Books, 2019)

Shapiro, Ian. "The Burkean Outlook." Yale Courses, *The Moral Foundations of Politics.* April 8th, 2011. https://www.youtube.com/watch?v=hkDqadw-fJE&t=3s

Shapiro, Ian. *The Moral Foundations of Politics.* (New Haven, CT: Yale University Press, 2003)

Shoikhedbrod, Igor. *Revisiting Marx's Critique of Liberalism: Rethinking Justice, Legality, and Rights.* (Cham, Switzerland: Palgrave MacMillan, 2019)

Smith, Miles. "Russell Kirk and the South." *The Imaginative Conservative,* September 15th, 2014

Sowell, Thomas. *Intellectuals and Society.* (New York, NY: Basic Books, 2009)

Sowell, Thomas. "Misinformed Electorate Shouldn't Vote." *Fox Business,* September 18th, 2015 https://www.youtube.com/watch?v=ENBKr2DZ0dI

Strauss, Leo. *The City and Man.* (Chicago, IL: The University of Chicago Press, 1978)

Strauss, Leo. *Natural Right and History.* (Chicago, IL: University of Chicago Press, 1953)

Strauss, Leo. "On German Nihilism" *Interpretation,* Vol 29, No 3, 1999

Strauss, Leo. *What is Political Philosophy? And Other Studies.* (Chicago, IL: University of Chicago Press, 1988)

Stephens, Alexander. "Cornerstone Speech." March 21st, 1861. https://www.battlefields.org/learn/primary-sources/cornerstone-speech

Suskind, Ron. "Faith, Certainty, and the Presidency of George W. Bush." *New York Times,* October 17th, 2004

Taylor, Hegel. *Hegel and Modern Society.* (Cambridge, UK: Cambridge University Press, 2015)

Taylor, Charles. *A Secular Age.* (Cambridge, MA: Harvard University Press, 2007)

Taylor, Charles. *Modern Social Imaginaries.* (Durham, NC: Duke University Press, 2004)

Taylor, Charles. *Sources of the Self: The Making of Modern Identity* (Cambridge, MA: Harvard University Press, 1992)

Teitelbaum, Benjamin R. *War for Eternity: Inside Bannon's Far-Right Circle of Global Power Brokers.* (New York, NY: Harper Collins, 2020)

The Project for the New American Century. "Rebuilding America's Defenses: Strategy, Forces, and Resources for a New Century." September 2000 at https://web.archive.org/web/20130817122719/http://www.newamericancentury.org/RebuildingAmericas Defenses.pdf

Tillich, Paul. *Dynamics of Faith.* (New York, NY: Harper Collins, 2001)

Tillich, Paul. *The Socialist Decision.* (Eugene, OR: WIPF and Stock Publishers, 1977)

Tocqueville, Alexis de. *Democracy in America and Two Essays on America,* trans. Gerald Bevan. (London, UK: Penguin Books, 2003).

Tolstoy, Leo. *The Kingdom of God is Within You,* trans. Constance Garnett. (Kshetra Books, 2016)

Toal, Gerard. *Near Abroad: Putin, The West, and the Contest Over Ukraine and the Caucasus.* (Oxford, UK: Oxford University Press, 2017)

Toth, Csaba. "Full Text of Victor Orban's Speech to the Baile Tusnad." *The Budapest Beacon.* July 29th, 2014

Traverso, Enzo. *The New Faces of Fascism: Populism and the Far Right.* (London, UK: Verso Books, 2019)

Trump, Donald. *The Art of the Deal.* (New York, NY: Ballantine Books, 2015)

Tuck, Richard. *Hobbes: A Very Short Introduction.* (Oxford, UK: Oxford University Press, 2002)

Vashem, Yad. "Extracts from Mein Kampf by Adolph Hitler." The World Holocaust Remembrance Center, 2022

Vermuele, Adrian. "All Human Conflict is Ultimately Theological." *Church Life Journal,* July 26th, 2019

Vermeule, Adrian. *Common Good Constitutionalism: Recovering the Classical Legal Tradition.* (Cambridge, UK: Polity Press, 2022)

Vico, Giambattista. *The New Science.* (London, UK: Penguin Books, 2000)

Villanova Center for Liberal Education. "Thomas Carlyle Resartus: Reappraising Carlyle for our Times" November 15th, 2010. https://www.youtube.com/watch?v=QbAlSqGouwY&t=20s

Von Mises, Ludwig. *Liberalism.* (Auburn, AL: Ludwig Von Mises Institute, 2018)

Von Mises, Ludwig. *Socialism: An Economic and Sociological Analysis.* (Mansfield Center, CT: Martino Publishing, 2012)

Von Mises, Ludwig. *The Anti-capitalistic Mentality.* (Indianapolis, IN: Liberty Fund Inc, 2006)

Watts, Galen. "The Religion of the Heart: Spirituality in Late Modernity" *American Journal of Cultural Sociology,* 2020 at pgs 1–33

Weber, Max. *Economy and Society,* trans. Keith Tribe. (Cambridge, MA: Harvard University Press, 2019)

Weber, Max. *The Protestant Work Ethic and the Spirit of Capitalism,* trans. Talcott Parsons. (Mineola, NY: Dover Publications, 1958)

Weber, Max. *The Vocation Lectures,* trans. Tracy B. Strong. (Indianapolis, IN: Hackett Publishing, 2004)

Wicks, Robert. *Nietzsche.* (Oxford, UK: Oneworld Publications, 2002)

Will, George F. *The Conservative Sensibility.* (New York, NY: Hachette Books, 2020)

Wilson, James Matthew. *The Vision of the Soul: Truth, Goodness and Beauty in the Western Tradition.* (Washington, DC: The Catholic University of America Press, 2017)

Wolin, Sheldon. *Politics and Vision: Continuity and Innovation in Western Political Thought-Expanded Edition.* (Princeton, NJ: Princeton University Press, 2016)

Wollstonecraft, Mary. *A Vindication of the Rights of Women.* (New York, NY: Norton Library, 1967)

Wood, Allen. *Kant's Ethical Thought.* (Cambridge, UK: Cambridge University Press, 1999)

Yarvin, Curtis. *A Gentle Introduction to Unqualified Reservations.* Unqualified Reservations, January 8th, 2009

Yarvin, Curtis. *Moldbug on Carlyle.* Unqualified Reservations, February 4th, 2010

Zizek, Slavoj. "Berlusconi in Tehran" *London Review of Books,* Vol 31, July 23rd, 2009

Zizek, Slavoj. *Less than Nothing: Hegel and the Shadow of Dialectical Materialism.* (London, UK: Verso Press, 2012)

Zizek, Slavoj. *The Fragile Absolute: Or Why Is the Christian Legacy Worth Fighting For?* (London, UK: Verso Books, 2009)

Zizek, Slavoj and Milbank, John. *The Monstrosity of Christ: Paradox or Dialectic?* (Boston, MA: MIT Press, 2011)

Zizek, Slavoj. *The Sublime Object of Ideology.* (London, UK: Verso Press, 2009)

INDEX